MW00986510

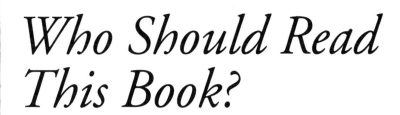

Who Should Read This Book?

"Read" may be the wrong word. "Engage" would be better, because this is not so much a book as it is a classic text, and Jewish classics are not read so much as they are engaged. Included here are a classic text of Jewish prayer, spanning 2,000 years of Jewish experience with the world and with God; and ten thoughtful commentaries on that text, each one reaching back in a different way, again through 2,000 years of time. The question ought to be "Who should engage this book in personal dialogue?"

If you like to pray, or find prayer services baffling: Whether you are Orthodox, Conservative, Reconstructionist, or Reform, you will find that *My People's Prayer Book* tells you what you need to know to pray.

- The Hebrew text here is the most authentic one we have, and the variations among the Jewish movements are described and explained. They are all treated as equally authentic.

- The translation is honest, altogether unique, and outfitted with notes comparing it to others' translations.

- Of special interest is a full description of the Halakhah (the "how-to") of prayer and the philosophy behind it.

If you are a spiritual seeker or Jewishly curious: If you have wondered what Judaism is all about, the prayer book is the place to begin. It is the one and only book that Jews read each and every day. The commentaries explain how the prayers were born and synopsize insights of founding Rabbis, medieval authorities, Chasidic masters, and modern theologians. The layout replicates the look of Jewish classics: a text surrounded by many marginal commentaries, allowing you to skip back and forth across centuries of insight.

If you are a teacher or student: This is a perfect book for adult studies, or for youth groups, teenagers, and camps. Any single page provides comparative insight from the length and breadth of Jewish tradition, about the texts that have mattered most in the daily life of the Jewish people.

If you are a scholar: Though written in friendly prose, this book is composed by scholars: professors of Bible, Rabbinics, Medieval Studies, Liturgy, Theology, Linguistics, Jewish Law, Mysticism, and Modern Jewish Thought. No other work summarizes current wisdom on Jewish prayer, drawn from so many disciplines.

If you are not Jewish: You need not be Jewish to understand this book. It provides access for everyone to the Jewish wisdom tradition. It chronicles the ongoing Jewish-Christian dialogue and the roots of Christian prayer in Christianity's Jewish origins.

The *My People's Prayer Book: Traditional Prayers, Modern Commentaries* series

Volume 1—The *Sh'ma* and Its Blessings
168 pp, ISBN 1-879045-79-6

Volume 2—The *Amidah*
240 pp, ISBN 1-879045-80-X

Volume 3—*P'sukei D'zimrah* (Morning Psalms)
240 pp, ISBN 1-879045-81-8

Volume 4—*Seder K'riat Hatorah* (The Torah Service)
264 pp, ISBN 1-879045-82-6

Volume 5—*Birkhot Hashachar* (Morning Blessings)
240 pp, ISBN 1-879045-83-4

Volume 6—*Tachanun* and Concluding Prayers
240 pp, ISBN 1-879045-84-2

Volume 7—Shabbat at Home
240 pp, ISBN 1-879045-85-0

Volume 8—*Kabbalat Shabbat* (Welcoming Shabbat in the Synagogue)
240 pp, ISBN 1-58023-121-7

Volume 9—Welcoming the Night: *Minchah* and *Ma'ariv* (Afternoon and Evening Prayer)
272 pp, ISBN 1-58023-262-0

Volume 10—*Shacharit* and *Musaf*
240 pp (est.), ISBN 1-58023-240-X Projected for Fall 2006

My People's Prayer Book

TRADITIONAL PRAYERS, MODERN COMMENTARIES

Vol. 9—Welcoming the Night: *Minchah* and *Ma'ariv* (Afternoon and Evening Prayer)

EDITED BY RABBI LAWRENCE A. HOFFMAN

CONTRIBUTORS

MARC BRETTLER	JOEL M. HOFFMAN
ELLIOT N. DORFF	LAWRENCE A. HOFFMAN
DAVID ELLENSON	LAWRENCE KUSHNER
ELLEN FRANKEL	DANIEL LANDES
ALYSSA GRAY	NEHEMIA POLEN

Jewish Lights Publishing
Woodstock, Vermont

My People's Prayer Book: Traditional Prayers, Modern Commentaries
Vol. 9—Welcoming the Night: Minchah *and* Ma'ariv *(Afternoon and Evening Prayer)*

2005 First Printing
© 2005 by Lawrence A. Hoffman

All rights reserved. No part of this book may be reproduced or transmitted in any form or by any means, electronic or mechanical, including photocopying, recording, or by any information storage and retrieval system, without permission in writing from the publisher.

For information regarding permission to reprint material from this book, please mail or fax your request in writing to Jewish Lights Publishing, Permission Department, at the address/fax number listed below, or e-mail your request to permissions@jewishlights.com.

The excerpts on pp. 143, 180, and 185 are reprinted from *Seder Tkhines*, © 2005, by Devra Kay, published by The Jewish Publication Society with the permission of the publisher, The Jewish Publication Society.

Library of Congress Cataloging-in-Publication Data
My people's prayer book : traditional prayers, modern commentaries / edited and with introductions by Lawrence A. Hoffman.
p.   cm.
Includes the traditional text of the siddur, English translation, and commentaries.
Contents: vol. 9. Welcoming the Night: *Minchah* and *Ma'ariv* (Afternoon and Evening Prayer).
ISBN 1-58023-262-0 (hc)
1. Siddur. 2. Siddurim—Texts. 3. Judaism—Liturgy—Texts.
I. Hoffman, Lawrence A., 1942– . II. Siddur. English & Hebrew.
BM674.39.M96 1997
296.4'5—dc21   97-26836
                                       CIP
First Edition

10 9 8 7 6 5 4 3 2 1

Manufactured in the United States of America

Published by Jewish Lights Publishing
A Division of LongHill Partners, Inc.
Sunset Farm Offices, Route 4, P.O. Box 237
Woodstock, VT 05091
Tel: (802) 457-4000   Fax: (802) 457-4004
www.jewishlights.com

Contents

ABOUT *MY PEOPLE'S PRAYER BOOK* vii

ANXIETY AND OPPORTUNITY: THE MOOD OF NIGHTTIME PRAYER 1
  Lawrence A. Hoffman

INTRODUCTION TO THE LITURGY: THE SHAPE OF *MINCHAH* AND *MA'ARIV* . . . 11
  Lawrence A. Hoffman

THE HALAKHIC STATUS OF *MINCHAH* AND *MA'ARIV* 25
  Daniel Landes

INTRODUCTION TO THE COMMENTARIES: HOW TO LOOK FOR MEANING
  IN THE PRAYERS 31
  Lawrence A. Hoffman

THE LITURGY

1. MA'ARIV *(WEEKDAY AND SHABBAT)* 36
   A. OPENING VERSES 36
      I. PSALM 134 36
      II. MISCELLANEOUS VERSES 36
      III. *V'HU RACHUM* ("HE IS MERCIFUL") 37
   B. THE *SH'MA* AND ITS BLESSINGS 47
      I. BLESSING ON CREATION: *MA'ARIV ARAVIM* ("WHO BRINGS ON EVENING") . . 47
      II. BLESSING ON REVELATION: *AHAVAT OLAM* ("ETERNAL LOVE") 57
      III. BLESSING ON REDEMPTION: *EMET VE'EMUNAH* ("TRUE AND TRUSTWORTHY") . . 66
      IV. BLESSING FOR A SAFE NIGHT: *HASHKIVENU* ("LIE US DOWN TO PEACE") . . 83
      V. A FIFTH EVENING BLESSING: *BARUKH ADONAI L'OLAM*
         ("BLESSED IS ADONAI FOREVER") 94
   C. ANNOUNCEMENT OF SACRED TIME 105
   D. THE *AMIDAH* 113

I. A *Havdalah* in the *Amidah* for Saturday Night 113

II. The *K'dushat Hayom* ("Sanctification of the Day") for Shabbat
Ma'ariv 121

III. The *Ma'ariv* Blessing for Peace: *Birkat Shalom* 131

E. *Magen Avot* ("Protecting Our Ancestors") 136

F. The Synagogue *Kiddush* 151

G. Counting the Omer 157

I. *Kavvanah* (Introductory Meditation) 157

II. Blessing on Counting 157

III. Counting 157

IV. Psalm 67 158

V. *Ana B'kho'akh* ("By the Might") 158

VI. *Kavvanah* (Closing Meditation) 159

H. Closing Prayers 179

I. Psalm 27 179

II. Psalm 49 190

2. Minchah *(Additions for Shabbat)* 201

A. The *Amidah* 201

I. The *K'dushat Hayom* ("Sanctification of the Day")
for Shabbat *Minchah* 201

II. *Tsidkat'kha Tsedek* ("Your Righteousness Is Right")
for Shabbat *Minchah* 209

About the Contributors 215

List of Abbreviations 219

Glossary 221

Contributors

Marc Brettler . . . . *Our Biblical Heritage*

Elliot N. Dorff . . . . *Theological Reflections*

David Ellenson . . . . *How the Modern Prayer Book Evolved*

Ellen Frankel . . . . *A Woman's Voice*

Alyssa Gray . . . . *Our Talmudic Heritage*

Joel M. Hoffman . . . . *What the Prayers Really Say*

Lawrence A. Hoffman . . . . *History of the Liturgy*

Lawrence Kushner and Nehemia Polen . . *Chasidic and Mystical Perspectives*

Daniel Landes . . . . *The Halakhah of Prayer*

About My People's Prayer Book

My People's Prayer Book is designed to look like a traditional Jewish book. Ever since the dawn of modern printing, Jews have arranged their books so that instead of reading in a linear fashion from the first line of the first page to the last line of the last one, readers were encouraged to linger on a single page and to consult commentaries across the gamut of Jewish thought, all at one and the same time. Every page thus contained a crosscut of the totality of Jewish tradition.

That intellectual leap across many minds and through the centuries was accomplished by printing a text in the middle of the page and surrounding it with commentaries. Readers could scan the first line or two of the various commentaries and then choose to continue the ones that interested them most, by turning the page— more or less the way newspaper readers get a sense of everything happening on a single day by glancing at all the headlines on page one, then following select stories as they are continued on separate pages further on.

Each new rubric (or liturgical section) is, therefore, introduced in traditional style: the Hebrew prayer with translation in the middle of the page, and the beginning lines of all the commentaries in the margins. Commentaries are continued on the next page or a few pages later (the page number is provided). Readers may dwell for a while on all the comments, deciding which ones to pursue at any given sitting. They may want to compare comments, reading first one and then another. Or having decided, after a while, that a particular commentator is of special interest, they may instinctively search out the opening lines of that commentator's work, as they appear in each introductory page, and then read them through to arrive at a summary understanding of what that particular person has to say.

Anxiety and Opportunity

The Mood of Nighttime Prayer

Lawrence A. Hoffman

Child. O mother, lay your hand on my brow!
O mother, mother, where am I now?
Why is the room so gaunt and great?
Why am I lying awake so late?

Mother. Fear not at all: the night is still.
Nothing is here that means you ill—
Nothing but lamps the whole town through,
And never a child awake but you.

Child. Mother, mother, speak low in my ear,
Some of the things are so great and near,
Some are so small and far away,
I have a fear that I cannot say.
What have I done, and what do I fear,
And why are you crying, mother dear?

Mother. Out in the city, sounds begin.
Thank the kind God, the carts come in!
An hour or two more and God is so kind,
The day shall be blue in the windowblind,
Then shall my child go sweetly asleep,
And dream of the birds and the hills of sheep.

Robert Louis Stevenson, "The Sick Child"

Thus does Robert Louis Stevenson conjure the plight of "The Sick Child," wracked by fear of the dark, the cold, and silence; and able to sleep only at the hint of another day. One need not be sick to experience the sense that "Night and Fear keep ghostly tryst" (Robert Burns Wilson, "Ballad of the Faded Field") or that night is the "mother of

Dread and Fear" (Shakespeare, "The Rape of Lucrece"). Mary Carolyn Davies ("A Girl's Songs") celebrates:

> Over and over
> > I tell the sky:
> > I am free—I!
>
> Over and over
> > I tell the sea:
> > —I am free!
>
> But when the night comes black and cold,
> I who am young, with fear grow old.

Come night, who does not revert, at least a little, to the fear of darkness imprinted in our brain when, eons ago, human beings learned to stand upright; when we traded in nighttime vision for the gift of looking heavenward, and began greeting the new day's dawn as the herald of possibilities both human and divine? We call pre-modernity "the dark ages," and modernity the Enlightenment. When Elie Wiesel chronicled his story of the Shoah, he could think of no better title than *Night*.

We have since invented streetlights to tear away the mask of darkness, but our liturgy took shape when night was lit only by stars, and on occasion, except for flickering candles and torches, not even that. Night brings out predators, both animal and human; it harbors ghosts like Hamlet's father; it reminds us of mortality.

It should come as no surprise, then, to see our nighttime liturgy awash with waves of fear for what the night may bring. *Ma'ariv* begins with the guarantee that God's mercy will sustain us through the darkness (*V'hu rachum*, "He is merciful"). The nighttime *Sh'ma* features *Hashkivenu*, a petition that God "lie us down to peace" and awaken us to life. Sleep, says the Talmud, is one-sixtieth of death, after all. Night is what you pray you will get through.

The liturgy speaks metaphorically, identifying the source of nighttime fear in *mazikin*, literally, "damagers"—spirits that haunt the night to inflict mischief upon us. *Sefer M'kor Hat'fillot* summarizes much of tradition when it cautions, "Nighttime requires being watched over because of *mazikin*." And it is not just we the living who should fear the night. As much as Christians, medieval Jews too believed in a "hell" where souls who sin are punished. Drawing on biblical roots, they named it *Gehinnom* but overlaid the biblical connotation with medieval fancy. In the Bible, *Gehinnom* is a shadowy place where the dead take up residence, far away from God, unable to offer customary praise. By the Middle Ages, it was thought that average sinners stop off there for up to eleven months (which is why, traditionally, the Mourner's *Kaddish* is said that long only, rather than for an entire year).

Tola'at Ya'akov is a commentary on our prayers by the influential Spanish-Turkish kabbalist R. Meir ibn Gabbai (1480/81–after 1543). He sums up everyday assumptions when he says we begin *Ma'ariv* with *V'hu rachum* (Ps. 78:38) "to seek mercy for the souls that suffer judgment every night, by three bands of destructive angels [*malakhei chevlah*]." Their names are *Mashchit*, *Af*, and *Chemah*, "Destruction,"

"Anger," and "Wrath." *V'hu rachum* contains the assurance *lo yashchit* (God "will not allow *Mashchit* to destroy"); indeed, God will restrain *apo* (his "ire," his *af*) and will not awaken *chamato* (his *chemah*, his "wrath"). The verse, moreover, has thirteen words, one for each of God's attributes of mercy. On Shabbat, says thirteenth-century Eliezer of Worms, the souls are set free from punishment for a day, but come *Minchah*, they prepare to return to *Gehinnom*; that is why we postpone the influential prayer *K'dushah D'sidra* from its usual weekday place in *Shacharit* and say it instead to start off Shabbat *Minchah*. "Its threefold reference to God as 'Holy, holy, holy' cools the fires of hell."

We need not literally believe in the punishment of wicked souls in hell to understand that those who did associated their torment with night and why they established prayers to comfort not just us, the living, but the dead as well. Fear of the dark goes deep indeed in the human psyche.

If *Shacharit* awakens hope of morning light, and *Ma'ariv* offers comfort from the dark, *Minchah* lies betwixt and between the two. Technically, *Minchah* corresponds to the afternoon sacrifice, so may be said long before sunset. But custom frequently combines *Minchah* and *Ma'ariv*, if only for convenience's sake—it is easier to gather just once at day's end and say both prayers than to take time off from work for *Minchah* and then assemble again just a few hours later for *Ma'ariv*. Think of *Minchah* as particularly sobering: it is the threshold of night; bidding day good-bye in anticipation of darkness.

But precisely because it falls when it is neither day nor night, *Minchah* may have extraordinary potential for creative good. In 1908, pioneering author Arnold Van Gennep investigated rites of passage, the twilight moments when we are neither here nor there, on the way from childhood, say, to maturity; on the verge of getting married; or on our deathbed, preparing for a journey to the beyond. There are, he said three stages to these all-too-human passage moments, and all three can be found in rituals devised to fill the time of being "in between." First, we say good-bye to where we have been; then we turn our attention to becoming fully part of wherever we are going. But there is also a middle stage, which Van Gennep called "liminal," from *limen*, the Latin word for the lintel, or wall, that frames a threshold or doorway connecting one space to another.

Imagine watching people move from room to room: from the place where they have been served hors d'oeuvres, perhaps, to the dining room for a formal meal. As comfortably animated as they may have been while chatting over wine and cheese, they naturally pause in the threshold to the dining room, in order to survey the new space and decide where they will sit. Visitors moving from the hallway into the synagogue sanctuary do the same thing: they stand in the doorway, prayer book in hand, figuring out who sits where. Thresholds in space are places to shift attention from the rules of behavior in the room you are leaving to the rules that obtain in the room you are entering. The threshold, or limen, is itself ruleless. It is experienced with the discomfort that is natural to transitions.

What is true of changing space is doubly certain for transitions in time. Historian of religion Mircea Eliade (d. 1986) emphasized rituals of transition that we use to protect ourselves from this liminal uncertainty, projected as downright dangerous. Think of the Chinese New Year, celebrated with costume and fireworks, associated with frightening off bad fortune; or the American New Year, for that matter, when we hand out noisemakers precisely at midnight. Think also of the traditional Jewish wedding, where the groom fasts on the day of the ceremony.

Coming of age is especially marked by initiation rites that engender fear of danger, but also structure the period of change to guarantee that people get through it safely. In African Ndembu culture, adult women dance while girls entering puberty lie naked and motionless wrapped in a blanket, as if returning briefly to the womb to be reborn as women themselves. In Cambodia, would-be Buddhist monks dress as a priestly Buddha and ride to the monastery while people pretend ritually to hinder their arrival. Hazing rites for fraternity initiants are a good example from our own day. Even the bar/bat mitzvah is not without its moments of fear for the child forced to display adult competence by errorlessly chanting the most sacred text of the Jewish people in full view of the assembled congregation.

Anthropologist Victor Turner (d. 1983) put the crowning touch on liminality theory by demonstrating not just its dangers but its stunning creativity. Both the old time or place that we are leaving and the new one that we are about to enter have rules that govern behavior. But the moment or space that is in between does not. That lack of formal structure is what makes it seem dangerous (there is nothing we can count on) and what leads us to rituals that make it passable. The same formlessness, however, gives us leave to invent new possibilities that we might never have imagined otherwise. Think of dreams, a liminal state between sleep and wakefulness, where what we imagine may be frightening but may also provide rare insight into who we are. We ask a bar/bat mitzvah—still just a child really, but for the moment, a pretend-adult—to project a vision of an adult future; rabbis give a charge to wedding couples; we make New Year's resolutions; we make wishes over candles on birthday cakes.

During the in-between time of pregnancy, when a child hasn't yet been born but is certainly on the way, we say the mother-to-be has conceived—the same verb we use for the mental act of "conceiving" a plan. Our Rosh Hashanah liturgy features the memorable line *hayom harat olam* (pronounced hah-YOHM hah-RAHT oh-LAHM), meaning, literally, "This is the day of the world's conception." We mean it in both senses: on Rosh Hashanah, the world was being born; it was also in God's thoughts, a plan for the future. What woman doesn't fear great danger while still imagining "great expectations" during the time of conception? In that in-between moment with the baby not yet formed, everything seems possible, both positively and negatively. So too with our celebration of the world's conception, as we look into the future frightened by world events but also imagining how wonderful the coming year might actually be, if we are fortunate. Liminality is both dangerous and promising.

Minchah and *Ma'ariv* are recited, traditionally, as liturgical brackets for the moment of nightfall, *Minchah* just before the stars appear, and *Ma'ariv* immediately after. No wonder these two brief services are seen as dangerous, filled with *mazikin* and demons. No wonder *Hashkivenu* looks ahead to a night of peace but worries about dangers from pestilence—even Satan himself (see p. 83). No wonder *V'hu rachum* at *Ma'ariv* evokes God's mercy. No wonder, also, tradition urges us especially to enter *Minchah* fully conscious of the mystery of the moment. As the Talmud (Ber. 6b) puts it, "A person should always be strict about praying *Minchah*, for Elijah was answered [by God] only because of *Minchah*, as it says (1 Kings 18:36–37): At *alot haminchah* [the time to offer up the *minchah* sacrifice], the prophet Elijah came forth … and said, 'Answer me, Adonai, answer me!'"

If they are said together, both *Minchah* and *Ma'ariv* are liminal, in that *Minchah* is the end of day and *Ma'ariv* is the beginning of night. All together, they take only a few minutes to go through, so are seen as a single span of time separating the real afternoon, when night is clearly not yet on its way, from the genuine night, when afternoon is long gone. The sense of urgency dominates *Minchah*; the sense of danger prevails in *Ma'ariv*. But there still remains a period that is the liminal within the liminal—I mean the few minutes or even just seconds when *Minchah* is over and *Ma'ariv* has not begun. It is dark, but not dark enough; the stars are arriving, but not yet clearly out; one star, says the Talmud (Shab. 34b) means day, three stars mean night, two stars are *ben hash'mashot*; it is that split second of absolute twilight, or, more colloquially, the "twilight zone," in that (being neither day nor night) it is absolutely anomalous, perfectly without rules. Anything that happens then is of dubious status: does it belong to the afternoon just ending or to the evening just beginning? A boy born *ben hash'mashot* is circumcised on the ninth day, not the eighth, since it is not quite clear what his birthday was, so we play it safe and assign his circumcision by counting from the first day that we know for sure he was alive (M. Shab. 19:5). If someone is found working *ben hash'mashot* between Shabbat and Yom Kippur, he is exempt from punishment, since the work cannot accurately be assigned to either day, and he is held guiltless for them both (M. Kritot 4:2).

But *ben hash'mashot* is not just the moment when ordinary things happen, albeit at an unordinary time. It is a moment so without rules that anything at all can be expected to occur. The Rabbis tell us how God used this liminal occasion in the act of creation (Avot 5:6):

Ten things were created *ben hash'mashot* on the first Friday of creation:

The mouth of the earth [that swallowed up Korah, Num. 16:32]
The mouth of the well [that fed the Israelites in the desert, Num. 21:16–18]
The mouth of the ass [that spoke to Balaam, Num. 22:28]
The rainbow [that appeared for Noah, Gen. 9:13]
The manna [that fell in the desert, Exod. 16:15]
The rod [used for miracles in Pharaoh's court, Exod. 4:17]

The *shamir* [the magical burrowing worm used by Solomon to build the Temple without having to use cutting tools (Git. 68a) and also the engraving on the High Priest's ephod (Sot. 48b)]
Script [that could be used for writing on the tablets]
Inscription [the actual writing on the tablets]
The tablets of stone [for the Ten Commandments, Exod. 32:15ff.]

Some people add also:

Demons *(shedim)*
The grave of Moses
The ram of Abraham [used in place of Isaac, Gen. 22:13]
And some say, the tongs made with tongs.

The list may look random at first, but it is not. The last item is the most interesting. Until about 1200 B.C.E., armies in the ancient Near East depended on bronze weapons. Iron had been available for a long time, but could not be melted in bronze era furnaces, so could not be separated from its ore. Mixed with slag (the impurities in the ore), it could be partly heated into wrought iron, but wrought iron was too soft for weaponry. By 1200 B.C.E., however, Hittite invaders had developed good iron, which they demonstrated in combat, smashing their enemies' bronze shields with newly designed iron swords. The secret was a process by which iron is repeatedly hammered and heated in a charcoal fire above 800 degrees centigrade. Exposure to carbon from the carbon monoxide gas creates steel, an alloy much harder than iron. By steeling the edge of the blade, a sharp hard edge can be developed, but by retaining the sword's haft as ordinary wrought iron, the sword absorbs the blow of an adversary rather than breaking. The new weapons were sharper, more durable, and stronger than their old bronze predecessors.

The health of society thus depended on skilled metallurgists, who required the technology for making very hot fires and then hammering and manipulating iron in the flame. For that, they needed tongs.

But here is the problem. The only way to make the tongs is to make them in the fire, for which you need tongs. Where, then, did the first tongs come from if there could not have been any prior tongs to make those tongs? The obvious answer was that God had prepared for just this necessity by creating primeval tongs at the beginning of time. They were an anomaly: the only set of tongs made without tongs; they were used just once, to make the first set of human tongs; and then they disappeared.

The rest of the list consists of equal anomalies, established by God for single use in future history that only God could know about in advance. A mouth in the earth to swallow Korah; a well to feed the Israelites, a talking donkey for Balaam; Noah's rainbow, the manna, Moses's miraculous rod, Moses's hidden burial place, the ram that saved Isaac, even the *shamir* worm that allowed the Temple to be built without heavy technology for it—and (somewhat its own category, but still an anomaly) the demons:

how did demons get created by a God who wanted only good for the world's creatures and who looked at creation and said it was good?

This midrash exists in many versions, with minor differences here and there, but always with the same overriding lesson. Anomalous times give rise to anomalous creations. *Ben hash'mashot* is that single anomaly that is neither day nor night, and is therefore frightening for what night will bring, but also rich in possibilities for inventing a future.

Day stands naturally for light and warmth; night for darkness and cold. As time goes on, secondary meanings accrue: day is good; night is evil; day is even "heaven," the end of time to which we aspire (our *Birkat Hamazon* [Grace after Meals] identifies it as *yom shekulo Shabbat um'nuchah l'chayei ha'olamim*, "the day that is entirely Shabbat and eternal rest"); while night is "hell"—the living kind on this earth, as in Wiesel's Auschwitz, or the eschatological variety where souls go at night for punishment.

The remarkable thing about human consciousness is our assumption that we can somehow control our destiny, lighting up the dark, literally with fire (now, electricity) or metaphorically with deeds of loving-kindness. Our barely human ancestors had no such aspirations. They accepted these basic oppositions as life's unchangeable givens. And then one day, someone invented a way to make fire, and all that changed. Fire is the ultimate gift of God, allowing us to make night into day, darkness into light, cold into warmth.

We know how Greek mythology explained the invention of fire. Knowing that Zeus cared little for his creatures, Prometheus, a god whose name means "foresight," stole it from him. Already, long before stealing fire, Prometheus had given mortals such necessary gifts as brickwork, woodworking, astronomy, numbers, healing, metallurgy, art, and even the alphabet to write things down—the very essence of cultural transmission. Now he completed the job of human independence in the face of nature: he gave them fire.

But Zeus, the mightiest of deities after taking the throne from his rival Kronos, intended human beings to live no better than other animals and eventually die off. Knowledge belonged to the gods alone. So, hearing of Prometheus's rebellion, he had him shackled to a crag, where, every day, an eagle would tear apart his flesh to devour his liver. Each night's frost, however, would heal the flesh, letting the eagle begin all over again the next day. More still, Zeus created a beautiful woman named Pandora, meaning "all giving," to entice human beings with the promise that they might have more of what Prometheus had intended for their welfare. Zeus gave her to Ephemetheus (brother of Prometheus), who accepted her willingly, only to discover that what she brought into the world was evil, mistrust, disease, and despair.

How different is the Jewish view: a merciful God, not a punishing one, who creates human beings as the very pinnacle of nature. Our midrash pictures God, *ben hash'mashot*, in the final liminal instant of twilight vision, making last-minute corrections to provide everything we will need when God's world-plan is likely to fall apart: a rainbow for the aftermath of universal destruction, a ram to save Isaac, manna for the desert, a hidden grave for Moses, writing (what Promotheus also had to steal from Zeus)—and fire, the gift of gifts, without which night and cold are here to stay.

Why doesn't our midrash about *ben hash'mashot* include the creation of fire, if, indeed, the twilight zone is the time to confront grave danger and to discover great inventions? The answer seems to be that rabbinic imagination saved the gift of fire for a separate midrash that is also about liminality's promise. How different it is from the Greek myth where humans are powerless and the mightiest god of all has only contempt for human discovery.

Adam was created on the sixth day, Friday. As Friday night fell, bringing with it Shabbat, Adam settled into pure bliss: not just Shabbat (perfect time), but Shabbat in the Garden of Eden (perfect space). What could be better? Meanwhile, unknown to him, at the very moment of light becoming dark, God was busy creating all the *ben hash'mashot* things that we have been talking about. But God had not anticipated the fear that would set in when Shabbat began to wane and Adam faced the prospect of an ordinary night, the first he had known. As Adam began to fear the worst, a pillar of fire appeared to him. He reached for it and used it to make *Havdalah*.

And that is how Jewish myth explains fire: not as human rebellion but as human intelligence taking advantage of opportunity. Unlike Prometheus, Adam is not exiled to eternally recurrent torture for disobedience. His expulsion from the Garden is altogether unrelated. God is, presumably, delighted that Adam will have fire to take with him into the world beyond.

In the story, Adam uses fire to make *Havdalah*, the ritual for Saturday night that distinguishes light from dark (see Volume 7, *Shabbat at Home*, pp. 164–190). But the midrash cannot just have had *Havdalah*, as ritual, in mind, for it provides Adam only with fire, not with the requisite wine and spices that *Havdalah* requires as much as it does fire. *Havdalah* here is not just the ritual, but the concept behind the ritual, the idea of being able to discern differences (see below, p. 113), the most obvious being life as a prehuman (without fire) and life as our prototypical human ancestor (with fire to free us from dark and cold). Fire for light, warmth, and creativity is not stolen from God; it is given, ready for Adam to find when he needs it. And he finds it *ben hash'mashot*.

Here lies the symbolic essence of *Minchah* and *Ma'ariv*. We should not assume our rabbinic ancestors were consumed only with superstitious tales about nighttime demons and dangers. When the Talmud says that sleep is one-sixtieth of death, it reflects the genuine fear that lingers deep within us, when we recognize that someday we will fall asleep and not wake up again. When fifteenth-to-sixteenth-century kabbalist Meir ibn Gabbai actually names the three bands of destructive angels (*malakhei chevlah*) whom the dead must fear, we should keep in mind that the entire kabbalistic scheme is metaphorical through and through; it is mythological the way the midrash is. Only a fool would identify everything the kabbalists describe as literal descriptions of premodern nonsense. We should remember that one of the rabbis who thinks that nighttime prayer "cools the fires of hell" (see p. 3) is Mordecai Jaffe of Poland (1535–1612), who was also a master of astronomy and philosophy in the day when those disciplines meant knowing Copernicus and Aristotle. When even Jaffe speaks of "cooling the fires of hell," we have a right to believe he is using language in a far deeper way than we generally give him credit for.

Sometimes when we say mythological, we mean mythic. "Mythological" is indeed the adjective we employ to characterize stories of the fabulous that we assume the ancients believed. Mythic is the larger-than-life quality those tales had. Our evening liturgy has mythic proportions, then. It should be approached with due regard for the human search for meaning in an uncontrollable universe, where day does indeed become night, where life will someday be death, and where good sometimes borders on evil. It should help us stop at *ben hash'mashot* to appreciate, as God did, the divine plan that threatens to founder at history's darkest moments, and to use that liminal time, as Adam did, to discover the potential for creative inventiveness. Our God is not an unfeeling Zeus; we need no Prometheus to save us from darkness. *Minchah* and *Ma'ariv* invite us to join with God in saving history's plan.

Introduction to the Liturgy

The Shape of *Minchah* and *Ma'ariv*

Lawrence A. Hoffman

When a king of flesh and blood strikes a coin, says the midrash, every single one comes out the same. Not so the ultimate ruler, God, who creates the human race without everyone looking exactly like each other. The midrash is onto something very deep: personalizing the shape of the things that matter.

THE WORK OF OUR HANDS

I look out my window and see some trees with buds, the first spring crocus, a squirrel or two, and driveways with automobiles. Like human beings, the trees, flowers, and animals are the work of God, each one different. All sheep, dogs, or monkeys look pretty much the same to me, but apparently, some animals, at least, distinguish each other's faces within their species just as humans do. All "life" forms are "alive" with their own uniqueness.

The automobiles are different. They are the Industrial Revolution's equivalent of coins struck by a king, modernity's mass productivity. Their uniformity provides the convenience of knowing in advance exactly what we will get: one Coca-Cola is exactly like the next; we needn't worry about the particular "cokemanship" of the person handing us the bottle. Likewise, fast food: Some years back, fast-food chains invaded restaurants in thruways and airports, where they were welcomed because hurried travelers are held hostage by limited restaurant availability. Rather than trust quick-service places we didn't know, we preferred fast food with no surprises. But mass production is distinctly impersonal, and by and large, except for the convenience, we hate it. We buy it, consume it, and trash the remains.

There is, however, a middle ground: manufactured products receive our personal touch when they become intimately involved with our private selves or are used to present a public image to others. These are the things that touch who we are; they display our taste, which we take to be revelatory of our inner quality.

Take clothing, for instance. Teenagers often dress pretty much the same, to indicate how "in with the crowd" they are. Adults usually have just the opposite goal. We buy fashionable clothes off the rack, knowing full well that the outfit is mass produced and available in the thousands. But we pretend that no one else we know is buying the same thing. No one brings home several copies of the same dress to distribute to friends and save them the time of shopping on their own (we really do not like it when other people show up at a party wearing what we have on). We use the mirror to make our clothes fit our own particular body shape, and we supplement what we wear with the personal touch of jewelry and "accessories."

Similarly, we have a special relationship to spaces where we spend a lot of private time, but are likely to be visited by others. We despise tract housing projects, for example; the minute we buy or rent a place, we decorate it to our taste, so as to make it truly "ours"; and we make sure to compliment others on how nicely they have fixed up their own homes. For professionals who identify closely with their work, there is also "the office," where we choose art for the wall and family photos or knickknacks for the desk. Secretarial assistants at workstations in the halls tend to do that less; they work in the open where, all day long, people pass them by without acknowledging their presence. Their mass-produced computer-equipped desks are the office equivalent of fast food: "fast furniture" which they occupy as indifferent consumers, putting in their time according to the rules and leaving for their private life back home. Lots of Americans identify also with their cars, plastering bumper stickers as telltale signs of self on the outside paint job.

The work of our hands, then, the way we personally modify what other people make and sell us, is the middle ground between the spectacularly individualized life forms that come from God and the undifferentiated and interchangeable output of mass production. We treat the work of our hands as extensions of ourselves. Psalm 90:17 echoes this relationship in a line that has become a favorite for public benedictions:

> May the favor of Adonai our God be upon us;
> Let the work of our hands prosper
> O prosper the work of our hands!

Wondering what it means to have the work of our hands prosper, medieval Jewish commentators refer the verse to the *mishkan*, the desert sanctuary that the Israelites build. Ibn Ezra says, "'To prosper' here means to be at one with the sentiment (Ps. 127:1), 'If Adonai does not build the house, its builders labor in vain.'" The work of our hands "prospers" when what we do is shared with God, when we (like God) create with individuality. When we endow what we make with "a life of its own," we reflect the creative power of our maker. Surely that is what human culture is all about: leaving our mark on the world as God did, etching evidence of our individual presence in the residue of time.

PRAYER AS THE WORK OF OUR HANDS

Whole peoples leave their mark, too. The Jewish People is more than the sum of individuals who compose it. We are a culture, growing through time, leaving our collective mark behind us through a tradition that we inherit, alter, and pass along to others. That is where our liturgy comes in. The prayer book is the work of our collective hands, our home in time, that generation after generation of Jews inherit and then re-outfit to express their collective spiritual mooring.

Better than any other cultural product, the liturgy reflects what we have lived through. Its contents reflect historical events, halakhic debates, our dialogue with each other, and our commentary on the world round about us. It changes in the same way that a family homestead does as new generations grow into adulthood, then possess and redecorate it. But through it all, the homestead keeps its essential shape. It looks enough the way it used to, to be recognizable. Knowledgeable visitors may pause to point out the extra porch that a grandfather added on, or the special molding in the den that his daughter, the present owner's mother, plotted.

To knowledgeable worshipers, reading the prayer book is like taking a walk through the family homestead, picking out each generation's alterations, but all the while thinking through what changes we will make to further prosper the work of our People's collective hands. Within the year, for instance (2006), North American Reform Jews will have a new prayer book, *Mishkan T'filah*. In 2001, liberal Jews in Germany wrote a Siddur marking the rebirth of Judaism even there, where so many of our people perished. The maturation of Israeli Conservative (Masorti) Judaism can be dated to *Siddur Va'ani Tefillati*, its first prayer book (1998). The clearest statement of Orthodox revival in America is the *ArtScroll Siddur*. These books are dynamic reflections of the ever-renewing Jewish soul. They are the work we do with God as our partner.

That has been the message of *My People's Prayer Book* from the very beginning. Our current volume continues the theme, by turning to a subject altogether new: the services we call *Minchah* and *Ma'ariv*.

THE EVENING SYMPHONY OF LITURGICAL IDEAS

Musicians speak of musical ideas that combine to form the structural backbone of longer works—like the memorable four opening notes of Beethoven's Fifth Symphony; so too, there are liturgical ideas embedded in the flow of our prayers. These ideas occur, recur, climax, and resolve, making our prayers no mere mishmash of verbiage, but a carefully constructed whole that moves smoothly and with purpose from beginning to end. Throughout the earlier volumes of *My People's Prayer Book*, we have been graphing that flow in the ups and downs of a largely horizontal line that traces how the service begins, mounts to a crescendo, and sinks back downward as it comes to a close.

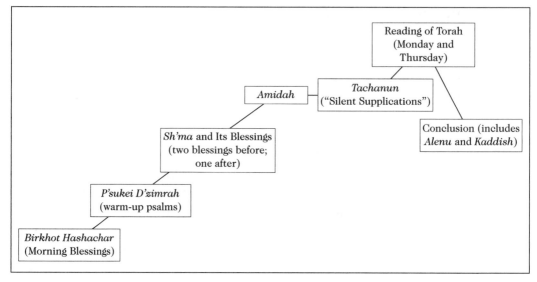

Weekday Morning Service (Shacharit)

What is true of morning *(Shacharit)* is true of afternoon *(Minchah)* and evening *(Ma'ariv)* as well. We can construct the afternoon and evening services on the model of the morning prototype.

The weekday *Minchah* (afternoon) service is simple to follow. It is composed of only four elements, each of which occurs elsewhere in the liturgy, their appearance here being, to some extent, predictable. The evening—called *Ma'ariv*, but also *Arvit*—is somewhat harder to figure out. But in both cases, once we arrive at the weekday set of prayers, we can expand them to reflect the liturgy for Shabbat. If we recall the basic pattern of the morning service and the rationale behind each of the rubrics it contains, we can generalize that pattern to the afternoon and evening.

Weekday Morning Service

1. *Birkhot Hashachar*, "Morning Blessings" (for detailed account, see Volume 5)
2. *P'sukei D'zimrah*, "warm-up psalms" (see Volume 3)
   Psalms 145–150 are central; Psalm 145 *(Ashre)* is the most important.
3. The *Sh'ma* and Its Blessings (see Volume 1)
   To be recited (as the *Sh'ma* itself instructs, Deut. 6:7) "when you lie down and when you rise."
4. The *Amidah* (see Volume 2)
   Said by the Rabbis to take the place of the regular weekday sacrifice from Temple times called *tamid* (meaning "regular" or "constant"; pronounced tah-MEED). The *tamid* was offered mornings and afternoons.
5. *Tachanun*, "supplications" (see Volume 6)
   Originally a daily confession; now a set of personal supplications.
6. Reading Torah (see Volume 4)

On Monday, Thursday, Shabbat, and holidays.
7. Concluding prayers (see Volume 6)
Primarily *Alenu* and *Kaddish*.

Now we apply our logic. As we go through each rubric, we can compile a tentative list of what we would expect. Later we will have to go back to amend the list on the basis of new information that could not be assumed from *Shacharit*. As we develop the list, an X indicates rubrics that are omitted. A question mark puts us on notice that our logic is insufficient to know for sure what to anticipate; we will have to return to the "question marked" entries with more information later on. We will use the standard Ashkenazi service as our liturgical baseline; the commentaries provide the major ways in which this baseline is altered in the Spanish-Portuguese and the Sefardi parallels.

Of the three central morning rubrics, the *Sh'ma* (#3), the *Amidah* (#4), and reading the Torah (#6), we can predict that in all likelihood:

- The *Sh'ma* (#3) will be said morning and evening (following its own instructions, "when you lie down and when you rise").
- The *Amidah* (#4) will be said morning and afternoon (when the *tamid* was offered—there was no sacrificial cult at night, if only because it was dark then, in an age without electric lights).
- Reading Torah (#6), which is relatively rare anyway, and generally limited to the mornings, will not occur in the afternoon or evening.

So, to start:

Weekday *Shacharit*	Weekday *Minchah*	Weekday *Ma'ariv*
3. *Sh'ma* and Its Blessings	X	Included
4. *Amidah*	Included	(No evening *tamid*)?
6 Torah reading	X	X

We are left with what we might consider not exactly minor rubrics—none of the prayers are unimportant—but rubrics that round out the service by building on the three major topics we just looked at: the *Sh'ma* (a conversation about God); the *Amidah* (a conversation with God); and reading Torah (confronting God's word and will, as members of covenanted Israel).

- The Morning Blessings (#1) are just that, *morning* blessings, intended to greet a new day. We would not expect to find them elsewhere.
- The warm-up psalms called *P'sukei D'zimrah* (#2), however, play a vital function—preparing individuals to constitute a community. At the very least, we should expect *some* form of psalms to start *Minchah* and, possibly, also *Ma'ariv*, especially when *Minchah* and *Ma'ariv* are not recited back to back, so that we

need to worry about reconstituting the community all over again when it meets for *Ma'ariv*.

So our list expands:

Weekday *Shacharit*	Weekday *Minchah*	Weekday *Ma'ariv*
1. Morning blessings	X	X
2. "Warm-up"	Included, but what psalms?	Included, but what psalms?
3. *Sh'ma* and Its Blessings	X	Included
4. *Amidah*	Included	(No evening *tamid*)?
6. Torah reading	X	X

Finally, we turn to the *Tachanun* (#5) and concluding prayers, especially *Alenu* and *Kaddish* (#7).

- The *Tachanun* (#5) developed out of a confession that follows and completes the silent prayer of the *Amidah*, so we might expect a repetition of *Tachanun* in *Minchah*, where the other *Amidah* (taking the place of the *tamid*) is found. There are, however, two kinds of *Tachanun* in the morning: a long variety for Monday and Thursday, and a short form for other days. We cannot easily predict which one will be said here.

The concluding prayers (#7) are easier to predict. Every service has a conclusion, and there is nothing about *Alenu* or *Kaddish* that makes them especially appropriate to the morning. So we get both of them in the afternoon and evening as well. Our fully filled-out tentative list, then, looks like this:

Weekday *Shacharit*	Weekday *Minchah*	Weekday *Ma'ariv*
1. Morning blessings	X	X
2. "Warm-up"	Included, but what psalms?	Included, but what psalms?
3. *Sh'ma* and Its Blessings	X	Included
4. *Amidah*	Included	(No evening *tamid*)?
5. *Tachanun*	Included, but which version?	X
6. Torah reading	X	X
7. *Alenu* and *Kaddish*	Included	Included

Now for the question marks.

An overriding concern of Jewish liturgy is the avoidance of *tirkha* (pronounced teer-KHAH, but, commonly, TEER-khah), "burden"—making it so burdensome for worshipers to pray that they stop coming. Because people have difficulty taking a lot of time off from afternoon work, and because they are tired at night, afternoon and evening prayers are shorter than their morning equivalents. So:

- The *Minchah* warm-up (#2) borrows only the most central psalm from the morning, the elaborated version of Psalm 145 that we call *Ashre*.
- Of the two versions of *Tachanun* (long and short), we use only the short one at *Minchah*.
- *Ma'ariv* includes almost no warm-up at all—just two lines from Psalms (78:38 and 20:10) that affirm God's compassion (*V'hu rachum*, "He is merciful"). When, however, *Ma'ariv* does not immediately follow *Minchah*, so we need to worry more about reestablishing a worshiping community, we add Psalm 134 (the shortest psalm in the Bible) and three other psalm verses that Jewish mystics tacked on.
- Finally, however, even though there was no *tamid* sacrifice at night, so that, technically, we need no *Amidah* then, we have one, added as an option originally, but treated by now as mandatory in practice. Still, theory retains some influence here: the *Ma'ariv Amidah* is not repeated by the prayer leader. People say it silently to themselves, and that is that.

There are other fine points also, some of them important.

- The *Sh'ma*, for instance, has an extra blessing at night, a fourth one called *Hashkivenu* ("Lie us down to peace") requesting safety in the nighttime darkness.
- And that is followed by a fifth blessing too, what we call here "an extended *Hashkivenu*" (*Barukh Adonai L'olam*).

But basically, both afternoon and evening services can now be listed, and then plotted horizontally on a par with the morning liturgy.

	Weekday *Shacharit*	Weekday *Minchah*	Weekday *Ma'ariv*
1.	Morning blessings	X	X
2.	"Warm-up"	Included, but only *Ashre*	Included: a. *V'hu rachum* b. When not immediately following *Minchah*, add Psalm 134 and three other verses
3.	*Sh'ma* and Its Blessings	X	Included, but: a. Add *Hashkivenu* b. Add extended *Hashkivenu—Barukh Adonai L'olam*
4.	*Amidah*	Included	Included: but silent only
5.	*Tachanun*	Included (short form)	X
6.	Torah reading	X	X
7.	*Alenu* and *Kaddish*	Included	Included

If we plot this horizontally, the way we did *Shacharit*, the three lines of service that demonstrate their "flow" look remarkably similar.

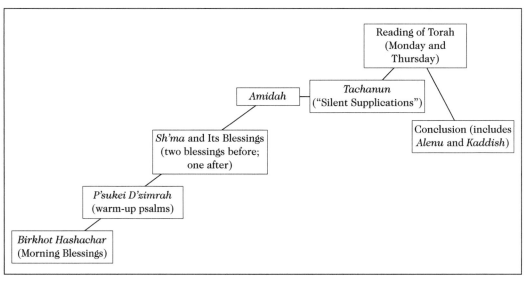

Weekday Morning Service (Shacharit)

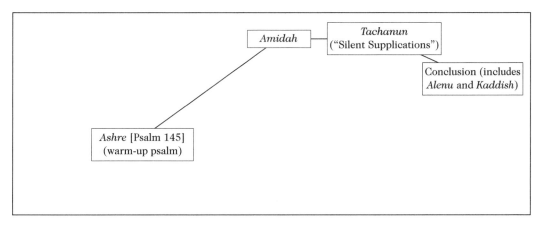

Weekday Afternoon Service (Minchah)

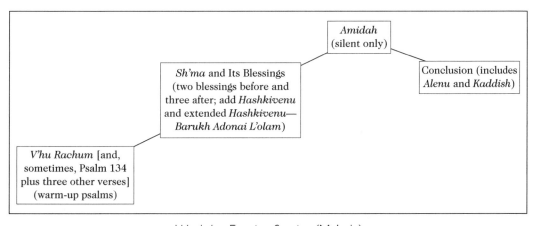

Weekday Evening Service (Ma'ariv)

Before moving on to the structure of *Minchah* and *Ma'ariv* for Shabbat, we should note simply that there is more to the conclusion of *Ma'ariv* than just *Alenu* and *Kaddish*. The end of the day seems naturally to call for psalms, so it is common to recite at least one psalm, and sometimes more, before disbanding for the night. But we could not do justice here to the enormous diversity of practice. We decided instead to include only two psalms that happen to be particularly widespread and well known. Psalm 27 is integral to the High Holy Day period, beginning with the preparatory month of Elul and continuing until Simchat Torah. Psalm 49 is associated with services in a mourner's home. We included these.

But there are others that we did not have room for. Psalm 16 (for example) is encountered on days when *Tachanun* is not said (e.g., Rosh Chodesh and Chanukah)—for rules of *Tachanun*, see Daniel Landes, "The Paradoxical Power of *Tachanun*," in Volume 6, *Tachanun and Concluding Prayers*, p. 19. Sefardi, Spanish-Portuguese, and Chasidic Jews add Psalm 23. Elsewhere, we find Psalms 83, 124, and other psalms as well.

The psalms we include should be seen as representative of the general role that psalms play in our liturgy. They are used as warm-up for every service, and they bring both the morning service (which starts our day) and the evening service (which ends it) to an appropriately spiritual end.

Early on, in this series, we said that even though more people are familiar with the service for Shabbat than with the set of weekday prayers, we were beginning with the weekday service anyway, because its daily staples are the skeletal backbone for every other occasion. The diagram that best represents the liturgy as a whole is a set of concentric circles, showing how the weekday prayers expand to represent Shabbat and holidays.

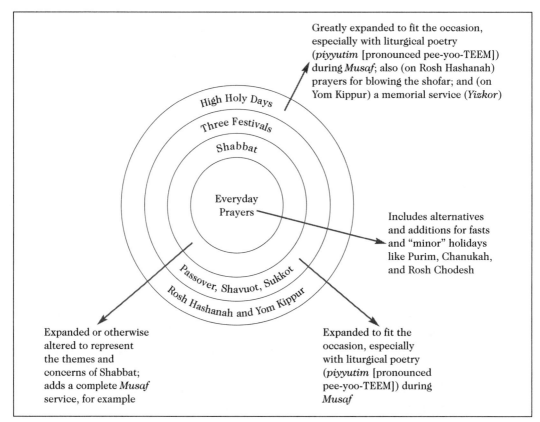

The Weekday Prayers Expand to Represent Shabbat and Holidays

The next volume (Volume 10) will complete the prayers of Shabbat (*Shacharit* and *Musaf*). Volume 8 began the liturgy of Shabbat, looking in depth at the lengthy and fascinating warm-up for *Ma'ariv* (Friday night). This volume (Volume 9) handles *Ma'ariv* itself, as well as *Minchah* before it—in both the Shabbat and the weekday service.

We have charted the weekday offerings; we now have to expand the map to indicate how *Minchah* and *Ma'ariv* are altered for Shabbat—how, that is, the core of the liturgy from Diagram 4 is outfitted for the next concentric circle outward, the one for Shabbat. The starting point is the two lines that mapped the weekday *Minchah* and *Ma'ariv* liturgy, but this time, we can indicate the changes for Shabbat in added boxes with dotted lines. The reasons for the changes are given in the commentaries, the pages for which occur inside the dotted boxes. A list of changes is also provided.

Above, we began with *Minchah*, since it was the easier of the two services to grasp. Here, we follow the order in which the services occur, first Friday night (Shabbat *Ma'ariv*), then Saturday afternoon (Shabbat *Minchah*). The changes for *Ma'ariv* are extensive; those for *Minchah* are minimal.

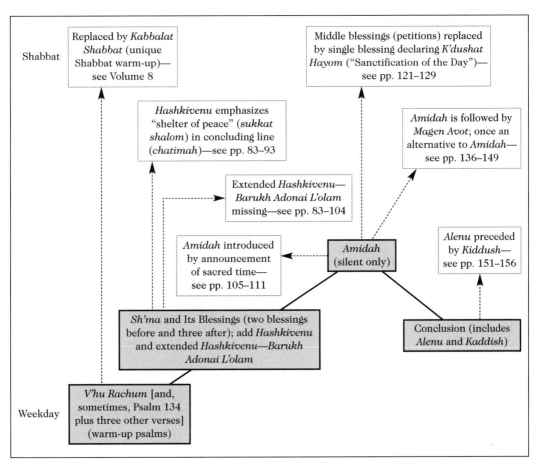

Evening Service (Ma'ariv): Weekdays and Shabbat

Shabbat changes in Ma'ariv *(Friday Night)*

1. Warm-up
   The usual psalms are replaced by *Kabbalat Shabbat* (the subject of Volume 8).

2. *Sh'ma* and Its Blessings
   a. *Hashkivenu* receives new ending emphasizing *sukkat shalom*, a "shelter of peace."
   b. The extended *Hashkivenu* (*Barukh Adonai L'olam*) is omitted.

3. *Amidah*
   a. Introduced by biblical verses announcing sacred time.
   b. Middle blessings (petitions) are replaced by a single blessing declaring *K'dushat Hayom* ("Sanctification of the Day").
   c. Followed by *Magen Avot* ("Protecting Our Ancestors"), originally an alternative *Amidah* in its own right.

4. Conclusion
   Alenu and *Kaddish* are preceded by *Kiddush*. Psalms conclude the service.

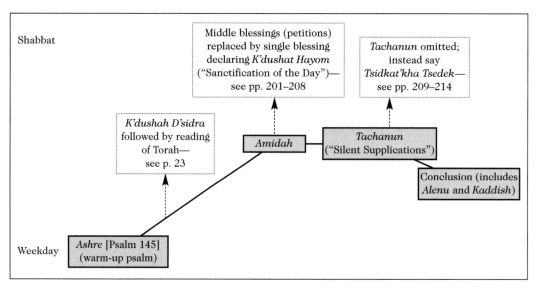

Afternoon Service (Minchah): *Weekdays and Shabbat*

Shabbat Changes in Minchah *(Saturday Afternoon)*

1. Torah reading added; preceded by *K'dushah D'sidra*, which is postponed from its usual place in the morning.

For a hundred years now, scholars have suggested the intriguing possibility that the Shabbat *Minchah* service reflects an ancient ritual for Saturday afternoons. To begin with, the Talmud (RH 31a) reports that in the days of the Temple, over a three-week period every Saturday afternoon, the Levites would alternate three songs from the Torah: the familiar *Shirat Hayam,* the Song of the Sea (divided into two, Exodus 15:1–10 and 11–18); and *Sh'irat B'er,* the Song of the Well (Num. 21:17–20). A second tradition *(Tanchuma Vayakhel)* associates Saturday afternoon outside the Temple as the locus for Torah study and midrashic sermons.

To this day, we read Torah on Shabbat afternoon, but the Talmud (Shab. 116b) recollects saying a *haftarah* also. Rashi (to Shab. 24a) too proclaims, "I have found in a geonic responsum that it was customary once to read a ten-verse prophetic reading [*haftarah*] at Shabbat *Minchah.*" Could it be that we once read more than just the Torah on Saturday afternoons? Other responsa trace an afternoon *haftarah* in Persia to as late as the eleventh century, and the thirteenth-century Italian work *Sefer Ha'ittim* confirms the reading of Prophets then— although as study before *Minchah* began, not, technically, as a *haftarah* within the service, as we have it in the morning. In 1909, pioneering scholar Louis Ginzberg (*Geonica* II, pp. 298–300) amassed evidence that the Saturday afternoon study regimen once also contained sections from the *K'tuvim* (the "Writings," the third section into which the Bible is divided, the first two being the Torah and the Prophets [*N'vi'im*]).

We have two prayers commonly associated with study, the familiar *Kaddish,* and the *K'dushah D'sidra* (see L. Hoffman, "A redeemer shall come," Volume 6, *Tachanun and Concluding Prayers,* pp. 112, 124–125). The former is ubiquitous, having spread throughout the prayer book, and is used now for many purposes (including a mourners' prayer), while the latter remains associated with study, forming a daily staple at that point in the morning service where the Torah is read. But Torah is also read at Shabbat *Minchah,* so on Shabbat, the *K'dushah D'sidra* is postponed from the morning service and used to introduce the afternoon Torah reading instead—at the place where introductory study would once have been common.

Later tradition explained the postponement on other grounds. It was said, for instance, that when Shabbat is over, the dead who are granted release for the day return to their punishment in *Gehinnom* (the equivalent of hell). At *Minchah,* then, as nighttime threatens to fall, we say a prayer that has the power "to cool the fires of hell" (Mordecai Jaffe, the *L'vush,* Poland, 1535–1612).

2. *Amidah*
Middle blessings (petitions) are replaced by a single blessing declaring *K'dushat Hayom* ("Sanctification of the Day").

3. *Tachanun*
Omitted; replaced by *Tsidkat'kha Tsedek.*

Readers of this series will recognize this introduction to *Minchah* and

Ma'ariv as one of a set of essays providing the structure of the service. Liturgy can best be appreciated by anticipating the "liturgical" ideas that constitute its symphony. The organization of *Minchah* and *Ma'ariv* are especially worth observing because they are so often taken for granted. More than any other services, these are prayed through rapidly or ignored altogether. But as we saw in "Anxiety and Opportunity: The Mood of Nighttime Prayer" (see pp. 1–9), the magic of twilight offers extraordinary opportunity for insight; the liturgy should be savored in the evening, no less than it is in the morning.

The Halakhic Status of Minchah and Ma'ariv

Daniel Landes

MINCHAH

Halakhah worries lest *Minchah* be overlooked, a surprising concern, really, since legally, *Minchah* has the same status as *Shacharit*. Both were created by patriarchs: Abraham, *Shacharit*; and Isaac, *Minchah*. Also like *Shacharit*, *Minchah* parallels an *olah*, the daily Temple sacrifice called the *tamid*. As *Shacharit* replaces the *tamid* of the morning, so *Minchah* replaces that of the afternoon. Nonetheless, the Talmud feels compelled to warn (Ber. 6b):

> A person should always be strict about praying *Minchah*, for Elijah was answered [by God] only because of *Minchah*, as it says (1 Kings 18:36), "At *alot haminchah* (the time to offer up the *minchah* sacrifice), the prophet Elijah came forth ... and said, 'Answer me, Adonai, answer me!'"

The context is Elijah's single-handed battle against Ba'al's prophets on Mount Carmel, for the souls of the People Israel. The Talmud evidently attributes God's validation of Elijah to Elijah's offering the *minchah* sacrifice—a clear and striking validation of *Minchah* the prayer.

The prayer Elijah offers parallels the threefold structure of the *Amidah*: praise *(shevach)*, petition *(bakashah)*, grateful thanksgiving *(hoda'ah)*. Elijah begins (1 Kings 18:36), "Adonai, God of Abraham, Isaac, and Israel! Let it be known today that You are God in Israel and that I am your servant, and that I have done all these things at your bidding"—language akin to the *Amidah*'s introductory three blessings of praise *(shevach)*. Then comes petition *(bakashah)*: "Answer me, Adonai, answer me, that this people may know that You, Adonai, are God" (v. 37). Finally there is grateful acknowledgment *(hoda'ah)*: "For You have turned their hearts backward." The Rabbis certainly saw in Elijah's prayer their definitional *Minchah Amidah*.

The *Tur* (Jacob ben Asher, 1270–1340, Spain; the main halakhic code after Maimonides' *Mishneh Torah*), explains the urgency of the Talmud's demand to take *Minchah* seriously:

Shacharit takes place in the morning: one arises from bed and prays immediately, before getting burdened by business *(tarud)*. Similarly *Ma'ariv* occurs upon coming home at night, when one is no longer burdened by business. But *Minchah* falls in the middle of the day when one is indeed burdened by business; it requires a concentrated effort to free oneself from business in order to pray it. But if one does so, the reward is very great.

The *P'rishah* (commentary on the *Tur*, by Rabbi Joshua Hakohen Falk, 1555–1614, Poland) explains the connection between Elijah and the urgency to take *Minchah* seriously: "Elijah was answered specifically through *Minchah*, and in our time too that prayer has a *s'gulah* [a special positive property], because its timing is burdensome." In other words, whether Elijah or the overtaxed businessperson, davening *Minchah* is always trying to beat the odds!

There are two possible times for *Minchah*. The rabbinic day, we must first understand, was variable in length, going from whenever the sun rose to whenever it set. The entire period was divided into twelve "hours." Throughout the year, these varied in duration, since they were a mathematical result of dividing daylight by twelve. These were not solar hours then, but "halakhic hours," *sha'ot z'maniyot* (pronounced shah-OHT z'-mah-nee-YOHT), as they are called. The more obvious time for *Minchah* in that system parallels the afternoon *tamid* for which it stands, and that sacrifice could be offered any time from 9½ *sha'ot z'maniyot* until the day's end. That 9½-hour starting time is called *minchah k'tanah* (pronounced min-KHAH k'-tah-NAH, or, popularly, MIN-khah k'TAH-nah), "the small *minchah*."

The other option is called *minchah g'dolah* (pronounced min-KHAH g'-doh-LAH, or, popularly, MIN-khah g'-DOH-lah), "the great *minchah*." It starts just after noon, three halakhic hours earlier (at 6½ *sha'ot z'maniyot*), and derives from the time of slaughtering the *tamid* on the day before Passover. They began early that day, so as to allow time for the many Passover offerings that would have to be dispatched for all the pilgrims arriving that day and needing to have their Passover offering completed for the Seder at nightfall.

Both *minchah k'tanah* (9½ halakhic hours onward) and *minchah g'dolah* (6½ halakhic hours onward) are halakhically valid for our *Minchah Amidah* today. The usual *tamid* time (9½ hours) is technically preferable, but the earlier *minchah g'dolah*, the earliest halakhically possible moment of opportunity, is always desirable.

A more substantive argument revolves around the end of *Minchah*. Mishnah Berakhot 4:4 cites Rabbi Eliezer: "A fixed prayer fails as a request for mercy." But what is a "fixed prayer" in this context? Of the many explanations for this enigmatic statement, the relevant one for us is that it refers to delaying prayer too long, or, as the Talmud puts it, "not praying with the reddening of the sun."

> Said Rabbi Chiyya bar Abba, in the name of Rabbi Yochanan, it is a *mitzvah* to pray while the sun is still red [at dawn and dusk]. Rabbi Zeira added: What verse teaches us this? "Let them fear You while the sun shines, before the moon rises" (Ps. 72:5). In the West [Land of Israel] they cursed those who prayed with the reddening of the sun. Why? Lest the time get away from him [better than waiting until the last

minute, one should arise before dawn for morning prayer and start evening prayer before dusk]. (Ber. 29b)

We can now outline the spectrum of nuanced *Minchah* spiritual experience as defined by Halakhah:

a. Pray at the beginning of *minchah g'dolah* (6½ hours), to fulfill the maxim, *Z'rizim makdimim l'mitzvot* ("The truly motivated perform commandments as soon as possible").

b. Since, however, the duration of *minchah g'dolah* falls in the midst of daytime business, try to set aside concern for money and affairs. Take time instead to proclaim, "Happy are those who dwell in Your house!" Thereby do you defeat your own daily idolatries, as Elijah did the idolatries of his day, at Mount Carmel.

c. But if you choose *minchah k'tanah* (9½ hours), the normal time for the *tamid*, know that your prayer is still your *avodah*—divine "service" precious in itself. "This *minchah* of the late afternoon is as dear and precious as the *N'illah* of Yom Kippur, *et ratson* ['a time of grace'] allowing us to take special joy" in completing the day and our service to God *(Arukh Hashulchan, O. Ch. 127)*.

d. "When the sun is red" at the very end of *minchah k'tanah* is an emotionally dramatic moment derived from observing the passage of day into night. *Minchah* converts this liminal experience into the awe of God. But the overwhelming nature of the event runs the risk of subverting Halakhah, since one could easily lose track of time and miss fulfilling the *mitzvah*. That is why authorities follow the practice of the Land of Israel in prescribing it as ideal. Nonetheless, it remains a halakhic possibility and has returned as normative, especially in Chasidic practice.

MA'ARIV

Ma'ariv is often the first or most predominant service that many people encounter—either as the synagogue liturgy Friday nights or a service in a house of mourning *(bet avel)*. Like *Shacharit* and *Minchah*, *Ma'ariv* too centers around the *Amidah*, but it has the weakest halakhic status of the three. The essential question is whether *Ma'ariv* is optional *(r'shut)* or obligatory *(chovah)*. If it is optional, then how optional; and if obligatory, where does its obligation come from?

In its classic discussion of the *Amidah* (Ber. 26b [see Volume 2, *The Amidah*, Landes, pp. 6–7]), the Talmud provides *Ma'ariv* with origins both patriarchal and sacrificial. The patriarchal piece involves Jacob (Gen. 28:11): While fleeing his brother's murderous rage, "he [Jacob] came [*vayifga*] upon a place [*bamakom*], when the sun had set." The Talmud reads *bamakom* literally, not just "He came upon *a place*," but *"the Place"*—*makom* meaning the Omnipresent (as it does frequently in rabbinic usage), a reference to God. *Vayifga*, moreover, is reminiscent of Jeremiah 7:16, *tifga bi*—"plead with Me," an allusion to prayer. So Jacob fled Esau "when the sun had set," at which time he came upon God and pleaded in prayer—the first *Ma'ariv*.

The sacrificial parallel comes from the nightly practice of burning the fat that was left over from the daily sacrifices. Because this burning took the whole night, the Mishnah says, *Ma'ariv* "has no set end time during the night beyond which it may not be recited. The problem with the talmudic discussion is that the patriarchal source is merely aggadic, so is secondary to the sacrificial rationale, but that rationale is also problematic because the burning of leftover fat is not itself an actual *avodah*, a "sacrifice." Indeed, in a subsequent discussion (Ber. 27a), the Mishnah's assertion that *Ma'ariv* "has no set end" is taken possibly to refer not to its time during the night, but to its status, which two Tannaim debate. Gamaliel calls it "obligatory" *(chovah)* but Joshua thinks it is optional *(r'shut)*. Famous Amoraic disputants continue this argument: "Abaye said the law follows the opinion that it is *chovah*; Rava says the law follows the opinion that it is *r'shut*."

Later halakhic authorities continue the debate. Isaac Alfasi (the RiF, 1013–1103, Morocco, to Ber. 4) rules, "The law follows Rava [*r'shut*]. Nonetheless, this applies only before it is prayed ["a priori," *mil'chat'chilah*]; once *Ma'ariv* has been prayed [*b'di'avad*, "ex post facto"], it is considered as if one has accepted it as a *chovah* … and nowadays everyone has accepted it upon themselves as a *chovah*." Thus, *Ma'ariv* is intrinsically optional, but only until it has been prayed, at which point it becomes mandatory, in that one has implicitly accepted the obligation of saying it. The source of the obligation is not *Ma'ariv* in and of itself, but one's implied acceptance of the practice of reciting it. This follows the general tendency of the traditionally observant world to transform matters of *r'shut* (option) into *chovah* (obligation).

Maimonides (1135–1204, Egypt; "Laws of Prayer" 1:6) reaches a similar, though not altogether identical conclusion, to which he provides a significant preamble:

> The Sages established that a person should pray a *Ma'ariv T'filah*, for the limbs of the perpetual sacrifice [the *tamid* offered earlier in the day] continued to be consumed all night long, as it says (Lev. 6:2), "The burnt offering itself shall remain where it is burned upon the altar all night until morning." Similarly it says (Ps. 55:18), "Evening, morning, and noon, I complain and moan, and He hears my voice." Not that *Ma'ariv* is obligatory (*chovah*) like *Shacharit* and *Minchah*, but all of Israel everywhere customarily pray *Ma'ariv*, having taken it upon themselves as an obligation.

Maimonides connects *Ma'ariv* to the Talmud's sacrificial rationale, omits the patriarchal narrative (which might be seen as homiletical rather than halakhic), and introduces a verse from Psalms to invoke the spiritual need for nighttime prayer. Going farther than Alfasi, he refrains from calling it *r'shut*, saying only that it is not a *chovah* in the same way that *Shacharit* and *Minchah* are; and then he immediately adds that all communities everywhere have accepted it as a *chovah*. For Alfasi, the transition from *r'shut* to *chovah* is activated by the *individual* worshiper; for Maimonides, *Ma'ariv*'s rightful status as *chovah* (because of its sacrificial roots) has been activated for us all by *community* practice.

A third viewpoint comes from the Tosafot (the School of Rashi, twelfth through fourteenth century, Franco-Germany), who maintain (Ber. 27b) that *r'shut* means more than "optional" or "permissible." It connotes actual obligation, which, however, may be considered optional when in conflict with a *mitzvah overet* (pronounced meets-VAH oh-VEH-reht), a "passing *mitzvah*," meaning a *mitzvah* whose proper time of performance will pass if not done immediately. Thus, if we are faced with praying *Ma'ariv* or performing a given *mitzvah* that must be done before its time runs out, *Ma'ariv* gives way to the "passing *mitzvah*." *Ma'ariv*, then, is a *mitzvah*, but without the same *chovah* status as *Shacharit* and *Minchah*, with regard to a competing "passing *mitzvah*." The latter two services might very well supersede the "passing *mitzvah*" or, if not, they will need to be "paid back" (by praying two *Amidah*s in a subsequent service). Not so *Ma'ariv* (see *Shiltei Gibborim* of Joshua Boaz ben Simon, d. 1492, commenting on Alfasi).

The upshot is that the Halakhah sees *Ma'ariv* as a *r'shut* that needs to be understood and treated as a *chovah*—it may not to be delayed, for example (Maimonides, Laws of Prayer 6:6). Nonetheless, elements of its *r'shut* status remain; for example, among the three prayer services, the *Amidah* of *Ma'ariv* alone has no *chazarat hashatz* (pronounced khah-zah-RAHT hah-SHAHTS), "repetition by the prayer leader." "Since it is not [technically] a *chovah*," Maimonides explains, "one should not recite blessings in vain in that there is no one who is so obligated that he [the prayer leader] need exempt him [through a repetition]" (Laws of Prayer 9:9).

The tension between *r'shut* and *chovah* within the understanding of *Ma'ariv*'s nature is one place that Halakhah reminds us of the balance in our prayer life, between the free will choosing the *option* of prayer and the consistency and seriousness of the *obligation* of turning to God.

Introduction to the Commentaries

How to Look for Meaning in the Prayers

Lawrence A. Hoffman

THE ART OF JEWISH READING

I remember the day I looked at a manuscript of a prayer book that no one could identify. It had been smuggled out of Russia (then the Soviet Union), and was obviously the liturgy for Rosh Hashanah, but who had written it? And when? It was handwritten, so the style told us much, but in addition, someone had written marginal notes in another handwriting, and yet a third person had written comments on the comments—a third unknown scholar of years gone by whose name we wanted to rescue from oblivion.

Standing before the massive volume, I reflected on the sheer joy of studying a traditional Jewish text. I had seen printed versions before, but never a handwritten instance. What a wonderful habit we Jews developed once upon a time: writing a text in the middle of the page and then filling up the margins with commentaries. Every page becomes a crosscut through Jewish history. Jewish Bibles come that way; so do the Talmud, the Mishnah, and the codes. We never read just the text. We always read it through the prism of the way other people have read it.

To be a Jewish reader, then, is to join the ranks of the millions of readers who came before us, leaving their comments in the margins, the way animals leave tracks in the woods. Go deep into the forest, and you will come across deer runs, for example: paths to water sources, carved out by hundreds of thousands of deer over time. The deer do not just inhabit the forest; they are part of the forest; they change the forest's contours as they live there, just as the forest changes them, by offering shelter, food, and water. There is no virgin forest, really; it is an ecosystem, a balance between the vegetation and the animals who live there.

So, too, there are no virgin texts. They too are ecosystems, sustaining millions of readers over time. When we read our classic texts, we tread the paths of prior readers, in search of spiritual nourishment. *My People's Prayer Book* is therefore not just the Siddur text; it is the text as read by prominent readers from among the people. You are invited to share our path, and even to break new ground yourself, passing on to others your own marginal notes, should you wish.

THE LITURGICAL TEXT WE USE

This volume is dedicated to *Minchah* and *Ma'ariv*, "afternoon" and "evening" prayer—for weekdays and for Shabbat. It therefore completes our study of weekday prayer (Volumes 1–6) and continues our journey through the liturgy for Shabbat (Volumes 7–8). As with prior volumes, our version depends primarily on the Siddur as provided by Philip Birnbaum. Back in 1949, Birnbaum labored over a Siddur that would contain the traditional liturgy in a modern scientific format. He combined the standard Ashkenazi rite with some modifications that had crept in and become popular in America. More than any other text, it is Birnbaum's that has met the test of time and that best represents the traditional liturgy most North Americans know best.

The final text was then translated by Joel M. Hoffman, in consultation with Marc Brettler. The translation of this particular volume benefited also from the wisdom of S. David Sperling, Richard White, and Danny Maseng. Our translation strives to reproduce not only the content of the original Hebrew, but also its tone, register, and style, so as to bring to modern readers the same experience (to the greatest extent possible) that the original authors would have conveyed with their words. In terms of content, we assume that by and large, words have meaning only to the extent that they contribute to sentences and concepts—as, for example, "by and large," which has nothing to do with "by" or "large."

We try to reproduce a tone and register similar to the original text: formal, but not archaic; prose or poetry, depending on the Hebrew. Where the Hebrew uses obscure words, we try to do the same, and where it uses common idiom, we try to use equally common idiom. Parallel structure and other similar literary devices found in the Hebrew are replicated as much as possible in the English translation. Our translations are best appreciated if they are read in conjunction with the running commentary by Joel Hoffman on why one set of words was chosen rather than another.

Our translation has not doctored the text to make it more palatable to modern consciousness. Blatant sexisms are retained, for instance, wherever we think the author intended them. We depend upon our commentaries to bridge the gap between the translation of the original and our modern sensibilities.

THE COMMENTARIES AND THEIR SOURCES

The heart and soul of *Minhag Ami* is its choice of commentaries that surround the prayerbook text. Translator Joel M. Hoffman explains his choice of words, provides alternatives, and compares his own translation with others. As always, Marc Brettler comments on the way the Bible is embedded in the Siddur. Ellen Frankel ("A Woman's Voice") and Elliot N. Dorff provide theological reflections on what the prayers might mean, should mean, could mean, cannot mean, or have to mean (even if we wish they didn't). Alyssa Gray presents talmudic commentary, and Daniel Landes gives us the Halakhah of prayer, the rules and traditions by which this sacred liturgical drama has traditionally been carried out. Lawrence Kushner and Nehemia Polen supply a kabbalistic commentary, adding wisdom from the world of Chasidic masters, and David Ellenson surveys liberal prayer books of the last two hundred years to see how their writers agonized over attempts to update this book of Jewish books for modern times.

My own historical commentary had to deal with the fact that the Birnbaum Siddur is only for Ashkenazi Jews, more specifically, the Ashkenazi version common in Eastern Europe, often under the influence of Elijah ben Solomon of Vilna, known as the *Gra*, or Vilna Gaon (1720–1797). To balance the picture, I cite Sefardi practice also. But the word "Sefardi" has two distinct meanings.

Nowadays, it usually describes Jews whose liturgy was influenced by Chasidism and the specific brand of Kabbalah initiated by Isaac Luria (the *Ari*), in sixteenth-century Palestine. Master liturgist and scholar of texts E. Daniel Goldschmidt compiled a scientific edition of this variant, and I used that to represent "Sefardi practice." But "Sefardi" can also mean the old Spanish-Portuguese custom carried by Jews from Spain in 1492 and then brought to the Netherlands, whence it moved to England (among other places) and eventually to America as well. When I want to draw attention to this Spanish-Portuguese custom, I call it that, using as my guide the standard work published in England at the turn of the twentieth century by Moses Gaster, *The Book of Prayer and Order of Service According to the Custom of the Spanish and Portuguese Jews*; and David de Sola Pool's more recent 1983 edition of *Book of Prayer According to the Custom of the Spanish and Portuguese Jews*. At times I cite *Seder Rav Amram* and *Siddur Saadiah*, the first two Jewish prayer books of which we are aware, from ninth- and tenth-century Babylon. And from the same era, roughly, I use the Genizah fragments, manuscripts telling us how Jews prayed in the Land of Israel prior to the Crusades.

As with all other volumes, I provide an introduction ("The Shape of *Minchah* and *Ma'ariv*," pp. 11–17) that examines the organization of the liturgy, so that readers can see the logic and aesthetics of its structure. Since *Minchah* and *Ma'ariv* are usually recited on either side of twilight, I provide yet one more introductory chapter ("Anxiety and Opportunity: The Mood of Nighttime Prayer," pp. 1–9) on the intriguing nature of twilight prayer in particular. It combines traditional comments on the liturgy with midrash about twilight—viewed through the lens of anthropological rites-of-passage theory to comprehend more deeply the psychological basis for the prayers in question. This book benefits also from an introductory essay by Daniel Landes on the overall halakhic status of *Minchah* and *Ma'ariv* (pp. 25–29).

As in previous volumes, our commentators are likely to refer to Halakhah (Jewish law), a topic that deserves its own introduction here, since it is so essential to Judaism, but is not easily accessible to Western readers. Frequently misunderstood as mere legalism, it is actually more akin to Jewish poetry, in that it is the height of Jewish writing, the pinnacle of Jewish concern, sheer joy to create or to ponder. It describes, explains, and debates Jewish responsibility, yet is saturated with spiritual importance. Jewish movements can be differentiated by their approach to Halakhah, but Halakhah matters to them all.

The topic of Halakhah is the proper performance of the commandments, said to number 613, and divided into positive and negative ones, numbering 248 and 365, respectively. Strictly speaking, commandments derived directly from Torah (mid'ora'ita) are of a higher order than those rooted only in rabbinic ordinance (called mid'rabbanan), but all are equally binding.

The earliest stratum of Halakhah is found primarily in the Mishnah, a code of Jewish practice promulgated about 200 C.E. The Mishnah is the foundation for further rabbinic discussion in the Land of Israel and Babylonia, which culminated in the two Talmuds, one from each center, called the Palestinian Talmud (or the Yerushalmi) and the Babylonian Talmud (or the Babli). While dates for both are uncertain, the former is customarily dated to about 400 C.E., and the latter between 550 and 650.

With the canonization of the Babli, Jewish law developed largely by means of commentary to the Talmuds and responsa, applications of talmudic and other precedents to actual cases. These are still the norm today, but they were initiated by authorities in Babylonia called Geonim (sing., Gaon) from about 750 to shortly after 1000. By the turn of the millennium, other schools had developed in North Africa and western Europe. Authorities in these centers are usually called Rishonim ("first" or "early" [ones]) until the sixteenth century, when they become known as Acharonim ("last" or "later" [ones]).

The first law code is geonic (from about 750), but it was the Rishonim who really inaugurated the trend toward codifying, giving us many works, including three major ones that are widely cited here: the *Mishneh Torah*, by Maimonides (Moses ben Maimon, 1135–1204), born in Spain, but active most of his life in Egypt; the *Tur*, by Jacob ben Asher (1275–1340), son of another giant, Asher ben Yechiel, who had moved to Spain from Germany, allowing Ashkenazi and Sefardi practice to intertwine in his son's magnum opus; and the *Shulchan Arukh*, by Joseph Caro (1488–1575), who also wrote influential commentaries on both the *Mishneh Torah* and the *Tur* before composing what would become the most widely used Jewish legal corpus ever.

Several commentaries here draw centrally on these sources, and not just for halakhic guidance, but for historical information as well. Most of what Jews have written through the ages has been halakhic in nature, so reconstructions of Jewish ritual at any stage of its development, and even the theological assumptions that underlie

Jewish practice, must often be reconstructed from legal sources that purport only to tell us what to do, but end up telling us why as well.

There is no way to convey the richness of even a single one of these works, let alone the legion of other sources in Jewish tradition on which *My People's Prayer Book* draws. Suffice it to say that the commentaries that follow access many of the greatest works of our people, from the close of the geonic era (1038) to the present.

The authors of the commentaries represent a panoply of contemporary scholars, all students of the prayerbook text, and all committed to a life of prayer, but representative of left, right, and center in the Jewish world. As editor, I could not ask for a more scholarly and helpful group of colleagues; I am indebted to every one of them, who have together made the editing of this series a joy. They are matched by the many people at Jewish Lights who support this volume energetically. Emily Wichland handles all publication details with the kind of love and care that is rare. Stuart Matlins, founder of Jewish Lights Publishing, takes personal pride in this series—as well he should. He helped conceptualize it from the start and remains its most ardent supporter. I am grateful for the privilege of working with a publisher as astute and spiritually committed as Stuart.

The people mentioned here represent all of us, all of *Am Yisrael*, all of those God had in mind when God said to Ezekiel (34:30), "They shall know that I, Adonai their God, am with them, and they, the House of Israel, are my people." Unabashedly scholarly and religious at one and the same time, *Minhag Ami*, "A Way of Prayer for My People," will be deemed a success if it provides the spiritual insight required to fulfill yet another prophecy (Isa. 52:6), that through our prayers,

> My people [*ami*] may know my name
> That they may know, therefore, in that day,
> That I, the One who speaks,
> Behold! Here I am.

1 | Ma'ariv
Weekday and Shabbat

[On weekdays, if Ma'ariv is recited immediately after Minchah, begin with "He is merciful" (p. 37); otherwise, begin here. On Saturday night, begin with Psalms 144 and 67 (not included here).

On Shabbat, begin with Kabbalat Shabbat and associated liturgy as described in volume 8. Then continue with the Sh'ma and Its Blessings.]

A. OPENING VERSES

I. PSALM 134

¹A song of ascent: Bless Adonai, all you who serve Adonai, you who stand in Adonai's house by night. ²Lift up your hands to what is holy and bless Adonai. ³May Adonai bless you from Zion, who made heaven and earth.

שִׁ֖יר הַמַּעֲלוֹת. הִנֵּה בָּרְכוּ אֶת יְיָ ¹
כָּל עַבְדֵי יְיָ, הָעֹמְדִים בְּבֵית יְיָ
בַּלֵּילוֹת. ²שְׂאוּ יְדֵכֶם קֹדֶשׁ, וּבָרְכוּ אֶת
יְיָ. ³יְבָרֶכְךָ יְיָ מִצִּיּוֹן, עֹשֵׂה שָׁמַיִם וָאָרֶץ.

II. MISCELLANEOUS VERSES

⁴The Lord of Hosts is with us, Jacob's God is our stronghold. ⁵Lord of Hosts, happy is the one who trusts in You. ⁶Adonai, save us. May our king answer us when we cry out.

יְיָ צְבָאוֹת עִמָּנוּ, מִשְׂגָּב־לָנוּ אֱלֹהֵי ⁴
יַעֲקֹב, סֶלָה. ⁵יְיָ צְבָאוֹת, אַשְׁרֵי אָדָם
בֹּטֵחַ בָּךְ. ⁶יְיָ, הוֹשִׁיעָה; הַמֶּלֶךְ יַעֲנֵנוּ
בְיוֹם קָרְאֵנוּ.

[Chatsi (Half) Kaddish is recited.]

36

III. *V'HU RACHUM* ("HE IS MERCIFUL")

[7] He is merciful, forgives iniquity, does not destroy, is quick to turn away his ire, and keeps his anger in check. [8] Adonai, save us! May our king answer us when we cry out.

[7] וְהוּא רַחוּם, יְכַפֵּר עָוֹן וְלֹא יַשְׁחִית; וְהִרְבָּה לְהָשִׁיב אַפּוֹ, וְלֹא יָעִיר כָּל חֲמָתוֹ. [8] יְיָ, הוֹשִׁיעָה; הַמֶּלֶךְ יַעֲנֵנוּ בְיוֹם קָרְאֵנוּ.

BRETTLER (BIBLE)

[1] *"A song of ascent"* This very short psalm concludes Psalms 120–134, a set of psalms called *Shir Hama'alot*, named after their first line. We are uncertain what *shir hama'alot* means. It is already called "Song of Ascents" in the Septuagint, the early Greek translation of the Bible, but the Aramaic translation, the *Targum*, renders it "rising up from the netherworld." Many connect the collection to the pilgrimage to Jerusalem, a context that fits many of these psalms, especially Psalm 122, which begins, "A song of ascents.... I rejoiced when they said to me, 'We are going to the House of Adonai,'" but also this one, which starts, "Bless Adonai, *(p. 41)*

DORFF (THEOLOGY)

[7] *"He is merciful"* The evening liturgy begins by acknowledging human vulnerability occasioned by nighttime darkness. God, we are assured, will save us from potential dangers. God will protect us from what we fear.

◆

ELLENSON (MODERN LITURGIES)

[1] *"A song of ascent"* Virtually all nineteenth-century prayer books omit these introductory lines from Psalm 134, probably because they have no evident relevance for what follows. Indeed, even the traditional Jewish sources that modern prayer *(p. 41)*

FRANKEL (A WOMAN'S VOICE)

[1] *"A song of ascent"* "Ascent" is commonly also understood as "pilgrim."

Do these phrases refer to female as well as to male pilgrims, to female Levites as well as male priests who nightly stood in the Temple?

Little is known about the daily lives and ritual roles of women in ancient Israel. We do know that in the biblical period, women sometimes sang and played instruments in levitical choirs. And, similarly, Israelite women *(p. 42)*

[For prayer instructions, see page 36.]

I. PSALM 134

[1] A song of ascent: Bless Adonai, all you who serve Adonai, you who stand in Adonai's house by night. [2] Lift up your hands to what is holy and bless Adonai. [3] May Adonai bless you from Zion, who made heaven and earth.

GRAY (OUR TALMUDIC HERITAGE)

[1] *"Who stand in Adonai's house by night"* The word *ba'leilot* ("by night"), say the Rabbis (Mid. T'hillim 134:1), refers to Torah study then. As a reward for a Jew's nighttime study, God considers it as if he or she were, literally, standing "in the house of God" (the Temple), not just praying, but engaging in the priestly Temple service, actually offering sacrifices.

Rabbinic tradition sees great value in nighttime Torah study. Resh Lakish (Hag. 12b) cites Psalm 42:9: *(p. 44)*

LANDES (HALAKHAH)

[1] *"Who stand in Adonai's house by night"* The rationale behind saying this psalm to begin *Ma'ariv* is found in this very verse: "Those who stand in Adonai's house by *night*" (*Shiltei Gibborim*, Ber. 1). Among other things, given the fact that *Ma'ariv* is technically just *r'shut* (an "option")—see Daniel Landes, "The Halakhic Status of *Minchah* and *Ma'ariv*," pp. 25–29—the psalm verse strengthens *Ma'ariv*'s claim upon us.

[2] *"Lift up your hands to what is holy and bless Adonai"* An introduction to

שִׁיר הַמַּעֲלוֹת. הִנֵּה בָּרְכוּ אֶת יְיָ כָּל עַבְדֵי יְיָ, הָעֹמְדִים בְּבֵית יְיָ בַּלֵּילוֹת. [2] שְׂאוּ יְדֵכֶם קֹדֶשׁ, וּבָרְכוּ אֶת יְיָ. [3] יְבָרֶכְךָ יְיָ מִצִּיּוֹן, עֹשֵׂה שָׁמַיִם וָאָרֶץ.

Bar'khu, the communal Call to Prayer (*Mishnah B'rurah* 237:2).

"*Chatsi [Half] Kaddish is recited*" Psalm 134 and the following three verses are followed by a *Chatsi* [Half] *Kaddish*, prior to "He is merciful," which is the beginning of *Ma'ariv* proper. The *Badai Hashulchan* (Rabbi Feivel Cohen, Brooklyn, NY, contemporary halakhic commentary to the *Shulchan Arukh*) explains the inclusion of psalm verses precisely because their recitation requires such a *Kaddish. Kaddish* brings the   *(p. 44)*

L. HOFFMAN (HISTORY)

OPENING VERSES: *WHEN* MA'ARIV *IS SAID IMMEDIATELY AFTER* MINCHAH, *SO THAT ONLY A MINIMAL WARM-UP IS REQUIRED, IT BEGINS WITH "*HE IS MERCIFUL*" (*V'HU RACHUM). *IF IT IS RECITED SOME TIME AFTER* MINCHAH, *THE WARM-UP EXPANDS TO INCLUDE* PSALM 134 *AND THE THREE OTHER MISCELLANEOUS VERSES.*

[1] *"A song of ascent … when we cry out"* *Ma'ariv* proper begins with *V'hu rachum* ("He is merciful"); but first, we have two sets of introductory verses: Psalm 134; and Psalms 46:8, 84:13, and 20:10. They serve as "warm-up," so are said only when *Minchah* has not just been recited. When *Minchah* and *Ma'ariv*   *(p. 45)*

J. HOFFMAN (TRANSLATION)

[1] *"Ascent"* Also commonly, "a Pilgrim Song." The introductions to Psalms are in general poorly understood, and this introduction, in particular, poses difficulty. The Hebrew word *ma'alot* usually means "stairs," but here and elsewhere (e.g., the well-known Ps. 122, added to *Birkat Hamazon* [Grace after Meals] on Shabbat and holidays), the word may refer to the pilgrims' ascent to Jerusalem during the three Pilgrimage Festivals.

[1] *"Bless"* Literally, "*hinei* bless." The Hebrew *hinei* literally means something like "here is" or "behold." But "behold, bless …" makes little sense.   *(p. 46)*

II. MISCELLANEOUS VERSES

⁴ The Lord of Hosts is with us, Jacob's God is our stronghold. ⁵ Lord of Hosts, happy is the one who trusts in You. ⁶ Adonai, save us. May our king answer us when we cry out.

⁴יְיָ צְבָאוֹת עִמָּנוּ, מִשְׂגָּב־לָנוּ אֱלֹהֵי יַעֲקֹב, סֶלָה. ⁵יְיָ צְבָאוֹת, אַשְׁרֵי אָדָם בֹּטֵחַ בָּךְ. ⁶יְיָ, הוֹשִׁיעָה; הַמֶּלֶךְ יַעֲנֵנוּ בְיוֹם קָרְאֵנוּ.

[Chatsi (Half) Kaddish is recited.]

III. *V'HU RACHUM* ("HE IS MERCIFUL")

⁷ He is merciful, forgives iniquity, does not destroy, is quick to turn away his ire, and keeps his anger in check. ⁸ Adonai, save us! May our king answer us when we cry out.

⁷וְהוּא רַחוּם, יְכַפֵּר עָוֹן וְלֹא יַשְׁחִית; וְהִרְבָּה לְהָשִׁיב אַפּוֹ, וְלֹא יָעִיר כָּל חֲמָתוֹ. ⁸יְיָ, הוֹשִׁיעָה; הַמֶּלֶךְ יַעֲנֵנוּ בְיוֹם קָרְאֵנוּ.

BRETTLER (BIBLE)

all you who serve Adonai, you who stand in Adonai's house."

[1] *"Bless Adonai, all you who serve Adonai, you who stand in Adonai's house"* We do not know who these "servants of Adonai" are, how they are expected to "bless Adonai," nor what special nocturnal role they had.

[2] *"Lift up your hands to what is holy"* Raising of hands was a typical biblical prayer position. "Holy" is typical priestly language (see Exod. 26:33), referring to the central section of the Jerusalem Temple, which was considered especially sacred.

[3] *"May Adonai bless you from Zion"* As the locus of Adonai's presence in the Jerusalem Temple, Zion figures prominently in all the *Shir Hama'alot* psalms (see "A song of ascent," above). Here, the idea that, from Zion, we bless God and God blesses us back appears in each of the three verses. But "May Adonai bless you from Zion" occurs in another *Shir Hama'alot* psalm (128:5), so it may be a stock phrase, like "God bless you," is used today.

[3] *"Who made heaven and earth"* This is probably a late phrase referring to Adonai as creator, an important theme for Jews in post-exilic times, who had experienced life outside of the Land of Israel and wanted to assert God's rulership over the entire world. The phrase occurs only in psalms toward the end of the Psalter (115:15, 121:2, 124:8, 146:6), which are likely late as well.

[4-5] *"Hosts"* God's heavenly retinue, who assist God in battle. The early Song of Deborah (c. twelfth century B.C.E.) notes (Judg. 5:20), "The stars fought from heaven."

[6] *"Adonai, save us"* There is ambiguity in the Hebrew here: Is Adonai saving the (Davidic) king, or is Adonai, as King, saving the People Israel?

[7] *V'hu Rachum [He Is Merciful]* From Psalm 78:38, which more broadly emphasizes God's continued acts of deliverance, despite Israel's repeated sins. It serves here to negate God's irrational anger, as found elsewhere in the Bible, prompting God, instead, to remember his "nice side."

———◆———

ELLENSON (MODERN LITURGIES)

books used as their basis were not in agreement on just what introductory verses (if any) were to be said (see L. Hoffman, "A song of ascent," p. 39). Isaac Mayer Wise was a notable exception in that he retained these passages in his *Minhag America* (1857). But otherwise, modern prayerbook editors wrote their own introductions, sometimes with aspects of Psalm 134 cited or paraphrased within them. David Einhorn's *Olath Tamid* (1858) and the American Reform 1895 *Union Prayer Book (UPB)*, for example, contain introductory paragraphs in the vernacular to start the service. The latter uses some translated lines from Psalm 134; and one of the evening prayer options in the 1948 *UPB* includes the Hebrew as well. The Hebrew was to be sung by a choir.

In the twentieth century, American Reform *Gates of Prayer* (1975) followed Einhorn (1858) and the *UPB* in offering an English introductory paragraph to the service. However, a number of liberal Siddurim reinstated these lines themselves. They include the Israeli Reform *Ha'avodah Shebalev* (1982); the two volumes for British Liberal Judaism, *Service of the Heart* (1967) and *Siddur Lev Chadash* (1995); and the German Reform *Das Jüdische Gebetbuch* (2001).

As the custom in Conservative congregations is for *Ma'ariv* to be recited immediately after *Minchah*, when these lines are omitted anyway, Conservative prayer books leave them out. This is true of the American *Siddur Sim Shalom* (1985) and the Israeli *Siddur Va'ani Tefillati* (1998), as well of the British Reform *Forms of Prayer* (1977) and the Reconstructionist Siddur *Kol Haneshamah* (1995).

[4] *"The Lord of Hosts is with us"* The Israeli Reform *Ha'avodah Shebalev* (1982) is the sole non-Orthodox prayer book to include these verses in its pages, though verse 6 ("Adonai, save us …") is omitted, probably because it is repeated as the end of *V'hu rachum* ("He is merciful"), which follows (v. 7). Whereas traditional prayer books often deliberately sought such redundancy, modern editors usually seek to leave it out.

[7] *"He is merciful"* In accord with accepted Ashkenazi liturgical custom, all Conservative Siddurim contain these passages as a prelude to the evening service, as does the Reconstructionist *Kol Haneshamah* (1995). With the exception of Abraham Geiger, nineteenth-century Reform prayerbook authors generally omitted them. However, several modern Reform prayer books have reinstated them. These include the Israeli *Ha'avodah Shebalev* (1982) and the German *Das Jüdische Gebetbuch* (2001).

—◆—

FRANKEL (A WOMAN'S VOICE)

flocked to Jerusalem together with their husbands to celebrate the three annual Pilgrimage Festivals—Passover, Shavuot, and Sukkot (Deut. 16:11, 16:14).

The Second Temple, shaped quite differently from the first, was equipped with a large *ezrat nashim*, a "courtyard for women." But women had little role in the sacrificial spectacle. The men proceeded through the women's courtyard and then up a few stairs into an area reserved only for them. From their closer vantage point, they could observe the sacrifices in the area more interior still, the place where the actual offerings took place. Any call to praise God would have emanated from the priests and Levites there, and it is not clear that it would have been heard by the women two courtyards away.

Although women did have their own celebrations—some of which are at least mentioned by rabbinic authors—the sacrifices were overwhelmingly done by men for men. Yet despite these and other undeniable gender divisions in biblical and rabbinic society, we can confidently assume that all the people in the Temple and outside of it, men and women, were meant to receive God's blessing.

[4] *"Our stronghold"* Whom can we call upon to protect us as we prepare to usher in the night?

For those living in the ancient world, devoid of electric light, safe transportation, and secure dwellings, night was a time of terror and uncertainty. Many feared nocturnal demons or all-too-human thieves. The end of daylight brought not only rest from labor but also exposure to predatory forces, both natural and supernatural.

To protect themselves from these forces, worshipers called upon the patriarch Jacob, "our fortress" *(misgav)*, who himself had experienced night terrors in the form of the Nameless Messenger who wrestled with him on the dark banks of the Jabbok.

In the early eighteenth century, Sore, daughter of Rabbi Yukil Segal Hurvitsk, who lived in Silesia, Poland, composed a Yiddish *tkhine* (pronounced t'-KHEE-n', "petitionary prayer") for the New Moon, in which she invoked the merits of the matriarchs to persuade God to accept Israel's prayers. In this prayer, she characterized Jacob's wife Rachel, *Rokhl*, as the matriarch who exercised the most influence with God. For from her roadside grave, Rachel tearfully watched her people go into Babylonian exile, and from her grave she will one day witness their return to Zion. Sore concludes this part of her prayer with an appeal to Rachel's intercession: "Through her merit You may illumine our eyes so that we may overcome darkness" (from *The Merits of Our Mothers*, comp. Tracy Guren Klirs; trans. by Tracy Guren Klirs, Ida Cohen Selavan, and Gella Schweid Fishman; annotated by Faedra Lazar Weiss and Barbara Selya. Cincinnati: Hebrew Union College Press, 1992, p. 86).

If Jacob is our fortress, guarding us from the perils of the night, then Rachel is our beacon, lighting our way home in the dark.

[7] *"He is merciful"* In this brief meditation before the *Bar'khu* ("Call to Prayer"), God is characterized as *rachum*, usually translated as "merciful." If we take the rest of the words and phrases of this prayer as defining precisely what "merciful" means in this context, we come to understand God's mercy as "restraint," more specifically "checked anger." Before we ask God to "save us when we call," we acknowledge that we may be partially responsible for arousing God's wrath. Why is God merciful? Because God "forgives iniquity," presumably ours. How is God merciful? By withholding all of the divine anger, which could destroy everything.

Before we call our community to worship God, we acknowledge that it is this quality of self-control, of restrained anger, that draws us near to God to allow us to unveil our shortcomings without fear of reprisal or excessive rebuke.

———◆———

GRAY (OUR TALMUDIC HERITAGE)

"By day Adonai commands the steadfast love of his faithful, and at night his song is with me," interpreted to mean that whoever studies Torah at night will be blanketed by divine protection during the day. The *Zohar* (2:46a) observes that while the daytime is filled with *mitzvot*, the night has no *mitzvot* to sustain it; nighttime study fills this lacuna. The *Zohar* also teaches that just as day is incomplete without night, so is daytime Torah study incomplete without its nighttime equivalent. The *Shulchan Arukh* (O. Ch. 238) thinks we should be even more zealous about study at night than study by day.

Siddur commentators Rabbis Samson Raphael Hirsch (a nineteenth-century founder of modern Orthodoxy) and J. H. Hertz (chief rabbi of Great Britain 1913–1946) cite the presumed allusion to nighttime study as the reason that this verse is recited only when there is a gap in time between *Minchah* and *Ma'ariv*, when, that is, we say *Minchah* at nightfall, but postpone *Ma'ariv* until later when night truly sets in.

[4-6] *"Adonai ... Adonai ... Adonai"* The Mishnah admonishes us to pray in a serious frame of mind. In that context, the Palestinian Talmud (Ber. 5:1, 8d) cites several prominent authorities as saying that these verses "should be on one's lips" as one rises to pray. Hence their appearance at the outset here.

[7] *"He is merciful"* Midrash Tanchuma *(Pinchas)* 12 cites Rabbi Judah bar Simon's belief that in Temple times, no one in Jerusalem ever went to sleep at night with unexpiated sin on their hands. At issue is the assumption that sacrifice atones for sin— the daily morning sacrifice *(shacharit)*, that is, atoned for sins of the previous night, while the daily afternoon sacrifice *(minchah)* atoned for sins committed earlier that day. But there was no evening *(ma'ariv)* sacrifice to atone for sins committed between *Minchah* and bedtime. So Judah cites the prophet Isaiah (1:21), "Justice resides [*yalin*] in Jerusalem." Since the Hebrew verb *yalin* ("resides") can also mean "sleeps," Judah deduces the lesson that expiation ("justice" for our sins) arrived with sleep time.

But Judah does not explain how it happened—how, that is, people managed to go to sleep sinlessly without actual sacrificial atonement. David Abudarham (fourteenth century, Spain) answers the question by pointing to "He is merciful." Though we have no nighttime sacrifice to effect atonement, we can at least *mention* atonement, acknowledging God's propensity to forgive even without a sacrificial offering.

---◆---

LANDES (HALAKHAH)

congregation to a higher spiritual realm, in preparation for being called formally to prayer by the *Bar'khu*.

---◆---

L. HOFFMAN (HISTORY)

are recited back to back, Psalm 145 (*Ashre*), with which *Minchah* begins, is considered sufficient warm-up for both.

Ashkenazi custom has included these verses since the sixteenth century (*Shiltei Gibborim* to Ber. 4b), so as to comply with a talmudic invitation to enter *Ma'ariv* only after studying Torah. Psalm 134 seemed apt, because it is short and because it refers to "all you who stand in Adonai's house by *night*." But Isaac Luria (sixteenth-century founder of Lurianic Kabbalah) preferred the three verses that follow. The *Gra* (the Vilna Gaon, 1730–1797) decried all these verses! "The general rule," say the instructions to his prayer book, "is to say no biblical verses and psalms in the public service, except for the psalm of the day." (For psalm of the day, see L. Hoffman, Volume 6, *Tachanun and Concluding Prayers*, p. 151.) The Spanish-Portuguese service adds other verses as well, beginning with Psalm 4:9, "Safe and sound, I lie down to sleep, for You alone, Adonai, keep me secure."

Nighttime study is advised elsewhere as well (Midrash T'hillim, for example—see Gray, "Who stand in Adonai's house by night …"), so had been considered desirable for centuries prior to the sixteenth century, when its status was suddenly enhanced, in part because the recent invention of coffee left people "wired" at night. Kabbalists therefore devised study rituals for midnight (*chatsot*), designed (in kabbalistic terminology) to effect a union of the disparate *s'firot* into which the unity of God had been shattered during the act of creation. Through *tikkun* (pronounced tee-KOON; plural *tikkunim*, pronounced tee-koo-NEEM), "repair," both God and the universe would be restored to wholeness. We know the term as the now popularized *tikkun olam* (pronounced tee-KOON oh-LAHM), "repairing the universe." For the kabbalists, *tikkun* was a cosmic process, but also any act that brought the process about. Kabbalists were to meet for penitential prayer at midnight to mourn the demise of the Temple; such a prayer gathering was called *tikkun chatsot* (pronounced tee-KOON khah-TSOT), a ritual to "repair the universe" *(tikkun)* that occurred "at midnight" *(chatsot)*.

Even Jews with no kabbalistic aspirations may keep some of these *tikkunim*— *tikkun leil shavuot* (pronounced tee-KOON layl shah-voo-OHT) for instance, a midnight study session for Shavuot eve, said to have been originated by Solomon Alkabetz, author of *L'kha Dodi* (see Volume 8, *Kabbalat Shabbat: Welcoming Shabbat in the Synagogue*, pp. 154–138), and Joseph Caro (author of the *Shulchan Arukh*), after the latter received a divine visitation then. Many people nowadays revise the "midnight" emphasis and simply meet for all-night study, but midnight was the essence of the ritual originally.

The practice today of scheduling *s'lichot* (pronounced s'-lee-KHOHT, meaning "penitential") services on the Saturday night prior to Rosh Hashanah predates medieval Kabbalah, but until then, people awoke early in the morning for *s'lichot*. Once coffee became common, kabbalists moved *s'lichot* to midnight as a *chatsot*. Modern practice may still hold *s'lichot* then, although some congregations have made a further change. Fearing that no one will come at midnight, they gather for study early in the evening, followed by *s'lichot* that end in time for people to get home before midnight even arrives.

[7] *"He is merciful"* "He is merciful" contains thirteen words, the number of the divine attributes associated with mercy. It is therefore associated with evoking God's compassion, especially at nighttime, when (unlike morning and afternoon) there was no ancient sacrifice to atone for sin. In addition, the Rabbis had spoken of "thirty-nine lashes" as the proper punishment for sin. It was assumed that souls being punished in the afterlife have these lashes administered, so some authorities advised saying the verse three times, one word of atonement corresponding to each of the lashes.

— ◆ —

J. Hoffman (Translation)

"Come, bless ..." (Birnbaum and *Siddur Lev Chadash*) makes sense, but is not supported by the Hebrew.

[1] *"By night"* The third-century B.C.E. Greek translation, the Septuagint, arranges this phrase as part of the next line, so the hand lifting—not the standing—happens at night. This sort of textual variation often suggests that the original text has become corrupted through oral or written transmission over the years.

[2] *"To what is holy"* Literally, "the holy," perhaps meaning "the sanctuary," or "to the sanctuary."

[3] *"Who made heaven and earth"* Clearly the intent is "May Adonai, who made heaven and earth, bless you from Zion." It is not clear why the phrase "from Zion" appears in such a grammatically awkward place, both in the Hebrew and, therefore, in our translation.

[4] *"Stronghold"* The Hebrew for "stronghold" here, *misgav*, comes from the root *s.g.v*, meaning "to be high," suggesting a military stronghold that owed its safety to its heights.

[6] *"May our king answer us"* A phrase that occurs frequently in the liturgy. See, for example, p. 42 in Volume 6, *Tachanun and Concluding Prayers*.

[7] *"Keeps his anger in check"* A possible interpretation for the Hebrew, which literally means "does not stir up all (or any of) his anger," as reflected in Birnbaum, for example. *Siddur Sim Shalom* gives us the interesting, "refuses to let rage be all consuming."

— ◆ ◆ ◆ —

[Begin with the Call to Prayer (Bar'khu)—see Volume 1, The Sh'ma and Its Blessings, p. 27. Then continue here.]

B. THE *SH'MA* AND ITS BLESSINGS

I. BLESSING ON CREATION: *MA'ARIV ARAVIM* ("WHO BRINGS ON EVENING")

¹Blessed are You, Adonai our God, ruler of the world, who brings on the evening with his word, ²opens gates with wisdom, changes one season into the next with reason, and turns one time of year into the next and arranges the stars in their trajectories in the sky as He sees fit, ³creating day and night, rolling light from darkness and darkness from light, making day pass and bringing the night, differentiating between day and night, "Lord of Hosts" is his name. ⁴The living and eternal God will continually rule over us forever. Blessed are You, Adonai, who brings on the evening.

בָּרוּךְ אַתָּה, יְיָ אֱלֹהֵינוּ, מֶלֶךְ הָעוֹלָם, אֲשֶׁר בִּדְבָרוֹ מַעֲרִיב עֲרָבִים. ²בְּחָכְמָה פּוֹתֵחַ שְׁעָרִים, וּבִתְבוּנָה מְשַׁנֶּה עִתִּים, וּמַחֲלִיף אֶת הַזְּמַנִּים, וּמְסַדֵּר אֶת הַכּוֹכָבִים בְּמִשְׁמְרוֹתֵיהֶם בָּרָקִיעַ כִּרְצוֹנוֹ. ³בּוֹרֵא יוֹם וָלָיְלָה, גּוֹלֵל אוֹר מִפְּנֵי חֹשֶׁךְ וְחֹשֶׁךְ מִפְּנֵי אוֹר, וּמַעֲבִיר יוֹם וּמֵבִיא לָיְלָה, וּמַבְדִּיל בֵּין יוֹם וּבֵין לָיְלָה, יְיָ צְבָאוֹת שְׁמוֹ. ⁴אֵל חַי וְקַיָּם, תָּמִיד יִמְלוֹךְ עָלֵינוּ, לְעוֹלָם וָעֶד. בָּרוּךְ אַתָּה, יְיָ, הַמַּעֲרִיב עֲרָבִים.

BRETTLER (BIBLE)

[1] *"With his word"* The accent on God's word echoes Psalm 33:6, "By the *word* of Adonai the heavens were made," but is modified significantly to emphasize God's continuing engagement in the world. This is not a deity who, as Genesis 1 may imply, created day and night just once only and was then done.

[2] *"Gates"* The gates of heaven through which the sun traveled, a common ancient near eastern image (see Dorff, *"Opens gates with wisdom,"* p. 50).

[2] *"Wisdom"* That God's "will" reflects God's "wisdom" is a notion found in Proverbs 3:19, "Adonai founded the earth by *(p. 50)*

DORFF (THEOLOGY)

[1] *"Who brings on the evening with his word"* With the first chapter of Genesis in mind, our prayer accentuates the uniqueness of God's use of language to create worlds. We humans do that morally, but God does so in a physical sense as well. *(p. 50)*

ELLENSON (MODERN LITURGIES)

[1] *"Who brings on the evening"* The *Hamburg Temple Prayer Books* (1819, 1841) contain only a vernacular rendering of this prayer. David Einhorn's *Olath Tamid* (1858) follows suit with his own text in the German alone. By contrast, the more *(p. 52)*

FRANKEL (A WOMAN'S VOICE)

[2] *"Opens gates"* Today we understand that the diurnal rhythm of our days results from the rotation of the earth. But in pre-Copernican times, the onset of evening was seen as an act of divine will—and therefore not completely predictable, even though night has dutifully been following day from time immemorial. Indeed, it was clearly within God's power to disrupt this orderliness and plunge the world back into primeval chaos—a world without light, without distinctions *(p. 54)*

[For prayer instructions, see page 47.]

I. BLESSING ON CREATION: *MA'ARIV ARAVIM* ("WHO BRINGS ON EVENING")

[1] Blessed are You, Adonai our God, ruler of the world, who brings on the evening with his word, [2] opens gates with wisdom, changes one season into the next with reason, and turns one time of year into the next and arranges the stars in their trajectories in the sky as He sees fit, [3] creating day and night, rolling

GRAY (OUR TALMUDIC HERITAGE)

[1] *"Brings on the evening* [ma'ariv aravim] *with his word"* Praising God for bringing on evening follows from the Torah's account of creation, whereby "there was evening [*erev*, the singular of *aravim*] and morning" (Gen. 1:5). But why the plural here, *aravim*, rather than the singular *erev*, as in Genesis? Abudarham links the choice to Exodus 12:6, where the word *arbayim* ("twilight") is employed. Grammatically, *arbayim* is the Hebrew "dual" construction, used to *(p. 55)*

KUSHNER & POLEN (CHASIDISM)

[2] *"Opens gates with wisdom"* Instead of reading "gates" as a poetic allusion to the sources of daylight and night dark, Rabbi Meir of Apt (1767–1831, a disciple of Yakov Yitzhak, the *Chozeh* or Seer of Lublin) in his 1850 work *Or Lashamayim* (*Y'sod Ha'avodah* 43), suggests it might refer to what William Blake once alluded to as "the doors of perception" in the human body. There are seven: two eyes, two ears, two nostrils, and one mouth. The "gates" here, in other words, refer to the holes in our heads! *(p. 55)*

L. HOFFMAN (HISTORY)

THE SH'MA AND ITS BLESSINGS ARE RECITED MORNING AND EVENING, EACH TIME PRECEDED BY THE BAR'KHU, THE OFFICIAL CALL TO PRAYER. WE THEN REACH THE FIRST OF THE BLESSINGS ASSOCIATED WITH THE SH'MA (THE ONE THAT FOLLOWS HERE)—ON THE THEME OF CREATION. THE MA'ARIV VERSION IS MA'ARIV ARAVIM, "WHO BRINGS ON EVENING" (FROM VERSE 1). FOR THE SHACHARIT VERSION (YOTSER OR, "WHO FORMS LIGHT"), SEE VOLUME 1, THE SH'MA AND ITS BLESSINGS, PP. 41–43.

[3] *"'Lord of Hosts' is his name... rule over us forever"* Careful scrutiny *(p. 56)*

בָּרוּךְ אַתָּה, יְיָ אֱלֹהֵינוּ, מֶלֶךְ הָעוֹלָם, אֲשֶׁר בִּדְבָרוֹ [1] מַעֲרִיב עֲרָבִים. בְּחָכְמָה פּוֹתֵחַ שְׁעָרִים, וּבִתְבוּנָה [2] מְשַׁנֶּה עִתִּים, וּמַחֲלִיף אֶת הַזְּמַנִּים, וּמְסַדֵּר אֶת הַכּוֹכָבִים בְּמִשְׁמְרוֹתֵיהֶם בָּרָקִיעַ כִּרְצוֹנוֹ. בּוֹרֵא יוֹם [3] וָלַיְלָה, גּוֹלֵל אוֹר מִפְּנֵי חֹשֶׁךְ וְחֹשֶׁךְ מִפְּנֵי אוֹר,

LANDES (HALAKHAH)

[1] *"Who brings on the evening.... Eternal love"* What is the connection between these two opening blessings? The first, "Who Brings on Evening" (*Ma'ariv Aravim*), attributes to God the entire order of the universe–the coming and going of night, sun, and stars. The second, "Eternal Love" (*Ahavat Olam*), discusses the impact of God's Torah on our lives. The two are set as parallel investigations of the universe–*Ma'ariv Aravim* the physical and *Ahavat Olam* the moral. Both have order *(p. 56)*

J. HOFFMAN (TRANSLATION)

[1] *"Brings on the evening"* Literally, the much more poetic "evenings the evening," a possibility excluded by English grammar. Both the noun "evening" (*erev*; plural, *aravim*) and the verb I coin here, "evenings" (*ma'ariv*), come from *ayin.r.b*, a confusingly common root that refers variously to "entering," "sunset" (as though the sun enters its home at night?), "west," and "evening." It not only gives us the name of the evening service (*Ma'ariv* or *Arvit*), but may be the original source, via Latin and Greek, of the English word "Europe," which is west of where Hebrew was spoken. (At least four other roots with the same letters further confuse the situation. Those *(p. 56)*

light from darkness and darkness from light, making day pass and bringing the night, differentiating between day and night, "Lord of Hosts" is his name. [4] The living and eternal God will continually rule over us forever. Blessed are You, Adonai, who brings on the evening.

וּמַעֲבִיר יוֹם וּמֵבִיא לָיְלָה, וּמַבְדִּיל בֵּין יוֹם וּבֵין לָיְלָה, יְיָ צְבָאוֹת שְׁמוֹ. ⁴אֵל חַי וְקַיָּם, תָּמִיד יִמְלוֹךְ עָלֵינוּ, לְעוֹלָם וָעֶד. בָּרוּךְ אַתָּה, יְיָ, הַמַּעֲרִיב עֲרָבִים.

BRETTLER (BIBLE)

wisdom." Biblically, this "wisdom" applies only to the creation of the world; in this prayer, however, God's continual cosmic involvement is emphasized. God sees to it that the sun and stars follow their expected patterns.

[3] *"Creating day"* This verse is replete with references to the first creation story, using words like "create," "day," "night," "light," "darkness," and "distinguish," but recontextualized to highlight God's perpetual care in continuing the work of creation (see above, v. 1, "With his word"). This emphasis sounds polemical, arguing against the idea that the universe is like a clock that God created and wound, but then abandoned.

[4] *"The living and eternal God"* Precisely because God still manages the world (the theme throughout—see comments above), God is "the living and eternal God." The prayer ends in the present tense, "who brings on the evening," emphasizing one final time God's ongoing activity.

DORFF (THEOLOGY)

[2] *"Opens gates with wisdom"* Until the discoveries of Copernicus (1473–1543), Kepler (1571–1630), Galileo (1564–1642), and Newton (1642–1727), most people thought the sun circled a flat earth. There were exceptions of course: around 560 B.C.E., the Greek philosopher Anaximander suggested that the earth was cylindrical, and Aristarchus of Samos (c. 310–230 B.C.E.) advanced the theory that the sun rested at the center of the sphere of fixed stars, and that the earth and the five known planets revolved around the sun. But by and large—and certainly in the Bible—people trusted

their immediate observation that the earth seemed obviously to extend outward on a flat plane, with the sun going around it, disappearing from sight at nighttime and reappearing every morning.

Similarly, the sky appeared to be a dome *(ra'ki'a)* enclosing the earth, moon, sun, and stars. Above the dome was water, which leaked through openings in the dome, causing rain; sunny days occurred when the openings closed. Noah's flood (says Gen. 7:11) came about because "the floodgates of the sky broke open," and the prophet Malachi (3:10) looked ahead to a happy time when God would "open the floodgates of the sky and rain down blessings."

To explain the nighttime movement of the sun, people imagined an opening in the dome on the west through which the sun slipped each evening. It then moved from west to east *on top of the dome*, which blocked its nocturnal journey from our sight, until it slipped back into view through another opening in the dome to the east. The "gates of heaven," then, is not just a metaphor; it describes how our ancestors actually conceived of the way the sun set and rose again.

We, of course, have a different understanding of how this happens, but still, hardly anyone proposes rewriting this paragraph to reflect modern science. Liturgy's purpose is frequently metaphorically suggestive, rather than literally descriptive, of natural processes. We maintain the traditional description of evening as a poetic metaphor of what actually happens. This is a good example of an important liturgical principle: *do not commit the genetic fallacy*. That is, do not limit the meaning of any piece of liturgy or ritual to the purpose it originally served. Since ritual attracts new meanings over time, the proper criterion for evaluating what to keep and what to change is the significance of the particular liturgical phrase or ritual *to us now*, with all the *new* meanings that the *old* form has taken on. If words or rituals become harmful to people, they should be changed for moral reasons. Sometimes, too, we omit them because they have lost all meaning; but most of the time, as here, we reinterpret the old form in light of our current understandings, putting new wine into old bottles. "The gates of heaven" is a phrase equally as compelling as Homer's "fingers of dawn," neither of which actually describes scientific reality, but both of which beautifully capture our feelings about the majesty of nature.

[2] *"Seasons … stars … sky"* People in antiquity knew a great deal about astronomy. Without electric lights, they could actually see the stars. Also, they used the movement of the heavens to set their calendar and navigate their ships. Consequently, our prayer recognizes the setting of the sun as part of a larger order of seasons and stars. Stopping to mark the sunset liturgically should help make us city folk aware of the broader orders of nature too!

[3] *"Rolling light from darkness and darkness from light"* The ancient cosmology described above (see *"Opens gates with wisdom"*) explains the use of the word "rolls": God is pictured as rolling the sun from east to west along the inside of the dome during the day and over the dome at night.

[3] *"'Lord of Hosts' is his name"* The prayer refers directly to an aspect of God most evident in nature, even for us, today. With all of our scientific advancements, we still cannot change the timing of dawn and dusk, let alone the fluctuation of seasons and the order of the stars. Thus, this prayer bespeaks something just as important for us to acknowledge as for our ancestors: the human powerlessness to control the orders of nature that depend on a power far beyond us, whom we name God.

In making these assertions, it is important to avoid the *fallacy of residue theology*, which limits God to what human beings cannot do, so that the more we learn to do, the less room there is for God. Jewish tradition is much wiser: it asserts that God is present also in what human beings do. Thus God is manifest when doctors, who act as God's agents, bring healing. God is present also when we "crack a problem" or otherwise become creative, inventive, or artistically imaginative. Still, God remains most dramatically evident in life's areas that we cannot control, like the eternal movement of sun, seasons, and stars.

[4] *"God will continually rule over us"* The Hebrew of this line may mean, "God *will* always rule over us" or "May God always rule over us." The former is a statement of faith; the latter a vision of hope, occasioned by the author's recognition that without God's continual ordering of nature, humanity would be in deep trouble. Either way, God is, as the phrase immediately before this one asserts, "a living and everlasting God," for only then could one trust or pray that the orders of nature will continue.

[4] *"Blessed are You, Adonai ..."* The mood of this entire prayer is not descriptive, but expressive—of awe, praise, and thanksgiving. We certainly may and should examine nature scientifically, but we must also appreciate the natural everyday wonders, which existed long before we understood them. Understanding should not dull our appreciation of still being as dependent on them as ever. That is the task of this prayer— to call attention to what we might otherwise take for granted.

—◆—

ELLENSON (MODERN LITURGIES)

traditional Geiger and Wise retain the traditional Hebrew alongside a translation. Virtually all twentieth-century Reform Siddurim reflect the model established by Geiger and Wise. The prayer in question is familiar—indeed, basic—after all, and not too long to prevent congregational recitation in the original.

The issue of Hebrew has a long history in modern prayer books. In America, a short Sabbath service, all in English, appeared briefly in 1830, the product of the Reform Society of Charleston. While it was short-lived, other rabbis—most notably Samuel Holdheim of Berlin and David Einhorn of Baltimore and Philadelphia—in nineteenth-century Europe and America preferred using as little Hebrew as possible. However, the majority of rabbis still considered Hebrew desirable. When an 1845 German rabbinic conference asserted that Hebrew was not "legally required" for the expression of Jewish prayer, Zacharias Frankel—the father of a Positive-Historical Jewish religious stance that later evolved into the ideological foundation for Conservative Judaism in America—walked out of the meeting in protest. Similarly, Abraham Geiger retained a strong attachment to Hebrew in Jewish liturgy, and Isaac Mayer Wise maintained that Hebrew should be retained "because our brethren in all parts of the world are conversant with the Hebrew service, and no Israelite should feel himself a stranger in the House of the Lord." Should Hebrew be abandoned as the principal language of Jewish prayer, Wise warned that Judaism would hopelessly be divided into sects, and the religious unity of the Jewish people would disappear.

Almost universally, the issue has not been whether to include Hebrew. Rather, the questions have been how to include and whether to include transliteration as well so that non-Hebrew readers might use it. This latter issue has exercised many rabbis because some contend that the use of transliteration would serve as a "crutch" that would have the effect of discouraging congregants from mastering Hebrew itself. This issue exercised the Conservative Movement when it issued its first official prayer book in 1946. The prototype of their book, prepared by Conservative rabbi Morris Silverman in Hartford, had employed transliteration quite liberally. However, the committee charged with the official Conservative liturgy broke with Silverman, refusing to concede the need for transliteration. Conservative Judaism insists on the principled position that people should learn to daven in Hebrew, and it remains the preferred position of the movement today. However, as the later editions of the Conservative *Sim Shalom* indicate, there has been a practical need to modify this stance somewhat in light of the sociological reality of a Jewish world where many Conservative worshipers simply do not know how to read Hebrew characters. Thus, *Sim Shalom* prints parts of the Torah service, including the blessings over the Torah, and *Kaddish* in transliteration. (See Volume 6, *Tachanun and Concluding Prayers*, pp. 155–156.) Indeed, even the Orthodox ArtScroll *Siddur Kol Ya'akov* does so.

Reform Judaism has generally omitted transliteration as well. However, because of the nontraditional nature of Reform worship, it was usually possible to conduct congregational readings in English and reserve the Hebrew parts for the rabbi, cantor, or choir (which usually sang from transliterated sheet music in any event). The forthcoming American Reform *Mishkan T'filah* was composed with the principle that every piece of Hebrew will appear with transliteration, precisely to empower worshipers to be able to say the Hebrew themselves without relying on "experts" to do it for them. A second edition without transliteration will appear as well, so as to satisfy a minority of Reform rabbis who believe—as do many of their Conservative counterparts—that transliteration impedes the learning of Hebrew and will set back the movement from the progress it is currently making in instilling Hebrew literacy among Reform worshipers.

[3] *"Creating day and night, rolling ... "* In 1892, I. S. Moses prepared a *Union Prayer Book* for the American Reform Movement. For reasons that are not altogether clear,

but probably having to do with the fact that it was deemed too traditional, it was quickly withdrawn from circulation and replaced by a *Union Prayer Book* that set the hallmark of what we now call classical Reform. Among other things, classical Reform exercised extreme care not to say anything that might be seen as medieval in thought. The 1892 edition had included the statement that "God rolls back," taking it as metaphoric, even poetic. (For its original meaning in biblical cosmology, see Dorff, "Rolling," p. 51.) Not so the series of *Union Prayer Books* that became the hallmark of American Reform worship until the *Gates of Prayer* (1975). The *UPB* series took out all but the philosophically acceptable epithet of God as "Creator of day and night."

[4] *"The living and eternal God"* The 1977 British *Forms of Prayer*, the 1995 British Liberal *Lev Chadas*, and the 2001 German *Gebetbuch* remove this line. *Minhag America* (1857) omits this line as well.

[4] *"Blessed are You"* Marcia Falk (*Book of Blessings*, 1996) labels this prayer "Blessing of Creation," but, typically for her, refuses to affirm a God who is totally "other" who stands above and beyond us. Instead, she prefers her own hallmark blessing formula, "Let us bless the source of life, source of darkness and light, heart of harmony and chaos, creativity and creation."

——◆——

FRANKEL (A WOMAN'S VOICE)

between day and night. It's significant—given this sense of human vulnerability to the forces of heaven—that we thank God for bringing on the evening, thereby asserting that daylight is the natural state of the world, and darkness a daily intervention.

How does this prayer depict the heavenly alternation of day and night? Not as the dance of the planetary spheres nor a cosmic clock, nor a grand celestial drama—but rather as a domestic scene: God opens the gates (*pote'ach sh'arim*), changes the seasons (*machalif et haz'manim*), orders the stars in their courses (*m'sader et hakokhavim b'-mishm'rotaeihem*). Like an efficient *baleh busteh* (pronounced bah-l' BUS-t' [the U of "BUS" rhymes with the OU of "could"], "homemaker"), God airs out the house each day, letting in the cool night air; changes the sheets, makes the beds, puts things to rights. Each day God rolls up the blinds of night; each night, rolls them down again. How comfortable it is to inhabit a world that is so well tended!

——◆——

describe two of anything, so rather than "twilight," it can be taken as implying two movements of the sun, each called *erev*: the first *erev* occurs when the sun passes its zenith in the afternoon and begins to tilt toward the west, while the second *erev* is the actual setting of the sun. Our blessing, says Abudarham, praises God for bringing about these two celestial movements every day.

[2] *"Opens gates"* Abudarham recalls patriarch Jacob's famous dream of the ladder stretching from earth to heaven. Jacob calls the place where the dream occurred *sha'ar hashamayim*, the "gate of heaven" (Gen. 28:17). The gates mentioned in our prayer must therefore be similar gates—in effect, our own (not just Jacob's) gates to heaven. The plural "gates" is employed to parallel Psalm 78:23, which refers to *daltayim*, "doors of heaven," in the plural.

[2] *"With wisdom … reason"* The juxtaposition of God's "wisdom" (*chochmah*) and "reason" (*t'vunah*) is based on Proverbs 3:19, where God is said to have established the earth through wisdom, and the heavens through reason.

[2] *"Turns one time of year into the next"* Abudarham identifies the "changing" here with the three times the day changes: evening, morning, and afternoon.

[2] *"Their trajectories [mish'm'roteihem]"* The Talmud (Ber. 3a) teaches, "The night has three watches [*mish'm'rot*]," using the same word for "watch" that we have translated as "trajectory." Even though our blessing represents God as the silent and efficient enforcer of natural law, the Talmud pictures Him at the conclusion of each watch "sitting and roaring like a lion … over [the destruction of] his beautiful place [the Temple in Jerusalem]."

◆

KUSHNER & POLEN (CHASIDISM)

And the operative question for him, and us, is how to bring these doors into alignment with God; or, in the language of the blessing, how can we open our own gates with wisdom? The answer to his rhetorical question comes from Job 28:12, where we read: *v'hachokhmah me'ayin timatsei*, "From where can wisdom be found?" But Meir of Apt, following a long tradition of kabbalistic interpretation, does not read the verse as a question, but as a statement. The word *me'ayin*, "from where," can also be read as meaning "from *ayin*," from "nothingness," that is, from the "divine nothingness." The source of wisdom is *ayin*, the divine nothingness, God. And, through making oneself *ayin*, "nothing"—both in the pietistic sense of humility and in the mystical sense of dissolution of self into the divine nothing (*bittul hayesh*), one can attain true wisdom. Through entering the ocean of the divine, we return to our own origins; we go back to zero. In the language of computers, we "restore the default configuration."

But Meir of Apt goes farther. He cautions us that thinking of ourselves as nothing can be a trap, a clever disguise of one's ego, for it can lead us into thinking that we now are in exclusive possession of the truth. How easy it is for us to forget that others too behold a dimension of the divine. Indeed, the ultimate *ayin* opens the doors for each person in a unique way. As important and sacred as it might be for us to realize that all wisdom comes from God, it may be more important to remember that for each creature this divine contact is a powerful and uniquely different experience.

———◆———

LANDES (HALAKHAH)

and beauty; both come from God. The first evokes awe; the second, love. But both universes are actually one, which find their resolution in the *Sh'ma*, our statement of God's unity.

———◆———

L. HOFFMAN (HISTORY)

reveals these as extra words. The prayer reads much better without them, going directly from "differentiating between day and night" to "Blessed are You, Adonai, who brings on the evening." Indeed, David Abudarham of twelfth-century Spain pointed this out. Most Sefardim (not all) omit these words, therefore, although the Spanish-Portuguese prayer book includes the first half, "Lord of Hosts is his name."

———◆———

J. HOFFMAN (TRANSLATION)

roots mean "to barter," "Arab," "to mix," and finally "to be pleasant.")

   [2] *"Gates"* Probably the gates of heaven.

   [2] *"One season into the next"* Literally, "changes the seasons."

   [2] *"Time of year into the next"* Literally, "turns the times of year."

   [2] *"Sees fit"* Or "wants."

   [3] *"Bringing"* Commonly, "bringing on," but we have already used that phrase in "bringing on the evening," and we want to use different phrases in English to reflect different phrases in Hebrew.

————————◆ ◆ ◆————————

II. BLESSING ON REVELATION:
AHAVAT OLAM ("ETERNAL LOVE")

[1] You have loved the House of Israel, your people, with an eternal love, teaching us Torah and commandments, laws and rules. [2] Therefore, Adonai our God, when we lie down and when we stand up, we will discuss your laws, and rejoice in the words of your Torah and your commandments forever. [3] For they are our life and the length of our days. We will meditate on them day and night. [4] Never remove your love from us! [5] Blessed are You, Adonai, who loves his People Israel.

[1] אַהֲבַת עוֹלָם בֵּית יִשְׂרָאֵל עַמְּךָ אָהָבְתָּ; תּוֹרָה וּמִצְוֹת, חֻקִּים וּמִשְׁפָּטִים, אוֹתָנוּ לִמַּדְתָּ; [2] עַל כֵּן, יְיָ אֱלֹהֵינוּ, בְּשָׁכְבֵּנוּ וּבְקוּמֵנוּ נָשִׂיחַ בְּחֻקֶּיךָ, וְנִשְׂמַח בְּדִבְרֵי תוֹרָתֶךָ וּבְמִצְוֹתֶיךָ לְעוֹלָם וָעֶד. [3] כִּי הֵם חַיֵּינוּ וְאֹרֶךְ יָמֵינוּ, וּבָהֶם נֶהְגֶּה יוֹמָם וָלָיְלָה. [4] וְאַהֲבָתְךָ אַל תָּסִיר מִמֶּנּוּ לְעוֹלָמִים. [5] בָּרוּךְ אַתָּה, יְיָ, אוֹהֵב עַמּוֹ יִשְׂרָאֵל.

BRETTLER (BIBLE)

[1] *"Eternal love"* The entire prayer is organized by two intersecting themes: God's love for Israel and the implications of chronology. Given God's past love for Israel, Israel has covenant obligations for the future. The result will be God's ongoing love in the present.

The opening phrase "Eternal love" is borrowed from Jeremiah's touching prophecy of consolation (31:3): "Eternal love I conceived for you then [in the wilderness]. Therefore, I continue my grace for you." "The House of Israel, your people" paraphrases Ezekiel's prophesy of restoration (34:30), "they, the House of Israel, are my people."

(p. 60)

DORFF (THEOLOGY)

[1] *"With an eternal love … Torah and commandments, laws and precedents"* This prayer *(Ahavat Olam)* says essentially the same thing as *Ahavah Rabbah*, the parallel prayer preceding the *Sh'ma* in the morning liturgy (see Volume 1, *The Sh'ma and Its Blessings*, pp. 67–82). But *(p. 61)*

ELLENSON (MODERN LITURGIES)

[1] *"Eternal love"* As with *Ma'ariv Aravim* ("Who Brings on Evening"), above, the *Hamburg Temple Prayer Books* (1819, 1841) and Einhorn's *Olath Tamid* (1858) offer a vernacular rendition alone of this prayer. But Geiger and Wise retain the Hebrew text. *(p. 61)*

FRANKEL (A WOMAN'S VOICE)

[2] *"Words of your Torah"* How do parents show their children that they are loved? Through their actions and their words—and through their abiding care. In this prayer, we single out God's words as the singular proof of divine concern. God's "eternal love" *(ahavat olam)* is manifested through our learning Torah and all that it holds—precepts, laws, and judgments. And we reciprocate that love through our *attention* to these words: we promise to meditate upon them day and night—*neh'geh yomam valaylah*. *(p. 62)*

II. BLESSING ON REVELATION: *AHAVAT OLAM* ("ETERNAL LOVE")

[1] You have loved the House of Israel, your people, with an eternal love, teaching us Torah and commandments, laws and rules. [2] Therefore, Adonai our God, when we lie down and when we stand up, we will discuss your laws, and rejoice in the words of your Torah and your commandments forever. [3] For they are our life and the length of our days. We will

GRAY (OUR TALMUDIC HERITAGE)

[1] *"Eternal love"* The Talmud (Ber. 11b) knows two versions of this prayer: *Ahavat Olam* ("Eternal Love") and *Ahavah Rabbah* ("Great Love"). Both express the theme of God's love for Israel through Torah. In a talmudic debate, Rabbi Judah (in the name of Samuel) and Rabbi Eleazar call for *Ahavah Rabbah* in the morning *(Shacharit)* service, while the majority opinion (the "Rabbis") prefer *Ahavat Olam* then, since it has biblical warrant in Jeremiah 31:3: "I [God] *(p. 63)*

L. HOFFMAN (HISTORY)

THIS, THE SECOND BLESSING BEFORE THE SH'MA, IS ON THE THEME OF GOD'S LOVE FOR ISRAEL, THE LOVE MANIFEST BY THE GIVING OF TORAH. THOUGH REFERRED TO AS AHAVAT OLAM, *"ETERNAL LOVE" (THE OPENING WORDS), THE BLESSING IS MORE TECHNICALLY AN EXAMPLE OF A* BIRKAT HATORAH, *"BLESSING ON TORAH." FOR THE* SHACHARIT *VERSION (*AHAVAH RABBAH, *"MOST LOVINGLY"), SEE VOLUME 1,* THE SH'MA AND ITS BLESSINGS, *P. 67*

[1] *"Eternal love"* The Talmud knows two versions of this prayer acknowledging Torah as the supreme demonstration of God's love: *Ahavah Rabbah*

(p. 63)

J. HOFFMAN (TRANSLATION)

[1] *"You have loved the House of Israel, your people, with an eternal love"* This line parallels the morning version of the same prayer (*Ahavah rabbah*), "You have loved us most lovingly." The Hebrew here, as in the morning version, doubles up the root *aleph.h.b*, using it once as the verb "to love" and again as the noun "love." As for "eternal" (*olam*), the Hebrew is both temporal and spatial. In *Ma'ariv Aravim* we translated it as "world." Here "eternal" is more appropriate. Unfortunately, we have no single English word to capture the ancient conflation of time and space. *Sim Shalom* offers "with constancy"; *Lev Chadash*, "unending love"; *Forms of Prayer* and *Kol Haneshamah*, "everlasting love."

(p. 65)

[1] אַהֲבַת עוֹלָם בֵּית יִשְׂרָאֵל עַמְּךָ אָהָבְתָּ; תּוֹרָה וּמִצְוֹת, חֻקִּים וּמִשְׁפָּטִים, אוֹתָנוּ לִמַּדְתָּ; [2] עַל כֵּן, יְיָ אֱלֹהֵינוּ, בְּשָׁכְבֵּנוּ וּבְקוּמֵנוּ נָשִׂיחַ בְּחֻקֶּיךָ, וְנִשְׂמַח בְּדִבְרֵי תוֹרָתְךָ וּבְמִצְוֹתֶיךָ לְעוֹלָם וָעֶד. [3] כִּי הֵם חַיֵּינוּ וְאֹרֶךְ יָמֵינוּ, וּבָהֶם נֶהְגֶּה יוֹמָם וָלָיְלָה. [4] וְאַהֲבָתְךָ אַל תָּסִיר מִמֶּנּוּ לְעוֹלָמִים. [5] בָּרוּךְ אַתָּה, יְיָ, אוֹהֵב עַמּוֹ יִשְׂרָאֵל.

meditate on them day and night.
[4] Never remove your love from us!
[5] Blessed are You, Adonai, who loves
his People Israel.

BRETTLER (BIBLE)

Together these allusions suggest an ideal future.

[2] *"When we lie down and when we stand up"* Paraphrasing Deuteronomy 6:7 and 11:19, which will follow in the *Sh'ma*. Here, however, the topic is Torah study in general, not just reciting the *Sh'ma*. "We will discuss your laws" paraphrases Psalm 119:23, which celebrates the virtues of such study. But the prayer goes farther than the psalms: it extols Torah study with language usually reserved by the Bible for God. The prayer promises, for instance, "We will rejoice … in the words of your Torah." Biblically, Jews are supposed to love, not rejoice in, Torah (e.g., see Ps. 119:97, 119:113, 119:163, 119:165). They rejoice in God (e.g., Pss. 9:3, 40:17, 85:7). This remarkable theology of implicitly likening Torah to God developed late in the biblical period (see Ps. 119) and continued with the Rabbis.

[3] *"For they are our life and …"* Paraphrasing Deuteronomy 30:20, "For He is your life and your length of days," again (see prior comment) applying to Torah a phrase used in the Bible of God. Verse 3 ends with a paraphrase of Joshua 1:8 and Psalm 1:2, from the opening of the *Nevi'im* (prophetic) and *Ketuvim* (writings) sections of the canon, both emphasizing the importance of perpetual Torah study.

[4] *"Never remove"* 1 Kings 10:9 mentions "Adonai's everlasting love for Israel," but otherwise the idea of God's *eternal* love for Israel is rarely found in the Bible. Love here is part of the Bible's covenant imagery, not love in an emotional sense, but love as support and assistance that follows upon mutual covenantal obligation.

[5] *"His People Israel"* The prayer circles back poetically at the end to reiterate the reference in verse 1, "the House of Israel, your people."

DORFF (THEOLOGY)

because Christians have taken over the language of "God loves us," Jews tend to shy away from it. The liturgy, however, has no such compunctions: both morning and evening, right before the *Sh'ma*, the central liturgical statement of Jewish faith, we insist that God loves us. Jewish liturgy has proclaimed this from antiquity; Jews should not be embarrassed to say the same thing today.

God's love, however, does not consist in saving us from sin through a supernatural intercessor, as Christians believe; that would deprive us of free will, a critical feature of our humanity. Instead, we say here that God loves us by giving us instruction (the literal meaning of Torah) and commandments as to how we should live. This is akin to the relationship between human parents and children: One of the primary ways in which parents express their love is by establishing and enforcing reasonable rules for their children. The absence of such rules is not love, but apathy. Even when children rail against the rules, enforcing them with care, concern, and energy is a clear and powerful expression of parental love. So our prayer perceives the Torah and commandments not as a burden, but as a gift of God's love, for which we rejoice, in gratitude to God who gives it.

2–3 *"When we lie down and when we stand up ... day and night"* These phrases are *merisms*, a biblical mode of expression in which the ends of a spectrum are meant to include everything in between as well. We speak of God's Torah and commandments not just day and night but always, "for they are our life and the length of our days"— that is, they give meaning to life itself.

———◆———

ELLENSON (MODERN LITURGIES)

In this regard, the two of them represent "moderate" Reform—Abraham Geiger in Germany, and Isaac Mayer Wise in America. Reform prayer books generally stake out ideological positions this way. The particulars of German law demanded a single unified communal structure, so that Geiger had to share a communal rabbinate in Breslau with the traditionalist Solomon Tiktin. He was consequently ever conscious of the need to be inclusive in his liturgical creations, hoping not to alienate somewhat traditional Jews who might side with him rather than his very Orthodox opponent in the Breslau rabbinate. By contrast, Hamburg was a free port city, which early on developed Reform prayer books without regard for rabbinic politics, and the Berlin *Reformgemeinde*, purposely located outside the communal structure that affected Geiger in Breslau, attracted radical Reformers to its pulpit, most notably Samuel Holdheim. Geiger did not necessarily disagree with Holdheim in principle, but in practice, he could not go as far as Holdheim in affirming extreme liturgical change.

In America, the dichotomy between "extreme" and "moderate" came in the form of the Einhorn-Wise debate. Isaac Mayer Wise, who arrived here in 1846, took it upon himself to create what he thought would be an umbrella reform of Judaism that would attract everyone, not just the radicals. Wise was eminently practical. David Einhorn assumed a pulpit in Baltimore in 1855, but brought a scholar's temperament to it. He had read and assimilated the best of German scholarship on the liturgy and would brook no compromises when it came to applying that scholarship to his prayer book. Among other things, he believed that German alone could best capture the spirit of Reform, whereas Wise preferred, whenever possible, to include Hebrew prayers, often to the point where traditionalists could daven it through on the right side of the page, ignoring the translation on the left. Wise was a proud reformer, of course—no less than Einhorn. But he was moved by a spiritual goal of unifying all American Jews in his 1857 *Minhag America* (literally, "American [prayer] Ritual"), while Einhorn's *Olath Tamid* (1858) stressed Reform as a matter of scholarly and ethical principle.

[4] *"Never remove your love from us"* Reconstructionist prayer book *Kol Haneshamah* (1995) employs the Sefardi "declarative mode," "Your love will never depart from us" *(lo tasur)*, in lieu of the imperative, "Never remove your love from us" *(al tasir)*. The accompanying comment to the prayer explains, "Divine love is available to every one of us when we fashion our lives into channels to receive and share it." The British Liberal *Lev Chadash* (1995) makes this change as well, but not necessarily for the same reason.

[5] *"Blessed are You"* Falk (see "Blessed are You," p. 54) labels this "Blessing of Revelation" and renders it, "Let us bless the source of life, source of the fullness of our knowing. May we learn with humility and pleasure, may we teach what we know with love, and may we honor wisdom in all its embodiments."

FRANKEL (A WOMAN'S VOICE)

It is significant that our love for God is not demonstrated through our performance of the *mitzvot*, but rather through our active engagement with them intellectually and emotionally. We commit ourselves to "speak of [them], and rejoice in [them] ... and meditate on them." By doing so, we hope to retain God's love.

Human parents know that children often fall short in doing what they've been taught is right. But wise parents know that their love for their children should not be based upon the latter's accomplishments, but must be unconditional. If parents teach them well, then their children will meditate upon these teachings and transmit them to their own children, and so on *l'olamim*, forever. Thus, both human and divine revelation unfold in teaching and learning.

GRAY (OUR TALMUDIC HERITAGE)

have loved you with eternal love [*ahavat olam*]." The Tosafot (twelfth to thirteenth centuries, France and Germany) point out that the disagreement is resolved by the compromise of placing the Rabbis' preferred *Ahavat Olam* in *Ma'ariv*, where it remains.

That is true, however, only for the Ashkenazi tradition. The classic Spanish-Portuguese tradition *(Minhag Sefarad)* and the Sefardi tradition influenced by Kabbalah *(Nusach Sefarad)* mix the two prayers. Their morning version begins with *Ahavat Olam*, but then continues with the rest of the words from *Ahavah Rabbah* (see L. Hoffman).

———◆———

L. HOFFMAN (HISTORY)

and *Ahavat Olam*. In talmudic times, when prayer was still oral, either one (or some other freely composed version on the same theme) might have appeared in any given service. All such prayers were called *Birkat Hatorah*, a "Blessing over Torah." Over time, the most common examples of a *Birkat Hatorah* were allocated as fixed elements throughout the liturgy, *Ahavah Rabbah* and *Ahavat Olam* before the *Sh'ma*, … *asher bachar banu* before an *aliyah*, … *asher natan lanu* after the *aliyah*, and so on. (See Volume 4, *Seder K'riat Hatorah* [*The Torah Service*], L. Hoffman, "Who chose us from all nations," p. 105; and Volume 5, *Birkhot Hashachar* [*Morning Blessings*], L. Hoffman, "Gave us his Torah," p. 115.)

The situation remained relatively fluid until Amram Gaon of Babylonia (c. 860) promulgated our first known prayer book. (See Volume 1, *The Sh'ma and Its Blessings*, L. Hoffman, "Our Diary of Prayer Across the Centuries," pp. 1–13.) Following his geonic forebears, he apportioned *Ahavah Rabbah* for the morning, and *Ahavat Olam* for the evening, as expressions of God's love for us prior to the *Sh'ma's* avowal of our love back to God.

The compromise on the two prayer versions seems insignificant, but a century after Amram, it exploded in debate. The last two great Geonim, Sherira and Hai (968–1038) described Amram's compromise as customary in only one very tiny academy, but not the main ones of Sura and Pumbedita. Alternating wording mornings and nights is a "mistaken custom" *(minhag ta'ut)*, they maintained. People should not say *Ahavah Rabbah* at all; they should limit themselves to *Ahavat Olam*, both *Shacharit* and *Ma'ariv*.

What makes the responsum intriguing is the fact that these two geonic authors almost never denounce local custom, in part through personal proclivity, perhaps, but also because the once-proud gaonate, center of the Jewish world, was beginning to totter. Jews in the Muslim empire dependent on Baghdad had once followed the marching orders of the Geonim who lived there, but by the tenth century, independent communities were being established throughout western Europe, each with its own local *yeshivot*, the graduates of which hardly needed advice anymore from far-off Babylonia. The gaonate, however, was increasingly dependent on financial support from the new and burgeoning Jewish centers in what is now Spain, France, and Germany. Among other things, requests for responsa came with money attached. What would happen if such requests dried up? It made no sense for Sherira and Hai to be too heavy-handed in their answers. Where possible, they benefited from applauding local custom, rather than pressuring new communities to change what they were doing just because they deviated in unimportant ways from Babylonian precedent. Why, then, did Sherira and Hai ban a custom that was in accord with an earlier geonic ruling?

A clue comes from the second geonic prayer book known to us, the one authored by Saadiah Gaon (c. 920). Saadiah follows Amram's precedent, but he changes the first two words of the morning *Ahavah rabbah* to *ahavat olam*. Like Sherira and Hai, then, Saadiah fought against at least the first two words of the morning version of this prayer. Now it may be that this is all Sherira and Hai objected to. The initial words are also the name of the prayer, so when they tell us not to say *Ahavah rabbah*, we do not know whether they meant to omit the entire prayer that begins that way or just to say the opening two words differently. But at the very least, all three of these authorities demand a change in the opening two words.

Their objection can be traced to the growing success of the movement we call Karaism. Begun in the eighth century, Karaism denied the rabbinic tradition that the Geonim championed, including the rabbinic prayer book. Karaite Jews limited their prayers to the Bible. Biblical idiom, they argued, was pure, since it was either the direct word of God to Moses and the prophets, or compositions by worthies like David (who wrote the psalms) and Solomon (who wrote Song of Songs and Ecclesiastes). Rabbinic prayers, by contrast, elected new and poorer wording—like comic-book English compared to Shakespeare! *Ahavah Rabbah* was purely rabbinic, so hardly as good as *Ahavat Olam*, which cites Jeremiah 31:3, "I [God] have loved you with eternal love [*ahavat olam*]."

Saadiah was the first Gaon to engage in polemic with the rising Karaite leadership. Karaism peaked, however, later, during the gaonate of Hai and Sherira. Saadiah changed at least the offending first two words. Hai and Sherira may even have tried to eradicate the entire prayer.

Amram's prayer book provided instructions in talmudic Aramaic, the universal rabbinic scholarly language. Saadiah wrote his instructions in Judeo-Arabic (Arabic written in Hebrew characters). The result was that most of Europe followed Amram, not Saadiah, whose language they did not understand. Tenth-century Spain, however, was still in the Muslim orbit, and its Jews learned in Arabic. Ashkenazi tradition, therefore, following Amram, reserves *Ahavat Olam* to the nighttime service, but Spanish-Portuguese practice (and Sefardi practice thereafter) influenced by Saadiah, has adopted at least the first two words, *Ahavat olam*, in the morning service as well.

J. HOFFMAN (TRANSLATION)

[1] *"Torah"* The Hebrew word *Torah* in the actual Torah meant more generally "teaching," or even "tradition" or "custom." But by the time the Rabbis wrote the liturgy, it had taken on the more specific meaning of "Torah."

[1] *"Commandments"* Or *mitzvot*, that is, "mitzvahs." The Hebrew *mitzvah* is a technical term, only approximated by the English "commandment." The "Ten Commandments," for example, are not all *mitzvot*. Also, the anglicized "mitzvah" is commonly (mis?)used to refer to any good deed, while the Hebrew denotes one of the specific set of commandments enjoined by God upon Israel.

[1] *"Laws and rules"* Birnbaum's "laws and judgments" more literally reflects the root of the second word, *sh.p.t*, which is also used for the verb "to judge," and the noun *shofet*, Hebrew for "a judge." But words do not, in general, get their meanings solely from their roots. As with *mitzvah* (see above "Commandments"), *mishpat* (here) has a technical meaning that we cannot capture entirely in English.

All translations struggle to provide parallels for the four words listed here. *Sim Shalom*, for example, offers, "Torah and *mitzvoth*, statutes and laws." *Forms of Prayer* prefers "teaching and practice, duty and justice." In the end, having a sequence of four words in translation is more important than the individual word choices.

[3] *"Life and the length of our days"* We translate this literally, on the assumption that it was meant poetically, and we do not want to destroy the poetry.

◆ ◆ ◆

[Recite the Sh'ma (see Volume 1, The Sh'ma and Its Blessings, p. 83); then continue here.]

III. BLESSING ON REDEMPTION: *EMET VE'EMUNAH* ("TRUE AND TRUSTWORTHY")

[1] True and trustworthy is all of this, and we are bound by it, for He is Adonai our God and there is none like Him, and we are Israel his people. [2] He is our savior from the hand of kings, our king, our redeemer from the fist of all tyrants. [3] He is God who exacts payment from our oppressors, paying all our mortal enemies in kind. [4] He does great things we cannot comprehend, and wondrous things we cannot count. [5] He gave us life, not letting our foot slip. [6] He lets us tread upon our enemies' altars, granting us victory over those who hate us, [7] granting us miracles and vengeance over Pharaoh, signs and wonders, in the land of the children of Cham. [8] He killed all the first-born of Egypt in his wrath, and brought his People Israel out of their midst into eternal freedom. [9] He let his children pass between the two halves of the Red Sea, drowning those who chased them and those who hated them in the depths. [10] His children saw his might, praised and glorified his name, and freely accepted his reign.

[11] Moses and the children of Israel most joyfully answered You in song, all of them singing:

[12] Who is like You among the gods, Adonai! Who is like You, adorned in holiness, revered in praise, worker of wonders!

[13] Your children saw your reign, as You split the sea before Moses.

[14] "This is my God," they responded, and said:

"Adonai will reign for ever and ever."

אֱ֝מֶת וֶאֱמוּנָה כָּל זֹאת, וְקַיָּם עָלֵינוּ [1] כִּי הוּא יְיָ אֱלֹהֵינוּ וְאֵין זוּלָתוֹ, וַאֲנַחְנוּ יִשְׂרָאֵל עַמּוֹ. [2] הַפּוֹדֵנוּ מִיַּד מְלָכִים, מַלְכֵּנוּ הַגּוֹאֲלֵנוּ מִכַּף כָּל הֶעָרִיצִים. [3] הָאֵל הַנִּפְרָע לָנוּ מִצָּרֵינוּ, וְהַמְשַׁלֵּם גְּמוּל לְכָל אֹיְבֵי נַפְשֵׁנוּ; [4] הָעֹשֶׂה גְדֹלוֹת עַד אֵין חֵקֶר, וְנִפְלָאוֹת עַד אֵין מִסְפָּר; [5] הַשָּׂם נַפְשֵׁנוּ בַּחַיִּים, וְלֹא נָתַן לַמּוֹט רַגְלֵנוּ; [6] הַמַּדְרִיכֵנוּ עַל בָּמוֹת אֹיְבֵינוּ, וַיָּרֶם קַרְנֵנוּ עַל כָּל שׂוֹנְאֵינוּ; [7] הָעֹשֶׂה לָּנוּ נִסִּים וּנְקָמָה בְּפַרְעֹה, אוֹתוֹת וּמוֹפְתִים בְּאַדְמַת בְּנֵי חָם; [8] הַמַּכֶּה בְעֶבְרָתוֹ כָּל בְּכוֹרֵי מִצְרָיִם, וַיּוֹצֵא אֶת עַמּוֹ יִשְׂרָאֵל מִתּוֹכָם לְחֵרוּת עוֹלָם. [9] הַמַּעֲבִיר בָּנָיו בֵּין גִּזְרֵי יַם סוּף; אֶת רוֹדְפֵיהֶם וְאֶת שׂוֹנְאֵיהֶם בִּתְהוֹמוֹת טִבַּע. [10] וְרָאוּ בָנָיו גְּבוּרָתוֹ; שִׁבְּחוּ וְהוֹדוּ לִשְׁמוֹ, וּמַלְכוּתוֹ בְּרָצוֹן קִבְּלוּ עֲלֵיהֶם.

[11] מֹשֶׁה וּבְנֵי יִשְׂרָאֵל לְךָ עָנוּ שִׁירָה בְּשִׂמְחָה רַבָּה, וְאָמְרוּ כֻלָּם:

[12] מִי־כָמֹכָה בָּאֵלִם, יְיָ; מִי־כָּמֹכָה נֶאְדָּר בַּקֹּדֶשׁ, נוֹרָא תְהִלֹּת, עֹשֵׂה פֶלֶא!

[13] מַלְכוּתְךָ רָאוּ בָנֶיךָ, בּוֹקֵעַ יָם לִפְנֵי מֹשֶׁה; [14] זֶה אֵלִי עָנוּ וְאָמְרוּ:

יְיָ יִמְלֹךְ לְעֹלָם וָעֶד.

[15] It has been said: "Adonai saved Jacob, redeeming him from a hand mightier than his own. [16] Blessed are You, Adonai, Israel's savior.

[15] וְנֶאֱמַר: כִּי פָדָה יְיָ אֶת יַעֲקֹב, וּגְאָלוֹ מִיַּד חָזָק מִמֶּנּוּ. [16] בָּרוּךְ אַתָּה, יְיָ, גָּאַל יִשְׂרָאֵל.

BRETTLER (BIBLE)

[1] *"True and trustworthy"* According to the Bible, God's power is manifest first in creation and then, in post-creation history, in Israel's deliverance. Working chronologically, the prayer before the *Sh'ma* emphasizes the former; the prayer after emphasizes the latter.

This prayer is a remarkable pastiche of (mostly) biblical phrases arranged in standard biblical poetic form.

[1] *"There is none like Him"* A statement of radical monotheism: Adonai is the only God rather than just the most powerful God among many. The Song of the Sea (see below, vv. 10–12, "His children saw ... Who is like You"), which was composed earlier, *(p. 71)*

DORFF (THEOLOGY)

[1] *"True [emet] and trustworthy [emunah] ..."* Literally, "truth and faith." The Conservative Movement's only official statement of belief, *Emet Ve'emunah: Statement of Principles of Conservative Judaism,* cites the opening of this prayer in its title. Rabbi Robert *(p. 72)*

ELLENSON (MODERN LITURGIES)

[1] *"True and trustworthy"* This prayer identifies God as the divine redeemer who liberated Israel from Egypt. In recounting that particularistic moment from ancient Israelite history, the Jew proclaims that the experience of redemption exists in an *(p. 75)*

FRANKEL (A WOMAN'S VOICE)

[11] *"Moses and the children of Israel"* As we build up to the *Amidah,* we rehearse our central story as a people: the Exodus from Egypt. We recall the plagues as miracles for us and vengeance upon our enemies. Our recitation climaxes at the Red Sea, where God vanquished the Egyptian army and led Israel to safety.

And where were the women during this epic drama?

In recent years, this moment at the Red Sea has become a flashpoint for feminist critique and liturgical *(p. 77)*

[For prayer instructions, see page 66.]

III. BLESSING ON REDEMPTION: *EMET VE'EMUNAH* ("TRUE AND TRUSTWORTHY")

[1] True and trustworthy is all of this, and we are bound by it, for He is Adonai our God and there is none like Him, and we are Israel his people. [2] He is our savior from the hand of kings, our king, our redeemer from the fist of all tyrants. [3] He is God who exacts payment from our oppressors, paying all our mortal enemies

GRAY (OUR TALMUDIC HERITAGE)

[1] *"True and trustworthy"* Possibly an amalgamation of Psalm 31:6, "You have redeemed me, Adonai, true God" *(el emet)* and Lamentations 3:23, "Great is your faithfulness" *(rabbah emunatekha).* Midrash T'hillim 25:2 explains that a human bailee (someone with whom items are deposited) may accidentally mistake one person's deposited items for another's. But God is not like that: a person does not wake up in the morning unable to locate her soul. Nor does she find her soul in the *(p. 77)*

LANDES (HALAKHAH)

"Recite the Sh'ma" Reciting *Sh'ma* (Deut. 6:4–8, 11:13–21; Num. 15:37–41) at night is as important a *mitzvah* as doing so by day, as the *Sh'ma* itself (v. 7) commands, "when you lie down and when you stand up" (Deut. 6:7; see Volume 1, *The Sh'ma and Its Blessings*, p. 83). The morning *Sh'ma* sets us out on a day of proper activity, while the nighttime *Sh'ma* guards our thoughts as day ends and we go to sleep (*Sefer Hachinukh*, Pinchas Halevi of Barcelona, 1523, Venice; *Mitzvah* 420).

The third paragraph of the *Sh'ma*

refers in the main to the *mitzvah* of *tzitzit*, the "tassel," but says explicitly, "When you see it" (Num. 15:21; see Volume 1, *The Sh'ma and Its Blessings*, p. 85). That paragraph is, therefore, technically obligatory only during the light of day, when we can truly *"see it."* Nonetheless, we recite it at night as well, for it mentions the Exodus from Egypt, which must be remembered both day and night (Maimonides, "Laws of Prayer" 1:3). We could, of course, remember the Exodus in other ways—indeed we do—but since we are used to saying this paragraph   *(p. 79)*

L. HOFFMAN (HISTORY)

THE BLESSINGS ON CREATION AND REVELATION ARE FOLLOWED BY THE SH'MA *ITSELF—THREE BIBLICAL PASSAGES (DEUT. 6:4–9, DEUT. 11:13–21, AND NUM. 15:37–41) RECITED MORNING AND EVENING (FOR TEXT AND COMMENTARY, SEE VOLUME 1,* THE SH'MA AND ITS BLESSINGS, *PP. 83–116). THE* SH'MA *IS FOLLOWED BY A THIRD BLESSING (ON THE THEME OF REDEMPTION), THE NIGHTTIME VERSION OF WHICH IS* EMET VE'EMUNAH, *"TRUE AND TRUSTWORTHY" (AFTER THE OPENING WORDS). FOR THE* SHACHARIT *VERSION (*EMET V'YATSIV, *"TRUE AND ESTABLISHED"), SEE VOLUME 1,* THE SH'MA AND ITS BLESSINGS, *P. 117.*

(p. 79)

אֱמֶת וֶאֱמוּנָה כָּל זֹאת, וְקַיָּם עָלֵינוּ כִּי הוּא יְיָ אֱלֹהֵינוּ וְאֵין זוּלָתוֹ, וַאֲנַחְנוּ יִשְׂרָאֵל עַמּוֹ. ²הַפּוֹדֵנוּ מִיַּד מְלָכִים, מַלְכֵּנוּ הַגּוֹאֲלֵנוּ מִכַּף כָּל הֶעָרִיצִים. ³הָאֵל הַנִּפְרָע לָנוּ מִצָּרֵינוּ, וְהַמְשַׁלֵּם גְּמוּל לְכָל אֹיְבֵי נַפְשֵׁנוּ; ⁴הָעֹשֶׂה גְדֹלוֹת עַד אֵין חֵקֶר, וְנִפְלָאוֹת עַד אֵין מִסְפָּר; ⁵הַשָּׂם

J. HOFFMAN (TRANSLATION)

[1] *"True and trustworthy"* As in Birnbaum. The two Hebrew words *(emet, emunah)* begin with the same two letters *aleph, mem* (together forming the sound *"em-"*), and we strive for a similar alliterative affect in English ("tr-"). In context, however, "certain" (as in *Lev Chadash*) may come closer to the meaning than "trustworthy."

[1] *"Is all of this"* We preserve the reversed word order of the Hebrew in order to start the passage with the content words ("true" and "trustworthy"), even though the English version is awkward. ("True and trustworthy is what all of this is" would be less awkward, but too colloquial.)

(p. 80)

in kind. [4] He does great things we cannot comprehend, and wondrous things we cannot count. [5] He gave us life, not letting our foot slip. [6] He lets us tread upon our enemies' altars, granting us victory over those who hate us, [7] granting us miracles and vengeance over Pharaoh, signs and wonders, in the land of the children of Cham. [8] He killed all the first-born of Egypt in his wrath, and brought his People Israel out of their midst into eternal freedom. [9] He let his children pass between the two halves of the Red Sea, drowning those who chased them and those who hated them in the depths. [10] His children saw his might, praised and glorified his name, and freely accepted his reign.

[11] Moses and the children of Israel most joyfully answered You in song, all of them singing:

[12] Who is like You among the gods, Adonai! Who is like You, adorned in holiness, revered in praise, worker of wonders!

[13] Your children saw your reign, as You split the sea before Moses.

[14] "This is my God," they responded, and said: "Adonai will reign for ever and ever."

[15] It has been said: "Adonai saved Jacob, redeeming him from a hand mightier than his own. [16] Blessed are You, Adonai, Israel's savior.

נַפְשֵׁנוּ בַּחַיִּים, וְלֹא נָתַן לַמּוֹט רַגְלֵנוּ; [6] הַמַּדְרִיכֵנוּ עַל בָּמוֹת אֹיְבֵינוּ, וַיָּרֶם קַרְנֵנוּ עַל כָּל שׂוֹנְאֵינוּ; [7] הָעֹשֶׂה לָּנוּ נִסִּים וּנְקָמָה בְּפַרְעֹה, אוֹתוֹת וּמוֹפְתִים בְּאַדְמַת בְּנֵי חָם; [8] הַמַּכֶּה בְּעֶבְרָתוֹ כָּל בְּכוֹרֵי מִצְרָיִם, וַיּוֹצֵא אֶת עַמּוֹ יִשְׂרָאֵל מִתּוֹכָם לְחֵרוּת עוֹלָם. [9] הַמַּעֲבִיר בָּנָיו בֵּין גִּזְרֵי יַם סוּף; אֶת רוֹדְפֵיהֶם וְאֶת שׂוֹנְאֵיהֶם בִּתְהוֹמוֹת טִבַּע. [10] וְרָאוּ בָנָיו גְּבוּרָתוֹ; שִׁבְּחוּ וְהוֹדוּ לִשְׁמוֹ, וּמַלְכוּתוֹ בְּרָצוֹן קִבְּלוּ עֲלֵיהֶם.

[11] מֹשֶׁה וּבְנֵי יִשְׂרָאֵל לְךָ עָנוּ שִׁירָה בְּשִׂמְחָה רַבָּה, וְאָמְרוּ כֻלָּם:

[12] מִי־כָמֹכָה בָּאֵלִם, יְיָ; מִי־כָּמֹכָה נֶאְדָּר בַּקֹּדֶשׁ, נוֹרָא תְהִלֹּת, עֹשֵׂה פֶלֶא!

[13] מַלְכוּתְךָ רָאוּ בָנֶיךָ, בּוֹקֵעַ יָם לִפְנֵי מֹשֶׁה; [14] זֶה אֵלִי עָנוּ וְאָמְרוּ: יְיָ יִמְלֹךְ לְעֹלָם וָעֶד.

[15] וְנֶאֱמַר: כִּי פָדָה יְיָ אֶת יַעֲקֹב, וּגְאָלוֹ מִיַּד חָזָק מִמֶּנּוּ. [16] בָּרוּךְ אַתָּה, יְיָ, גָּאַל יִשְׂרָאֵל.

still displays the idea that Adonai is only the strongest of "the gods." True monotheism developed relatively late in the biblical period—as in the anonymous exilic prophet whom we call Deutero-Isaiah (Isa. 45:5): "There is none like You and there is no other God but You."

[2-3] *"Our savior ... our redeemer"* We see here a poetic pattern borrowed from the Bible (sometimes called synonymous parallelism): the second part of a line paraphrases or "seconds" the first.

[4] *"He does great things we cannot comprehend ..."* Paraphrasing Job—quite remarkably, the verse is recited once by Job (9:10) and once by his antagonistic friends (5:9).

[5] *"Not letting our foot slip"* Psalm 66:9.

[6-7] *"Lets us tread"* Again (as in vv. 2–3, above), various biblical phrases are combined in synonymous parallelism.

[8] *"Eternal freedom"* A post-biblical expression, and therefore of particular interest, since the Rabbis chose it deliberately, even though it obscures the fact, well-known to them, that even after Israel's deliverance from Egypt, it suffered periods of subjugation.

[10-12] *"His children saw ... Who is like You"* Almost universally, contemporary prayerbook editors who separate this prayer into paragraphs divide it as we do here, following convention. The paragraph break occurs just before line 11. The second paragraph is the Song of the Sea *(Mi Khamoka)*, duly introduced with the opening statement anticipating what is to come: "Moses and the children of Israel most joyfully answered You in song" (v. 11).

But that arrangement is probably wrong. Rabbinic theology understood the Song as the means by which Israel accepted God's rule; that is its whole point. The introductory line should therefore begin not with verse 11, but in the middle of verse 10, "They freely accepted his reign [as] Moses and the children of Israel most joyfully answered You in song." The first thought (and the first paragraph, therefore) runs from verse 1, "True and trustworthy" through just the first half of verse 10, not all of it. God's trustworthiness (God's *emunah*, v. 1) is displayed through God's saving power (vv. 2–9), which Israel sees and duly praises (v. 10a).

The second thought, accepting God's rule by singing *Mi Khamokhah*, follows from the first, but is a separate idea conceptually, and the whole point of the prayer. The covenant was not imposed on Israel, but was accepted willingly, as in Exodus 19:8, before the giving of the Decalogue: "All that Adonai has spoken we will do!"

For a similar issue, see below vv. 13–15, "They responded ... it has been said."

[12] *"Who is like You"* From the Song of the Sea (Exod. 15:11), where it is a statement of Adonai's comparability to other gods, not of his absolute monotheism. See above, v.

1, "There is none like him," and (for details) Volume 1, *The Sh'ma and Its Blessings*, Brettler, p. 130. In this context, however, the introductory "and there is none like Him" corrects the earlier notion to provide true monotheism.

13–15 *"They responded ... it has been said"* Here too—just like "His children saw ... Who is like you" (see above, vv. 10–12)—the usual prayerbook editing misunderstands the point being made. Usually, the Song of the Sea is organized on the page so that verse 14 (translated literally), "'This is my God,' they answered, and they said," is a single verse. In fact, it should be two. The first half, "'This is my God,' they answered," sums up all that has come in the paragraph so far. The second half, "They said," introduces what is to follow, namely, "Adonai will reign for ever and ever," which constitutes the answer.

The editor has selected two biblical texts, "This is my God," from Exodus 15:2, and "Adonai will reign for ever and ever," from Exodus 15:18, so that one reinforces and completes the other—a case of synthetic parallelism. Exodus 15:18 is the first time the Bible explicitly calls God king, a sentiment that is rare in the Torah, but frequent elsewhere, especially in Psalms (see Brettler, "*Kabbalat Shabbat:* A Liturgy from Psalms," pp. 23–25 in Volume 8, *Kabbalat Shabbat* [*Welcoming Shabbat in the Synagogue*]).

15 *"Adonai saved Jacob"* Jeremiah 31:11, complementing the earlier quotation of Jeremiah 31:3, *ahavat olam*, "eternal love" (see p. 58), with which the *Sh'ma* was introduced. The *Sh'ma* is thus bracketed by a promise of God's love and the deliverance that flows from it.

16 *"Israel's savior"* The Hebrew is in the past tense, suggesting that God redeemed Israel before; the person praying is supposed to infer that God will do so again.

———◆———

DORFF (THEOLOGY)

Gordis, chair of the commission that produced the statement (the Commission on the Philosophy of Conservative Judaism), thereby intended to indicate that our fundamental convictions are sometimes "truths" that human beings can fathom, but sometimes they are beyond our comprehension, requiring faith in their truthfulness. Faith need not imply blind leaps without thought; on the contrary, we are duty bound to wrestle with significant issues and to determine what we can about them before we take the further step of asserting what we believe even in the absence of firm knowledge. Since "God's seal is truth" (Shab. 55a), we are to imitate God in striving to know the truth, but we will never know "everything"; some things require faith.

Martin Buber (1878–1965), however, alerted us to another kind of faith, more deeply rooted in Judaism. Faith *that* something is true is what Buber calls "p-faith," after the Greek word *pistis*. Jewish faith, however, is not usually of that type, for while

Judaism surely has some central beliefs, there is no official list of beliefs, no creed that a Jew must affirm in order to be Jewish. Instead, Judaism emphasizes "e-faith," after the Hebrew word used here in the liturgy, *emunah*. It is faith *in* something or someone, in this case, God. We *trust* God. Like p-faith, e-faith should also not be blind: we need to evaluate the grounds for such trust before we affirm it. (See Martin Buber, *Two Types of Faith*, trans. Norman P. Goldhawk [London: Routledge and Paul, 1951].)

It is precisely this latter kind of faith that our prayer asserts. We do not believe *that* God exists, so much as we believe in the *relationship* that we have *with* God, "that He is Adonai our God, and there is none like him, and we are Israel his People."

[2] *"Redeemer from the fist of all tyrants"* As God redeemed Israel in the past, especially in the Exodus from Egypt, so God can be trusted to redeem us now and in the future from those who oppress us. Much of the latter part of this prayer and the blessing that closes it are in the past tense—God redeemed us—but the paragraph asserts here that God "*redeems* us from kings [now!]." God's past record justifies such confidence.

In a post-Holocaust world, however, present-tense assertions of God's redemptive power ring hollow. God's failure to save the victims of the Shoah have led Jewish thinkers to produce a significant body of thought known as "post-Holocaust theology." Even though I myself have written about this, I think it is only accurate to admit that no theology adequately justifies God's not stepping in to stop the Holocaust.

The argument that comes closest to successfully justifying God, in my view, is the "free-will defense," an argument proposed by medieval theologians like Maimonides. According to that argument, God cannot intervene in history to make things right when people do evil, for that would rob us of free will. Free will makes sense only if human beings have the ability to choose badly, even if their choices occasion terrible suffering. To the extent that God stops history to prevent such evil, the human actors involved lose their ability to make choices and to act upon them.

It is critical, both for God and for us, that we retain free will, for without it, we would be mere machines, programmed to act as God wants. We are instead, as the Garden of Eden story asserts, people who must choose. To be sure, this does not get God off the hook for natural disasters that kill or injure the innocent or for undeserved illnesses where the victims bear no responsibility—like leukemia in a three-year-old. True, like a parent, God needs to back off to let people make choices and learn their consequences, but at some point good parents intervene to ensure that their children do not suffer, and the Holocaust was surely such an event. Thus as much as the free-will defense provides at least some plausibility as to why God did not stop the Holocaust, it is not completely adequate.

Beyond the free-will argument, it seems to me that we have only three substantive ways of retaining belief in a just, redeeming God. They may be used separately or in combination. (1) We can scream at God and/or call God to justice, a response going back to Abraham and Job (see, e.g., *Arguing with God: A Jewish Tradition*, by Anson Laytner, or *Facing the Abusing God: A Theology of Protest*, by David Blumenthal). (2) We can take refuge in our lack of knowledge about why God lets good things happen to bad people and bad things happen to good (notice, incidentally, that both sides of the issue challenge God's justice, even though the latter is usually the only one discussed), thus leaving the problem unresolved, except to say that ultimately God's mysterious behavior demands faith beyond our understanding. Or (3), we can distinguish between the God of the philosophers and the God of Abraham, Isaac, and Jacob (see chapter 5 of my book, *Knowing God: Jewish Journeys to the Unknowable*, and chapter 7 in Harold Schulweis, *For Those Who Cannot Believe*). The God of the philosophers is an intellectual construct acknowledging that a God of sheer power cannot legitimately be expected to be moral. (Schulweis calls this God Elohim, the divine name associated talmudically with justice.) The God of our ancestors is the God we meet in personal interactions like prayer, the God who calls us to alleviate the pain of others. (Schulweis calls this God Adonai, the name associated with love.) All the while, we challenge God and confess our inability to understand how God would let a Holocaust happen.

[7-8] *"Granting us miracles and vengeance over Pharaoh … and brought his people out of their midst into eternal freedom"* Why does the liturgy constantly use the Exodus to exemplify God's redeeming power? Why not refer to more recent events, even something later in the Bible—God's delaying the setting of the sun for Joshua (Josh. 10:12–14), for example, or rescuing the Israelites from the Philistines under Deborah, Gideon, or Samson (Judges 4–5, 6–8, 13–16)?

One answer is that the Exodus is the birth event of the Jewish People. Individuals celebrate birthdays as the day they came into existence and, thus, the birth of whatever it is for which they stand. So, too, nations use their birthdays (like July 4) to communicate their values and character, especially with their birth stories. Consider what is being communicated about the nature of the United States, for example, in our tales about the Boston Tea Party, George Washington, or the Declaration of Independence. The Exodus-Sinai narrative exemplifies divine redemption from slavery to freedom and human responsibility as the story that best describes not only the fact of our birth, but our character as a people.

[12] *"Who is like You among the gods …"* Coming from Exodus 15, whose archaic Hebrew forms indicate that it is among the earliest layers of Torah, this verse may mean either "Who is like You among the other existing gods?" or "Who is like you among what other nations wrongfully *think* are gods?" In the first case, the verse would articulate henotheism, the belief that there are many gods, with one of them supreme over the rest, leading us to the conclusion that our ancestors were henotheists first, and monotheists only later (perhaps by the time of Isaiah in the eighth century B.C.E.). The latter interpretation is consistent with monotheism, suggesting that Jewish monotheism came as early as the twelfth century B.C.E.

◆

"eternal present." Liberal Jews have always seen the experience of ancient freedom as paradigmatic of modern times, when Jewish freedom (this time from medieval marginality and persecution) finally arrived. Traditional Judaism too had seen God's deliverance in Egypt as providential for their future, but for nineteenth-century Reformers especially, that providence had already begun to unfold. For liberal Jews, then, this assertion of God's deliverance has always constituted a particularly powerful proclamation of faith, making this prayer highly popular among liberal prayerbook authors.

At the same time, these liberal prayerbook writers have found elements of "chauvinism" and "vengeance" within this prayer disturbing to their sensibilities and offensive to their conscience. Consequently, this prayer has been treated in many different ways.

The *Hamburg Temple Prayer Books* (1819, 1841) offer this prayer in the vernacular alone and (in its German offering) emphasize only the universal themes of divine redemption. David Einhorn does the same in his 1858 *Olath Tamid*.

By contrast, the moderation and caution that characteristically mark the liturgy of Abraham Geiger (see "Eternal love," p. 58) caused him to retain a great deal of the traditional Hebrew. However, he omits verses 3, 6, and 9 in their entirety, as he believed they paint a picture of a vengeful God, totally unbecoming and unworthy of affirmation today. Similarly, the phrase at the beginning of verse 7 that asserts that God took "vengeance over Pharaoh" was emended to "who performed miracles in Egypt." He also omitted the first parts of verse 8 and the second part of verse 9, which speak of God's slaying of the Egyptian first-born.

Numerous Reform and Reconstructionist prayer books have followed Geiger's model. The American Reform *Union Prayer Book* (1895) and *Gates of Prayer* (1975) virtually replicate Geiger. The current British Liberal *Lev Chadash* (1995) as well as British Reform *Forms of Prayer*, (1977) and the new German *Das Jüdische Gebetbuch* (2001) abbreviated verses to emphasize the most universalistic dimensions of this prayer.

Isaac Mayer Wise had been much more conservative in his *Minhag America* (1857), where he omitted only the first part of verse 8 ("he killed … Egypt"), though in line 7 he emulated the pattern established by Geiger and stated that "God hath wrought miracles for us in Egypt," thereby eliminating reference to the "vengeance" God took upon Pharaoh.

It is not just Reform liturgies that have been troubled by these themes of destruction and drowning. Marcus Jastrow and Benjamin Szold were early American rabbis whom we might nowadays identify as Conservative. Szold came to the United States in 1858, where he assumed the pulpit of Congregation Oheb Shalom in Baltimore. The congregation was then on its way to becoming Reform, a move that Szold tried to temper, in part (in 1867) by replacing Wise's 1857 *Minhag America* with his own *Avodath Yisrael*, a prayer book he had written four years earlier while still in Germany.

Jastrow arrived later than Szold (1866), becoming rabbi of Temple Rodeph Shalom in Philadelphia. In 1885, he revised Szold's work, translated it into English, and introduced it as part of a campaign against the radicals (as he thought of them) Isaac Mayer Wise, David Einhorn (who had died in the interim [1879], but whose influence was still felt), and Einhorn's son-in-law in Chicago, Emil Hirsch.

Jastrow-Szold was hardly a radical prayer book! But, like Geiger, it altered the first part of verse 8 and the second part of verse 9. In the latter instance, after asserting that God had brought the children of Israel through the Red Sea, Jastrow-Szold concludes, "Thus was Thy marvelous power made known to them," in lieu of "their pursuers and their enemies were drowned in the deep."

Similarly, while the 1998 *Sim Shalom* retains the Hebrew text of this prayer in its entirety, its authors find the manifest content of some of the prayer troubling. Typifying American Conservative liturgy, *Sim Shalom* employs translation to mute the meaning of the Hebrew. Thus, in verse 7, no English mention is made regarding divine vengeance upon Pharaoh. Rather, we read that God vindicates "us with miracles before Pharaoh."

Kol Haneshamah (Reconstructionist, 1995) and *Ha'avodah Shebalev* (British Liberal, 1982) offer the most noteworthy alterations in this liturgy. As Arthur Green states in his commentary to the former, the version offered in *Kol Haneshamah* "omits those portions of the text that glory in the enemy's fall or see in God a force for vengeance." At the same time, this Reconstructionist Siddur rewrites the latter part of the prayer that "includes reference to the Holocaust, from which there was no redemption, and the return to Zion, a fulfillment of Israel's ancient dream. The same divine spirit that gave Israel the courage to seek freedom from Egypt in ancient times inspired those who fought for Israel's freedom in our own day."

Ha'avodah Shebalev (Israeli Reform, 1982) displays an identical sensibility and after verse 9 inserts the following alternative wording: "Who guides His people in the desert to bring them to the border of His holy [land], Who commanded judges to rescue them, and prophets to cause them to return to Him. Who scatters Israel among the nations, and gathers His dispossessed as a shepherd gathers his flock. Even those who walked through the valley of the shadow of death, six million in pillars of smoke, He remembered their last remnants, and He showed them the beginning of his redemption as He brought and planted them on the mount of his possession." Here the capacity of the traditional text to offer a broad horizon of interpretations and inspiration is readily apparent.

[11] *"Moses"* Several contemporary Siddurim such as *Kol Haneshamah* (Reconstructionist, 1995) display their impulse toward gender-inclusiveness by adding "Miriam" to her brother Moses as those who led Israel in rejoicing after the crossing of the Red Sea. That pattern continues in the forthcoming American Reform *Mishkan T'filah*.

◆

FRANKEL (A WOMAN'S VOICE)

creativity. After all, even in the Torah, Miriam's leadership is acknowledged in this scene, albeit in only two verses as opposed to her brother's twenty-one: "Then Miriam the prophetess, Aaron's sister, took a timbrel in her hand, and all the women went out after her in dance with timbrels. And Miriam chanted for them: 'Sing to the Lord, for He has triumphed gloriously; Horse and rider He has hurled into the sea'" (Exod. 15:20–21). Some scholars believe that Miriam's song was originally much longer, perhaps as long as Moses's, but that it was later censored or lost. Elsewhere in the Bible, we see evidence of biblical women's roles as singers of battle songs—in the song of Deborah, for example (Judges 5). Such traditions involving women drummers, dancers, and singers linger to this day in east Mediterranean cultures.

To commemorate this ancient tradition symbolized by Miriam and the women at the Sea, contemporary Jewish feminists have composed new songs such as "Miriam's Song" by Debbie Friedman, created Miriam's tambourines, and decorated ritual objects such as *tallitot* and *tallit* bags, synagogue decorations, and *challah* covers with images of the Israelite women at the Sea. Songs and poems celebrating Miriam's leadership are also being included at Seder tables, along with Miriam's cup.

The Reconstructionist prayer book *Kol Haneshamah* has formally added Miriam to this part of the liturgy: "Moses and Miriam and the Children of Israel ..." *(Moshe umiryam uv'nei yisrael). Mishkan T'filah,* the forthcoming American Reform prayer book, is likely to do the same.

◆

GRAY (OUR TALMUDIC HERITAGE)

body of someone else, and that person's soul in her. This is because "Adonai [is a] true God" *(el emet)*. Rabbi Alexandri adds that, given the way the world works, a bailee may be given brand-new items for safekeeping, only to return them used up and worn out. With God, the opposite is the case: a person going to sleep at night deposits his tired, weary body and soul with God, only to wake up refreshed and invigorated. This renewal each morning demonstrates how "great is your [God's] faithfulness" *(rabbah emunatekha)*.

[12] *"Who is like You among the gods* [Mi khamokha ba'elim]" The Mekhilta D'rabbi Yishmael (*B'shalach* 8) says that it was not only Israel that joyfully sang, "Who is like You!" The other nations of the world were equally glad that Pharaoh's tyrannical reign was ending and his idolatry shown to be worthless, so they too joined in the singing. In messianic times also, idolatrous peoples will reject their false gods and join Israel in *Mi khamokha.*

The Mekhilta interprets *Mi khamokha* to mean, "Who is like You among those *who see themselves* as gods?" Pharaoh, the Assyrian tyrant Sennacherib, and the Babylonian conqueror Nebuchadnezzar all saw themselves as gods, yet ultimately were shown to have no substance at all. God, however, is the one true, living, and liberating God.

Another midrash (Shir Hashirim Rabbah 2:45) interprets "I am my beloved's and my beloved is mine" (Song of Songs 2:16) to refer to a mutual exchange of affection between God and Israel. Israel says of God, "Who is like You!" *(Mi khamokha)*, and God answers, "Who is like Israel, one nation in all the earth!" (2 Sam. 7:23).

The Talmud (Git. 56b) turns these midrashim on their head to make a bold theological statement, in a fascinating and characteristic way. As part of their extended series of legends pertaining to the destruction of the Second Temple, the Rabbis read *mi khamokha ba'elim* as *mi khamokha b'ilmim* (plural of *ilem*, meaning "deaf-mute"). That is to say, "Who is like You, God, who sees the destruction of your holy house, yet keeps silent?" With the mere addition of the Hebrew letter *mem*, the Rabbis are saying that during the Temple's destruction, the very same God whom we lavishly praise as greater than all the so-called gods who are really powerless turns out instead to be the greatest of those who are physically incapable of speaking on their own behalf.

[12] *"Revered in praise"* Rabbi Yudan interpreted this to mean that no amount of praise can do justice to God. When a mortal king enters a city, everyone reveres him for his wealth, strength, and so forth—that is, for what they can *see* of him. But with God, who is invisible, so much lies beyond what we can see, and is far in excess of any praise we can offer Him (Mid. T'hillim 106:2)!

[13] *"Saw your reign"* Rabbi Eliezer taught that even a humble maidservant standing at the Red Sea saw visions greater than those of the prophet Ezekiel (Mekhilta D'rabbi Yishmael, B'shalach 3)!

[16] *"Israel's savior"* The *Sh'ma* and Its Blessings customarily precede the *Amidah*. Rashi explains that the issue concerns the topic of this, the last of the *Sh'ma*'s blessings: redemption. It makes sense, he says, to praise God for redeeming us in the past, before moving on to the *Amidah*, our main petitionary prayer, which asks God for yet more favors. But that "customary" order was not always taken for granted in the evening service. In a talmudic debate (Ber. 4b), Rabbi Yochanan supports making the evening the same as the morning—as we now have it—going so far as to say that someone who says things in that order is worthy of the world-to-come. Rabbi Joshua ben Levi argues against that order, because (in his view) all the *Amidah* prayers of the day must fall between the morning and the evening *Sh'ma*.

Their positions are argued on the basis of logic and scripture. Joshua reasons that although redemption from Egypt occurred partly at night, its completion took place the following day. Since it is the completion of redemption that we celebrate, the evening part of the redemption is of lesser importance and need not precede the petitions of the evening *Amidah*. Yochanan holds that *all* redemption is important, the evening beginning no less than the morning conclusion, so that praise for redemption should come first in the evenings as well.

Scripturally speaking, both parties cite Deuteronomy 6:7, which prescribes saying the *Sh'ma* "when you lie down and when you rise up," implying that the evening prayers ("when you lie down") should resemble the morning prayers ("when you rise up"). But how are they similar? Joshua holds that in the morning, a person recites the *Sh'ma* close to the time he has been in bed; in the evening, then, he should recite the *Sh'ma* close to the time that he *will* be in bed. Yochanan sees a different similarity: according to him, the *Sh'ma* precedes the *Amidah* in the morning, so should precede the *Amidah* in the evening as well.

——◆——

LANDES (HALAKHAH)

from the morning prayers, we say it in the evening also, toward this purpose of remembering (*Tosafot Yom Tov*, Ber. 1; Rabbi Yom Tov Lipman Heller, fourteenth-century commentary on the Mishnah).

[7] *"True and trustworthy"* For the nighttime recitation of the *Sh'ma*, the Mishnah (Ber. 1:4) demands two blessings before and two blessings after. The Palestinian Talmud (Ber. 1:5) and the *Tur* (O. Ch. 236) connect this practice to Psalm 119:64, "I praise you seven times each day," implying a tally of seven: four blessings to bracket the evening *Sh'ma*, and three to bracket the morning one (see "Lie us down," p. 85).

According to the Babylonian Talmud (Ber. 12a) "One who does not recite 'True and Established' [*Emet V'yatsiv*] following *Sh'ma* in the morning [see Volume 1, *The Sh'ma and Its Blessings*, p. 121], and 'True and Trustworthy' [*Emet Ve'emunah*] here at night, has not fulfilled his obligation 'to proclaim in the morning your grace and your trustworthiness at night'" (Ps. 92:3). The *Bayit Chadash* (the *BaCH*, Joel Sirkes, 1561–1640, Poland) considers the night symbolic of our as yet unredeemed exilic existence, making this a prayer for our future redemption.

——◆——

L. HOFFMAN (HISTORY)

[16] *"Israel's savior"* The summarizing last line is in the past tense, referring back to redemption in Egypt. But Rashi captures the prayer's intent when he says (Ber. 12a), "'True and trustworthy' refers even to the future, in which we anticipate the fulfillment of God's divine promise and God's faithfulness in redeeming us from rulers and tyrants."

——◆——

J. HOFFMAN (TRANSLATION)

[1] *"We are bound by it"* This represents a parsing of the Hebrew in which the literal "[it] endures upon us" *(kayyam aleinu)* is a continuation of the first thought. Birnbaum starts a new sentence here, and renders *kayyam* as "certain"—"We are certain that …," even though there is little support for translating the Hebrew "endure" as "certain." *Kol Haneshamah* wishes to combine the first thought with the second (as we do), giving us, "Our faith and truth rest on all this, which is binding upon us."

[2] *"He is"* For the purposes of rendering the text in English sentences, we add punctuation, such as full stops, and repeat "he is." The original Hebrew was written without punctuation, which had not yet been invented.

[2] *"Fist"* "Hand," really, but not *yad*, the word for "hand" in the line above. A different word is used in the Hebrew (and English here) to produce two lines in parallel.

[3] *"In kind"* More literally, "paying … a reward." The Hebrew word for "reward" represents anything one deserves, good or bad, but the English "reward" implies only what is good. We therefore opt for "in kind." (We have translated this elsewhere as "just reward.")

[4] *"Great things we cannot comprehend"* Literally, "great things beyond comprehension," but this line parallels the next ("wondrous things we cannot count"), and we want to maintain the syntactic similarity between the two. Also, the Hebrew is "greats" here, and "wonders" below, but "greats" in English does not mean "great things."

[4] *"We cannot count"* Literally, "beyond counting"—see previous note, "Great things…."

[5] *"Gave us life"* More literally, "put our bodies in life" (the word *nefesh*, popularly associated now with "soul," meant the physical body in biblical times). We assume this line (from Psalm 66:9) is a poetic phrase meaning "gave us life," but it may reflect a deeper meaning that we have not discerned.

[6] *"Tread upon our enemies' altars"* Hebrew, *bamot*. In the Bible, this word means "high places" and, more specifically, "altar." By rabbinic times, it was used predominantly to mean "altar." (The English word "altar," too, comes from the Latin *altare*, "to be high.") The idea may be that victory comes when we trample the shrines that our enemies erect to their gods.

[6] *"Granting us victory"* Once again, we see the ubiquitous idiom of "raising our horn." See Volume 2, *The Amidah*, p. 143, J. Hoffman.

[7] *"Granting"* Literally, "doing," but while "doing miracles" makes a bit of sense, "doing vengeance" does not, and once again we want to preserve the poetic parallelism in the Hebrew.

[7] *"Miracles and vengeance"* Or, perhaps, "miracles as vengeance," as reflected in *Siddur Sim Shalom's* "vindicating us with wonders."

[7] *"Wonders"* This is different from the word for "wonder" used above (v. 4). Some translations prefer "signs and portents" here, but "portent" seems arcane to us.

[7] *"Childen of Cham"* That is, Egypt. Noah's son Cham represents the northern African countries of Egypt, Ethiopia, and so on, and probably because Egypt played such a prominent role in the life of the ancient Hebrew, Cham came to be associated with Egypt in particular.

[9] *"Two halves"* Literally, "divided parts," from the root *g.z.r*, "to cut."

[9] *"Those who chased them and those who hated them"* The Hebrew, like our English, is ambiguous, leaving open the improbable interpretation that not everyone chasing the Jews hated them.

[10] *"Reign"* Or "kingdom," but below we will need "reign" for this word, so we use it here for consistency.

[11] *"Singing"* Literally, "saying." We could, perhaps, have omitted this word, since it is used (here and elsewhere) in place of quotation marks, which had not yet been invented.

[12] *"[The] gods"* Birnbaum: "mighty gods," perhaps to avoid even the implication that we might consider the possibility of other gods. For similar reasons, *Gates of Prayer* translates, "gods that are worshipped."

[12] *"Adonai!"* Certainly an exclamation, not a question.

[12] *"Wonders!"* The Hebrew provides three sets of two words each; so our English too gives three parallel two-word phrases. Other translations of this famous line include "glorious in holiness, awe-inspiring in renown, doing wonders" (Birnbaum), "majestic in holiness, awesome in splendor, working wonders" *(Sim Shalom)*, and "majestic among the holy-ones, Feared-One of praises, Doer of Wonders" (Fox). We prefer "wonders" to "miracles," because miracles are extrascientific, and nothing can be extrascientific in an era that predated science.

[15] *"His own"* Literally, "a hand mightier than him."

◆ ◆ ◆

IV. BLESSING FOR A SAFE NIGHT: *HASHKIVENU* ("LIE US DOWN TO PEACE")

[1] Lie us down to peace, Adonai our God, and raise us up to life, our king, and spread over us the shelter of your peace, and direct us with good advice before You, and save us for the sake of your name, [2] and look out for us, and keep enemies, plagues, swords, famines, and troubles from our midst, [3] and remove Satan from in front of us and from behind us, [4] and cradle us in the shadow of your wings, for You are God who guards us and saves us, for You are God, our gracious and merciful king. [5] Guard our departure and our arrival to life and to peace, from now and ever more. *[6] Blessed are You, Adonai, who guards his People Israel forever.

הַשְׁכִּיבֵנוּ, יְיָ אֱלֹהֵינוּ, לְשָׁלוֹם; [1]
וְהַעֲמִידֵנוּ, מַלְכֵּנוּ, לְחַיִּים; וּפְרוֹשׂ
עָלֵינוּ סֻכַּת שְׁלוֹמֶךָ, וְתַקְּנֵנוּ בְּעֵצָה
טוֹבָה מִלְּפָנֶיךָ, וְהוֹשִׁיעֵנוּ לְמַעַן שְׁמֶךָ;
[2] וְהָגֵן בַּעֲדֵנוּ, וְהָסֵר מֵעָלֵינוּ אוֹיֵב, דֶּבֶר
וְחֶרֶב וְרָעָב וְיָגוֹן; [3] וְהָסֵר שָׂטָן מִלְּפָנֵינוּ
וּמֵאַחֲרֵינוּ, [4] וּבְצֵל כְּנָפֶיךָ תַּסְתִּירֵנוּ; כִּי
אֵל שׁוֹמְרֵנוּ וּמַצִּילֵנוּ אָתָּה, כִּי אֵל
מֶלֶךְ חַנּוּן וְרַחוּם אָתָּה. [5] וּשְׁמוֹר צֵאתֵנוּ
וּבוֹאֵנוּ לְחַיִּים וּלְשָׁלוֹם, מֵעַתָּה וְעַד
עוֹלָם. *[6] בָּרוּךְ אַתָּה, יְיָ, שׁוֹמֵר עַמּוֹ
יִשְׂרָאֵל לָעַד.

*[*On Shabbat, substitute the following:]*

[7] And spread over us the shelter of your peace. Blessed are You, Adonai, who spreads a shelter of peace over us, over all of his People Israel, and over Jerusalem.

[7] וּפְרוֹשׂ עָלֵינוּ סֻכַּת שְׁלוֹמֶךָ. בָּרוּךְ
אַתָּה, יְיָ, הַפּוֹרֵשׂ סֻכַּת שָׁלוֹם עָלֵינוּ,
וְעַל כָּל עַמּוֹ יִשְׂרָאֵל, וְעַל יְרוּשָׁלָיִם.

BRETTLER (BIBLE)

[1] *"Lie us down"* The entire paragraph comes as a corrective to the preceding one, by emphasizing that the redemption Israel seeks is bloodless and peaceful, a result not of war, but of God's watchful guardianship. It too shares many features of biblical parallelism. Verses 1–2, for instance, display synonymous style (verse 2 echoes and strengthens verse 1). They are even syntactically parallel, both opening with an imperative. Verse 2 concludes with a paraphrase of Psalm 106:8, "Yet He saved them, as befits his name," meaning that Israel was not deserving, but God was concerned that abandoning Israel *(p. 86)*

DORFF (THEOLOGY)

[1] *"Lie us down to peace, Adonai our God, and raise us up to life … and save us for the sake of your name"* Our prayer reflects the prescientific belief—and the intuition of children too—that losing consciousness in sleep is dangerous, for there is no guarantee that we will continue living during that *(p. 87)*

ELLENSON (MODERN LITURGIES)

[1] *"Adonai our God"* This is an extremely popular prayer in liberal prayer books. As was their custom elsewhere, the authors of the *Hamburg Temple Prayer Books* (1819, 1841) and David Einhorn (1858) offered only translations, but virtually all other non-Orthodox *(p. 88)*

FRANKEL (A WOMAN'S VOICE)

[1] *"Lie us down"* Only in modern Western countries—and then only among the middle and upper classes—do people go to bed at night and arise in the morning with a sense of relative physical security. Though we may suffer personal setbacks in the form of illness, economic reversal, or natural disaster, we do not tend to conclude from these experiences that the world has suddenly become inhospitable to human life.

But the world has always been a more perilous place than we *(p. 89)*

IV. BLESSING FOR A SAFE NIGHT: *HASHKIVENU*, ("LIE US DOWN TO PEACE")

[1] Lie us down to peace, Adonai our God, and raise us up to life, our king, and spread over us the shelter of your peace, and direct us with good advice before You, and save us for the sake of your name, [2] and look out for us, and keep enemies, plagues, swords, famines, and troubles from our midst, [3] and remove Satan from in front of us and from behind us, [4] and

GRAY (OUR TALMUDIC HERITAGE)

[1] *"Lie us down"* R. Yochanan holds that the blessing following the *Sh'ma* (the *G'ullah*) is supposed to lead directly into the *Amidah* with absolutely nothing in between (Ber. 4b). That works in the morning, but at night, *Hashkivenu* comes in the middle. The Talmud solves the problem with a legal fiction: we consider *G'ullah* and *Hashkivenu* as a single *G'ullah*.

This issue of juxtaposition should have been raised earlier, in connection with the debate between *(p. 89)*

KUSHNER & POLEN (CHASIDISM)

[1] *"Spread over us the shelter of your peace"* Rabbi Chayim Tchernovitz, in his *Siduro shel Shabbat* (*Y'sod Ha'avodah* 44), wonders why the liturgy employs the complicated poetic expression "spread over us the shelter of your peace" rather than the simple and direct "grant us peace." He goes on to explain that peace, here, is not just an absence of strife, but the blessed state of balance. And that is the divine protection that is sought. For, once we get everything in balance,   *(p. 90)*

WHILE THE BENEDICTION ON REDEMPTION CONCLUDES THE MORNING RECITATION OF THE SH'MA, THE EVENING SH'MA IS CHARACTERIZED BY EXTRA BLESSINGS FOLLOWING IT. THE FIRST IS HASHKIVENU ("LIE US DOWN [TO PEACE]"), A PRAYER FOR SAFE PASSAGE THROUGH THE NIGHT.

[7] *"Shelter of peace"* On Shabbat, we alter the prayer's conclusion to reiterate the thought from verse 1: our desire for a "shelter of peace." The Yerushalmi (Ber. 4:8) implies that it was said every day (see also Midrash T'hillim 6), so in the third or fourth centuries, and possibly later, it was the normal   *(p. 92)*

¹הַשְׁכִּיבֵנוּ, יְיָ אֱלֹהֵינוּ, לְשָׁלוֹם; וְהַעֲמִידֵנוּ, מַלְכֵּנוּ, לְחַיִּים; וּפְרוֹשׂ עָלֵינוּ סֻכַּת שְׁלוֹמֶךָ, וְתַקְּנֵנוּ בְּעֵצָה טוֹבָה מִלְּפָנֶיךָ, וְהוֹשִׁיעֵנוּ לְמַעַן שְׁמֶךָ; ²וְהָגֵן בַּעֲדֵנוּ, וְהָסֵר מֵעָלֵינוּ אוֹיֵב, דֶּבֶר וְחֶרֶב וְרָעָב וְיָגוֹן; ³וְהָסֵר שָׂטָן מִלְּפָנֵינוּ וּמֵאַחֲרֵינוּ, ⁴וּבְצֵל כְּנָפֶיךָ תַּסְתִּירֵנוּ; כִּי אֵל שׁוֹמְרֵנוּ וּמַצִּילֵנוּ אָתָּה, כִּי אֵל מֶלֶךְ חַנּוּן וְרַחוּם.

LANDES (HALAKHAH)

[1] *"Lie us down"* The Tannaim left us with what seems at first glance to be contrary liturgical demands.

The Mishnah (Ber. 1:4) requires one blessing after the *Sh'ma* in the morning, but two blessings in the same place at night. That single morning blessing, and the first of the two evening ones, is on the theme of redemption—in Hebrew, *G'ullah*. But the Talmud says also (Ber. 4b) that, according to Rabbi Yochanan, it is necessary to connect the   *(p. 91)*

J. HOFFMAN (TRANSLATION)

[1] *"To peace"* Almost always, "in peace," which does make more sense; but "to peace" sets the stage for "to life," immediately below, and so we translate "to peace" here.

[2] *"Enemies"* This word and the ones following it are singular in Hebrew, but English grammar requires the plural.

[2] *"Plagues"* Commonly, "pestilence," one of the plagues. We avoid "pestilence" because not many people know what it means; in general, we try to translate common Hebrew words into common English words (and rare Hebrew words into rare English words) so as to better convey the flavor of the Hebrew.

[2] *"From our midst"* Literally,   *(p. 93)*

cradle us in the shadow of your wings, for You are God who guards us and saves us, for You are God, our gracious and merciful king. [5]Guard our departure and our arrival to life and to peace, from now and ever more. *[6]Blessed are You, Adonai, who guards his People Israel forever.

אָתָּה. ⁵וּשְׁמוֹר צֵאתֵנוּ וּבוֹאֵנוּ לְחַיִּים וּלְשָׁלוֹם, מֵעַתָּה וְעַד עוֹלָם. *⁶בָּרוּךְ אַתָּה, יְיָ, שׁוֹמֵר עַמּוֹ יִשְׂרָאֵל לָעַד.

[On Shabbat, substitute the following:]

[7]And spread over us the shelter of your peace. Blessed are You, Adonai, who spreads a shelter of peace over us, over all of his People Israel, and over Jerusalem.

⁷וּפְרוֹשׁ עָלֵינוּ סֻכַּת שְׁלוֹמֶךָ. בָּרוּךְ אַתָּה, יְיָ, הַפּוֹרֵשׂ סֻכַּת שָׁלוֹם עָלֵינוּ, וְעַל כָּל עַמּוֹ יִשְׂרָאֵל, וְעַל יְרוּשָׁלָיִם.

BRETTLER (BIBLE)

would reflect poorly on God (a common biblical theme).

[2] *"Enemies … famines, and troubles"* Afflictions mentioned in the Bible, often together; all but "troubles," for instance, appear in Jeremiah 21:7.

[3] *"Satan"* Satan appears in 1 Chronicles 21:1, possibly as a particular character; elsewhere, however, *satan* implies a role, "the adversary," either terrestrial (e.g., 1 Kings 11:14) or celestial (e.g., Job 1:6). When post-biblical and rabbinic Jews further developed angelology, Satan emerged more clearly as a specific individual.

[4] *"Cradle us in the shadow of your wings"* From Psalm 17:8, expressing God's care for the supplicant. This is followed by another couplet based on biblical phrases. The phrase "gracious and merciful" or "merciful and gracious" appears eleven times in the Bible. The order found here is more typical of later biblical texts, like Nehemiah 9:31.

[5] *"Guard …"* A paraphrase of Psalm 121:8, "Adonai will guard your going and coming now and forever." The phrase "to life and to peace" reiterates themes of verse 1, "Lie us down to peace … and raise us up to life."

[6] *"Guards his People Israel"* From Psalm 121:4, but expanded. Indeed, this entire prayer can almost be seen as a midrash on Psalm 121, building on the imagery of Adonai as guardian and protector.

[7] *"Shelter of your peace"* Although the phrases *pores sukkah* ("spread a shelter") and *sukkat shalom* ("shelter of peace") are post-biblical, they build on the following common biblical images: the *sukkah* or hut functioning to protect people from the hot Mediterranean sun (see Jonah 4:5), Adonai offering a protective *sukkah* (e.g., Isa. 4:6; Ps. 31:21), and Adonai's *"pores*-ing," representing an act of protection (e.g., Deut. 32:11; Ezek. 16:8).

◆

DORFF (THEOLOGY)

state and regain consciousness when sleep is over. For similar reasons, an early morning blessing thanks God "who restores souls to dead corpses" (see Volume 5, *Birkhot Hashachar*, p. 119, and "My God, the soul," p. 131).

Why would adults who normally believe both science and their own repeated experience say these words? Perhaps they remind us that it is a gift to sleep and then awaken—not something to take for granted. Blessings always call attention to what might otherwise be passed over as routine. The late Conservative rabbi and seminary professor Max Kadushin called this function of liturgy "normal mysticism" (see his books, *Organic Thinking*, pp. 237ff.; *Worship and Ethics*, pp. 13–17), in that they briefly interrupt the normal, everyday activities of life with ritualized words or acts that make us aware of the large theological and moral meanings embedded in what we do daily. Life is not just a series of humdrum repetitive acts without significance—a kind of existence portrayed by existentialist Jean-Paul Sartre (1905–1980) in his devastating play *No Exit*. Even ordinary life is an endless stream of things to notice and appreciate. By punctuating each day with such prayers and rituals, Judaism underscores the significance of life's inherent meaning.

[1] *"Lie us down to peace, Adonai our God ... "* At camp, once, I asked rabbinical students to write down whatever words came to mind as they free-associated about night. Some described feelings of security and repose—rest, sleep, peace, and a warm, snuggly blanket. Others fastened on danger, fear, and vulnerability—their inability to see well, and therefore to notice potential threats like snakes or even human adversaries. The Mishnah (*Avot* 3:4 [3:5 in some editions]) even cautions that one who goes out alone at night is held culpable for taking his or her own life! Opposite as these feelings are, they are both accurate.

I then asked the students to write prayers that articulate both sets of feelings. Despite their own wonderful creativity, they found they could do no better than this traditional prayer in expressing both sides of the coin. We ask God to "lay us down ...

to peace" and "spread over us the shelter of your peace" but also to "keep enemies, plagues, swords, famines, and troubles from our midst, and remove Satan from in front of us and from behind us, and cradle us in the shadow of your wings."

The rabbinical students and I then took a silent walk together to feel all of these nuances of night. Try the exercise yourself. You will never utter this prayer the same way again.

[4] *"For You are God who guards and saves us, for You are God, our gracious and merciful King"* Since God is also depicted elsewhere as bellicose and judgmental, the prayer has us remind God of those aspects of His character that would lead Him to grant us rest and safety. We use the same technique to encourage people (not just God) to act on their better instincts. We might say, "I believe you will forgive me, because you are a kind and forgiving person." People, like God, can sometimes be led to a higher moral plane by hearing a positive image of themselves and wanting to prove that they deserve to be seen that way.

ELLENSON (MODERN LITURGIES)

Siddurim included the Hebrew text. However, in verse 1, a number of Reform prayer books—the British Reform *Forms of Prayer* (1977), the French *Siddour Taher Libeinu* (1997), and the German *Das Jüdische Gebetbuch* (2001)—substitute "our Father" for "Adonai our God." In so doing, they follow the alternative used in the Spanish-Portuguese rite.

[3] *"Satan"* This mention of Satan has proved troublesome to many Reform authors. Geiger and even the American Reform *Gates of Prayer* retain the line, but Wise as well as the older Reform *Union Prayer Book* simply omit it. In contrast, *Ha'avodah Shebalev* (Israeli Reform, 1982) and *Lev Chadash* (British Liberal, 1995) substitute the phrase *V'harchek mimenu avon vafesha* ("distance sin and iniquity from us"). The Hebrew remains untranslated in the Israeli volume, of course, but the latter prayer book renders it, "Keep us from wrongdoing"—a very liberal understanding of "Satan"! Whatever *satan* implied in the past, the word was hardly identified with internal problems of conscience.

Typically also, *Sim Shalom* (American Conservative, 1985) retains the Hebrew, but renders it in English, "Remove the evil forces that surround us." Unlike "Keep us from wrongdoing," the translation here at least retains the notion of some external source of evil, albeit muting the blatant "angelology" (and, perhaps, what was seen as a Christianized notion of sin) implicit in the original Hebrew *satan*.

[6] *"Who guards his People Israel forever"* The Shabbat version of this prayer provides a different concluding line *(chatimah)*: not "who guards his people," but "who spreads a shelter of peace.... " A number of liberal Siddurim substitute the Shabbat *chatimah* for

the normal weekday text. Others add a universal element to the prayer. Thus, in *Minhag America* (1857), Wise asked that God cause peace to descend not only "upon us," but upon "all those who revere Your Name"—*al kol yirei sh'mekha*. More recently, *Lev Chadash* (British Liberal, 1995) states, "May Your sheltering peace descend on us and all the world," while Reconstructionist *Kol Haneshamah* (1995) requests that God "ever guards all who dwell on earth."

———◆———

FRANKEL (A WOMAN'S VOICE)

like to imagine, for Jews, of course, but for others as well—rife with disease, drought, flood, famine, war, persecution, and exile. Especially in earlier times, when a person lay down to sleep, it was often with a sense of dread, and it still is so in areas around the world where war is the normal state of things, and where one's final thoughts before falling asleep are likely to be, "What calamity will tomorrow bring? Will there even be a tomorrow?"

Perhaps that is why this prayer invokes the image of the *Shekhinah*, God's indwelling presence. As a mother bird shelters its young underneath its wings, so God is here called upon to shield us beneath the shadow of the divine wings, *b'tzel k'nafekha*, from the perils of the night.

———◆———

GRAY (OUR TALMUDIC HERITAGE)

Rabbi Joshua ben Levi and Yochanan (see "Israel's savior," p. 78) over saying the *Sh'ma* and its blessings before or after the evening *Amidah*. Yochanan upheld the custom of saying it beforehand in the evening as well as in the morning, whereas Joshua wanted to say the evening *Amidah* first. But in fact, the issue was not raised there! It is first mentioned by the mid-fourth century Babylonian Amora Mar bar Ravina. It might be, then, that *Hashkivenu* began to be recited somewhere between the mid-third century (the time of Yochanan) and the mid-fourth (Mar bar Ravina).

[1] *"Spread over us the shelter of your peace"* For technical reasons (see above, "Lie us down"), *Hashkivenu* and the blessing before it, *G'ullah*, are considered one long prayer on the theme of redemption. Abudarham sees an impact of that on the text of the blessing itself. "Spread over us" is an adaptation of a biblical expression referring to redemption. At Ezekiel 16:8, God (as the passing helpful stranger) tells Israel (symbolized by a sick, homeless girl) "I spread my cloak over you [to save you]." Similarly, at Ruth 3:9, Ruth tells Boaz to spread his robe over her, because he is the "redeeming relative" (*go'el*, there used as a technical legal term).

[5] *"Guard our departure and our arrival"* From Deuteronomy 28:6 ("Blessed are you

in your coming in, and blessed are you in your going out"), which the Talmud (B.M. 107a) interprets to mean that a person's exit from this world should be like her entrance. Just as she entered the world without sin, so should she leave it that way.

[6] *"Who guards his People Israel forever"* The *Sh'ma* and Its Blessings in *Shacharit* consist of seven separate passages to recite, each a *mitzvah* in itself: (1) the *Yotser*, (2) *Ahavah Rabbah*, (3–5) the three paragraphs of the *Sh'ma*, (6) the first half of the *G'ullah* (beginning *Emet v'yatsiv*), and (7) its last half, with *Mi Khamokha* (see Volume 1, *The Sh'ma and Its Blessings*, for contents). The third paragraph of the *Sh'ma* (#5) however, contains the commandment to wear *tsitsit*, which does not apply at night. We therefore "miss" that *mitzvah* during the evening recitation of the *Sh'ma*. To compensate, we add this extra blessing for God's protection (Mid. T'hillim 6:1).

---◆---

KUSHNER & POLEN (CHASIDISM)

then we experience everything that comes to us as love. And that is the meaning of "shelter of peace."

Erev Shabbat is a time of great mercy. God becomes, as it were, says Rabbi Chayim Tchernovitz, like a mother hovering over her child who depends on its mother for protection from heat and cold, storm and rain. And, in much the same way, God spreads God's wings over us, making a canopy for shade to save us from the fowler's snare and destructive pestilence. The "two wings" of the *Shekhinah* are a metaphor for the balance of different pairs of divine attributes—for example, judgment and mercy. And when these attributes work harmoniously with one another, we experience everything that happens as a gesture of maternally divine protection and love.

[7] *"And over Jerusalem"* The Midrash teaches that Jerusalem was first called *Shalem* (meaning "wholeness"). But Abraham came along and called it *Yireh* ("seeing"), as in the verse "And Abraham named the place Adonai-yireh ["Adonai will see"]; whence the present saying, 'On the mount of Adonai there is seeing" (Gen. 22:14). God combined the two names ("seeing" and "wholeness") to make up *Yerushalayim* [*Yeru*, like *yireh*, and *shalayim*, like *shalem*] (Gen. Rab., 51:10).

What this means is that at first God ran the world purely with divine grace, the love God gives although no one has even earned it. There was, therefore, no need for human works. Then Abraham came along and set the stage for a new dispensation, whereby humans might strive toward spiritual goals by their own achievements based on piety ("fear of God") [*yirah*, which means piety, is related here to *yireh*, "seeing"; piety is equated with vision].

Really, both dispensations remain necessary. God initially gave the world a reserve of grace. But we must demonstrate our receptivity by our vision. The assurance that our vision will reach completion is alluded to by the Hebrew *shalem* ("wholeness").

So every worthy project in life begins with the gift of God's grace. But we must then follow up by doing our part, as Abraham did, adding "seeing" to reach "wholeness." And when our efforts are crowned with success, we must lift up the fruits to heaven, in recognition that it is all a gift from God.

That is the meaning of the verse, "I am the first and I am the last" (Isa. 44:6). The initial flash of creative possibility comes from God. And at the very end, the successful conclusion, the sense of fullness and closure, is also God's gift. What remains for us is the vast and crucial middle—the time of anxious effort when nothing is assured, nothing is taken for granted, and everything is at risk. This is the time for striving, for our effort, the time sustained by our vision.

Jerusalem was the place of sacrifice (avodah), which also means work, a reference to our own striving to achieve our vision. The Hebrew term for God's grace is chesed, a concept that also includes the legacy we inherit from our ancestors (avot). This means the entire received tradition of Jewish life, practice, and cultural values, as well as the memory of loved ones now departed whose example continues to inspire and instruct us; without this legacy, this chesed, we could not hope to begin our own quest for a sacred and meaningful life.

All human work is unfinished. Whatever we achieve is based on divine assistance and the legacy of those who preceded us (avot). We function in the "in-between time." This is our arena of action, of receiving the gift of our legacy and providing ("seeing ahead") for the future.

The time for our work is now; but God is always the first and the last. The fusion of both perspectives—vision and completion—is Jerusalem.

◆

LANDES (HALAKHAH)

G'ullah to the *T'fillah*—the rabbinic word for the *Amidah* (*lismokh g'ullah lit'fillah* [pronounced lis-MOKH g'-oo-LAH li-t'-fee-LAH]). There is no problem in the morning, when the *G'ullah* is indeed followed immediately by the *Amidah*. The problem arises at night, however, when the *Amidah* does not come next. Instead we get the *Hashkivenu* ("Lie us down"), the fourth blessing of the nighttime *Sh'ma*. Since it follows the *G'ullah*, it interrupts the connection between the *G'ullah* and the *Amidah*. If we are supposed to join the *G'ullah* to the *Amidah*, how can there be an additional blessing after the *G'ullah* at night?

The *Tur* explains that *Hashkivenu* (pronounced hahsh-kee-VAY-noo) should be thought of as an intensification and elaboration of the *G'ullah* theme: salvation; it is "like a great *G'ullah*" (*g'ulah arichta*, pronounced g'-oo-LAH ah-RIKH-tah). *Bet Yosef*, Joseph Caro's major sixteenth-century commentary on the *Tur*, agrees, arguing that *Hashkivenu* recollects the fears of the Israelites when they saw their Egyptian oppressors being destroyed and thought they too would be engulfed in the Red Sea's waters. So *Hashkivenu* counts formally as a separate blessing (as per the Mishnah), but it constitutes no interruption of the *G'ullah* theme, which remains connected to the *Amidah* (as per Rabbi Yochanan).

But we still face *Barukh Adonai L'olam* (pronounced bah-RUKH ah-doh-NA'i l'-oh-LAHM), and the Half *Kaddish* that follows it. The *Tur* explains *Barukh Adonai L'olam* as a prayer invented originally for field laborers who feared nighttime brigands and wished to rush home from work as soon as darkness settled in. They were able to substitute these verses (which mention God's name nineteen times) for the evening weekday *Amidah*. They would gather hastily together, say these verses and a concluding *Kaddish*, and hurry home. Later, when the need for this prayer no longer existed, because people were leaving work earlier and praying in established synagogues in towns, the custom of reciting the extra verses and the *Kaddish* remained.

Since the verses had begun as a substitute for the *Amidah*, they cannot be considered as interrupting the flow between the *G'ullah* and the *Amidah*. The underlying assumption in this discussion is that only truly extraneous material creates a *hefsek* (pronounced HEF-sayk), an "interruption" in consciousness between these two liturgical staples.

Since, however, laborers would never have been found working late in the fields on Friday nights and *Chol Hamo'ed* (pronounced khol hah-moh-AYD, the intermediary days of festivals), the prayer is not said then.

It is also not said in the Land of Israel, but the *Kaddish* is nonetheless retained there, even if *Baruch Adonai L'olam* is omitted.

(See also "The children of Israel shall keep Shabbat," p. 107.)

L. HOFFMAN (HISTORY)

conclusion in Eretz Yisra'el for weekdays also. The version without the "shelter of peace" conclusion—the one that we use on weekdays—may have been said in Babylonia. Eventually, we adopted both, using one for Shabbat and one for weekdays.

The metaphor of a "shelter of peace" has enjoyed remarkable resonance throughout the centuries. In the sixteenth century, it was the name of a mystical fellowship founded by Elazar Azikri (or Azkari), author of *Y'did Nefesh* (see Volume 7, *Shabbat at Home*, pp. 135–146). Nowadays, it is the name of congregations worldwide (in Israel, Scotland, Germany, and the United States). Of late, it has spawned prayers for victims of abuse, who, we pray, will feel the protection of a divine "shelter of peace."

"from over us," setting the stage for "from in front of us and from behind us" ("over … in front … behind"), a trick we miss in English.

[4] *"Saves us"* The Hebrew for "saves us" sounds like the word for "shadow" above, since both words contains the root letters *ts.l.* ("Shadow" comes from *ts.l.l* and "save" from *n.ts.l,* but the two end up sounding alike because *nuns* and double letters both sometimes drop out of words in Hebrew. In this case, the *nun* in *n.ts.l* drops out, and so does one of the *lameds* in *ts.l.l.*)

[4] *"Our [gracious and merciful…]"* Once again, we need to add "our" to the English to make it parallel the Hebrew.

◆ ◆ ◆

MA'ARIV (WEEKDAY AND SHABBAT)

[On Shabbat, continue on p. 105, with the announcement of sacred time.

On weekdays, Sefardim and communities in Israel continue with a Chatzi Kaddish (Half Kaddish) and the Amidah (p. 113).

On weekdays in the diaspora, prior to the Chatsi Kaddish and Amidah, Ashkenazi liturgy continues here.]

V. A FIFTH EVENING BLESSING: *BARUKH ADONAI L'OLAM* ("BLESSED IS ADONAI FOREVER")

¹Blessed is Adonai forever. Amen and amen. ²Blessed is Adonai from Zion, as He dwells in Jerusalem. Halleluyah. ³Blessed is Adonai, God, Israel's God, who alone does wonders. ⁴And blessed is his glorious name forever; He will fill the whole earth with his glory. Amen and amen. ⁵May Adonai's glory be forever. May Adonai rejoice in his creations. ⁶May Adonai's name be blessed, from now and to eternity. ⁷For Adonai will not abandon his people for the sake of his great name, for Adonai has decided to make you into his nation. ⁸And all the people saw and fell upon their faces, crying out, "Adonai is God! Adonai is God!" ⁹Adonai shall become king over the entire earth. On that day, Adonai shall be one and his name shall be one. ¹⁰Adonai, be kind to us, as we have always wanted. ¹¹Save us, Adonai, our God, and gather us from among the other nations, to gratefully acknowledge your holy name, to exalt in your glory. ¹²All the nations You created will come and bow down before You, Adonai, and they will honor your name; ¹³for You are great, a worker of wonders. You alone are God. ¹⁴And we are your people, the sheep of your pasture. We will gratefully acknowledge You forever; from generation to generation we will tell of your glory.

¹בָּרוּךְ יְיָ לְעוֹלָם, אָמֵן וְאָמֵן. ²בָּרוּךְ יְיָ מִצִּיּוֹן, שֹׁכֵן יְרוּשָׁלָיִם; הַלְלוּיָהּ. ³בָּרוּךְ יְיָ אֱלֹהִים, אֱלֹהֵי יִשְׂרָאֵל, עֹשֵׂה נִפְלָאוֹת לְבַדּוֹ. ⁴וּבָרוּךְ שֵׁם כְּבוֹדוֹ לְעוֹלָם, וְיִמָּלֵא כְבוֹדוֹ אֶת כָּל הָאָרֶץ, אָמֵן וְאָמֵן. ⁵יְהִי כְבוֹד יְיָ לְעוֹלָם; יִשְׂמַח יְיָ בְּמַעֲשָׂיו. ⁶יְהִי שֵׁם יְיָ מְבֹרָךְ, מֵעַתָּה וְעַד עוֹלָם. ⁷כִּי לֹא יִטֹּשׁ יְיָ אֶת עַמּוֹ בַּעֲבוּר שְׁמוֹ הַגָּדוֹל; כִּי הוֹאִיל יְיָ לַעֲשׂוֹת אֶתְכֶם לוֹ לְעָם. ⁸וַיַּרְא כָּל הָעָם וַיִּפְּלוּ עַל פְּנֵיהֶם, וַיֹּאמְרוּ: יְיָ הוּא הָאֱלֹהִים, יְיָ הוּא הָאֱלֹהִים. ⁹וְהָיָה יְיָ לְמֶלֶךְ עַל כָּל הָאָרֶץ; בַּיּוֹם הַהוּא יִהְיֶה יְיָ אֶחָד וּשְׁמוֹ אֶחָד. ¹⁰יְהִי חַסְדְּךָ יְיָ עָלֵינוּ, כַּאֲשֶׁר יִחַלְנוּ לָךְ. ¹¹הוֹשִׁיעֵנוּ, יְיָ אֱלֹהֵינוּ, וְקַבְּצֵנוּ מִן הַגּוֹיִם, לְהוֹדוֹת לְשֵׁם קָדְשֶׁךָ, לְהִשְׁתַּבֵּחַ בִּתְהִלָּתֶךָ. ¹²כָּל גּוֹיִם אֲשֶׁר עָשִׂיתָ יָבוֹאוּ וְיִשְׁתַּחֲווּ לְפָנֶיךָ, אֲדֹנָי, וִיכַבְּדוּ לִשְׁמֶךָ. ¹³כִּי גָדוֹל אַתָּה וְעֹשֵׂה נִפְלָאוֹת; אַתָּה אֱלֹהִים לְבַדֶּךָ. ¹⁴וַאֲנַחְנוּ, עַמְּךָ וְצֹאן מַרְעִיתֶךָ, נוֹדֶה לְךָ לְעוֹלָם, לְדוֹר וָדוֹר נְסַפֵּר תְּהִלָּתֶךָ.

¹⁵ Blessed is Adonai by day. Blessed is Adonai by night. Blessed is Adonai when we lie down. Blessed is Adonai when we stand up. For in your hand are the souls of the living and the dead. ¹⁶ In his hand is the soul of all that lives, and the spirit of all flesh. ¹⁷ In your hand I trust my soul. I am the one You have redeemed, Adonai, God of truth. ¹⁸ Our God in heaven, unite your name, and preserve your kingdom eternally, and rule over us forever.

¹⁹ Let our eyes see and our heart rejoice, and our soul celebrate in your true salvation, telling Zion, "Your God is king." ²⁰ Adonai is king, was king, and will be king forever. ²¹ The kingdom is yours, and You will always rule in glory, for we have no king other than You! ²² Blessed are You, Adonai, the king who in his glory will always rule over us forever— and over all his creatures.

¹⁵בָּרוּךְ יְיָ בַּיּוֹם, בָּרוּךְ יְיָ בַּלַּיְלָה; בָּרוּךְ יְיָ בְּשָׁכְבֵּנוּ, בָּרוּךְ יְיָ בְּקוּמֵנוּ; כִּי בְיָדְךָ נַפְשׁוֹת הַחַיִּים וְהַמֵּתִים. ¹⁶אֲשֶׁר בְּיָדוֹ נֶפֶשׁ כָּל חָי, וְרוּחַ כָּל בְּשַׂר אִישׁ. ¹⁷בְּיָדְךָ אַפְקִיד רוּחִי; פָּדִיתָה אוֹתִי, יְיָ, אֵל אֱמֶת. ¹⁸אֱלֹהֵינוּ שֶׁבַּשָּׁמַיִם, יַחֵד שִׁמְךָ וְקַיֵּם מַלְכוּתְךָ תָּמִיד, וּמְלוֹךְ עָלֵינוּ לְעוֹלָם וָעֶד.

¹⁹יִרְאוּ עֵינֵינוּ וְיִשְׂמַח לִבֵּנוּ, וְתָגֵל נַפְשֵׁנוּ בִּישׁוּעָתְךָ בֶּאֱמֶת, בֶּאֱמֹר לְצִיּוֹן מָלַךְ אֱלֹהָיִךְ. ²⁰יְיָ מֶלֶךְ, יְיָ מָלָךְ, יְיָ יִמְלֹךְ לְעוֹלָם וָעֶד. ²¹כִּי הַמַּלְכוּת שֶׁלְּךָ הִיא, וּלְעוֹלְמֵי עַד תִּמְלֹךְ בְּכָבוֹד, כִּי אֵין לָנוּ מֶלֶךְ אֶלָּא אָתָּה. ²²בָּרוּךְ אַתָּה, יְיָ, הַמֶּלֶךְ בִּכְבוֹדוֹ תָּמִיד יִמְלֹךְ עָלֵינוּ, לְעוֹלָם וָעֶד, וְעַל כָּל מַעֲשָׂיו.

BRETTLER (BIBLE)

[1] *"Blessed is Adonai forever"* The whole prayer is a pastiche of biblical verses, most of which request help from God, who is depicted as a powerful king. It begins with a particularly interesting choice, Psalm 89:53, a verse that demarcates the division between Books Three and Four of Psalms. Such verses of praise, called "doxologies," divide the biblical Book of Psalms into five parts (each called a "book" in itself), to parallel the Torah (the Five "Books" of Moses). (See Brettler, *"Kabbalat Shabbat:* A Liturgy from Psalms," p. 22, in Volume 8, *Kabbalat Shabbat* [*Welcoming Shabbat in the Synagogue*].) *(p. 99)*

DORFF (THEOLOGY)

[1] *"Blessed is Adonai forever ..."* In the prior prayer, we asked God to protect us *personally*. Now we ask God to safeguard us *as a nation*, by bringing about messianic times when God alone will rule. That theme is intertwined with asking God to ensure our safe passage through sleep, when we are more vulnerable than we are when awake.

———◆———

ELLENSON (MODERN LITURGIES)

[1] *"Blessed is Adonai forever"* While Conservative prayer books include this set of verses in its entirety, most Reform prayer books do not, not for polemical reasons, but probably just to shorten the service. Their editors *(p. 101)*

GRAY (OUR TALMUDIC HERITAGE)

[1] *"Blessed is Adonai forever"* As we saw (see "Lie us down," p. 84), the Talmud considers *Hashkivenu* and the prior blessing, *G'ullah*, to be one long prayer on the theme of redemption (Ber. 4b), followed immediately by the *Amidah*. It knows nothing about what we are here calling the "extended" *Hashkivenu*, a further addition still. The Tosafot (Ber. 4b, s.v. *d'amar*) appear to believe that it was instituted by the Talmud anyway and consider it to be just more of the lengthy *G'ullah*, reasoning *(p. 101)*

[For prayer instructions, see page 94.]

V. A FIFTH EVENING BLESSING: *BARUKH ADONAI L'OLAM* ("BLESSED IS ADONAI FOREVER")

[1] Blessed is Adonai forever. Amen and amen. [2] Blessed is Adonai from Zion, as He dwells in Jerusalem. Halleluyah. [3] Blessed is Adonai, God, Israel's God, who alone does wonders. [4] And blessed is his glorious name forever; He will fill the whole earth with his glory. Amen and amen. [5] May Adonai's

SINCE THE MIDDLE AGES, ASHKENAZI JEWS ADD YET A FIFTH BLESSING, BARUKH ADONAI L'OLAM (AFTER ITS OPENING WORDS, "BLESSED IS ADONAI FOREVER"). SEFARDI JEWS AND JEWS IN ISRAEL OMIT IT.

[1] *"Blessed is Adonai forever* [Barukh adonai l'olam]*"* The *Mishnah* demands one blessing (the *G'ullah*) after the *Sh'ma* in the morning, and two (the *G'ullah* followed by the *Hashkivenu*) after the *Sh'ma* in the evening. But simultaneously, Halakhah requires us to go directly from the *G'ullah* to the *Amidah*—a patent impossibility, given the need to add the *Hashkivenu* (p. 83) in the middle.   *(p. 102)*

בָּרוּךְ יְיָ לְעוֹלָם, אָמֵן וְאָמֵן. [2]בָּרוּךְ יְיָ מִצִּיּוֹן, שֹׁכֵן יְרוּשָׁלָיִם; הַלְלוּיָהּ; [3]בָּרוּךְ יְיָ אֱלֹהִים, אֱלֹהֵי יִשְׂרָאֵל, עֹשֵׂה נִפְלָאוֹת לְבַדּוֹ. [4]וּבָרוּךְ שֵׁם כְּבוֹדוֹ לְעוֹלָם, וְיִמָּלֵא כְבוֹדוֹ אֶת כָּל הָאָרֶץ, אָמֵן וְאָמֵן. [5]יְהִי כְבוֹד יְיָ לְעוֹלָם; יִשְׂמַח יְיָ בְּמַעֲשָׂיו. [6]יְהִי שֵׁם יְיָ מְבֹרָךְ,

J. HOFFMAN (TRANSLATION)

[1] *"Forever"* That is, "from now and forever more."

[1] *"Amen and amen"* This repetition of *amen* in English matches the Hebrew, but we suspect that the Hebrew reflects an idiomatic usage that we have not fully understood.

[8] *"Fell upon their faces"* Or more idiomatically in English, "bowed down low." We prefer to keep the literal translation here because the imagery seems so powerful.

[8] *"Crying out"* Commonly, "saying."

[10] *"Be kind to us"* Literally, "Let your kindness be upon us," but, as   *(p. 103)*

glory be forever. May Adonai rejoice in his creations. [6] May Adonai's name be blessed, from now and to eternity. [7] For Adonai will not abandon his people for the sake of his great name, for Adonai has decided to make you into his nation. [8] And all the people saw and fell upon their faces, crying out, "Adonai is God! Adonai is God!" [9] Adonai shall become king over the entire earth. On that day, Adonai shall be one and his name shall be one. [10] Adonai, be kind to us, as we have always wanted. [11] Save us, Adonai, our God, and gather us from among the other nations, to gratefully acknowledge your holy name, to exalt in your glory. [12] All the nations You created will come and bow down before You, Adonai, and they will honor your name; [13] for You are great, a worker of wonders. You alone are God. [14] And we are your people, the sheep of your pasture. We will gratefully acknowledge You forever; from generation to generation we will tell of your glory.

[15] Blessed is Adonai by day. Blessed is Adonai by night. Blessed is Adonai when we lie down. Blessed is Adonai when we stand up. For in your hand are the souls of the living and the dead. [16] In his hand is the soul of all that lives, and the spirit of all flesh. [17] In your hand I trust my soul. I am the one You have redeemed, Adonai, God of truth. [18] Our God in heaven, unite

מֵעַתָּה וְעַד עוֹלָם. [7] כִּי לֹא יִטּשׁ יְיָ אֶת עַמּוֹ בַּעֲבוּר שְׁמוֹ הַגָּדוֹל; כִּי הוֹאִיל יְיָ לַעֲשׂוֹת אֶתְכֶם לוֹ לְעָם. [8] וַיַּרְא כָּל הָעָם וַיִּפְּלוּ עַל פְּנֵיהֶם, וַיֹּאמְרוּ: יְיָ הוּא הָאֱלֹהִים, יְיָ הוּא הָאֱלֹהִים. [9] וְהָיָה יְיָ לְמֶלֶךְ עַל כָּל הָאָרֶץ; בַּיּוֹם הַהוּא יִהְיֶה יְיָ אֶחָד וּשְׁמוֹ אֶחָד. [10] יְהִי חַסְדְּךָ יְיָ עָלֵינוּ, כַּאֲשֶׁר יִחַלְנוּ לָךְ. [11] הוֹשִׁיעֵנוּ, יְיָ אֱלֹהֵינוּ, וְקַבְּצֵנוּ מִן הַגּוֹיִם, לְהוֹדוֹת לְשֵׁם קָדְשֶׁךָ, לְהִשְׁתַּבֵּחַ בִּתְהִלָּתֶךָ. [12] כָּל גּוֹיִם אֲשֶׁר עָשִׂיתָ יָבוֹאוּ וְיִשְׁתַּחֲווּ לְפָנֶיךָ, אֲדֹנָי, וִיכַבְּדוּ לִשְׁמֶךָ. [13] כִּי גָדוֹל אַתָּה וְעֹשֵׂה נִפְלָאוֹת; אַתָּה אֱלֹהִים לְבַדֶּךָ. [14] וַאֲנַחְנוּ, עַמְּךָ וְצֹאן מַרְעִיתֶךָ, נוֹדֶה לְךָ לְעוֹלָם, לְדוֹר וָדוֹר נְסַפֵּר תְּהִלָּתֶךָ.

[15] בָּרוּךְ יְיָ בַּיּוֹם, בָּרוּךְ יְיָ בַּלָּיְלָה; בָּרוּךְ יְיָ בְּשָׁכְבֵנוּ, בָּרוּךְ יְיָ בְּקוּמֵנוּ; כִּי בְיָדְךָ נַפְשׁוֹת הַחַיִּים וְהַמֵּתִים. [16] אֲשֶׁר בְּיָדוֹ נֶפֶשׁ כָּל חָי, וְרוּחַ כָּל בְּשַׂר אִישׁ. [17] בְּיָדְךָ אַפְקִיד רוּחִי; פָּדִיתָה אוֹתִי, יְיָ, אֵל אֱמֶת. [18] אֱלֹהֵינוּ שֶׁבַּשָּׁמַיִם, יַחֵד שִׁמְךָ וְקַיֵּם מַלְכוּתְךָ תָּמִיד, וּמְלוֹךְ עָלֵינוּ לְעוֹלָם וָעֶד.

[19] יִרְאוּ עֵינֵינוּ וְיִשְׂמַח לִבֵּנוּ, וְתָגֵל נַפְשֵׁנוּ בִּישׁוּעָתְךָ בֶּאֱמֶת, בֶּאֱמֹר לְצִיּוֹן מָלַךְ אֱלֹהָיִךְ. [20] יְיָ מֶלֶךְ, יְיָ מָלָךְ, יְיָ יִמְלֹךְ לְעוֹלָם וָעֶד. [21] כִּי הַמַּלְכוּת שֶׁלְּךָ

your name, and preserve your kingdom eternally, and rule over us forever.

[19] Let our eyes see and our heart rejoice, and our soul celebrate in your true salvation, telling Zion, "Your God is king." [20] Adonai is king, was king, and will be king forever. [21] The kingdom is yours, and You will always rule in glory, for we have no king other than You! [22] Blessed are You, Adonai, the king who in his glory will always rule over us forever—and over all his creatures.

הִיא, וּלְעוֹלְמֵי עַד תִּמְלֹךְ בְּכָבוֹד, כִּי אֵין לָנוּ מֶלֶךְ אֶלָּא אָתָּה. [22] בָּרוּךְ אַתָּה, יְיָ, הַמֶּלֶךְ בִּכְבוֹדוֹ תָּמִיד יִמְלֹךְ עָלֵינוּ, לְעוֹלָם וָעֶד, וְעַל כָּל מַעֲשָׂיו.

BRETTLER (BIBLE)

[2] *"Blessed is Adonai from Zion"* Psalm 135:21.

[3–4] *"Blessed is Adonai, God"* Psalm 72:18–19, concluding the four-part "blessed" *(barukh)* opening of this prayer.

[5–6] *"May Adonai's glory ... May Adonai's name"* Psalms 104:31 and 113:2, both opening with *y'hi*, to express a wish.

[7] *"For Adonai will not abandon"* A powerful verse from 1 Samuel 12:22, where Saul becomes the first Israelite king. It emphasizes God as Israel's ultimate king, who, unlike human kings, is fully trustworthy and will never abandon his people.

[8] *"And all the people saw"* 1 Kings 18:39, the competition between Elijah and the prophets of Baal on Mount Carmel. In this climactic verse, Elijah has just proved that Adonai is more powerful than His Canaanite "opposition."

[9] *"On that day"* Zechariah 14:9 is the only verse in the entire Bible that recognizes (and paraphrases) the initial verse of the *Sh'ma* (Deut. 6:4). It is chosen also to conclude the *Alenu* (see Volume 6, *Tachanun and Concluding Prayers*, p. 136). Zechariah may actually be two books, not just one, with chapters 9–14 written as late as the sixth–fourth century B.C.E., by which time Deuteronomy 6:4 was becoming especially popular.

[10] *"Be kind to us"* Psalm 33:22. *Chesed* is a complex biblical notion involving loyalty, goodness, graciousness, and (only occasionally) mercy.

[11] *"Save us"* Psalm 106:47, clearly a late composition, since it imagines Israel as dispersed. As elsewhere in the Bible, it is not on account of its own merit that Israel requests deliverance, but for God's sake, so that Israel may continue praising God. The Israelites believed that God enjoyed being praised.

[12-13] *"All the nations"* Psalm 86:9–10, expressing a particular vision of the ideal future, similar to Zechariah 14:9. Less parochial images are found elsewhere; in Isaiah 2:1–4, for example, the nations will be instructed by God, but do not necessarily embrace God as their only deity.

[14] *"Your people, the sheep of your pasture"* Psalm 79:13.

[15] *"For in your hand are the souls of the living"* The notion of a bipartite body and soul entered Judaism under Greek influence, sometime after the fourth century B.C.E., at which time it was assumed that God controls all souls, living and dead. The word *nefesh* came then to mean "soul"; in the Bible, it had meant just a general sense of one's life-force. It disappeared upon death, when one entered Sheol, the world of the dead, far away from God.

Verse 16 cites Job 12:10 ("in his hand is the soul of all that lives") as a proof text for the later understanding, but there too, in its biblical context, it meant only life-force. Similarly, verse 17 follows with Psalm 31:6 ("in your hand I trust my soul"), as if God's care for our *ruach* demonstrated his care of our soul (our *nefesh*) after death. But *ruach* in the Bible just means "wind" or "breath."

[18] *"Unite your name"* A post-biblical text, influenced by the growing influence of the *Sh'ma*. (See above, v. 9, "On that day.")

[20] *"Adonai is king, was king, and will be king"* The idea that Adonai was, is, and will be king combines three separate biblical verses, but is never found together in one place in the Bible. Their combination here constitutes the poetic device called a *tricolon*, relatively rare biblically, compared to the common *bicolon*.

We recite this also when removing the Torah from the ark. (See detailed discussion in Volume 4, *Seder K'riat Hatorah (The Torah Service)*, p. 52, Brettler, v. 3, "Adonai is King."

[21-22] *"In glory ... in his glory"* An emphatic conclusion associating God and *kavod*. Exactly what *kavod* means in these two lines is unclear, but it probably refers back to Psalm 24, where Adonai is "king of *hakavod*."

———◆———

ELLENSON (MODERN LITURGIES)

knew that their recitation has been halakhically questionable anyway (see L. Hoffman, "Blessed are You," p. 148) and is not part of the ritual as practiced in the Land of Israel, so they had ample precedent for removing it. Abraham Geiger is the most notable exception to this, retaining all of verses 1–14, with the exception of verses 2 and 11. He omits the former because of its particularistic focus on Zion, and the latter because it calls for a return of Jewish exiles to Israel. Typically (see "Eternal love," p. 58), Geiger tries to be as traditional as his sensibilities allow, but he opposes any idea of Zion-centrism or the diaspora as exile. Geiger also omits that part of verse 15 that asserts that the "souls of the living and the dead" are in the hand of God.

A number of Reform and Reconstructionist prayer books such as the Israeli *Ha'avodah Shebalev* (1967), *Kol Haneshamah* (Reconstructionist, 1995), and *Das Jüdische Gebetbuch* (German Reform, 2001) do include elements of verses 15–22.

◆

GRAY (OUR TALMUDIC HERITAGE)

that the Talmud instituted it on account of people who arrived late in the synagogue. This extension could be recited by worshipers who had finished praying the *Amidah* while waiting for latecomers to say their own *Amidah*. Afterward, everyone could leave together.

Asher ben Yechiel (Rabbenu Asher, or the Rosh; 1250–1327, Germany and Spain) presents a similar explanation, but with a critical difference. He claims that people themselves began to recite these verses because in talmudic times, their synagogues were out in the fields where they worked and they were afraid to tarry too long out there after dark. Consequently, they began to recite these verses, which mention God's name (Adonai) eighteen times (prior to verse 19, the beginning of the blessing's conclusion), corresponding to the eighteen blessings of the *Amidah*. These verses were a *substitute* for the full *Amidah*, and by reciting them instead, people would be able to leave sooner for home. Even though we now recite *Ma'ariv* in a synagogue and, naturally, recite the full *Amidah* as part of it, "the early *minhag* [of reciting the verses of the extended *Hashkivenu*] was not nullified." Abudarham quotes the *"Ba'al Haminhagot,"* who sees the recitation of these verses as a replacement for the *Amidah* during a time of persecution, when Jews were prohibited from gathering for evening prayers. The persecution was eventually lifted, but the practice remained. Abudarham knows major scholars (including the Rambam) who objected to the recitation of these verses, but he rejects them because "the *minhag* [custom] of our ancestors is Torah, as we say (PT B.M. 7:1, 11b) '*minhag* nullifies *halakhah*.'"

◆

L. HOFFMAN (HISTORY)

But there, at least, we have Mishnaic precedent explaining the deviation, since the Mishnah itself stipulates the "extra" blessing. In the morning, we do move directly from *G'ullah* to *Amidah*; in the evening, we include *Hashkivenu*, but in order to say we go directly from *G'ullah* to *Amidah*, we categorize it (by legal fiction) as a single "long [or extended] *G'ullah*" (*g'ullah arichta*).

But *Hashkivenu* is not the only problem, because in *Baruch Adonai l'olam*, we get yet a third blessing after the *Sh'ma*—complete with a concluding *chatimah* ("seal" or "concluding line," typical of blessings), "Blessed are You ... and over all his creatures" (p. 94).

We really do not know how this extra blessing got here. Halakhah explains it away by lumping it together with the preceding *Hashkivenu* as just more of the extended *G'ullah*, but even if Halakhah is right, "explaining away" is not the same as "explaining," and we just have no really plausible historical explanation for this blessing.

Still, since the Middle Ages, traditional sources have explained *Barukh Adonai l'olam* as a stand-in for the normal evening *Amidah*, because it mentions God's name eighteen times.

The reasons given for such a stand-in vary. Perhaps people once prayed in the fields and were afraid to travel to synagogue in the dark; this was an easy prayer they could say in the fields on their own, without having to take the time to go through the entire *Amidah* of eighteen benedictions. Or perhaps they were tempted not to say the *Ma'ariv Amidah* at all, since they knew that technically, there being no evening sacrifice to justify it, it was merely optional—in which case, saying *Barukh Adonai l'olam* would at least provide them with an equivalent of the missing *Amidah*. Maybe too, the problem was Rabbi Meir's second-century regulation that everyone recite a hundred blessings daily. Without the eighteen of the *Amidah* (for those who omitted the *Amidah* as optional), people might fall short; treating each citation of God's name in *Barukh Adonai l'olam* as if it were a blessing would make up the difference. Whatever the rationale, the eighteenfold mention of the divine name Adonai is central.

The only problem with all of these explanations is that the prayer mentions God's name more than eighteen times! Rather than eighteen, or even nineteen (the *Amidah* nowadays has nineteen, not eighteen, blessings, so nineteen would be acceptable also), and counting only the four-letter name of God (YHVH) but omitting *elohim* and ADNY (spelled *alef, dalet, nun, yod*), we still have twenty-four references in all.

To get even near the number eighteen, tradition omits from the count the last paragraph, "Let our eyes see ..." (*yir'u eineinu*). As the twelfth- to thirteenth-century Tosafot put it (Ber. 4b, s.v. *d'amar*), the writers composed the necessary eighteen references, but then, "Having instituted the recitation of those verses anyway, they instituted also the conclusion, 'Let our eyes behold' [*agav shetiknu lomar otam p'sukim tiknu lomar chatimah shel yir'u eineinu*]." But this "gratuitous addition" provides only four citations of Adonai, still leaving us with twenty. How do we get from twenty to eighteen?

The only way to do so is to count no more than one reference in any single sentence. The lengthy paragraph from "Blessed is Adonai forever" to the add-on "Let our eyes see" contains twenty names of God, but within only eighteen biblical verses. To get the necessary eighteen references to God's name, our medieval ancestors must have counted the sentences, not the names themselves, getting one sentence for each blessing of the original eighteen-benediction *Amidah*.

Seeing these eighteen biblical verses as an eighteen-blessing *Amidah* led some halakhists, including such eminent Polish authorities as the sixteenth-century Mordecai Jaffe (the *L'vush*) and Moses Isserles *(Darkhei Moshe)* to stand during their recitation. But most authorities overruled them, lest people get the idea that saying the paragraph exempted them from reciting the "real" *Amidah* that follows.

Sefardi practice solves the problem of *Barukh Adonai l'olam* by just omitting it, a practice going back at least as far as Isaac ibn Ghayyat (1038–1089), who says he omits it specifically to go from the end of *Hashkivenu* to the *Amidah*. Maimonides concurs.

On Friday night, *Baruch Adonai l'olam* is missing from the Ashkenazi service, too. By the time of the Tosafot (twelfth to thirteenth centuries), its absence was explained by noting that, first of all, the *Amidah* for Friday night has only seven, not eighteen, blessings, so we hardly need eighteen citations of the divine name then. But we would, of course, still need seven citations, and that is why the *Ma'ariv Amidah* for Shabbat is followed by *Magen Avot*. The eighteen-benediction *Amidah* of weekday evenings comes with *Barukh Adonai l'olam*, which mentions God's name eighteen times; the seven-benediction *Amidah* for Shabbat evening carries *Magen Avot*, a single blessing "in place of seven." (See *Magen Avot*, ["Protecting Our Ancestors"], p. 136.)

This legal explanation was arrived at ex post facto, however. Already in the eighth century, Natronai Gaon omitted *Barukh Adonai l'olam* on Friday nights without knowing exactly why. He reasoned that nighttime demons threaten to derange people running home for the *mitzvah* of Shabbat; we therefore shorten the service to make sure everyone is safely home and off the streets before dark.

◆

J. HOFFMAN (TRANSLATION)

we have frequently pointed out, proper translation need not always translate nouns as nouns or verbs as verbs. Birnbaum uses "may thy kindness rest on us" to set the stage for his translation of the next line, "as our hope rest in Thee."

[10] *"Wanted"* The Hebrew verb is stronger, but "as we have always yearned" doesn't seem to make much sense in English. Birnbaum's "as our hope rests in Thee" poetically matches his "may Thy kindness rest on us," but the Hebrew doesn't match up the way his English does, and so our English doesn't either.

[11] *"Gather us"* The notion here is clearly "gather us in," that is, "end our exile."

[11] *"The other nations"* Here, as frequently elsewhere, the Hebrew doesn't explicitly say "other," but certainly that was the point.

[11] *"To exalt in your glory"* Not only isn't it clear exactly what the Hebrew means here, it's not clear who is doing the exalting, "us" or "God."

[15] *"Souls"* Elsewhere, we have translated this word as "mind" (see Volume 1, *The Sh'ma and Its Blessings*, p. 100), but the translation "mind" applies to the biblical use of the word, while here we see the rabbinic usage of the word.

[16] *"Soul"* Alas, in contrast to the previous line (see above), here "soul" is not our most accurate translation. But we want to keep the same word in English to match the repeated word in Hebrew.

[19] *"Celebrate"* Or "be glad." We prefer an active verb, to match "see" and "rejoice."

[19] *"Telling"* The gerund "telling" seems out of place, and it is, because this is actually a quotation from Isaiah 52:7. The composers of our liturgy frequently included quotations without bothering to harmonize the grammar.

◆ ◆ ◆

[On weekdays, continue with a Chatsi Kaddish (Half Kaddish) and the weekday Amidah (for the entire text, see Volume 2, The Amidah).

On Shabbat and holidays, continue here. Then say a Chatsi Kaddish (Half Kaddish) and the Shabbat or holiday Amidah.]

C. ANNOUNCEMENT OF SACRED TIME

[On Shabbat]

[1] The children of Israel shall keep Shabbat, observing Shabbat throughout their generations as an eternal covenant. [2] It is an eternal sign between Me and the children of Israel, for in six days Adonai made heaven and earth, and on the seventh day He rested.

וְשָׁמְרוּ בְנֵי יִשְׂרָאֵל אֶת הַשַּׁבָּת, לַעֲשׂוֹת אֶת הַשַּׁבָּת לְדֹרֹתָם בְּרִית עוֹלָם. בֵּינִי וּבֵין בְּנֵי יִשְׂרָאֵל אוֹת הִיא לְעֹלָם, כִּי שֵׁשֶׁת יָמִים עָשָׂה יְיָ אֶת הַשָּׁמַיִם וְאֶת הָאָרֶץ, וּבַיּוֹם הַשְּׁבִיעִי שָׁבַת וַיִּנָּפַשׁ.

[On Passover, Shavuot, and Sukkot]

[3] Moses explained Adonai's holidays to all the children of Israel.

וַיְדַבֵּר מֹשֶׁה אֶת מֹעֲדֵי יְיָ אֶל בְּנֵי יִשְׂרָאֵל.

[On Rosh Hashanah]

[4] Blow the shofar on the new moon, on the full moon for our holiday. That is the law of Israel, the ruling of Jacob's God.

תִּקְעוּ בַחֹדֶשׁ שׁוֹפָר, בַּכֶּסֶה לְיוֹם חַגֵּנוּ. כִּי חֹק לְיִשְׂרָאֵל הוּא, מִשְׁפָּט לֵאלֹהֵי יַעֲקֹב.

[On Yom Kippur]

[5] For this very day will atone for you to purify you; you will be pure of all your sins before Adonai.

כִּי בַיּוֹם הַזֶּה יְכַפֵּר עֲלֵיכֶם לְטַהֵר אֶתְכֶם, מִכָּל חַטֹּאתֵיכֶם לִפְנֵי יְיָ תִּטְהָרוּ.

BRETTLER (BIBLE)

1–2 *"The children of Israel shall keep Shabbat"* Exodus 31:16–17 is also found as a common introduction to Saturday afternoon *Kiddusha Rabbah* (see Volume 7, *Shabbat at Home*, pp. 156–157). The passage was composed by priestly authors in, or after the return from, Babylonian exile, where Shabbat became especially significant. The verses occur in the middle of the instructions for constructing the Tabernacle (Exod. 31:12–17). This placement of the ban on Shabbat labor in the middle of the Tabernacle account served as the basis for the rabbinic decision to define forbidden Shabbat work as activities involved in the construction of the Tabernacle. *(p. 108)*

DORFF (THEOLOGY)

1–2 *"The children of Israel shall keep Shabbat ..."* In just two verses the Torah (Exod. 31:16–17) provides the two rationales for observing the Sabbath, as articulated in the two versions of the Decalogue (Exod. 20:8–11 and Deut. 5:12–15). First, God created the universe in *(p. 109)*

ELLENSON (MODERN LITURGIES)

"Announcement of Sacred Time" Included in all non-Orthodox prayer services—as we would expect. Liberal Judaism began as part of the nineteenth century's discovery of history. Situated at the cutting edge of intellectual thought, liberal Jews gloried *(p. 109)*

GRAY (OUR TALMUDIC HERITAGE)

1 *"The children of Israel shall keep Shabbat"* These verses follow the extended blessing on redemption to demonstrate that if the Jewish people observe Shabbat properly, they will immediately be redeemed (Abudarham).

3 *"Moses explained"* Leviticus 23:44, cited in the Talmud (R.H. 24a) as a proof text for the Mishnah's contention that the head of the rabbinic court would proclaim the new month by exclaiming "It is sanctified! It *(p. 110)*

[For prayer instructions, see page 105.]

[On Shabbat]

1 The children of Israel shall keep Shabbat, observing Shabbat throughout their generations as an eternal covenant. 2 It is an eternal sign between Me and the children of Israel, for in six days Adonai made heaven and earth, and on the seventh day He rested.

KUSHNER & POLEN (CHASIDISM)

1 *"The children of Israel shall keep ..."* According to *Parashat Ki Tisa* (Exod. 30:11–34:35), the very last thing God said to Moses at the conclusion of his first ascent up Mount Sinai was the *V'shamru*—"And the children of Israel shall keep Shabbat ..." (Exod. 31:16–17).

Noting this juxtaposition of the Shabbat commandment with the receiving of the Torah, Rabbi Yehuda Aryeh Lieb of Ger in his *S'fas Emes* (1895) (5657, s.v. *Ki Tisa*), *(p. 110)*

LANDES (HALAKHAH)

[1] *"The children of Israel shall keep Shabbat" V'sham'ru* also interrupts the flow between the *G'ullah* and the *Amidah* (*Tur*, O. Ch. 367), but it too is not considered a *hefsek* (see "Lie us down," p. 85). The Rabbis taught that if we observe two *Shabbatot* in a row, we will immediately be redeemed. *V'shamru* instructs us to keep Shabbat, so is thematically consonant with redemption. The verses introducing the other holidays function similarly to refer to the *G'ullah* theme.

L. HOFFMAN (HISTORY)

THE SH'MA AND ITS BLESSINGS IS FOLLOWED BY AN AMIDAH, THE SECOND OF THE TWO CENTRAL UNITS IN OUR SERVICE. ON SHABBAT AND HOLIDAYS, IT IS PRECEDED BY AN ANNOUNCEMENT OF SACRED TIME.

[1] *"The children of Israel shall keep Shabbat"* The *Amidah* is altered to fit particular occasions. It is introduced by an announcement of sacred time, an oral reminder, drawn from the Bible, of the particular day in question. We include here the announcement of Shabbat, and holidays as well, so that the Shabbat announcement can be seen in context. The *(p. 111)*

(p. 111)

[1] וְשָׁמְרוּ בְנֵי יִשְׂרָאֵל אֶת הַשַּׁבָּת, לַעֲשׂוֹת אֶת הַשַּׁבָּת לְדֹרֹתָם בְּרִית עוֹלָם. [2] בֵּינִי וּבֵין בְּנֵי יִשְׂרָאֵל אוֹת הִיא לְעֹלָם, כִּי שֵׁשֶׁת יָמִים עָשָׂה יְיָ אֶת הַשָּׁמַיִם וְאֶת הָאָרֶץ, וּבַיּוֹם הַשְּׁבִיעִי שָׁבַת וַיִּנָּפַשׁ.

J. HOFFMAN (TRANSLATION)

[4] *"That is the law of Israel, the ruling of Jacob's God"* This is typical biblical poetry, stating the same thing twice with synonyms. In this case, "Israel" = "Jacob" and "law" = "ruling."

Nonetheless, *Machzor Vitry* (by Simchah of Vitry, student of Rashi, d. 1105, France) advises reciting these verses quietly—in order not to interrupt the flow from *G'ullah* to *Amidah*, and the Gra (the Gaon Elijah of Vilna, 1730–1797) did not recite them at all, lest they constitute a *hefsek*. This is also the custom of Jerusalem.

[On Passover, Shavuot, and Sukkot]

³ Moses explained Adonai's holidays to all the children of Israel.

³וַיְדַבֵּר מֹשֶׁה אֶת מֹעֲדֵי יְיָ אֶל בְּנֵי יִשְׂרָאֵל.

[On Rosh Hashanah]

⁴ Blow the shofar on the new moon, on the full moon for our holiday. That is the law of Israel, the ruling of Jacob's God.

⁴תִּקְעוּ בַחֹדֶשׁ שׁוֹפָר, בַּכֶּסֶה לְיוֹם חַגֵּנוּ. כִּי חֹק לְיִשְׂרָאֵל הוּא, מִשְׁפָּט לֵאלֹהֵי יַעֲקֹב.

[On Yom Kippur]

⁵ For this very day will atone for you to purify you; you will be pure of all your sins before Adonai.

⁵כִּי בַיּוֹם הַזֶּה יְכַפֵּר עֲלֵיכֶם לְטַהֵר אֶתְכֶם, מִכָּל חַטֹּאתֵיכֶם לִפְנֵי יְיָ תִּטְהָרוּ.

BRETTLER (BIBLE)

³ *"Moses explained"* Leviticus 23:44. The Torah provides four main accounts of the Jewish calendar, in whole or in part: Exodus 23:14–19; Leviticus 23:1–44; Numbers 28:9–29:39; and Deuteronomy 16:1–17. The earliest, from Exodus, dates back to about the eighth century B.C.E. The Deuteronomy calendar is part of the Bible edited by the party we call the Deuteronomist and can be dated to the seventh century B.C.E. The other two calendars (Leviticus and Numbers) reflect priestly concerns with the details of the sacrificial cult and are the most recent, probably composed about the sixth century B.C.E.

The verse in question here concludes the Leviticus account.

⁴ *"Blow"* Psalm 81:4–5, two extremely difficult verses, which may not even refer to Rosh Hashanah. Of the four main calendrical accounts in the Bible (see above, v. 3, "Moses explained"), what we consider Rosh Hashanah is known in the priestly versions of Numbers 29 and Leviticus 23, but it is not called by that name in either source because Rosh Hashanah means "new year," and the biblical new year was Nisan 1, the month of the Exodus, not Tishrei 1, which is the seventh month, not the first. The Numbers calendar (29:1) just says, "the seventh day, on the first of the month," giving the day no title at all. Leviticus 23:24 gives the same chronological date, but more

detail, calling the day *shabbaton zikhron t'ruah mikra kodesh*—"[a day of] complete rest, a sacred occasion commemorated with loud blasts."

Sukkot (Tishrei 15) was probably the original new year. Exodus 34:22 calls it *t'kufat hashanah*, "the turn of the year"; this was replaced by Passover, originally celebrated on the first of Nisan, and thus according to the Bible, there are two new years. (According to the Rabbis, there are four!) The reference here to *yom chageinu* ("our holiday") parallels Deuteronomy 16:14, where Sukkot is called *chag*, "festival," suggesting that this verse originally referred to Sukkot, but when that new year was replaced by Rosh Hashanah, these verses became understood as denoting that Rosh Hashanah (Tishrei 1, that is, not Tishrei 15).

[5] *"For this very day"* Leviticus 16:30. The bulk of this chapter describes the Yom Kippur cleansing or purgation (Hebrew root *k.p.r*) of impurities from the Tabernacle. This verse is unusual in that it highlights the cleansing of the *people*, anticipating the rabbinic idea of Yom Kippur.

———◆———

DORFF (THEOLOGY)

six days and desisted from creative acts on the seventh, so we should model ourselves after God and do likewise; second, God took us out of Egypt to enter a covenant with God, of which Shabbat is a symbol. These verses juxtapose the universal with the particular: God created the entire universe, but God also established a special relationship with the Jewish People. As the Rabbis put it, "Between Me and the children of Israel" implies its own negative: "Not between Me and the other nations of the world" (*Mekhilta D'rabbi Yishmael, Ki Tisa*, on Exod. 31:17). Shabbat is thus not one of the seven duties for which non-Jews are responsible, under the terms of God's covenant with them as the universal children of Noah (Sanh. 56a). Shabbat is God's gift specifically for Jews, even as it also reminds us of God's larger gift of creating all the universe.

———◆———

ELLENSON (MODERN LITURGIES)

in Darwinism and evolution. But unlike Darwin, where evolution is always to higher forms of life, Jewish liberals asserted a second side to the phenomenon of development. Yes, humanity was slowly evolving to a better state. But antiquity was considered superior to the "dark ages" that separated classical thought from the modern enlightenment.

This privileging of antiquity was not solely Jewish; Jews learned it from German academicians who typified the romantic era by searching out ancient roots for culture. As the universities saw it, antiquity provided Hebrew, Greek, and Roman genius. These were largely lost until the Renaissance and were becoming clear once again in the Enlightenment.

Liberal Jews accepted the notion of biblical genius and agreed that the Middle Ages had dulled the clear insights of the ancients. That was how they explained the reforms necessary when facing talmudic legislation, which, being medieval, could not always uphold pure biblical truths.

Here, then, liberal prayerbook editors jumped at the chance to include the relevant biblical verses commanding Jewish holy day celebration.

Gray (Our Talmudic Heritage)

is sanctified!" As Moses declared the time aloud, so did the court, and so, therefore, do we, by citing this verse to herald sacred time ourselves.

Kushner & Polen (Chasidism)

reminds us of a midrash (Exodus Rabbah 41:6): "Rabbi Abahu said: The whole forty days Moses was on high, he was learning Torah. But he forgot it all. 'God,' Moses said, 'I have had forty days with You, but I cannot remember a thing.' So what did God do? After the forty days were completed, the Holy One gave him the Torah, as a gift!"

The *S'fas Emes* then draws a parallel: The six days of creation, he proposes, correspond to Moses's forty days on Mount Sinai. And just as Moses was unable to remember what he had learned from God, the six days of creation are likewise under the sway of forgetfulness. Furthermore, just as the Torah is an undeserved, divine gift to our deteriorating memories, so too is Shabbat a day of *being able to remember everything*. Indeed, says the Gerer, the commandment mentioned back in Exodus 20:8 to "remember Shabbat" might also be read as the promise of a reward: On Shabbat, *you will be able to remember*. Indeed, we wear *t'fillin* during the six days precisely because they are "a sign to remember," if you will, a mnemonic device! *T'fillin* help us remember things during the forgetfulness of the six days of creation. In the same way, Shabbat day and the Torah are both instruments of memory, mechanisms for recalling everything we have forgotten. And what we remember on Shabbat is why we were created.

L. HOFFMAN (HISTORY)

four announcements demonstrate three kinds of holy time: Shabbat is in a category by itself. The three Pilgrimage Festivals (Passover, Shavuot, and Sukkot) are tied to the agriculture season, two spring harvests (Passover and Shavuot) and the autumn harvest (Sukkot); Rosh Hashanah is a preparation for Yom Kippur, which has its own status as a *tsom*, "fast." And Yom Kippur is the most important fast day of the Jewish year, the only one mandated by Torah.

Four other fast days connected to the Temple's fall are mentioned biblically:

1. Tish'a B'av (ninth of Av), when the destruction occurred (Jer. 52:12–13, where, however, the date is given as the tenth)
2. The seventeenth of Tammuz, when the walls of Jerusalem were breached (Jer. 39:2, where, however, the date is given as the ninth)
3. The tenth of Tevet, commemorating the Babylonian siege of Jerusalem
4. *Tsom Gedaliah* ("The Fast of Gedaliah," third of Tishrei, from Jer. 41:2, 2 Kings 25:25), in memory of the death of Jerusalem's governor

For all but Yom Kippur, fasts call for the standard *Amidah* with additions to recognize the mournful quality of the day, but have no biblical preamble in the liturgy.

◆

[Continue with the Amidah *(for the entire weekday text, see Volume 2, The Amidah). On Saturday night, the fourth blessing reads as follows. For the normal benediction on all other nights, see Volume 2, The Amidah, pp. 100–101.]*

D. THE *AMIDAH*

I. A *HAVDALAH* IN THE *AMIDAH* FOR SATURDAY NIGHT

[1] You favor people with knowledge, and teach mortals understanding. [2] You favored us with knowledge of your Torah, and taught us to do the laws of your will. [3] You distinguished, Adonai our God, between holy and ordinary, between light and dark, between Israel and the other nations, between the seventh day and the six days of creation. [4] Our father, our king, let the days now approaching us begin with peace, devoid of sin, and cleansed of transgression, and full of awe for You. [5] Favor us with your knowledge, understanding, and wisdom. [6] Blessed are You, Adonai, who favors people with knowledge.

א[1] תָּה חוֹנֵן לְאָדָם דַּעַת, וּמְלַמֵּד לֶאֱנוֹשׁ בִּינָה. [2]אַתָּה חוֹנַנְתָּנוּ מַדַּע תּוֹרָתֶךָ, וַתְּלַמְּדֵנוּ לַעֲשׂוֹת חֻקֵּי רְצוֹנֶךָ; [3]וַתַּבְדֵּל, יְיָ אֱלֹהֵינוּ, בֵּין קֹדֶשׁ לְחֹל, בֵּין אוֹר לְחֹשֶׁךְ, בֵּין יִשְׂרָאֵל לָעַמִּים, בֵּין יוֹם הַשְּׁבִיעִי לְשֵׁשֶׁת יְמֵי הַמַּעֲשֶׂה. [4]אָבִינוּ מַלְכֵּנוּ, הָחֵל עָלֵינוּ הַיָּמִים הַבָּאִים לִקְרָאתֵנוּ לְשָׁלוֹם, חֲשׂוּכִים מִכָּל חֵטְא, וּמְנֻקִּים מִכָּל עָוֹן, וּמְדֻבָּקִים בְּיִרְאָתֶךָ. [5]חָנֵּנוּ מֵאִתְּךָ דֵעָה, בִּינָה וְהַשְׂכֵּל. [6]בָּרוּךְ אַתָּה, יְיָ, חוֹנֵן הַדָּעַת.

BRETTLER (BIBLE)

[2] *"You favored us with knowledge"* The language and the flow of this additional section are quite difficult, but the sense seems to be that the uniquely human ability to distinguish between various entities implies the necessity to differentiate Shabbat from secular time, and virtue from sin.

[3] *"You distinguished"* Four pairs through which God has created distinctions. Each pair is longer than the preceding one, following a general rule called the law of increasing members, by which lists move from short to long items. This list concludes climactically with Shabbat itself, but the preceding elements of the   *(p. 116)*

DORFF (THEOLOGY)

[3] *"You distinguished, Adonai our God, between holy and ordinary … between the seventh day and the six days of creation"* The late Perry London, professor of psychology at the University of Southern California and later Harvard (may his memory be a blessing), once asked me how   *(p. 117)*

ELLENSON (MODERN LITURGIES)

[3] *"Between Israel and the other nations"* Geiger omits "between Israel and the other nations," just as he does in his version of *Havdalah* at home. In so doing, he reflects his desire to purge Jewish liturgy of what he regards as an unnecessary emphasis on particularity.

(p. 117)

FRANKEL (A WOMAN'S VOICE)

[5] *"Favor us with your knowledge"* In the following excerpt from an early twentieth-century Yiddish *tkhine* to be recited before *Havdalah*, the author asks God to protect her family and community in the week ahead:

> Who, other than You, heavenly Father, knows the hard life of Your people Israel? [Who knows] their bitter spirit, how hard it is for every Jew to earn his piece of bread? With what worry and heartache, with what fear and hardship he gathers his bleak living! Who among all
>
> *(p. 117)*

[For prayer instructions, see page 113.]

I. A *HAVDALAH* IN THE *AMIDAH* FOR SATURDAY NIGHT

[1] You favor people with knowledge, and teach mortals understanding. [2] You favored us with knowledge of your Torah, and taught us to do the laws of your will. [3] You distinguished, Adonai our God, between holy and ordinary, between light and dark, between Israel and the other nations, between

GRAY (OUR TALMUDIC HERITAGE)

[1] *"You favor people with knowledge"* The Mishnah (Ber. 5:2) records three views on where to include *Havdalah* in the *Amidah* on Saturday night:

1. The first view, given anony-mously (called, "first teacher"— *tanna kamma*) wants to include it as we have it here: an inclusion in the fourth blessing (*Binah*, "Knowledge") of the weekday *Amidah*.

(p. 117)

KUSHNER & POLEN (CHASIDISM)

2 *"You favored us with knowledge"* The fourth blessing of the evening *Amidah* (the blessing for knowledge) at the conclusion of Shabbat is longer than its counterpart on weekdays. It is called *Atah chonantanu*, "You favored us with knowledge," after one of its additions. The blessing is also referred to as *Havdalah*—not to be confused with the liturgy for the ceremony of the braided candle, spice box, and wine marking the end of Shabbat that comes later in the liturgy just prior to the *(p. 118)*

L. HOFFMAN (HISTORY)

TEXT AND COMMENTARY FOR THE WEEKDAY MORNING AMIDAH CAN BE FOUND IN VOLUME 2, THE AMIDAH. OF THE ENTIRE AMIDAH, WE INCLUDE HERE JUST THE CHANGES REQUIRED FOR THE EVENING VERSION. THE FIRST THREE BLESSINGS ARE THE SAME AS FOR THE MORNING, EXCEPT FOR THE FACT THAT THE EVENING AMIDAH HAS NO READER'S REPETITION, SO THE USUAL ELABORATION OF ITS THIRD BLESSING (THE K'DUSHAT HASHEM) IS LACKING.

THE FOURTH BLESSING, WHICH FOLLOWS (BINAH, DISCERNMENT), IS ALTERED ON SATURDAY NIGHT, SO AS TO REFLECT HAVDALAH, THE (p. 119)

¹אַתָּה חוֹנֵן לְאָדָם דַּעַת, וּמְלַמֵּד לֶאֱנוֹשׁ בִּינָה. ²אַתָּה חוֹנַנְתָּנוּ מַדַּע תּוֹרָתֶךָ, וַתְּלַמְּדֵנוּ לַעֲשׂוֹת חֻקֵּי רְצוֹנֶךָ; ³וַתַּבְדֵּל, יְיָ אֱלֹהֵינוּ, בֵּין קֹדֶשׁ לְחֹל, בֵּין אוֹר לְחֹשֶׁךְ, בֵּין יִשְׂרָאֵל לָעַמִּים, בֵּין יוֹם הַשְּׁבִיעִי לְשֵׁשֶׁת יְמֵי הַמַּעֲשֶׂה. ⁴אָבִינוּ מַלְכֵּנוּ, הָחֵל עָלֵינוּ הַיָּמִים הַבָּאִים

LANDES (HALAKHAH)

2 *"You favored us [Atah chonantanu]"* *Havdalah* is part of the double *mitzvah* of demarcating the Sabbath day—by *Kiddush*, as it arrives, and by *Havdalah* as it departs (Maimonides, "Laws of the Sabbath" 29:1).

Most authorities (including Maimonides, 29:6) maintain that the double *mitzvah* of *Kiddush*/*Havdalah* is *d'rabbanan*, "rabbinic" in origin, but some consider it *d'ora'ita*, deriving from Torah (see SMaG [*Sefer Mitzvot Gadol*] by Moses of Coucy [thirteenth *(p. 118)*

J. HOFFMAN (TRANSLATION)

2 *"Favored us with knowledge"* Even though this word *(mada)* is not the same word for "knowledge" we see immediately above *(de'ah)*, it comes from the same root. (In modern Hebrew, *mada* means "science.")

3 *"Ordinary"* Others, "profane," but profane has a negative connotation in English that the Hebrew *chol* lacks.

4 *"Full of"* Literally, "stuck with" or "clung to."

◆◆◆

the seventh day and the six days of creation. ⁴ Our father, our king, let the days now approaching us begin with peace, devoid of sin, and cleansed of transgression, and full of awe for You. ⁵ Favor us with your knowledge, understanding, and wisdom. ⁶ Blessed are You, Adonai, who favors people with knowledge.

לִקְרָאתֵֽנוּ לְשָׁלוֹם, חֲשׂוּכִים מִכָּל חֵטְא,
וּמְנֻקִּים מִכָּל עָוֹן, וּמְדֻבָּקִים בְּיִרְאָתֶֽךָ.
⁵ חָנֵּֽנוּ מֵאִתְּךָ דֵּעָה, בִּינָה וְהַשְׂכֵּל.
⁶ בָּרוּךְ אַתָּה, יְיָ, חוֹנֵן הַדָּֽעַת.

BRETTLER (BIBLE)

list are connected, since Shabbat is holy, ends at darkness, and is a sign of God's special relationship with Israel. Each of the first three pairs has a biblical basis: in Genesis 1:4, God distinguishes between light and darkness; in Leviticus 10:10, priests are told to distinguish between holy and ordinary; and in Leviticus 20:24, God distinguishes Israel from other nations. The only phrase without explicit biblical precedent is the fourth and climactic one distinguishing Shabbat from the six days of creation, but it is assumed here, and subsumed into the biblical pattern used for the other three.

⁴ *"Our father, our king"* God is called both "father" and "king" in the Bible, but these epithets are never used together, as they are here and elsewhere in the liturgy. The image of a tender "father" mitigates the concept of a powerful "king," making God more accessible and compassionate.

DORFF (THEOLOGY)

I thought people gain meaning in life. I told him that if people have overarching goals, then everything that they do to accomplish those goals takes on meaning. My high school biology course had relatively little meaning for me, for example, in that it was just the next thing students on the academic track took. By contrast, it had much deeper meaning for a friend who wanted to be a dentist. Perry agreed, but observed (I am quoting him exactly), "Your Bubbie [grandmother] and mine did not know about long-term goals." They did, however, know that the morning, afternoon, and evening services occurred in their proper set time; they also knew the round of seasons—the life cycle of a given year, if you like—and the life cycle of the people they loved. Punctuating time so as to discriminate one moment from another gave our grandmothers' lives meaning. In this prayer, then, we thank God for making distinctions that add meaning to our lives.

———◆———

ELLENSON (MODERN LITURGIES)

While most Reform liturgies exclude this prayer altogether, the generally more traditional Israeli Reform *Ha'avodah Shebalev* (1982) includes it, as do all Conservative prayer books, and the Siddurim of Reconstructionism and British Reform.

———◆———

FRANKEL (A WOMAN'S VOICE)

the nations of the world regards a new week with such trepidation as Your poor, driven children? We face the new week with new worries and cares, new fears and sorrows.... May it therefore be Your will, Almighty One, that You open for us the doors of compassion in the coming week.... (Rochel-Esther bas Avihayil of Jerusalem, quoted in Norman Tarnor, *A Book of Jewish Women's Prayers*, [Northvale, NJ: Jason Aronson, 1995], p. 50)

———◆———

GRAY (OUR TALMUDIC HERITAGE)

2. Akiba thinks it should be a fourth blessing unto itself.
3. Eliezer allocates it to the seventeenth blessing, *modim* ("Thanksgiving").

The Yerushalmi (Ber. 5:2, 9b) supports our practice (#1) by citing a rhetorical question asked by the Mishnah's reputed editor, Judah Hanasi (called, simply, "Rabbi"). The blessing in question ("Knowledge") is one of the thirteen intermediate ones, recited only on weekdays, but Rabbi had wondered why it is not recited on Shabbat, because "if there is no knowledge, how can we have prayer?" That is, without a discerning intellect, how can a person pray altogether? The Yerushalmi extends Rabbi's point: Without a discerning intellect, one can make no distinctions at all; so *Havdalah*, the prayer of distinguishing, is appropriately included within the blessing on knowledge.

That opinion did not immediately settle matters, however, as we see from the Babylonian Talmud (Ber. 29a), where the early fourth-century Amora Rabbah bar Shmuel still sides with Akiba, though we know of no one who does so today.

The Talmud (Ber. 33a) also discusses the relative merit of *Havdalah* at home and in the synagogue. Some regard *Havdalah* in the *Amidah* as having greater religious value. But the Talmud concludes that both are equally necessary.

—◆—

KUSHNER & POLEN (CHASIDISM)

Alenu. The logic seems obvious: if you lack discernment, how can you make distinctions?

The *S'fas Emes* (*Naso*, 5651) reminds us that there were *two* trees in the Garden of Eden: the tree of knowledge of good and evil and the tree of life. During the week we need to repair the tree of knowledge of good and evil from the damage done to it by Adam and Eve when they ate of its fruit. We do this by wearing the *t'fillin* of the head. With the phylactery set on our foreheads, we are again able to clarify, discern, distinguish, and make a distinction between good and evil. And, in this way, we restore the universe to its original harmony. For this reason, we also refrain from wearing *t'fillin* on Shabbat: Shabbat remains under the sway of the tree of life; Shabbat is already within redemptive time. Thus, on Shabbat, not only do we live under the tree of life, but our discernment of the difference between good and evil is also sustained. At this time, then, our prayer is to keep the knowledge we have attained on Shabbat intact throughout the entire week.

—◆—

LANDES (HALAKHAH)

century, France], "Positive Commandments" 29). It may also be that while both *Havdalah* and *Kiddush* are *d'ora'ita*, *Kiddush* is of greater significance (*Migdal Oz*, Rabbi Shem Tov Hasefardi, medieval Spain, Shab. 26) and takes priority if, for example, there is not enough wine for both.

Just announcing the end of Shabbat in our own words is sufficient to permit the doing of work. But since the *Anshei K'nesset Hag'dolah* (Men of the Great Assembly) have left us with a formal *Havdalah* formula, it should be used (*Minchat Chinukh*, an analytic commentary on the 613 commandments, by Yosef Babad, 1801–1874, Tarnapol, Safed).

Havdalah is said twice: (1) at home, in what is called *Havdalah al hakos* (pronounced hahv-dah-LAH ahl hah-KOHS), meaning "*Havdalah* over a cup [of wine]," and (2) here, the institutionalized synagogal prayer form of separating Shabbat from the week. (For *Havdalah* at home, see Volume 7, *Shabbat at Home*, pp. 164–165.) The first and major *Havdalah* is this one (*Havdalah* over wine at home came later), so even if one has already heard *Havdalah* at home, one must say it here in the *Amidah* (*Shulchan Arukh D'rav* of Shneur Zalman of Liadi, founder of Chabad Hasidism, nineteenth century, Russia, 294).

Atah chonantanu goes back to a debate between Rabbi Akiba, Rabbi Eliezer, and the anonymous "Sages" (the majority opinion). Akiba makes it as a blessing in its own right; Eliezer places it within the second to last blessing of the *Amidah* (the *Hoda'ah*, "Grateful Acknowledgment"); the Sages place it within the fourth blessing (*Binah*, "Knowledge") as we have it here, because "knowledge" implies the ability to distinguish (as Rashi says) "the holy from the profane, the pure from the impure." The Talmud supports the Sages' view by noting that we omit the middle petitionary blessings on Shabbat, but then begin adding them back into our *Amidah* on Saturday night. "Knowledge" (the first of those middle blessings) is therefore the first petition that we make during the new week—signaling the end of Shabbat (Ber. 33a).

Havdalah is not an easy prayer. Saying good-bye to sanctity and drawing distinctions is harsh. Perhaps that is why we surround the home *Havdalah* with intoxicating wine, fragrant spices, and the soft light of the candle. I write this close to the *siyyum* (completion) of the seven-year cycle of *Daf Yomi*, the talmudic page-a-day study, instituted by Rabbi Meir Shapiro (d. 1934), founder of the famed Yeshivah of Chochmei Lublin and member of the Polish Parliament (Sejm). I remember a remark made by him to my grandfather, the *M'nachem Tziyon* (Rabbi Menachem Sacks, Jerusalem, Chicago): "The Jews of America have learned to make *Kiddush*; they still need to learn to make *Havdalah*."

———◆———

L. Hoffman (History)

DISTINCTION BETWEEN SHABBAT (JUST PAST) AND ORDINARY WEEKDAY TIME (JUST BEGINNING).

[1] *The Amidah* The *Amidah* is considered a replacement for the *tamid* (pronounced tah-MEED), the daily sacrifice that was once offered mornings *(Shacharit)* and afternoons *(Minchah)*. Since there was no *tamid* for the evening *(Ma'ariv)*, the evening *Amidah* is theoretically optional—but only in theory; since the twelfth century, it has been considered required.

Kabbalah added reasons for this mandatory status, including the striking notion that the three daily recitations of the *Amidah* correspond to the three Pilgrimage Festivals (Passover, Shavuot, and Sukkot), each considered by Torah as a time to appear before God. *Ma'ariv* corresponds to the fall of night, so is likened to Sukkot, in that

Sukkot, coming in the autumn, anticipates the approaching long nights of winter. As a proof text, kabbalists pointed to the talmudic tradition that the *Ma'ariv Amidah* was ordained by Jacob, of whom it is said (Gen. 33:17), "He journeyed to [a place called] Sukkot."

Reciting the three instances of the *Amidah* recapitulates the uniqueness of all three times of year, each a unique opportunity for divine contact.

A further insight from Kabbalah comes from the fact that in the kabbalistic system (see Volume 8, *Kabbalat Shabbat* [*Welcoming Shabbat in Synagogue*], p. 36), the created universe parallels the emanation of God, which is identical with the ongoing flow of history, so that outstanding biblical personalities may be aligned with specific aspects of the divine. The three patriarchs are thus assigned positions in the divine map of creation, with Jacob standing for the *s'firah* known as *Tiferet* (pronounced tee-FEH-reht), the masculine principle through which blessing flows. The feminine principle is the tenth *s'firah*, *Malkhut* (pronounced mahl-KHOOT), known also as *Shekhinah*; as the last of the emanations, it is dependent upon the *s'firot* higher up for its light, so is functionally equivalent to night, which receives only reflected light from the moon. The *Ma'ariv Amidah*, specifically established by Jacob, thus spreads blessing in the form of light (from *Tiferet*) throughout the night *(Shekhinah)*. Without it, the night (the *Shekhinah*) would be darkened, and we, who receive our blessing from *Shekhinah* (the feminine principle), would be bereft.

———◆———

[On Shabbat, the middle benediction of the Amidah *reads as follows. For the thirteen middle blessings for weekdays that are superseded by this single Shabbat benediction, see Volume 2,* The Amidah, *pp. 95–99.]*

II. THE *K'DUSHAT HAYOM* ("SANCTIFICATION OF THE DAY") FOR SHABBAT *MA'ARIV*

[1] You sanctified the seventh day for your name, as the end of the creation of heaven and earth, and You blessed it beyond all other days and sanctified it beyond all other times, as is written in your Torah: [2] Heaven and earth and everything associated with them were completed. [3] On the seventh day, God completed the work He had done. On the seventh day, He rested from all the work He had done. [4] God blessed the seventh day and sanctified it, for on it He rested from all the work God created to do.

[5] Our God and our ancestors' God, accept our rest, [6] sanctify us through your commandments, and grant us a share in your Torah. [7] Satisfy us with your goodness, and gladden us with your salvation. [8] And purify our heart to serve You in truth. [9] And, Adonai our God, lovingly and adoringly grant us as our inheritance your holy Shabbat, that all of Israel, who sanctify your name, might rest on it. [10] Blessed are You, Adonai, who sanctifies Shabbat.

[1] אַתָּה קִדַּשְׁתָּ אֶת יוֹם הַשְּׁבִיעִי לִשְׁמֶךָ, תַּכְלִית מַעֲשֵׂה שָׁמַיִם וָאָרֶץ, וּבֵרַכְתּוֹ מִכָּל הַיָּמִים וְקִדַּשְׁתּוֹ מִכָּל הַזְּמַנִּים, וְכֵן כָּתוּב בְּתוֹרָתֶךָ: [2] וַיְכֻלּוּ הַשָּׁמַיִם וְהָאָרֶץ וְכָל צְבָאָם. [3] וַיְכַל אֱלֹהִים בַּיּוֹם הַשְּׁבִיעִי מְלַאכְתּוֹ אֲשֶׁר עָשָׂה, וַיִּשְׁבֹּת בַּיּוֹם הַשְּׁבִיעִי מִכָּל מְלַאכְתּוֹ אֲשֶׁר עָשָׂה. [4] וַיְבָרֶךְ אֱלֹהִים אֶת יוֹם הַשְּׁבִיעִי וַיְקַדֵּשׁ אֹתוֹ, כִּי בוֹ שָׁבַת מִכָּל מְלַאכְתּוֹ אֲשֶׁר בָּרָא אֱלֹהִים לַעֲשׂוֹת.

[5] אֱלֹהֵינוּ וֵאלֹהֵי אֲבוֹתֵינוּ, רְצֵה בִמְנוּחָתֵנוּ. [6] קַדְּשֵׁנוּ בְּמִצְוֹתֶיךָ, וְתֵן חֶלְקֵנוּ בְּתוֹרָתֶךָ; [7] שַׂבְּעֵנוּ מִטּוּבֶךָ, וְשַׂמְּחֵנוּ בִּישׁוּעָתֶךָ; [8] וְטַהֵר לִבֵּנוּ לְעָבְדְּךָ בֶּאֱמֶת. [9] וְהַנְחִילֵנוּ, יְיָ אֱלֹהֵינוּ, בְּאַהֲבָה וּבְרָצוֹן שַׁבַּת קָדְשֶׁךָ, וְיָנוּחוּ בָהּ יִשְׂרָאֵל מְקַדְּשֵׁי שְׁמֶךָ. [10] בָּרוּךְ אַתָּה, יְיָ, מְקַדֵּשׁ הַשַּׁבָּת.

BRETTLER (BIBLE)

[1] *"You sanctified"* The Bible contains cases where either God or Israel sanctifies the Sabbath. Genesis 2:1–4a has God sanctifying it. Jeremiah 17:22, among other places, has Israel doing so. "End" reflects the Genesis depiction of Shabbat as the final culminating act of creation. As the sequel to this creation story makes clear, even though other parts of creation are *blessed* (Genesis 1), only Shabbat is *sanctified*. This idea of having to *sanctify* Shabbat parallels the priestly notion found in Leviticus 19:2, instructing the Israelites "to be holy," because neither they nor Shabbat are intrinsically so. (See also Volume 7, *Shabbat at Home*, Brettler, "Sanctifies Shabbat," p. 96.   *(p. 124)*

DORFF (THEOLOGY)

[1] *"Creation of heaven and earth"* Creation, revelation, and redemption represent an ideological trilogy in Judaism. The blessings surrounding the *Sh'ma* address them (as to the meaning and importance of this trilogy, see my comments in Volume 1, *The Sh'ma and Its Blessings,*   *(p. 125)*

ELLENSON (MODERN LITURGIES)

[5] *"Our ancestors' God"* This blessing remains standard in non-Orthodox prayer books. But a number of them (e.g., Reconstructionist *Kol Haneshamah*, 1995) add the *imahot*, the "matriarchs" of the Jewish people.

———◆———

FRANKEL (A WOMAN'S VOICE)

[6] *"Grant us a share in your Torah"* In virtually all prayers that mention Shabbat, we find the same divine paradigm: God creates the world in six days and then rests on the seventh. Created in the divine image, we are commanded to model our behavior on God's, working for six days and then ceasing from our labor on the seventh day.

For Jewish men, Shabbat has long been a haven from relentless toil, a sanctuary in which to renew   *(p. 125)*

[For prayer instructions, see page 121.]

II. THE *K'DUSHAT HAYOM* ("SANCTIFICATION OF THE DAY") FOR SHABBAT *MA'ARIV*

[1] You sanctified the seventh day for your name, as the end of the creation of heaven and earth, and You blessed it beyond all other days and sanctified it beyond all other times, as is written in your Torah: [2] Heaven and earth and everything associated with them were completed. [3] On the seventh day, God

GRAY (OUR TALMUDIC HERITAGE)

[2–3] *"Heaven … completed … God completed"* Abudarham (fourteenth century, Spain) knows people who skip these verses, beginning only with the next one (verse 4), "God blessed." He objects because of the Talmud's dictum (Shab. 119b) that an individual who recites *"Heaven … completed"* (verse 1) makes himself a partner with God in the work of creation. In a different context, Abudarham admonishes us that reciting this verse serves as testimony that God created   *(p. 126)*

LANDES (HALAKHAH)

[2] *"Heaven and earth ... were completed [vay'khulu]"* This middle section of the *Amidah* consists of one blessing, *K'dushat Hayom*, which expresses the theme of the day. Every Shabbat *Amidah* has such a section, always ending with the *chatimah* (pronounced chah-tee-MAH, the final summary line of a blessing), "Blessed are You, Adonai, who sanctifies Shabbat." Though the endings are the same, the introductions vary, giving us different perspectives on Shabbat.   *(p. 126)*

L. HOFFMAN (HISTORY)

TEXT AND COMMENTARY FOR THE WEEKDAY MORNING AMIDAH *CAN BE FOUND IN VOLUME 2,* THE AMIDAH. *WE INCLUDE HERE JUST THE CHANGES REQUIRED FOR THE EVENING VERSION. THE MIDDLE THIRTEEN BLESSINGS (BLESSINGS 4–16) ARE THE SAME AS THOSE IN* SHACHARIT. *ON SHABBAT, HOWEVER, THOSE BLESSINGS, CONSIDERED PETITIONARY AND THEREFORE UNFITTING FOR SO SACRED A DAY, ARE REPLACED BY A SINGLE PRAYER (BOTH MORNING AND EVENING) CALLED* K'DUSHAT HAYOM *("SANCTIFICATION OF THE DAY"). THE* K'DUSHAT HAYOM *FOR FRIDAY NIGHT* MA'ARIV *IS* ATAH KIDASHTA, *"YOU SANCTIFIED [THE SEVENTH DAY]."*

¹אַתָּה קִדַּשְׁתָּ אֶת יוֹם הַשְּׁבִיעִי לִשְׁמֶךָ, תַּכְלִית מַעֲשֵׂה שָׁמַיִם וָאָרֶץ, וּבֵרַכְתּוֹ מִכָּל הַיָּמִים וְקִדַּשְׁתּוֹ מִכָּל הַזְּמַנִּים, וְכֵן כָּתוּב בְּתוֹרָתֶךָ: ²וַיְכֻלּוּ הַשָּׁמַיִם וְהָאָרֶץ וְכָל צְבָאָם. ³וַיְכַל אֱלֹהִים בַּיּוֹם הַשְּׁבִיעִי מְלַאכְתּוֹ אֲשֶׁר עָשָׂה, וַיִּשְׁבֹּת בַּיּוֹם הַשְּׁבִיעִי מִכָּל מְלַאכְתּוֹ אֲשֶׁר

¹*"You sanctified [atah kidashta] the seventh day"* The word *K'dushah* is widely employed to mean the third blessing of the *Amidah*. But liturgically, there are two kinds of *K'dushah*: *K'dushat Hashem* (pronounced k'-doo-SHAHT hah-SHEHM), meaning "Sanctification of the Name" (declaring the holiness of God); and *K'dushat Hayom* (k'-doo-SHAHT hah-YOHM), "Sanctification of the Day" (announcing the holiness of Shabbat or a festival). The "Sanctification of the Name" denotes the third blessing of the *Amidah* and is recognizable by its summary *chatimah* (final *Barukh* line in a blessing): "Blessed are You, Adonai, the holy God." The "Sanctification of the Day" is any blessing for Shabbat   *(p. 127)*

completed the work He had done. On the seventh day, He rested from all the work He had done. [4] God blessed the seventh day and sanctified it, for on it He rested from all the work God created to do.

[5] Our God and our ancestors' God, accept our rest, [6] sanctify us through your commandments, and grant us a share in your Torah. [7] Satisfy us with your goodness, and gladden us with your salvation. [8] And purify our heart to serve You in truth. [9] And, Adonai our God, lovingly and adoringly grant us as our inheritance your holy Shabbat, that all of Israel, who sanctify your name, might rest on it. [10] Blessed are You, Adonai, who sanctifies Shabbat.

עָשָׂה. 4וַיְבָרֶךְ אֱלֹהִים אֶת יוֹם הַשְּׁבִיעִי וַיְקַדֵּשׁ אֹתוֹ, כִּי בוֹ שָׁבַת מִכָּל מְלַאכְתּוֹ אֲשֶׁר בָּרָא אֱלֹהִים לַעֲשׂוֹת.

5אֱלֹהֵינוּ וֵאלֹהֵי אֲבוֹתֵינוּ, רְצֵה בִמְנוּחָתֵנוּ. 6קַדְּשֵׁנוּ בְּמִצְוֹתֶיךָ, וְתֵן חֶלְקֵנוּ בְּתוֹרָתֶךָ; 7שַׂבְּעֵנוּ מִטּוּבֶךָ, וְשַׂמְּחֵנוּ בִּישׁוּעָתֶךָ; 8וְטַהֵר לִבֵּנוּ לְעָבְדְּךָ בֶּאֱמֶת. 9וְהַנְחִילֵנוּ, יְיָ אֱלֹהֵינוּ, בְּאַהֲבָה וּבְרָצוֹן שַׁבַּת קָדְשֶׁךָ, וְיָנוּחוּ בָהּ יִשְׂרָאֵל מְקַדְּשֵׁי שְׁמֶךָ. 10בָּרוּךְ אַתָּה, יְיָ, מְקַדֵּשׁ הַשַּׁבָּת.

BRETTLER (BIBLE)

[5] *"Accept our rest"* Using the technical verb *r'tseh* ("accept"), elsewhere found with sacrifices, in which God "takes pleasure." Clearly, for the author of this prayer, Shabbat takes the place of these biblical sacrifices.

[7] *"Satisfy … gladden"* Both phrases appear biblically in eschatological contexts (Jer. 31:14; Isa. 25:9), making this prayer implicitly a request for eschatological salvation.

[8] *"Purify our heart to serve"* From Psalm 51:12, "Fashion a pure heart for me, O God," and 1 Samuel 12:24, "Above all, you must revere Adonai and serve Him faithfully with all your heart."

[9] *"Grant us as our inheritance"* Biblically, the verb *n.ch.l* is used in the context of apportioning property, usually in the Land of Israel. Its use here suggests that possession of the holy Shabbat is an appropriate surrogate for possession of the holy Land of Israel. "Your holy Shabbat" is mentioned in Nehemiah 9:14 in a list of gifts bestowed upon Israel by God.

[9] *"Who sanctify your name"* Nowadays, the idiom suggests *kiddush hashem*, a technical medieval term for martyrdom; here, it means simply sanctifying God through praise and observance of the commandments.

[10] *"Who sanctifies Shabbat"* A poetic recapitulation of the opening theme: it is God who sanctifies Shabbat.

◆

DORFF (THEOLOGY)

pp. 112–113). So, too, do the middle sections of the Shabbat *Amidah*. Here, in the evening service, we find creation, beginning with verse 1, and continuing with a citation of Genesis 2:1–3 (vv. 2–4, here). The middle section of the Shabbat morning *(Shacharit) Amidah* celebrates revelation and the gift of Shabbat that makes Moses rejoice and that distinguishes Jews from non-Jews. The Shabbat afternoon *(Minchah) Amidah* anticipates redemption, when the One true God will be recognized throughout the world, so that, following God's will, we will know universal peace.

◆

FRANKEL (A WOMAN'S VOICE)

body and spirit before returning to daily pressures. But for women, Shabbat may just intensify such working pressure. The house must be cleaned and set in order; food must be purchased, prepared, served, and put away; guests must be accommodated and hospitality reciprocated. Children need to be cleaned and specially dressed. All this and—increasingly, nowadays—a full-time career that does not stop for Friday preparation time!

What, then, of a woman's own spiritual needs, her need for rest? Women must truly take to heart the petition articulated within the third paragraph of this prayer: "Grant us a share in your Torah." If we delight in our rest, then God will as well. We say to God, "Accept our rest ... and purify our heart to serve You truth." What a perfect recipe for sanity!

◆

GRAY (OUR TALMUDIC HERITAGE)

the world in six days and rested on the seventh. We stand while saying it, because witnesses in court give testimony standing (Deut. 19:17 refers to the witnesses "standing" to testify).

(For further traditions associated with these verses, see Volume 7, *Shabbat at Home*, Gray, pp. 93, 100–102.)

[8] *"Purify our heart to serve You in truth"* Abudarham links "heart" and "purity" by means of Psalm 51:12 ("God created in me a pure heart"). On the strength of the talmudic principle that "the one who wishes to be purified will receive help from heaven" (Yoma 38b), we ask God to purify our hearts for divine service.

The addition of "in truth" stems from Jeremiah's reference (10:10) to the "God of truth."

[10] *"Blessed are You … who sanctifies Shabbat"* The parallel conclusion for *yom tov* (a holy day) is, "Blessed are You who sanctifies Israel and the *z'manim* ['times'']." Why is Israel not mentioned in the Shabbat conclusion also? The eighth-century Palestinian work *Massekhet Soferim* 13:14 explains that Shabbat preceded Israel chronologically. God created Shabbat on the seventh day, after all, long before there was Israel. The holidays, however, were not part of creation; Israel must declare them in accord with the lunar calendar that it observes, from year to year. There is reason, therefore, to link holidays to Israel, but not Shabbat.

———◆———

LANDES (HALAKHAH)

Friday night emphasizes the theme of creation, Shabbat being the *takhlit* (pronounced tahkh-LEET), the "epitome" and purpose of creation. So our blessing contains *Vay'khulu*, the account of creation from Genesis 1. The Talmud (Shab.119b) vocalizes it *vay'khalu* (active voice) not *vay'khulu* (passive), so as to imply, "They [God and human beings] finish [creation]"—that is, by reciting *Vay'khulu* (= *vay'khalu*) Friday night, we become God's active, not passive, partner in the act of creation. Creation needs both the actual doing (by God) and its acknowledgment (by man), for it to be a divine act. So the first two paragraphs of our prayer center upon God's act of creation, sealed, as it were, by man's equally active witness.

The *K'dushat Hayom* replaces the thirteen middle blessings of petition (see Volume 2, *The Amidah*, pp. 95–147), which are omitted on Shabbat because they are considered a *tirkha* (pronounced teer-KHAH, but, commonly, TEER-khah), "a bother or burden" that interferes with *k'vod Shabbat*, "respect for Shabbat." Abudarham (fourteenth century, Spain) objects further that the petitionary blessings evoke our deficiencies, lacks, needs, and suffering, the very thought of which causes pain on a day when we are to avoid pain. Thus the Palestinian Talmud (Shab. 15:3) states: "It is forbidden to demand or seek one's needs on Shabbat."

⁵ *"Rest"* The third paragraph of the middle *Amidah* blessing concentrates on the halakhic implication of our duty to rest on Shabbat. Two terms are employed for rest: *shabbat* and *m'nuchah*. The first connotes cessation from labor—indeed, the modern Hebrew word for strike, *sh'vitah*, is derived from it. The second term, *m'nuchah*, connotes "letting go." Halakhically they refer to two forms of rest: "ceasing" from weekday acts of creation and work; and "letting go" of discussion about such activities. A third term, *vayinafash* (from Exod. 31:17) occurs in the *Shacharit* service and in the introduction to the *Kiddush (Kiddusha Rabbah)* for Shabbat day (see Volume 7, *Shabbat at Home*, p. 155). It can be translated as "to en-soul," connoting positive, spiritual activities (e.g., *Kiddush*, Torah study, festive eating) that are to be done on Shabbat.

◆

L. HOFFMAN (HISTORY)

and holidays that ends, "Blessed are You, Adonai, who sanctifies [the day in question]." We have three of these: (1) the middle blessing of the *Amidah*, (2) the *Kiddush* for the eve of Shabbat and holidays, and (3) the last blessing over the *Haftarah*.

The "Sanctification of the Day" is the same for all holiday services, but surprisingly it varies from service to service on Shabbat. Its style is generally similar: (1) a variable introduction (*Atah kidashta* ["You sanctified …"], here; *Atah echad* ["You are One …"] for *Minchah*—see p. 201); and (2) an invariable final paragraph (beginning "Our God and our ancestors' God, accept our rest," and ending with the necessary *chatimah* for a "Sanctification of the Day" ("Blessed … who sanctifies Shabbat"—see below, "Who sanctifies Shabbat").

In between (1) and (2), we get (3) a variable citation from Torah dealing with Shabbat. Here *(Ma'ariv)* we have an account of Shabbat being created (Genesis 2:1–3): "Heaven and earth … were completed." The *Shacharit* service features the commandment to keep Shabbat (Exod. 31:16–17): "The children of Israel shall keep Shabbat….") The *Musaf* service, which in general has retained its original thematic connection to the sacrificial cult, provides Numbers 28:9–10, an account of the offerings required at the Temple.

But having a different version for each and every Shabbat service over a twenty-four-hour period is a relatively late innovation. The tenth-century Gaon, Saadiah, remarks, "I have found a custom [!] whereby the middle blessing for the *Amidah* of the four Shabbat services varies from service to service." It was just a local custom at the time, apparently. The custom goes back at least a century earlier, when another Gaon, Natronai, was asked whether it was necessary to alter the blessing depending on the service. Natronai responds that Babylonian custom did indeed feature different blessings, but the one he names for *Ma'ariv* is not the one we have here.

The interesting philosophical issue is the extent to which custom determines practice. Amram composed our very first prayer book in 860 C.E., with the express intent of forcing Babylonian customs on Palestinian Jews, who still considered their own Talmud (the *Yerushalmi*), not the Babylonian version (the *Bavli*), definitive and who prayed quite differently from Jews in the geonic academies in and around Baghdad. But there is no reason to believe that Palestinian Jews capitulated to him, and still in Saadiah's day (mid-tenth century), manuscript copies of prayer books were rare, and localisms prevailed. Even in Babylonia itself, custom must have varied over time, since in the case we are talking about here, Saadiah seems surprised by a custom that Natronai, about fifty years before, already knew.

Saadiah—a well-traveled Gaon who had lived and worked in Egypt, Palestine, and Babylonia—generally accepted localisms as long as there was no overriding reason to oppose them (as long, that is, as they followed certain aesthetic strictures that he considered proper and did not support the Karaite schism, against which Saadiah polemicized with vigor). The last two great Babylonian leaders, Sherira and Hai Gaon (968–1038), were even more open to liturgical diversity.

But conditions hardened thereafter, especially in western Europe, where communities in present-day Spain, Provence, France, and Germany forged their own unique way of praying and composed written prayer books and commentaries that justified their local customs. The growth of fixed and firm prayer wording is a direct result of the spread of manuscript prayer books, which itself was fueled by the need for local communities to develop their own sense of identity. To this day, "How we pray is who we are"—that is, local communities pride themselves on one set of words rather than another, and become vociferously upset at attempts to change even the tiniest liturgical custom that they consider sacrosanct.

[10] *"Who sanctifies Shabbat"* This concludes the middle benediction specifically for Shabbat. The parallel for holidays differs, not only because it mentions "holidays" instead of "Shabbat," but because it inserts the word "Israel": "Blessed are You, Adonai, who sanctifies *Israel and* the holidays." The standard halakhic explanation for the added word is that unlike Shabbat, which falls unfailingly (by definition) every seventh day, holidays depend for their timing on the moon. Judaism keeps a solar year, but lunar months, each one roughly 29½ days in duration. Months must therefore, in practice, be rounded off to be either 29 or 30 days. Since the fourth century, the length of the months has been mathematically set so that we do not have to worry about it all the time, but before that, the beginning of each month had to be established by observation. The exact day of Passover, for instance, a holiday that falls in the middle of the month, would not be known until Jewish officials declared the month to have begun (on either the thirtieth or the thirty-first day after the beginning of the month before). The day of the new moon was itself a holy day, so when the new moon appeared in the sky (on the night of the twenty-ninth or the thirtieth day—it had to be one or the other), the officials in charge would announce, *m'kudash*, "It [the moon] is sanctified." In that sense, Israel sanctifies the holidays, which fall when they do only because of an official declaration. That is said to be why "Israel" is mentioned prior to "the holidays" in the festival version of the prayer.

The explanation is appealing, if only because of the theological implications of our own human role (with God) in establishing the sacred.

It is not historically valid, however. The Genizah fragments show us that Jews in Eretz Yisrael included "Israel" in the concluding line for Shabbat as well: "Blessed are You, Adonai, who sanctifies Israel and Shabbat."

The full blessing, which is quite lovely, goes as follows:

> Adonai our God, out of the love with which You have loved your People Israel, and, our king, out of the care with which You have cared for the children of your covenant … You have given us this great and holy seventh day in love, for greatness, for holiness, for rest, for thanksgiving, for a sign of the covenant, and to give us your peace and blessing. Blessed are you, Adonai, who sanctifies Israel and Shabbat.

♦ ♦ ♦

[The final blessing of the Minchah and Ma'ariv Amidah reads as follows. For the Shacharit form of the blessing, see Volume 2, The Amidah, pp. 176–178.]

III. THE *MA'ARIV* BLESSING FOR PEACE: *BIRKAT SHALOM*

[1] Let it be great peace that You give your people forever, for You are king and master of all peace, and You see fit to bless your People Israel with your peace every hour and every minute. *[2] Blessed are You, Adonai, who blesses his People Israel with peace.

שָׁ¹לוֹם רָב עַל יִשְׂרָאֵל עַמְּךָ תָּשִׂים לְעוֹלָם, כִּי אַתָּה הוּא מֶלֶךְ אָדוֹן לְכָל הַשָּׁלוֹם, וְטוֹב בְּעֵינֶיךָ לְבָרֵךְ אֶת עַמְּךָ יִשְׂרָאֵל בְּכָל עֵת וּבְכָל שָׁעָה בִּשְׁלוֹמֶךָ. ²בָּרוּךְ אַתָּה, יְיָ, הַמְבָרֵךְ אֶת עַמּוֹ יִשְׂרָאֵל בַּשָּׁלוֹם.

[*From Rosh Hashanah to Yom Kippur, substitute the following:]

[3] Let it be the book of life, blessing and peace, and good fortune, in which we are remembered and written before You, we and all your people the house of Israel, for good life and for peace. [4] Blessed are You, Adonai, who creates peace.

³בְּסֵפֶר חַיִּים, בְּרָכָה וְשָׁלוֹם וּפַרְנָסָה טוֹבָה, נִזָּכֵר וְנִכָּתֵב לְפָנֶיךָ, אֲנַחְנוּ וְכָל עַמְּךָ בֵּית יִשְׂרָאֵל, לְחַיִּים טוֹבִים וּלְשָׁלוֹם. ⁴בָּרוּךְ אַתָּה, יְיָ, עוֹשֶׂה הַשָּׁלוֹם.

BRETTLER (BIBLE)

[1] *"Let it be great peace"* The prayer opens with a democratization of Psalm 119:165: "Those who love your teaching enjoy well-being; they encounter no adversity." The wish that this be "forever" may reflect eschatological prophecies such as Ezekiel 37:26, "I will make a covenant of friendship [*shalom*] with them—it shall be an everlasting covenant with them." Most kings use their might to battle others; the sentiment here, following Psalm 29:10–11, is that God, as king, is a peacemaker, assuring Israel's well-being. (See Brettler, "Adonai will give strength… peace," Volume 8, *Kabbalat Shabbat* [*Welcoming Shabbat in the Synagogue*], p. 103.)

—◆—

DORFF (THEOLOGY)

[1] *Let it be great peace* … The parallel blessing in the morning, when we face a whole new day, is fuller, asking God not only for peace but for "grace, kindness, and mercy … Torah of life, a love of grace, righteousness, blessing, mercy, life, and peace." By evening we have dealt with the day's challenges, but still, we are left with the request for peace. That is no small matter: as the Rabbis contend, "Great is peace, for all blessings are contained in it…. Great is peace, for God's name is peace" (Num. Rab. 11:7).

—◆—

[For prayer instructions, see page 131.]

III. THE *MA'ARIV* BLESSING FOR PEACE: *BIRKAT SHALOM*

[1] Let it be great peace that You give your people forever, for You are king and master of all peace, and You see fit to bless your People Israel with your peace every hour and every minute. *[2] Blessed are You, Adonai, who blesses his People Israel with peace.

GRAY (OUR TALMUDIC HERITAGE)

[1] *"Let it be great peace"* In the *Shacharit* service (see Volume 2, *The Amidah*, pp. 177–178), the blessing for peace begins with *Sim shalom* ("Grant peace"), not *Shalom rav* ("Let it be great peace"). It also includes the Priestly Blessing, which is missing in the evening service. Moses Isserles (the R'ma, 1525–1575, Poland) says (O. Ch. 127:2) that *Sim shalom* occurs alongside the Priestly Blessing because that blessing expresses the hope, *v'yasem lekha shalom* ("and [may God] grant you peace"); *(p. 134)*

LANDES (HALAKHAH)

[1] *"Great peace"* This version is recited by Ashkenazim for *Minchah* and *Ma'ariv* (*R'ma* 127:3), except when *Minchah* includes (1) a Priestly Blessing *(Birkat Kohanim)*, for example, on fast days, (2) a weekday Torah reading (*Kri'at Hatorah*)—again, on fast days—in which case, we recite *Sim Shalom*. The latter version includes the phrase "for in the light of your face" which can refer to blessing or to the Torah itself.

The *Arukh Hashulchan* 127:4 (Yechiel Michal Epstein, 1829–1888, Russia) opines that *Shalom Rav* is a

L. HOFFMAN (HISTORY)

TEXT AND COMMENTARY FOR THE WEEKDAY MORNING AMIDAH CAN BE FOUND IN VOLUME 2, THE AMIDAH. WE INCLUDE HERE JUST THE CHANGES REQUIRED FOR THE EVENING VERSION. OF THE FINAL THREE BLESSINGS (BLESSINGS 17–19), THE FIRST TWO ARE THE SAME AS THOSE OF THE MORNING. THE LAST BLESSING, HOWEVER, CALLED BIRKAT SHALOM ("THE BLESSING FOR PEACE") OR BIRKAT KOHANIM ("THE PRIESTLY BLESSING"), CHANGES. THE ACTUAL PRIESTLY BENEDICTION FROM NUMBERS 6:24–26 IS OMITTED; AND INSTEAD OF THE VERSION STARTING SIM SHALOM ("GRANT US PEACE"), WE SAY SHALOM RAV ("GREAT PEACE").

◆

שָׁלוֹם רָב עַל יִשְׂרָאֵל עַמְּךָ תָּשִׂים לְעוֹלָם, כִּי אַתָּה הוּא מֶלֶךְ אָדוֹן לְכָל הַשָּׁלוֹם, וְטוֹב בְּעֵינֶיךָ לְבָרֵךְ אֶת עַמְּךָ יִשְׂרָאֵל בְּכָל עֵת וּבְכָל שָׁעָה בִּשְׁלוֹמֶךָ. ²בָּרוּךְ אַתָּה, יְיָ, הַמְבָרֵךְ אֶת עַמּוֹ יִשְׂרָאֵל בַּשָּׁלוֹם.

J. HOFFMAN (TRANSLATION)

[1] *"Let it be great peace"* The Hebrew emphasizes "great peace," and we try to do the same in English (as one might hope, "Let it be me who wins the lottery this time").

[1] *"Hour ... minute"* The two words in Hebrew both roughly mean "time." We don't have two such words in English, so we resort to "hour" and "minute," which, in this context, combine to capture the point of the Hebrew.

darker version of the prayer, suitable for a regular *Minchah* and *Ma'ariv*, which are known as "a time of judgment" *(sha'at din)*. He is left in a quandary, however, as to why *Shalom Rav* would be recited on *Ma'ariv* of Friday night *(lel Shabbat)*, which is certainly *not* a time of judgment.

◆

◆ ◆ ◆

[*From Rosh Hashanah to Yom Kippur, substitute the following:]

³ Let it be the book of life, blessing and peace, and good fortune, in which we are remembered and written before You, we and all your people the house of Israel, for good life and for peace. ⁴ Blessed are You, Adonai, who creates peace.

³בְּסֵפֶר חַיִּים, בְּרָכָה וְשָׁלוֹם וּפַרְנָסָה טוֹבָה, נִזָּכֵר וְנִכָּתֵב לְפָנֶיךָ, אֲנַחְנוּ וְכָל עַמְּךָ בֵּית יִשְׂרָאֵל, לְחַיִּים טוֹבִים וּלְשָׁלוֹם. ⁴בָּרוּךְ אַתָּה, יְיָ, עוֹשֵׂה הַשָּׁלוֹם.

GRAY (OUR TALMUDIC HERITAGE)

v'yasem comes from the same root as *sim*. Otherwise, he concludes, we default to the *Shalom rav* version.

◆

134

MA'ARIV (WEEKDAY AND SHABBAT)

[On Shabbat, after the Amidah, continue here, after which, say the synagogue Kiddush (p. 151). On weekdays, continue with a Full Kaddish (Kaddish Shalem) and Alenu (for text, see Volume 6, Tachanun and Concluding Prayers, pp. 129–133).]

E. MAGEN AVOT ("PROTECTING OUR ANCESTORS")

[1] Heaven and earth and everything associated with them were completed. [2] On the seventh day, God completed the work He had done. On the seventh day, He rested from all the work He had done. [3] God blessed the seventh day and sanctified it, for on it He rested from all the work God created to do. [4] Blessed are You, Adonai, our God and our ancestors' God: Abraham's God, Isaac's God, and Jacob's God, great, mighty, and revered God, creator of heaven and earth.

[5] Protecting our ancestors with his word, reviving the dead with his speech, He is the unequaled holy God, [6] who lets his people rest on his holy day of Shabbat, for He loves them, letting them rest. [7] We will serve Him with awe and fear, and gratefully acknowledge his name every day forever, with the blessings. [8] God of grateful acknowledgment, master of peace, He sanctifies Shabbat and blesses the seventh day, and in holiness lets this joyful people rest, in memory of acts of creation.

[9] Our God and our ancestors' God, accept our rest, sanctify us through your commandments, and grant us a share in your Torah. [10] Satisfy us with your goodness, and gladden us with your salvation. And purify our heart to serve You in truth. [11] And, Adonai our God, lovingly and adoringly grant us as our inheritance your holy Shabbat, that all of Israel, who sanctify your name, might rest on it. [12] Blessed are You, Adonai, who sanctifies Shabbat.

וַ[1] יְכֻלּוּ הַשָּׁמַיִם וְהָאָרֶץ וְכָל צְבָאָם. [2] וַיְכַל אֱלֹהִים בַּיּוֹם הַשְּׁבִיעִי מְלַאכְתּוֹ אֲשֶׁר עָשָׂה, וַיִּשְׁבֹּת בַּיּוֹם הַשְּׁבִיעִי מִכָּל מְלַאכְתּוֹ אֲשֶׁר עָשָׂה. [3] וַיְבָרֶךְ אֱלֹהִים אֶת יוֹם הַשְּׁבִיעִי וַיְקַדֵּשׁ אֹתוֹ, כִּי בוֹ שָׁבַת מִכָּל מְלַאכְתּוֹ אֲשֶׁר בָּרָא אֱלֹהִים לַעֲשׂוֹת.

[4] בָּרוּךְ אַתָּה, יְיָ אֱלֹהֵינוּ וֵאלֹהֵי אֲבוֹתֵינוּ, אֱלֹהֵי אַבְרָהָם, אֱלֹהֵי יִצְחָק, וֵאלֹהֵי יַעֲקֹב, הָאֵל הַגָּדוֹל הַגִּבּוֹר וְהַנּוֹרָא, אֵל עֶלְיוֹן, קוֹנֵה שָׁמַיִם וָאָרֶץ.

[5] מָגֵן אָבוֹת בִּדְבָרוֹ, מְחַיֶּה מֵתִים בְּמַאֲמָרוֹ, הָאֵל הַקָּדוֹשׁ שֶׁאֵין כָּמוֹהוּ. [6] הַמֵּנִיחַ לְעַמּוֹ בְּיוֹם שַׁבַּת קָדְשׁוֹ, כִּי בָם רָצָה לְהָנִיחַ לָהֶם. [7] לְפָנָיו נַעֲבֹד בְּיִרְאָה וָפַחַד, וְנוֹדֶה לִשְׁמוֹ בְּכָל יוֹם תָּמִיד מֵעֵין הַבְּרָכוֹת. [8] אֵל הַהוֹדָאוֹת, אֲדוֹן הַשָּׁלוֹם, מְקַדֵּשׁ הַשַּׁבָּת וּמְבָרֵךְ שְׁבִיעִי, וּמֵנִיחַ בִּקְדֻשָּׁה לְעַם מְדֻשְּׁנֵי עֹנֶג, זֵכֶר לְמַעֲשֵׂה בְרֵאשִׁית.

[9] אֱלֹהֵינוּ וֵאלֹהֵי אֲבוֹתֵינוּ, רְצֵה בִמְנוּחָתֵנוּ; קַדְּשֵׁנוּ בְּמִצְוֹתֶיךָ, וְתֵן חֶלְקֵנוּ בְּתוֹרָתֶךָ; [10] שַׂבְּעֵנוּ מִטּוּבֶךָ, וְשַׂמְּחֵנוּ בִּישׁוּעָתֶךָ; וְטַהֵר לִבֵּנוּ לְעָבְדְּךָ

136

בֶּאֱמֶת: [11]וְהַנְחִילֵנוּ, יְיָ אֱלֹהֵינוּ, בְּאַהֲבָה וּבְרָצוֹן שַׁבַּת קָדְשֶׁךָ, וְיָנוּחוּ בָהּ יִשְׂרָאֵל מְקַדְּשֵׁי שְׁמֶךָ. [12]בָּרוּךְ אַתָּה, יְיָ, מְקַדֵּשׁ הַשַּׁבָּת.

BRETTLER (BIBLE)

[4] *"Creator of heaven and earth"* Genesis 14:19.

[5] *"Protecting our ancestors"* The blessing to Abram in Genesis 15:1, "I am a shield to you," is extended to all the patriarchs.

[5] *"Reviving the dead"* Similar sentiment is found in Akkadian prayers that request restoring the gravely ill to good health. That is its biblical meaning too. Only rabbinically did it come to mean reviving the dead.

[5] *"The unequaled holy God"* Based on Hannah's prayer (1 Sam. 2:2), "There is no holy one like Adonai."

[7] *"We will serve Him with awe and fear"* As *(p. 141)*

DORFF (THEOLOGY)

[4] *"Creator of heaven and earth"* An abbreviated version of the *Amidah* that succinctly identifies the theme of the middle section of Friday night's *Amidah* as creation. See above, "Creation of heaven and earth." *(p. 141)*

ELLENSON (MODERN LITURGIES)

[4] *"Our ancestors' God"* The trend toward gender-inclusiveness causes virtually all current non-Orthodox prayer books to mention also the *imahot*, "[fore]mothers," wherever "God of our [fore]fathers" is found. While one would expect these changes *(p. 142)*

FRANKEL (A WOMAN'S VOICE)

Magen Avot In this prayer, we praise God for "protecting our ancestors" *(magen avot)*. Yet unlike shields made by human craftsmen, this one consists of the word of God *(d'varo)*, which not only protects our ancestors, but also revives the dead *(m'chayei metim)*.

In premodern times, resurrection of the dead had considerable currency among the Jewish common folk, offering them a second chance for happiness, beyond the misery they often experienced in their *(p. 143)*

[For prayer instructions, see page 136.]

E. MAGEN AVOT ("PROTECTING OUR ANCESTORS")

[1] Heaven and earth and everything associated with them were completed. [2] On the seventh day, God completed the work He had done. On the seventh day, He rested from all the work He had done. [3] God blessed the seventh day and sanctified it, for on it He rested from all the work God created to do.

GRAY (OUR TALMUDIC HERITAGE)

[4] *"Creator of heaven and earth"* [koneh shamayim va'aretz] The Hebrew *koneh* is a unique appellation for God, found only twice in the Bible (Gen. 14:19 and 22), both in the context of the same narrative: Abraham's (still called "Abram") war with the kings of Canaan. After the final battle, Abram is blessed by Melchizedek, the king of Salem, who refers to God as the *koneh* of heaven and earth. In his public declaration that he will not accept any booty from the war for himself, and taking *(p. 143)*

KUSHNER & POLEN (CHASIDISM)

[1] *"Heaven and earth ... were completed"* When Yechiel Yehoshuah ben Yerachmiel Tzvi of Biala (the Bialer rebbe), a descendant of the *Yehudi Hakadosh* of Przysucha, and author of *Siddur Chelkat Yehoshuah*, would make *kiddush*, he would call heaven and earth to testify that God had created them. Then a great awesomeness would fall upon all who were present, for they would all sense the presence of the *Shekhinah*. (Some say that those present could even see the *Shekhinah*   *(p. 145)*

וַיְכֻלּוּ הַשָּׁמַיִם וְהָאָרֶץ וְכָל צְבָאָם. [1] וַיְכַל אֱלֹהִים בַּיּוֹם הַשְּׁבִיעִי מְלַאכְתּוֹ אֲשֶׁר עָשָׂה, וַיִּשְׁבֹּת בַּיּוֹם הַשְּׁבִיעִי מִכָּל מְלַאכְתּוֹ אֲשֶׁר עָשָׂה. [2] וַיְבָרֶךְ אֱלֹהִים אֶת יוֹם הַשְּׁבִיעִי וַיְקַדֵּשׁ אֹתוֹ, כִּי בוֹ שָׁבַת מִכָּל מְלַאכְתּוֹ אֲשֶׁר בָּרָא אֱלֹהִים לַעֲשׂוֹת. [3]

LANDES (HALAKHAH)

[1] *"Heaven and earth ... were completed [vay'khulu]"* This section from Genesis 1 is recited three times on Friday night: (1) privately, within the *Amidah* (p. 113); (2) communally, after the *Amidah* (here); and (3) at home, as part of the *Kiddush* (see Volume 7, *Shabbat at Home*, p. 91). Its significance is that it makes the reciter God's partner in creation (see "Heaven and earth ... were completed [*vay'khulu*]," p. 123). It is recited silently within the *Amidah* (1) because it defines prayer for   *(p. 146)*

L. HOFFMAN (HISTORY)

THE MA'ARIV AMIDAH *NORMALLY RECEIVES NO READER'S REPETITION. BUT ON FRIDAY NIGHT, IT IS FOLLOWED BY A UNIQUE FORM OF* AMIDAH *(CALLED* MEI'EIN*), WHICH USES A SINGLE BLESSING (RATHER THAN SEVEN) TO EXPRESS THE SEVEN BLESSINGS OF THE* SHABBAT AMIDAH. *IT IS THEREFORE CALLED A* B'RACHAH ACHAT MEI'EIN SHEVA *("ONE BLESSING IN PLACE OF SEVEN"), BUT KNOWN ALSO BY THE TWO KEY WORDS OF VERSE 5,* MAGEN AVOT.

Magen Avot ("Protecting Our Ancestors") Halakhah goes to great lengths to explain this prayer, which seems to be an altogether   *(p. 147)*

J. HOFFMAN (TRANSLATION)

[4] *"Creator"* See Volume 1, *The Sh'ma and Its Blessings*, "Your creatures," pp. 49–50.

[5] *"Protecting our ancestors"* We would like to translate this phrase as "Our ancestors' protector," to make clear the connection between this line and the end of our standard version of *Avot* ("Abraham's protector"; see Volume 2, *The Amidah*, p. 62). In both places the Hebrew construction is the same. But translating "Our ancestors' protector" would make it awkward to introduce the adverbial "with his word" ("Our ancestors' with-his-word-protector...").

[5] *"He is"* The Hebrew is not actually a sentence. We add these words to make the English grammatical.   *(p. 149)*

[4] Blessed are You, Adonai, our God and our ancestors' God: Abraham's God, Isaac's God, and Jacob's God, great, mighty, and revered God, creator of heaven and earth.

[5] Protecting our ancestors with his word, reviving the dead with his speech, He is the unequaled holy God, [6] who lets his people rest on his holy day of Shabbat, for He loves them, letting them rest. [7] We will serve Him with awe and fear, and gratefully acknowledge his name every day forever, with the blessings. [8] God of grateful acknowledgment, master of peace, He sanctifies Shabbat and blesses the seventh day, and in holiness lets this joyful people rest, in memory of acts of creation.

[9] Our God and our ancestors' God, accept our rest, sanctify us through your commandments, and grant us a share in your Torah. [10] Satisfy us with your goodness, and gladden us with your salvation. And purify our heart to serve You in truth. [11] And, Adonai our God, lovingly and adoringly grant us as our inheritance your holy Shabbat, that all of Israel, who sanctify your name, might rest on it. [12] Blessed are You, Adonai, who sanctifies Shabbat.

[4] בָּרוּךְ אַתָּה, יְיָ אֱלֹהֵינוּ וֵאלֹהֵי אֲבוֹתֵינוּ, אֱלֹהֵי אַבְרָהָם, אֱלֹהֵי יִצְחָק, וֵאלֹהֵי יַעֲקֹב. הָאֵל הַגָּדוֹל הַגִּבּוֹר וְהַנּוֹרָא, אֵל עֶלְיוֹן, קוֹנֵה שָׁמַיִם וָאָרֶץ.

[5] מָגֵן אָבוֹת בִּדְבָרוֹ, מְחַיֶּה מֵתִים בְּמַאֲמָרוֹ, הָאֵל הַקָּדוֹשׁ שֶׁאֵין כָּמוֹהוּ. [6] הַמֵּנִיחַ לְעַמּוֹ בְּיוֹם שַׁבַּת קָדְשׁוֹ, כִּי בָם רָצָה לְהָנִיחַ לָהֶם. [7] לְפָנָיו נַעֲבֹד בְּיִרְאָה וָפַחַד, וְנוֹדֶה לִשְׁמוֹ בְּכָל יוֹם תָּמִיד מֵעֵין הַבְּרָכוֹת. [8] אֵל הַהוֹדָאוֹת, אֲדוֹן הַשָּׁלוֹם, מְקַדֵּשׁ הַשַּׁבָּת וּמְבָרֵךְ שְׁבִיעִי, וּמֵנִיחַ בִּקְדֻשָּׁה לְעַם מְדֻשְּׁנֵי עֹנֶג, זֵכֶר לְמַעֲשֵׂה בְרֵאשִׁית.

[9] אֱלֹהֵינוּ וֵאלֹהֵי אֲבוֹתֵינוּ, רְצֵה בִמְנוּחָתֵנוּ; קַדְּשֵׁנוּ בְּמִצְוֹתֶיךָ, וְתֵן חֶלְקֵנוּ בְּתוֹרָתֶךָ; [10] שַׂבְּעֵנוּ מִטּוּבֶךָ, וְשַׂמְּחֵנוּ בִּישׁוּעָתֶךָ; וְטַהֵר לִבֵּנוּ לְעָבְדְּךָ בֶּאֱמֶת; [11] וְהַנְחִילֵנוּ, יְיָ אֱלֹהֵינוּ, בְּאַהֲבָה וּבְרָצוֹן שַׁבַּת קָדְשֶׁךָ, וְיָנוּחוּ בָהּ יִשְׂרָאֵל מְקַדְּשֵׁי שְׁמֶךָ. [12] בָּרוּךְ אַתָּה, יְיָ, מְקַדֵּשׁ הַשַּׁבָּת.

BRETTLER (BIBLE)

in Psalm 2:11, "Serve Adonai in awe; tremble with fright," though the opposite sentiment is also found in the Bible—as in Psalm 100:2, "Worship Adonai in gladness; come into his presence with shouts of joy."

[7] *"Gratefully acknowledge"* As in Psalm 145:2, "Every day will I bless You and praise Your name forever and ever."

[8] *"Sanctifies Shabbat and blesses the seventh day"* Quotation marks did not exist in antiquity, so sometimes when a later source cites an earlier one, it inverts the order of the original. This may be seen here, in the inverted citation of Genesis 2:3, "And God blessed the seventh day and sanctified it."

[8] *"Joyful people* [am m'dush'nei oneg]*"* The root *d.sh.n* (from which we get *m'dush'nei*) sometimes refers to sacrificial offerings; since Shabbat is called *oneg* ("joy"), the two words together may imply that Shabbat has replaced sacrifices. See also "Grant us as our inheritance" above, p. 124, where we saw that Shabbat replaces ownership of the Land of Israel as well.

[8] *"Joyful"* Isaiah 58:13, defines "joy" as crucial to Shabbat, perhaps to counterbalance many priestly texts that consider the desecration of Shabbat a capital offense.

[8] *"In memory of acts of creation"* Following the tradition of Genesis 2 and the version of the Decalogue in Exodus 20, rather than Deuteronomy 5 (where Shabbat commemorates the Exodus, not creation).

DORFF (THEOLOGY)

[5] *"Protecting our ancestors ..."* Because in the Temple of old there was no communal sacrifice at night, there really should not be an *Amidah* in the evening service, for the *Amidah* replaces the communal sacrifices of the Temple period (specifically the *tamid*, offered mornings and afternoons, and the *musaf* added for festive occasions). As a result, the evening *Amidah* is recited only individually. Wanting, however, to acknowledge the special character of Shabbat, the Rabbis created this paragraph for the evening when Shabbat begins. It consists of snippets from an old Palestinian version of the seven Shabbat *Amidah* blessings, followed by a return to the reason why this paragraph is being said in the first place, namely (end of v. 8), to celebrate the sanctity and joy of Shabbat. The final paragraph (vv. 9–12) reiterates the prose that ends the *Amidah's* fourth blessing, the one praising God for sanctifying the Sabbath.

Quite a clever way to devise a publicly recited *Amidah* without actually repeating it aloud! And a good example of one way in which Judaism preserves tradition while changing it.

141

Ellenson (Modern Liturgies)

in Reform and Reconstructionist liturgies, it is noteworthy that the matriarchs have been added into contemporary Conservative liturgy as well. It took place in stages: the 1985 *Sim Shalom* provides no mention of them alongside their husbands, neither here nor in the full *Amidah* that comes prior; and not in the short reference to God of our fathers in verse 5 here—although a "creative" *Amidah* in English alone does supply them. But the revised gender-sensitive version of 1998 gives an option to include the foremothers, though it also allows worshipers to choose the original text, where God is just "God of our fathers." The Israeli *Va'ani Tefillati* (later still, 1998) provides the same options.

[5] *"Protecting our ancestors"* From the days of the Hamburg Temple, where our first modern liberal prayer books emerged (1819, 1841), this prayer has generally been included. Editors knew that as "one blessing in place of seven" (see L. Hoffman, *"Magen Avot"*), it constituted an alternative to the established longer version of the *Amidah* that took up seven entire blessings, instead of just brief references to the theme of each one. Wanting to shorten the service, but wanting also to do so within bounds of Halakhah and tradition (broadly conceived), they hit upon the idea of using this short prayer instead of the *Amidah*—a particularly useful strategy, given the talmudic theory that an entire evening *Amidah* is not required anyway (see Landes, "The Halakhic Status of *Minchah* and *Ma'ariv*," pp. 25–29). The original *Union Prayer Book* (American Reform, 1895) did not have separate services for each week in the month, but once the latest editions did, it was decided to dedicate one version to using this prayer instead of an entire *Amidah*, as a short but valid way of including the *Amidah*.

[5] *"Reviving the dead"* Resurrection is a classical Jewish belief of the Rabbis, held firmly through the centuries, and questioned in modern times. Once questioned, prayerbook editors could either change the Hebrew or leave the Hebrew intact but alter the translation so as to obviate the clear message of the original. In our time, prayer books like the American Reform *Gates of Prayer* (1975) and Reconstructionist *Kol Haneshamah* (1995) alter the Hebrew. The former substitutes *hakol* ("everything") for *metim*—God gives life to everything all the time. The latter prefers *m'chayei kol chai* ("gives life to all life") and translates the line as divine "speech enlivening all human beings."

———◆———

FRANKEL (A WOMAN'S VOICE)

lifetime. Many of the Yiddish *tkhines* that Jewish women composed and recited make reference to this belief, including *tkhines* meant to be recited at the cemetery. They would often recite such *tkhines* at the graves of their loved ones as a substitute for *Kaddish*, which was reserved for men alone to say. An anonymous *tkhine* from the mid-seventeenth century, to be recited by the worshiper when prostrating herself upon a grave, concludes with the following words:

> So you rest in eternal rest,
> among your friends, the saintly men and women,
> till the time when God, blessed be He,
> will let the dead fall from Heaven,
> and make them live again,
> and lead them, with great honor,
> in their piety, to become worthy
> to see the radiance of the Holy Divine Presence,
> with all saintly men and women.

> (From Devra Kay, *Seyder Tkhines: The Forgotten Book of Common Prayer for Jewish Women* [Philadelphia: Jewish Publication Society, 2004], p. 178)

◆

GRAY (OUR TALMUDIC HERITAGE)

his cue from Melchizedek, Abram also refers to God as *koneh*. Why is this rare name for God selected for this blessing on Friday night?

One clue may be the beginning of the next paragraph, *magen avot* ("protecting [literally, 'shield'] our ancestors"). At Genesis 15:1, immediately after Abram refers to God as *koneh*, God tells Abraham that He will be a "shield" *(magen)* for him. Since we are beginning a prayer alluding to God's being a shield to our ancestors, the introductory lines refer to Abraham's use of *koneh* in describing God.

But what does *koneh* mean in this context? Although many translations say "creator," the Hebrew root *k.n.h* can also mean "to acquire"—a meaning we allude to when we translate it here as "master" (see J. Hoffman on this verse). We acquire the right to ownership by buying what we own or by creating it from scratch. Since God created the universe, God can thereby be said to have "acquired" it. Psalm 104:24 thus says the earth is full of God's *kinyanim* ("creations" or "acquisitions").

In the supplementary sixth chapter of *Pirkei Avot* (6:11), the Mishnah speaks of five such *kinyanim* (by which the Mishnah clearly means "acquisitions") that God created in this world: (1) Torah, (2) heaven and earth (taken together as "universe"), (3) Abraham, (4) the People Israel, and (5) the Jerusalem Temple (each is proved a *kinyan* by the citation of verses). The Talmud (Pes. 87b) and the midrash called *Mekhilta D'rabbi Yishmael (B'shalach)* 9 both shorten the list to four by eliminating Abraham (3), while the midrash called *Sifre D'varim* 309 shortens it to three by eliminating both Abraham (3) and heaven and earth (2). Rabbinic texts typically display variations like these, reflecting different priorities as to what should be emphasized. The result is several versions of lists that get taught orally, memorized, and recorded eventually in writing.

5–8 *"Protecting our ancestors* [magen avot]*"* Tradition regards *magen avot* as an "all-in-one" short version of the seven-benediction Shabbat *Amidah*, called *B'rakhah achat mei'ein sheva*, literally, "One blessing in place of seven" (see L. Hoffman, "Magen Avot").

1. *Magen avot* ("protecting our ancestors") corresponds to *magen Avraham* ("Abraham's protector"), the first blessing in the Shabbat *Amidah*.
2. *M'chayei metim* ("reviving the dead") corresponds to *m'chayei hametim* ("gives life to the dead"), the second blessing.
3. *Ha'el hakadosh* repeats *ha'el hakadosh* ("the holy God"), the third blessing.
4. *"Hameniach l'amo"* ("lets his people rest") denotes the reference to Shabbat rest that forms the content of the all-important middle blessing of the Shabbat *Amidah*, called *K'dushat Hayom*, "The Sanctification of the Day."
5. *L'fanav na'avod* ("we will serve Him") refers to the fifth blessing, the *Avodah* (from the same root as *na'avod*), a reference to God's accepting our worship, originally a Temple sacrifice over which the sacrificer "stood."
6. *Nodeh lishmo* ("gratefully acknowledge his name") corresponds to the sixth blessing *Hoda'ah* ("Grateful Acknowledgment"). *Hoda'ah* and *nodeh* stem from the same root (*y.d.h*). It is followed by *El hahoda'ot*, "God of grateful acknowledgment," another reference to the same benediction.
7. We then get *adon hashalom*, "master of peace," denoting the seventh benediction, on the theme of *shalom*.

7 *"With the blessings"* The Talmud (Ber. 40a) cites Psalm 68:20, *Barukh Adonai yom yom ya'amos lanu*, "Blessed is God. Day by day [He will support us]." But the Rabbis drop the last part, reading what is left (*Barukh Adonai yom yom*) as "Blessed be God every day," in order to raise the rhetorical question: "Do we bless God only during the day and not at night?" Surely (goes the answer), "the verse means to say that each and every day, we should [bless God] with an abstract [*mei'ein*] of all his blessings." Rashi (1040–1105, France) explains that the wording we choose for blessing should be appropriate to the day: Shabbat blessing should reflect Shabbat matters, festival blessings reflect festival issues, and so on.

KUSHNER & POLEN (CHASIDISM)

speaking through his throat.) And then everyone began to think of *t'shuvah* ("repentance") and returning home to God. *Kiddush*, in other words, not only sanctifies Shabbat day but it also restores the pristine purity of a newly created world.

The story is told of a man who desperately needed a miraculous intervention and who came to the rebbe to intercede on his behalf. The rebbe told him to return on Friday evening when he would make *Kiddush*. So the man did, and the salvation was effected! An explanation is offered in Chayim ben Attar's *Or Hachayim* (Sephardi, eighteenth century). There we read that the world was created in six days, and on Shabbat, all creation arrived at a state of renewal. Indeed, according to the Talmud (Shab. 119b), the meaning of *vay'khulu* (Gen. 2:1, customarily vocalized in the passive voice as meaning "and they [the heavens and the earth] were finished"), should instead be vocalized in the active voice: "and they finished." In other words, on Shabbat they (we) all become partners with God in completing the work of creation. By *our* rest, we effectively channel the *Shekhinah back into* the world.

The text then cites the *No'am Elimelekh* of Rabbi Elimelekh of Lizhensk, which rhetorically asks, How can a *tsadik* perform a miracle or reverse a divine decree? The answer is that if you can enter the place of renewing the world, that is, Shabbat, then the world you have created is a *new* world, different from the one that God created when the divine decree went forth. You are thus, as in the personal case of *t'shuvah*, effectively pressing the *restore default configuration* button, beginning anew, fresh, pure, and pristine.

[5] *"Reviving the dead"* The following legend of the wonder-working abilities of the Baal Shem Tov (the BeSHT), founder of Chasidism, is related by the contemporary Tosher rebbe of Montreal. The BeSHT would customarily spend an unusually long time reciting the *Minchah* liturgy on *Erev Shabbat*. When questioned by Reb Zev Kitzes, the BeSHT explained, "That is when souls ascend on high. They all come to me seeking *tikkun*, 'repair.' Indeed, if you prepare yourself all week, then when you put on your *tallis*, you too will be able to see the souls that come to you." Reb Zev Kitzes nodded, and the BeSHT took his own *tallis* and placed it over both himself and Kitzes. When they reached the blessing *m'chayei hametim*, "who resurrects the dead," overwhelmed by the onslaught of souls, Reb Kitzes fainted.

The legend continues that at the time of the afternoon service on *Erev Shabbat*, we too (though in a much more modest way, to be sure) can visualize all the dead ends of the past week, all the unfinished chores yearning for repair, and elevate them. We can comprehend now how, even in their incompleteness, our unfinished business becomes done, completed, finished, repaired, healed—on Shabbat.

◆

the Sabbath day; it is recited after the *Amidah* (2) because there are times (like the *Amidah* for a Shabbat eve that falls on a holiday) when it is not recited within the *Amidah*, but can be recited here, at least. It is recited at home as part of *Kiddush* (3), so that the family may participate together in this transformational experience.

Vay'khulu here (2) is customarily recited or sung together. Anyone who has finished the *Amidah* late, and missed this group recitation, should ask another person to recite it with him: *Vay'khulu* is a form of *edut*, "witnessing" (in the juridical sense), to God's creation of the world; since "witnessing requires at least two people present" *(ein edut pachot mishnayim)*, a partner is needed for it (*Shulchan Arukh* O. Ch. 268:7).

Given its "witnessing" nature, *Vay'khulu* here should be said standing—the way one witnesses in a Jewish court.

Magen Avot ("Protecting Our Ancestors") Unlike other services (*Shacharit, Minchah, Musaf*), we have no repetition of the *Amidah* in *Ma'ariv* (see Daniel Landes, "The Halakhic Status of *Minchah* and *Ma'ariv*," pp. 25–29). Yet, clearly, a form of repetition has been created here. *Magen Avot* (as it is called) begins with a version of the *Amidah's* first blessing; it then evokes the second and the third blessings and provides an extended meditation upon the sanctity of Shabbat, ending with the telltale "Blessed are You, Adonai, who sanctifies Shabbat" (see "Heaven and earth ... were completed [*vay'khulu*]," p. 123). It is "saved" from being an *actual* repetition by the fact that it lacks the last three blessings.

Why was this virtual repetition created? The Mordecai (Mordecai ben Hillel, Germany, latter half of the thirteenth century, Shab. 24b) considers it a holdover from when Jews prayed in makeshift synagogues in the fields and it was dangerous to walk home alone. This added section recited by the prayer leader would give those who were late in their prayer recital time to catch up and leave safely with everyone else. Once this prayer was established, it was never nullified, even when conditions changed.

But why not? There must be some compelling need to retain at least a "virtual" repetition of the *Amidah* for Friday night. Along with *Vay'khulu* (See "Heaven and earth ... were completed [*vay'khulu*]," p. 123), it continues the public and group declaration of Shabbat's sanctity and witnesses to God's act of creation. In this sense, while *Ma'ariv* remains a technical option (*r'shut*, pronounced r'-SHOOT), it has certainly become, for all intents and purposes, *k'chovah* (pronounced k'-choh-VAH), "like an obligation." It is indeed arguable that through its recitation we fulfill a Torah obligation to proclaim the Sabbath day publicly as a community. No wonder *Magen Avot*, once instituted for altogether different reasons, was joyously held on to.

One sign of its being a *chazarat hashatz* is the gradual acceptance of *korim*—bowing at the beginning of the first blessing (*Y'sodai Y'shurun, Siddur L'Shabbat*, p. 283, Gedaliah Felder, eminent halakhic authority, Toronto, mid- to late twentieth century, and *Tzitz Eliezer*, Eliezer Waldenberg, major Israeli responder and Head Judge of Rabbinical Courts, 7:23). Another sign is that while authorities allow the group singing of *Magen Avot*, many mandate that the *shatz* (the prayer leader) repeat it out loud (see

Mishnah B'rurah 269:22; for a dissenting view, see *Kitzot Hashulchan* in *Badei Hashulchan* 77:24). The definitive sign of the prayer functioning formally as a repetition, however, is that if for some reason a person does not pray the Shabbat evening *Amidah*, or if he recites the weekday service by mistake, he may fulfill his obligation by hearing this prayer from the *shatz*. He should stand with his feet together and say it word for word, or simply listen with the intention of fulfilling his obligation, and say *Amen* at the end (*Shulchan Arukh*, O. Ch. 268:13 and discussion in the contemporary prayer compendium *Ishei Yisrael* 36:41).

◆

L. HOFFMAN (HISTORY)

unnecessary repetition of the *Amidah* (cf. Landes and Gray, *"Protecting our ancestors"*). That it is an *Amidah* of sorts is clear from the fact that it incorporates all the necessary seven Shabbat benedictions, not with the words we are used to, and not in seven separate benedictions, but in one (see below, "Blessed are You"). The halakhic problem is Jewish law's aversion to "blessings said in vain," that is, blessings said without cause. Since the *Ma'ariv Amidah* is at least theoretically optional (see "The *Amidah*," p. 113), it is the sole instance of an *Amidah* with no reader's repetition. The repetition, after all, was to absolve people who were unable to say the prayer on their own (a common instance when there were no written prayer books). They could simply listen to the prayer leader and answer *"Amen"* to each benediction. Adding what seems like a repetition to what is technically merely an optional prayer that people are free to omit looks like a patent case of "a blessing said in vain."

This particular form of having several blessings condensed as one is called *mei'ein* (pronounced may-AYN), meaning (roughly) "in place of"—in our instance here, *b'rakhah achat mei'ein sheva*, "one blessing in place of seven.") Our liturgy has two other *mei'ein* blessings also:

1. Corresponding to the normal eighteen-blessing *Amidah* is *b'rakhah achat mei'ein sh'moneh esreh*, "one blessing in place of eighteen"; it is also called by its opening Hebrew word, *Havineinu* ("Grant us wisdom"). *Havineinu* is nowadays recited if there is insufficient time to say the entire daily *Amidah* (see Volume 2, *The Amidah*, pp. 192–193).

2. Our normal Grace after Meals *(Birkat Hamazon)* has four blessings, but originally there were only three, so it corresponds to *b'rakhah achat mei'ein shalosh*, "one blessing in place of three." The long *Birkat Hamazon* concludes meals with bread; when there is no bread, we use a shorter form. This *mei'ein shalosh* follows consumption of "the seven species" of food grown in the Land of Israel, as stipulated in Deuteronomy 8:7–8 (wheat, barley, grapes, figs, pomegranates, olives, honey [from dates, not bees]). Its language varies to reflect the specific food eaten. After the fourth cup of wine at the Passover Seder, for instance, we customarily say a version thanking God "for vines and the fruit of the vine."

Our *mei'ein* blessing here, *b'rakhah achat mei'ein sheva*, "one blessing in place of seven" (meaning the seven standard blessings for Shabbat), is also known by its opening words, *Magen Avot* (pronounced mah-GAYN ah-VOT, *"Protecting Our Ancestors"*).

But how did it get here? And why? Especially since it looks like a blessing said in vain! The commonest medieval explanation is connected to the extended *Hashkivenu* (see "Blessed is Adonai forever [*Barukh Adonai l'olam*]," p. 93). But it is hardly convincing and is, in any event, circular, since it explains *Barukh Adonai l'olam* with reference to the extended *Hashkivenu*, but also explains the extended *Hashkivenu* by referring to *Barukh Adonai l'olam*!

Sometimes, the liturgy developed independently of the Halakhah that was being systemized to explain it. Rules that we now take for granted may not have fit liturgical situations already in place when the rules were formulated. It might once have been the preferred Friday night Amidah in Eretz Yisrael from the days when it was not yet clear that you needed separate blessings for each Amidah theme.

In any event, it is a clear case of a *mei'ein* blessing, a *b'rakhah achat mei'ein sheva*, and an interesting one at that, because it replicates a short version of the Palestinian *Amidah* (not the Babylonian one that we customarily use)—a form that is otherwise available to us only in the Genizah fragments (see Volume 2, *The Amidah*, pp. 37–42). Since our prayer book was composed by Babylonian authorities, we almost never have whole instances of ancient Palestinian prayers in it. *Magen Avot* is an exception.

[1] *"Heaven and earth ... completed"* The evening *Amidah* is preceded by an announcement of sacred time, taken from Torah (see p. 105). As an *Amidah* in its own right (see above *Magen Avot*), *Magen Avot* begins that way as well.

[3] *"Blessed are You ..."* This is an alternative early version of the Shabbat *Amidah*, in which all seven themes occur, but in a single benediction rather than in seven separate ones (see above, *"Magen Avot"*). But the themes receive unequal treatment. This is certainly no synopsis of an already existent larger text, therefore, but a creative composition in its own right. Verse 3 introduces the first theme (*avot*, the merit of the forefathers) at some length, after which the other themes follow in short order, each one given a few words only. The last theme in the *Amidah* is *shalom*, "peace," represented here by *adon hashalom*, "master of peace" (v. 8). But unlike the standard *Amidah* that we are used to, the author of this one circles back to end with a repetition of the all-important middle blessing, the *K'dushat Hayom*, the "Sanctification of the Day," which specifies the sacred occasion for which this *Amidah* was composed. After "master of peace," the text celebrates again "[God who] sanctifies Shabbat and blesses the seventh day, and in holiness lets this joyful people rest, in memory of acts of creation." We then find wording that we are used to, the only paragraph that occurs in every one of the Shabbat versions of the *Amidah*, "Our God and our ancestors' God," but here, the text is not buried internally in the fourth blessing. Rather, the prayer ends with it.

[7] *"With the blessings* [mei'ein hab'rakhot]" This prayer originated in medieval or

ancient Palestine (see above, *"Magen Avot"*). We therefore find parallels in the Genizah fragments, where other liturgical remnants of Eretz Yisra'el were recovered at the end of the nineteenth century. But these Genizah versions read *ma'on hab'rakhot*, not *mei'ein hab'rakhot*, as we have it here. The *ma'on* reading is correct; *mei'ein* is probably a scribal error that crept in under the influence of the prayer's title, *mei'ein* [*sheva*].

It is not even clear what *mei'ein b'rakhot* could mean. We translate it simply, "with the blessings." Birnbaum says "the fitting form of blessing"; ArtScroll gives us "appropriate blessings." *Mei'ein* could also mean "source," or even "wellspring," giving us a God who is the source of blessing. But *ma'on hab'rakhot* is much more interesting. It means "the abode of blessing," implying that God is the place where blessings lie in wait for us, not just the source of them. As source, God would be like a fountain, spraying blessings down upon us. But as "abode," God is a place where we can enter and feel at home, a spiritual destination where we ourselves can go to find the blessings we seek.

Siddur Sim Shalom (the Conservative Siddur for North America) has changed the text back to *ma'on*, but translates it merely "source of blessing."

J. HOFFMAN (TRANSLATION)

[6] *"Lets"* Or "makes."

[6] *"Holy day of Shabbat"* Or "day of his holy Shabbat." In English, they mean the same thing. (English grammar allows adjectives [e.g., "holy"] to float around a bit in main phrases ["day of Shabbat"]. A similar example can be found in the common expression "good cup of coffee," where, of course, the coffee is good, not necessarily the cup.)

[6] *"He loves them, letting them rest"* Birnbaum's simpler "He is pleased to let them rest" may be the point here.

[7] *"With"* Probably a technical term implying "with a shortened form of ...," implying, as well, "in place of." See L. Hoffman, *Magen Avot* (*"Protecting Our Ancestors"*).

[8] *"He"* Literally, "who." Once again, we strive to translate the Hebrew in full sentences.

[8] *"Seventh day"* Literally, "seventh."

[On Shabbat continue here.]

F. THE SYNAGOGUE *KIDDUSH*

[1] Blessed are You, Adonai our God, ruler of the world, creator of the fruit of the vine. [2] Blessed are You, Adonai our God, ruler of the world, who sanctified us with his commandments and adored us, lovingly and adoringly granting us his holy Shabbat as our inheritance, in memory of acts of creation. [3] For it is the first day of holy festivals, a memorial of the Exodus from Egypt. [4] For you have chosen us and sanctified us above all nations, lovingly and adoringly granting us your holy Shabbat as our inheritance. [5] Blessed are You, Adonai, who sanctifies Shabbat.

[1] בָּרוּךְ אַתָּה, יְיָ אֱלֹהֵינוּ, מֶלֶךְ הָעוֹלָם, בּוֹרֵא פְּרִי הַגָּפֶן. [2] בָּרוּךְ אַתָּה, יְיָ אֱלֹהֵינוּ, מֶלֶךְ הָעוֹלָם, אֲשֶׁר קִדְּשָׁנוּ בְּמִצְוֹתָיו וְרָצָה בָנוּ, וְשַׁבַּת קָדְשׁוֹ בְּאַהֲבָה וּבְרָצוֹן הִנְחִילָנוּ, זִכָּרוֹן לְמַעֲשֵׂה בְרֵאשִׁית; [3] כִּי הוּא יוֹם תְּחִלָּה לְמִקְרָאֵי קֹדֶשׁ, זֵכֶר לִיצִיאַת מִצְרָיִם. [4] כִּי בָנוּ בָחַרְתָּ וְאוֹתָנוּ קִדַּשְׁתָּ מִכָּל הָעַמִּים, וְשַׁבַּת קָדְשְׁךָ בְּאַהֲבָה וּבְרָצוֹן הִנְחַלְתָּנוּ. [5] בָּרוּךְ אַתָּה, יְיָ, מְקַדֵּשׁ הַשַּׁבָּת.

151

FRANKEL (A WOMAN'S VOICE)

[2] *"Ruler of the world"* In recent years, some liberal Jews have objected to the gendered language in this ancient blessing over Shabbat and holiday wine. As in all traditional Hebrew blessings, God is here addressed literally as "king of the world," an unambiguously male metaphor. In addition, the verbs and possessive suffixes are all in masculine forms, since Hebrew does not permit neutral conjugation.

As an alternative, Marcia Falk, a feminist liturgist, has offered different wording for this prayer that goes beyond neutralizing gender; her alternative *Kiddush* actually feminizes God:

> *N'vareykh et eyn hahayim matzmihat p'ri hagefen unkadeysh et yom hash'vi'i— yom hashabbat—zikaron l'ma'aseyh v'reyshit ki hu yom t'hilah l'mikra'ey kodesh, zeykher litzi'at mitzrayim.*
>
> Let us bless the source of life that ripens fruit on the vine as we hallow the seventh day—the Sabbath day—in remembrance of creation, for the Sabbath is first among holy days, recalling the exodus and the covenant. (From Marcia Falk, *The Book of Blessings* [San Francisco, HarperSanFrancisco, 1996], pp. 128–29)

Falk has proposed two innovations here: first, she changes the initial word in the traditional blessing, *barukh*, "Blessed [be]"—a masculine passive participle—into first-person plural, *n'varekh*, "Let us bless." Gender is thereby eliminated altogether. And by changing the verb from a *(p. 154)*

GRAY (OUR TALMUDIC HERITAGE)

The Synagogue Kiddush The third-century Amora Samuel (Pes. 101a) is said to be of the view that *Kiddush* may be recited only as part of a meal. The anonymous, editorial voice of the Talmud (dated as late as the sixth century) asks how Samuel would explain the practice of reciting *Kiddush* in the synagogue on Friday night, and answers on Samuel's behalf that the synagogue *Kiddush* is specifically meant to fulfill the obligations of guests who will be eating, drinking, and sleeping in the synagogue (see also Maimonides,

F. THE SYNAGOGUE *KIDDUSH*

[1] Blessed are You, Adonai our God, ruler of the world, creator of the fruit of the vine. [2] Blessed are You, Adonai our God, ruler of the world, who sanctified us with his commandments and adored us, lovingly and adoringly granting us his holy Shabbat as our inheritance, in memory of acts of creation. [3] For it is the first day of holy festivals, a memorial of the Exodus from Egypt. [4] For you have chosen us and

"Laws of Shabbat" 29:8). From this talmudic editorial attribution, we see that the recitation of the synagogue *Kiddush* had become a well-known practice by the time of the late editors (sixth century C.E.).

R. Natronai Gaon (ninth century C.E., Babylonia) is credited with going further. We recite the synagogue *Kiddush* even in the absence of guests, he says, because the *Kiddush* wine has healing properties; people are to take some of the wine and put it on their eyes because of a tradition according to which taking long strides *(p. 155)*

L. HOFFMAN (HISTORY)

AS THE SHABBAT MA'ARIV *SERVICE APPROACHES ITS END, WE PAUSE TO MAKE* KIDDUSH—*AS WE WILL AT HOME LATER, BUT WITHOUT THE BIBLICAL PREAMBLE (*GEN. *1:31, 2:1–3) THAT WAS ADDED TO THE HOME* KIDDUSH *DURING THE* MIDDLE AGES.

[2] *"Creator of the fruit of the vine"* Tradition has struggled with saying *Kiddush* in synagogue, since (at the very least) it seems redundant to the *Kiddush* that will be said afterward, at Shabbat dinner. Halakhah holds, moreover, that a proper *Kiddush* requires sitting down for a fixed meal—patently not the case in services. An early justification revolved about the assumption that travelers passing through would spend Shabbat in town, until Halakhah permitted them to resume their travels. Given the tiny homes and large families that characterized late antiquity and the Middle Ages, such guests would be billeted in the synagogue. The congregational *Kiddush* would be for them.

But guests were not a weekly occurrence, and to later commentators, anyway, it was obvious that people said the synagogue *Kiddush* even without them. So other justifications prevailed. A common one (reported by the *BaCH*, Joel Sirkes, sixteenth century, Poland) was that in years past, when the *Kiddush* really had been said for guests, the locals got into the bad habit of saying it with them in the *(p. 155)*

[1] בָּרוּךְ אַתָּה, יְיָ אֱלֹהֵינוּ, מֶלֶךְ הָעוֹלָם, בּוֹרֵא פְּרִי הַגָּפֶן.

[2] בָּרוּךְ אַתָּה, יְיָ אֱלֹהֵינוּ, מֶלֶךְ הָעוֹלָם, אֲשֶׁר קִדְּשָׁנוּ בְּמִצְוֹתָיו וְרָצָה בָנוּ, וְשַׁבַּת קָדְשׁוֹ בְּאַהֲבָה וּבְרָצוֹן הִנְחִילָנוּ, זִכָּרוֹן לְמַעֲשֵׂה בְרֵאשִׁית; [3] כִּי הוּא יוֹם תְּחִלָּה לְמִקְרָאֵי קֹדֶשׁ, זֵכֶר לִיצִיאַת מִצְרָיִם. [4] כִּי בָנוּ בָחַרְתָּ וְאוֹתָנוּ קִדַּשְׁתָּ מִכָּל הָעַמִּים, וְשַׁבַּת קָדְשְׁךָ בְּאַהֲבָה

sanctified us above all nations, lovingly and adoringly granting us your holy Shabbat as our inheritance. [5] Blessed are You, Adonai, who sanctifies Shabbat.	וּבְרָצוֹן הִנְחַלְתָּנוּ. ⁵בָּרוּךְ אַתָּה, יְיָ, מְקַדֵּשׁ הַשַּׁבָּת.

FRANKEL (A WOMAN'S VOICE)

participle into the collective invitational form, "Let us," she transforms the worshipers into agents of blessing together with God. Instead of simply declaring: "Blessed are You!" we call each other to bless God together. Falk also gives God a new name, *ein hachayim*, literally, "fountain" or "wellspring" of life, translated by Falk as "source of life." Since the Hebrew term is feminine, the verb takes a feminine form, *matzmichat*. So, even though a fountain displays no explicitly female characteristics, its grammatical form suggests that God acts as a female agent.

[4] *"For you have chosen us … above all nations"* A second objection to the words of the *Kiddush* (for the first objection, on gendered language, see above, *"Ruler of the World"*) has to do with the concept of Israel's chosenness. Like many other prayers, this one too asserts that God has chosen Israel from among all nations. Many liberal Jews reject this notion of the Jewish people's privileged status. The founder of Reconstructionism, Mordecai Kaplan, argued strenuously against the notion and preferred changing the simple Hebrew word *mikol* ("from all") into the similar sounding *im kol* ("together with all"), saying thereby, "You chose us *together with* all [other] peoples." He had in mind, no doubt, the talmudic view that God made a covenant with all descendents of Noah, not just with Jews.

The current Reconstructionist prayer book, *Kol Haneshamah*, refuses to go as far as Kaplan. It opts for a different solution that affirms Israel's chosenness but designates being chosen as a status of responsibility rather than privilege. It rewrites the words to read: "For you have called to us and set us apart to serve you" (*ki eleinu karata … v'otanu kidashta la'avodatekha*). Some individuals have chosen to retain the phrase *ki vanu vacharta*, "You have chosen us," but again, only with Kaplan's bold emendation, *im kol ha'amim*. This outright rejection of Jewish chosenness usually argues that claims of specialness inevitably lead to envy and resentment among those excluded. Some writers make this a specifically Jewish argument, concluding that if only we did not make such claims about ourselves, anti-Semitism would be lessened. Kaplan's point had been more universal. He had in mind the moral lesson that our prayers and theology should say only what we can believe and should never have immoral consequences, not just upon Jews, but by Jews who inevitably imply by their chosenness that they are better than anyone else.

———◆———

GRAY (OUR TALMUDIC HERITAGE)

diminishes 1/500th of the light of a person's eyes. This lost gleam can be restored through the healing properties of the *Kiddush* wine. Since people undoubtedly had taken long strides in order to arrive at the synagogue on time Friday night, this healing is clearly desirable. R. Jonah Gerondi (thirteenth century, Spain) also believed that the synagogue *Kiddush* should be recited even without guests present, but for a different reason. There are two kinds of *mitzvot*: biblical *(d'ora'ita)* and rabbinic *(d'rabbanan)*. Sanctifying Shabbat through the recitation of *Kiddush* is especially important as a biblical commandment, but not everyone knows how to do it. The synagogue *Kiddush* makes it possible for people who do not know how to make *Kiddush* at home to fulfill the *mitzvah*.

R. Jacob ben Asher (1269–1343, Germany and Spain, author of the *Tur*) says the synagogue *Kiddush* is a widespread practice in his day, but despite the explanations of his rabbinic predecessors, he still finds the practice surprising in light of Samuel's talmudic requirement for saying it at a meal. He considers reciting it without guests present as being "close to a blessing in vain [*b'rakhah l'vatalah*]" (*Tur*, O. Ch. 269).

R. Joseph Caro (1488–1575, Land of Israel) was similarly ambivalent about the practice. The practice of housing guests in the synagogue had passed away by his time, but the synagogue *Kiddush* remained. Caro did not ban it—he probably couldn't have done so successfully—but he ruled "it is better to institute [a practice] of not reciting the synagogue *Kiddush*" (*Shulchan Arukh*, O. Ch. 269), and he asserted that the practice of Jewish communities in the Land of Israel was, in fact, not to recite it.

———◆———

L. HOFFMAN (HISTORY)

synagogue and then omitting it afterward at home. That was an error, of course, but people were doing it anyway, and omitting *Kiddush* from services might only exacerbate the situation. They just might stop saying *Kiddush* altogether. So the synagogue *Kiddush* had been continued as the lesser of two evils. The historical logic of the *BaCH*'s position is questionable, but one wonders whether his characterization of his own time is accurate. Is it possible that in sixteenth-century Poland, *Kiddush* at home was not as universal as we imagine?

Long before the *BaCH*, the ninth-century Babylonian Gaon, Natronai, knew also that *Kiddush* was recited even without visitors. He arrived at another rationale, based on several interesting talmudic discussions about people who are always in a hurry to get things done—the Talmud calls it *p'siyah gasah*, "a big stride" (= "rushing") to get where they want to go. Presumably, *p'siyah gasah* on the way to perform a *mitzvah* is commendable, but sometimes people hurry to *avoid mitzvot*, or just to get their mundane business done faster and better. Modern men and women who fall into the latter category can appreciate the stress such hurry entails; and so did the Talmud, which opined, "Every *p'siyah gasah* takes away 1/500th of a person's eyesight" (Ber. 41b). Apparently, people in a hurry did not slow down on account of that teaching (any more than they do today, despite doctors' warnings on stress-related illnesses), so the medieval commentators called Tosafot had to face the fact that 500 such steps by the average busy person ought to have occasioned total blindness—a conclusion contrary to what they observed. To save the talmudic ruling, they interpreted the remark to mean that every large step takes away 1/500th of whatever eyesight a person has, the first step reducing perfect eyesight by 1/500th, the second step 1/500th of that, and so on.

The Talmud had already provided a "medicinal" way out: eyesight is restored, the Rabbis said, by the evening *Kiddush*. Natronai reasoned that the real purpose for providing synagogue *Kiddush* wine was not just so that worshipers could say *Kiddush* and fulfill their obligation, but so that they could heal their eyesight. In his view, synagogue-goers would not drink the wine; they would put it directly on their eyelids, like a wonder-working salve. They would then return home for the *Kiddush* over dinner, at which time, they could drink wine to fulfill their obligation to make a proper *Kiddush*.

◆ ◆ ◆

[Prior to Alenu:

From the second night of Passover to the night before Shavuot, continue here with counting the Omer.

On Tish'a B'av, the biblical Book of Lamentations (Eichah) and related poetry (piyyutim) are recited.

On Purim, the biblical Book of Esther (the Megillah) is read.

Otherwise, continue with Alenu and Kaddish Yatom (Mourner's Kaddish). For text and commentary, see Volume 6, Tachanun and Concluding Prayers, pp. 133–157.]

G. Counting the Omer

I. *Kavvanah* (Introductory Meditation)

[1] I am fully prepared to perform the positive commandment of counting the Omer, in accordance with what is written in the Torah: [2] Count from the day after the holiday; from the day you wave the Omer offering, there must be seven full weeks. Until the day after the seventh week, you shall count fifty days.

הִנְנִי מוּכָן וּמְזֻמָּן לְקַיֵּם מִצְוַת עֲשֵׂה [1]
שֶׁל סְפִירַת הָעֹמֶר, כְּמוֹ שֶׁכָּתוּב
בַּתּוֹרָה: [2]וּסְפַרְתֶּם לָכֶם מִמָּחֳרַת הַשַּׁבָּת,
מִיּוֹם הֲבִיאֲכֶם אֶת עֹמֶר הַתְּנוּפָה, שֶׁבַע
שַׁבָּתוֹת תְּמִימֹת תִּהְיֶינָה; עַד מִמָּחֳרַת
הַשַּׁבָּת הַשְּׁבִיעִית תִּסְפְּרוּ חֲמִשִּׁים יוֹם.

II. Blessing on Counting

[3] Blessed are You, Adonai our God, ruler of the world, who sanctified us with his commandments and commanded us regarding the counting of the Omer.

בָּרוּךְ אַתָּה, יְיָ אֱלֹהֵינוּ, מֶלֶךְ [3]
הָעוֹלָם, אֲשֶׁר קִדְּשָׁנוּ בְּמִצְוֹתָיו
וְצִוָּנוּ עַל סְפִירַת הָעֹמֶר.

III. Counting

[4] Today we are one day into the counting of the Omer.

[5] May the Merciful One bring the Temple sacrifice back to its proper place for us, quickly in our day. Amen.

הַיּוֹם יוֹם אֶחָד לָעֹמֶר. [4]
הָרַחֲמָן, הוּא יַחֲזִיר לָנוּ עֲבוֹדַת [5]
בֵּית הַמִּקְדָּשׁ לִמְקוֹמָהּ בִּמְהֵרָה בְיָמֵינוּ.
אָמֵן סֶלָה.

IV. PSALM 67

⁶For the conductor of instrumental music a psalm, a song. ⁷May God treat us graciously and bless us, shining his face among us forever ⁸so that we know your way on earth, your salvation among all the peoples. The nations will praise You, God. ⁹All the nations will praise You! ¹⁰Every nationality will greatly rejoice, as You rule the nations justly, and guide the nationalities on earth, forever. ¹¹The nations will praise You, God. All the nations will praise You! ¹²The earth had yielded its produce. God, our God, will bless us! ¹³God will bless us, and the ends of the earth will revere Him!

V. ANA B'KHO'ACH ("BY THE MIGHT")

¹⁴By the might of your great right hand set free the captive.

¹⁵Accept the song of your people. Strengthen and purify us, Awesome One.

¹⁶Mighty One, guard those who seek You like the apple of your eye.

¹⁷Bless them. Purify them, and have mercy on them, forever granting them your righteousness.

¹⁸Strong One, Holy One, in your greatness guide your people.

¹⁹Only One, Exalted One, turn to your people who remember your holiness.

²⁰Accept our prayer, hear our cry, knower of secrets.

²¹Blessed is the One the glory of whose kingdom is renowned forever.

⁶לַמְנַצֵּחַ בִּנְגִינֹת מִזְמוֹר שִׁיר. ⁷אֱלֹהִים יְחָנֵּנוּ וִיבָרְכֵנוּ; יָאֵר פָּנָיו אִתָּנוּ, סֶלָה. ⁸לָדַעַת בָּאָרֶץ דַּרְכֶּךָ, בְּכָל גּוֹיִם יְשׁוּעָתֶךָ. יוֹדוּךָ עַמִּים, אֱלֹהִים; ⁹יוֹדוּךָ עַמִּים כֻּלָּם. ¹⁰יִשְׂמְחוּ וִירַנְּנוּ לְאֻמִּים, כִּי תִשְׁפֹּט עַמִּים מִישׁוֹר; וּלְאֻמִּים בָּאָרֶץ תַּנְחֵם, סֶלָה. ¹¹יוֹדוּךָ עַמִּים, אֱלֹהִים; יוֹדוּךָ עַמִּים כֻּלָּם. ¹²אֶרֶץ נָתְנָה יְבוּלָהּ; יְבָרְכֵנוּ אֱלֹהִים אֱלֹהֵינוּ. ¹³יְבָרְכֵנוּ אֱלֹהִים, וְיִירְאוּ אוֹתוֹ כָּל אַפְסֵי אָרֶץ.

¹⁴אָנָּא, בְּכֹחַ גְּדֻלַּת יְמִינְךָ תַּתִּיר צְרוּרָה,

¹⁵קַבֵּל רִנַּת עַמְּךָ, שַׂגְּבֵנוּ, טַהֲרֵנוּ, נוֹרָא.

¹⁶נָא, גִבּוֹר, דּוֹרְשֵׁי יִחוּדְךָ כְּבָבַת שָׁמְרֵם.

¹⁷בָּרְכֵם, טַהֲרֵם, רַחֲמֵם, צִדְקָתְךָ תָּמִיד גָּמְלֵם.

¹⁸חֲסִין קָדוֹשׁ, בְּרֹב טוּבְךָ נַהֵל עֲדָתֶךָ.

¹⁹יָחִיד גֵּאֶה, לְעַמְּךָ פְּנֵה, זוֹכְרֵי קְדֻשָּׁתֶךָ.

²⁰שַׁוְעָתֵנוּ קַבֵּל וּשְׁמַע צַעֲקָתֵנוּ, יוֹדֵעַ תַּעֲלוּמוֹת.

²¹בָּרוּךְ שֵׁם כְּבוֹד מַלְכוּתוֹ לְעוֹלָם וָעֶד.

VI. *KAVVANAH* (CLOSING MEDITATION)

22 Master of the universe, you commanded us through Moses your servant to count the Omer, in order to cleanse us of our evil and impurities, in accordance with what You wrote in your Torah: 23 Count from the day after the holiday; from the day you wave the Omer offering, there must be seven full weeks. Until the day after the seventh week you shall count fifty days— 24 so that all the souls of your People Israel be cleansed of their filth.

25 And so may it be your will, Adonai our God and our ancestors' God, that, in consideration of the Omer that I have counted today, everything I have done wrong be fixed by the counting, that I might be cleansed and sanctified with sanctity on high. Amen.

22 רִבּוֹנוֹ שֶׁל עוֹלָם, אַתָּה צִוִּיתָנוּ עַל יְדֵי מֹשֶׁה עַבְדְּךָ לִסְפּוֹר סְפִירַת הָעֹמֶר, כְּדֵי לְטַהֲרֵנוּ מִקְּלִפּוֹתֵינוּ וּמִטֻּמְאוֹתֵינוּ, כְּמוֹ שֶׁכָּתַבְתָּ בְּתוֹרָתֶךְ: 23 וּסְפַרְתֶּם לָכֶם מִמָּחֳרַת הַשַּׁבָּת, מִיּוֹם הֲבִיאֲכֶם אֶת עֹמֶר הַתְּנוּפָה, שֶׁבַע שַׁבָּתוֹת תְּמִימוֹת תִּהְיֶינָה; עַד מִמָּחֳרַת הַשַּׁבָּת הַשְּׁבִיעִית תִּסְפְּרוּ חֲמִשִּׁים יוֹם. 24 כְּדֵי שֶׁיִּטַּהֲרוּ נַפְשׁוֹת עַמְּךָ יִשְׂרָאֵל מִזֻּהֲמָתָם.

25 וּבְכֵן, יְהִי רָצוֹן מִלְּפָנֶיךָ, יְיָ אֱלֹהֵינוּ וֵאלֹהֵי אֲבוֹתֵינוּ, שֶׁבִּזְכוּת סְפִירַת הָעֹמֶר שֶׁסָּפַרְתִּי הַיּוֹם יְתֻקַּן מַה שֶּׁפָּגַמְתִּי בִּסְפִירָה, וְאֶטָּהֵר וְאֶתְקַדֵּשׁ בִּקְדֻשָּׁה שֶׁל מַעֲלָה. אָמֵן סֶלָה.

159

BRETTLER (BIBLE)

Counting the Omer An omer is a biblical dry measure (slightly larger than two quarts). Here, it refers to the omer of new grain brought to the Temple, which the priest will elevate "after the Sabbath" (Lev. 23:9–14). The grain in question would have been barley, which ripened at Passover time, well before the wheat harvest that coincided with Shavuot, roughly seven weeks later. This ritual was important for two reasons: (1) no new grain in any form was permitted until the omer of barley and the attendant sacrifices were offered (v. 14); and (2) the offering began a period of counting (*s'firah*), until fifty days later when, for the wheat harvest, a festival would be   (p. 164)

DORFF (THEOLOGY)

Omer (literally, "sheaf") refers to an offering from the barley crop that was brought to the Temple on the sixteenth of Nisan, the eve of the second day of Passover. By extension, the word is used to designate the entire Passover to Shavuot season, each day of which (according   (p. 166)

ELLENSON (MODERN LITURGIES)

Omer The restoration of this prayer into so many contemporary non-Orthodox prayer books testifies to the "return to tradition" that is so prevalent today. The forthcoming American Reform *Mishkan T'filah* restores the ceremony of counting the Omer after   (p. 167)

FRANKEL (A WOMAN'S VOICE)

Counting the Omer With the exception of the phases of the moon, time does not naturally parse into discrete units. We live in an analog universe—day and night flow into each other as the earth turns; yearly time flows from season to season as the earth orbits the sun.

But the human mind craves measurement, to give us a measure of control over the wild diversity of nature. And so we have created a digital world, divided into quantifiable units—inches and meters,   (p. 168)

[For prayer instructions, see page 157.]

I. KAVVANAH (INTRODUCTORY MEDITATION)

[1] I am fully prepared to perform the positive commandment of counting the Omer, in accordance with what is written in the Torah: [2] Count from the day after the holiday; from the day you wave the Omer offering, there must be seven full weeks. Until the day after the seventh week, you shall count fifty days.

GRAY (OUR TALMUDIC HERITAGE)

[2] *"The day after the holiday* [shabbat]*"* The Talmud reports that the Boethusians (alleged opponents of the Pharisees prior to the Temple's destruction in 70 C.E., and probably related to the Sadducees, the more general name of their opponents in Halakhah) read the phrase (from Lev. 23:15) to mean literally "the day after Shabbat" (Sunday). This meant that Shavuot would also always fall on a Sunday seven weeks off. The Pharisees, by contrast (and the talmudic   (p. 168)

KUSHNER & POLEN (CHASIDISM)

Counting the Omer According to kabbalistic tradition, the ten *s'firot* are frequently divided into the top three and the bottom seven. These lower seven are distinguished from the upper three by their relative accessibility to our human awareness. We stand a chance at comprehending them, whereas the top three are unknowable. It is hardly surprising, therefore, that the seven weeks between the beginning of Pesach and Shavuot should find a "s'firotic" analogue. The *(p. 169)*

L. HOFFMAN (HISTORY)

THE BIBLE INSTRUCTS US TO COUNT THE DAYS AND WEEKS IN THIS PERIOD OF TIME—A PRACTICE KNOWN AS COUNTING THE OMER (PRONOUNCED OH-MEHR, A TECHNICAL TERM MEANING A SHEAF OF [FRESH] PRODUCE, AND, ALSO, THE PERIOD WHEN THE PRODUCE RIPENS); OR JUST S'FIRAH (PRONOUNCED S'FEE-RAH, BUT, COMMONLY, S'-FEE-RAH), "COUNTING." THE CUSTOM IN SOME PLACES IS TO DO THE COUNTING AFTER ALENU, BUT FOLLOWING THE MORE GENERAL CUSTOM, WE INCLUDE IT BEFORE.

Counting the Omer We include the counting of the Omer before *Alenu* *(p. 172)*

הִנְנִי מוּכָן וּמְזֻמָּן לְקַיֵּם מִצְוַת עֲשֵׂה שֶׁל סְפִירַת¹ הָעֹמֶר, כְּמוֹ שֶׁכָּתוּב בַּתּוֹרָה: ²וּסְפַרְתֶּם לָכֶם מִמָּחֳרַת הַשַּׁבָּת, מִיּוֹם הֲבִיאֲכֶם אֶת עֹמֶר הַתְּנוּפָה, שֶׁבַע שַׁבָּתוֹת תְּמִימֹת תִּהְיֶינָה; עַד מִמָּחֳרַת הַשַּׁבָּת הַשְּׁבִיעִית תִּסְפְּרוּ חֲמִשִּׁים יוֹם.

LANDES (HALAKHAH)

Counting the Omer On the night of the sixteenth of Nisan (the second night of Passover; in the diaspora, the night of the second Seder), we begin the practice of *s'firat ha'omer*, counting the days and weeks from the time of the *omer* sacrifice to the biblical holiday of *Atzeret* (which we call Shavuot). The crucial verse is Leviticus 23:15, which I render in my own translation, following the understanding of the Talmud: "You all are to count from the morrow of the rest day. From the day you *(p. 170)*

J. HOFFMAN (TRANSLATION)

¹*"Fully prepared"* Literally, "ready and invited," but this Hebrew pair—*muchan* and *m'zuman*—clearly forms an idiom best not translated literally.

¹*"Positive commandment"* As opposed to negative commandment.

²*"Holiday"* Others: "Shabbat" or (Birnbaum) "day of rest." The Hebrew word *shabbat* refers, obviously, to what we variously call "Shabbat," "the Sabbath," "the day of rest," and so forth, but also more generally to time off from the usual routine. Yom Kippur, for example, is called *shabbat* in the Torah, as is the seventh year, in which the land is to rest. This *(p. 174)*

II. BLESSING ON COUNTING

[3] Blessed are You, Adonai our God, ruler of the world, who sanctified us with his commandments and commanded us regarding the counting of the Omer.

בָּרוּךְ אַתָּה, יְיָ אֱלֹהֵינוּ, מֶלֶךְ הָעוֹלָם, [3] אֲשֶׁר קִדְּשָׁנוּ בְּמִצְוֹתָיו וְצִוָּנוּ עַל סְפִירַת הָעֹמֶר.

III. COUNTING

[4] Today we are one day into the counting of the Omer.

[5] May the Merciful One bring the Temple sacrifice back to its proper place for us, quickly in our day. Amen.

הַיּוֹם יוֹם אֶחָד לָעֹמֶר. [4]

הָרַחֲמָן, הוּא יַחֲזִיר לָנוּ עֲבוֹדַת בֵּית [5] הַמִּקְדָּשׁ לִמְקוֹמָהּ בִּמְהֵרָה בְיָמֵינוּ. אָמֵן סֶלָה.

IV. PSALM 67

[6] For the conductor of instrumental music a psalm, a song. [7] May God treat us graciously and bless us, shining his face among us forever [8] so that we know your way on earth, your salvation among all the peoples. The nations will praise You, God. [9] All the nations will praise You! [10] Every nationality will greatly rejoice, as You rule the nations justly, and guide the nationalities on earth, forever. [11] The nations will praise You, God. All the nations will praise You! [12] The earth had yielded its produce. God, our God, will bless us! [13] God will bless us, and the ends of the earth will revere Him!

לַמְנַצֵּחַ בִּנְגִינֹת מִזְמוֹר שִׁיר. [7] אֱלֹהִים [6] יְחָנֵּנוּ וִיבָרְכֵנוּ; יָאֵר פָּנָיו אִתָּנוּ, סֶלָה. [8] לָדַעַת בָּאָרֶץ דַּרְכֶּךָ, בְּכָל גּוֹיִם יְשׁוּעָתֶךָ. יוֹדוּךָ עַמִּים, אֱלֹהִים; [9] יוֹדוּךָ עַמִּים כֻּלָּם. [10] יִשְׂמְחוּ וִירַנְּנוּ לְאֻמִּים, כִּי תִשְׁפֹּט עַמִּים מִישׁוֹר; וּלְאֻמִּים בָּאָרֶץ תַּנְחֵם, סֶלָה. [11] יוֹדוּךָ עַמִּים, אֱלֹהִים; יוֹדוּךָ עַמִּים כֻּלָּם. [12] אֶרֶץ נָתְנָה יְבוּלָהּ; יְבָרְכֵנוּ אֱלֹהִים אֱלֹהֵינוּ. [13] יְבָרְכֵנוּ אֱלֹהִים, וְיִירְאוּ אוֹתוֹ כָּל אַפְסֵי אָרֶץ.

V. *Ana B'kho'ach* ("By the Might")

[14] By the might of your great right hand set free the captive.

[15] Accept the song of your people. Strengthen and purify us, Awesome One.

[16] Mighty One, guard those who seek You like the apple of your eye.

[17] Bless them. Purify them, and have mercy on them, forever granting them your righteousness.

[18] Strong One, Holy One, in your greatness guide your people.

[19] Only One, Exalted One, turn to your people who remember your holiness.

[20] Accept our prayer, hear our cry, knower of secrets.

[21] Blessed is the One the glory of whose kingdom is renowned forever.

VI. *Kavvanah* (Closing Meditation)

[22] Master of the universe, you commanded us through Moses your servant to count the Omer, in order to cleanse us of our evil and impurities, in accordance with what You wrote in your Torah: [23] Count from the day after the holiday; from the day you wave the Omer offering, there must be seven full weeks. Until the day after the seventh week you shall count fifty days— [24] so that all the souls of your

אָנָּא, בְּכֹחַ גְּדֻלַּת יְמִינְךָ תַּתִּיר צְרוּרָה. [14]

קַבֵּל רִנַּת עַמְּךָ, שַׂגְּבֵנוּ, טַהֲרֵנוּ, נוֹרָא. [15]

נָא, גִבּוֹר, דּוֹרְשֵׁי יִחוּדְךָ כְּבָבַת שָׁמְרֵם. [16]

בָּרְכֵם, טַהֲרֵם, רַחֲמֵם, צִדְקָתְךָ תָּמִיד גָּמְלֵם. [17]

חֲסִין קָדוֹשׁ, בְּרֹב טוּבְךָ נַהֵל עֲדָתֶךָ. [18]

יָחִיד גֵּאֶה, לְעַמְּךָ פְּנֵה, זוֹכְרֵי קְדֻשָּׁתֶךָ. [19]

שַׁוְעָתֵנוּ קַבֵּל וּשְׁמַע צַעֲקָתֵנוּ, יוֹדֵעַ תַּעֲלוּמוֹת. [20]

בָּרוּךְ שֵׁם כְּבוֹד מַלְכוּתוֹ לְעוֹלָם וָעֶד. [21]

רִבּוֹנוֹ שֶׁל עוֹלָם, אַתָּה צִוִּיתָנוּ עַל יְדֵי [22] מֹשֶׁה עַבְדְּךָ לִסְפּוֹר סְפִירַת הָעֹמֶר, כְּדֵי לְטַהֲרֵנוּ מִקְּלִפּוֹתֵינוּ וּמִטֻּמְאוֹתֵינוּ, כְּמוֹ שֶׁכָּתַבְתָּ בְּתוֹרָתֶךָ: [23] וּסְפַרְתֶּם לָכֶם מִמָּחֳרַת הַשַּׁבָּת, מִיּוֹם הֲבִיאֲכֶם אֶת עֹמֶר הַתְּנוּפָה, שֶׁבַע שַׁבָּתוֹת תְּמִימֹת תִּהְיֶינָה; עַד מִמָּחֳרַת הַשַּׁבָּת הַשְּׁבִיעִית תִּסְפְּרוּ חֲמִשִּׁים יוֹם. [24] כְּדֵי שֶׁיִּטַּהֲרוּ

People Israel be cleansed of their filth.

נַפְשׁוֹת עַמְּךָ יִשְׂרָאֵל מִזֻּהֲמָתָם.

25 And so may it be your will, Adonai our God and our ancestors' God, that, in consideration of the Omer that I have counted today, everything I have done wrong be fixed by the counting, that I might be cleansed and sanctified with sanctity on high. Amen.

²⁵וּבְכֵן, יְהִי רָצוֹן מִלְּפָנֶיךָ, יְיָ אֱלֹהֵינוּ וֵאלֹהֵי אֲבוֹתֵינוּ, שֶׁבִּזְכוּת סְפִירַת הָעֹמֶר שֶׁסָּפַרְתִּי הַיּוֹם יְתֻקַּן מַה שֶּׁפָּגַמְתִּי בִּסְפִירָה, וְאֶטַּהֵר וְאֶתְקַדֵּשׁ בִּקְדֻשָּׁה שֶׁל מַעְלָה, אָמֵן סֶלָה.

BRETTLER (BIBLE)

celebrated (vv. 15–21).

The Bible has several calendars. (For the different calendars, see v. 3, "Moses explained," p. 108.) The earliest one (Exod. 23:16) knows of a first-fruits festival, but not of the counting, which is emphasized in the later priestly and Deuteronomic calendars, possibly as a magical means to protect the growing crop of wheat that would have to mature throughout the counting period.

Of the later calendars, the earliest, Deuteronomy (16:9–10) contains no prohibition against eating new grain, saying only, "You shall count off seven weeks; start to count the seven weeks when the sickle is first put to the standing grain. Then you shall observe the Feast of Weeks [Shavuot] for Adonai your God." Leviticus 23 does not name the festival, though Numbers 28:26 does, beginning, "On the day of the first fruits, your Feast of Weeks [Shavuot], when you bring an offering of new grain to Adonai…."

Obviously, it is the weeks and days, not the omer, that are counted. The term *s'firat ha'omer* is thus shorthand for counting the days after bringing the omer of the first barley to the priest (Lev. 23:10).

The biblical injunction (Lev. 23:15–16) is to "count off seven weeks … fifty days," so the liturgical counting mentions both weeks and days—for example (on the tenth day), "Today is ten days, which is one week and three days from [the time] the omer [was brought]."

Psalm 67 This psalm is from a section of psalms that stands out because it prefers to call God *elohim* rather than Adonai, so is known as "Elohistic Psalter" (Psalms 42–83). Unlike most psalms, it is phrased in the plural, as a communal, not an individual, prayer for a successful harvest—which the nations will notice, causing them to praise both God and his people, Israel (see line 12). Though there is no evidence to suggest that this psalm was associated in antiquity with the Omer, it is an appropriate liturgical choice, since it reflects the first crops beginning to ripen.

[6] *"For the conductor of instrumental music"* Like many superscriptions in Psalms, the technical terms used here are obscure.

[7] *"Treat us graciously and bless us"* A paraphrase of the Priestly Blessing, Numbers 6:24–25 (see Volume 2, *The Amidah*, pp. 177–183):

> May Adonai bless you and keep you.
> May Adonai shine his face toward you and treat you graciously.
> May Adonai lift his face toward you and grant you peace.

This must have been a popular blessing in antiquity, since it is paraphrased in several biblical texts.

[8–9] *"Peoples … nations"* Psalms often assume an implied audience of nations who will praise God for watching over Israel—as in Psalm 117, the shortest psalm of all: "Praise Adonai, all you nations; extol Him, all you peoples, for great is his steadfast love toward us; the faithfulness of Adonai endures forever. Halleluyah."

Line 4 is repeated as line 6, serving as a refrain, and expressing a sentiment that may be a revision of Psalm 57:10 (cf. 108:4), "I will praise You among the peoples, Adonai; I will sing a hymn to You among the nations."

[10] *"Greatly rejoice"* Here the nations play the role usually assigned to nature (as in Ps. 98:4–9) or to Israel itself in the form of "Zion and the daughters of Judah" (Ps. 97:8). See Volume 8, *Kabbalat Shabbat (Welcoming Shabbat in the Synagogue)*, p. 77. The occasion for praise is God's justice, a theme found elsewhere also, as in Psalm 99:4, "Mighty king who loves justice, it was You who established equity, You who worked righteous judgment in Jacob."

[12–13] *"Earth … earth"* Clearly a couplet, two statements on the same theme, but reverse word order: "a,b," then "b,a." The same word ("land") begins line 12 and ends line 13. Also, the start of line 8 *(y'var'khenu elohim, "May God … bless us")* echoes the end of line 12. Both parts return to the theme established in line 7 *(elohim … y'var'khenu)*.

[12] *"God, our God"* The verse probably once read "Adonai our God," but when the Elohistic Psalter was created, and most references to *Adonai* were changed to *elohim* (God), the tautological phrase "God, our God" was created.

[13] *"God will bless us … revere Him"* A summary of the psalm as a whole, stressing the blessing of the land and its implication for the world's nations.

[22] *"Master of the universe"* In the Bible, the counting of the Omer is purely agricultural. This kabbalistic petitionary prayer reflects its remarkable transformation

into a mystical ritual.

22–23 *"You wrote in your Torah...."* Leviticus 23:15–16a. The ritual is described only there, nowhere else in the Bible.

25 *"Counted"* The Hebrew is a pun: The root *s.f.r* gives us the word "to count [the Omer]"; hence the counting period is called the *s'firah* (time of counting). But mystically speaking, *s'firah* is one of the primeval spheres of creation that need repairing.

———◆———

DORFF (THEOLOGY)

to the Bible) is to be numbered. This counting (*s'firat ha'omer*, pronounced s'-fee-RAHT hah-OH-mehr) links the two festivals, agriculturally and theologically. Agriculturally, the barley harvest of Passover is joined to the wheat harvest of Shavuot, when the "first fruits" (*bikurim*, pronounced bee-koo-REEM) of wheat were brought to the Temple. Counting these days raises our appreciation of these two harvests on which we so sorely depend. Theologically, we link the Exodus (on Passover) to the revelation of Torah (on Shavuot). The purpose of freedom is not freedom from, but freedom to take on adult responsibility to God and to others. Rabbi Jules Harlow explains (*Siddur Sim Shalom*, p. 236), "On our personal journeys in life, we each have our own enslavements, revelations and promised lands. As we often count the days leading to significant events in our personal lives, so we count the days in the life of our people, times past and present, culminating, in this instance, with the revelation of Torah, essential for our spiritual sustenance."

1 *"I am fully prepared"* The ritual may not be done mechanically; to fulfill the commandment and benefit from its meaning, one must focus on what one is doing.

2 *"From the day after the holiday [shabbat]"* Exactly when the Omer was to begin was a matter of great debate in the first century. The Sadducees understood *"shabbat"* here to refer to the usual Sabbath at the end of the week (the Sabbath of creation); so for them, the Omer always began on Sunday. Since the count is fifty days in all, Shavuot always fell on a Sunday. Preferring to understand *Shabbat* here literally—a day on which one desists from work—the Pharisees (precursors of the Rabbis) identified it with the first day of Passover, making the onset of the Omer the night that concludes that first day. As rabbinic Jews we follow the Pharisees.

4 *"Today we are one day"* From the end of the first week on, the counting mentions both days and weeks—for instance, "This is the ninth day, that is, one week and two days of the Omer." We thereby literally fulfill the Torah's mandate to count both "fifty days" and "seven full weeks." Some authorities hold that we may not start Shavuot until sunset so that the full forty-nine days have passed. Most, however, allow people to begin Shavuot before the entire forty-nineth day of the Omer has concluded at sunset. The principle that allows this interpretation is, "We may add from the ordinary to the sacred" (R.H. 9a). Moreover, since (as in sitting shivah [pronounced SHI-vah], "observing the seven days of mourning") part of a day counts as a whole day, even part of the last day of the Omer can be considered "whole."

——◆——

ELLENSON (MODERN LITURGIES)

over a hundred years of its absence. A tentative commentary in the draft version holds that the Omer represents an index of "what we need to sustain us."

In *Kol Haneshamah* (Reconstructionist, 1995) the counting of the Omer is seen as connecting "the idea of freedom, associated with Pesach, with the idea of Torah, associated with Shavuot," so that *s'firat ha'omer* ("counting the Omer") teaches, "Only one who engages in the study of Torah is truly free." That line goes back to the Reconstructionist *Daily Prayer Book* of 1963 and is a patent polemic against the traditional notion that the Omer recollects and prays for a Temple cult in Jerusalem. The French *Siddour Taher Libeinu*, still retains the original idea: the counting actually appears with the words, "May the Merciful One restore the temple to its place."

Ana B'kho'ach The Israeli Reform *Ha'avodah Shebalev* (1982) retains Psalm 67, but not the following *Ana B'kho'ach*, which has mystical overtones that Reform prayer books regularly omitted. One idea, however, of the *Ana B'kho'ach* appealed to the Israeli Reform community: freedom. They added this newly composed paragraph: "Those enslaved to time are the slaves of slaves. Only a servant of God is free. Blessed is Adonai who took us from Egyptian bondage, and commanded us to count fifty days so that He could bring us near to His service. May He open our hearts to His Torah, to serve Him in awe as in days of yore."

In the 1998 *Sim Shalom*, Psalm 128, asking that God bless us from Jerusalem, replaces Psalm 67. A concluding prayer states, "Our personal journeys in life are marked by enslavements and liberations, revelations and promised lands. Just as we mark the approach of significant moments in our own life, so we count such days in the life of our people. As we pause to recall our ancestors' bond with the soil ... and their gratitude for the annual harvest of grain, we also give thanks to God for renewing for us a year of life and of blessing."

The Israeli Conservative *Va'ani Tefillati* (1998) reinterprets the fifty days of the counting of the Omer. We have moved from the "attainment of bodily freedom [in Egypt] to the attainment of spiritual freedom [through the reception of the Torah at Sinai]." Passages from Psalm 28:9 and 1 Kings 8:59–60 follow the counting of the day.

——◆——

MA'ARIV (WEEKDAY AND SHABBAT)

FRANKEL (A WOMAN'S VOICE)

miles and fathoms; minutes and days, months and years.

For women, measurement, specifically counting, is more natural than it is for men. Women's bodies train them to count—days between menstrual periods, months until giving birth, hours between feedings, years between mammograms.

Counting the Omer gives all of us—men and women—a chance to keep track of time on several levels: the Israelites' trek from Egypt to Sinai; the agricultural countdown in Israel from spring to summer; the kabbalist's inner journey through the seven lower *s'firot*; an individual's passage from liberation to revelation.

The psalmist urges us to "number our days" so that we might attain a heart of wisdom. Counting the Omer makes us mindful of how quickly our own days are passing, and how precious each one is.

GRAY (OUR TALMUDIC HERITAGE)

Rabbis after them), interpreted it to mean "the day after *yom tov*," meaning the day after the first day of Passover, in which case Shavuot would not necessarily fall on a Sunday.

The Boethusians appear to have had the literal meaning of the word *shabbat* going for them, but for its own polemical purposes, the Talmud (Men. 65a–b) portrays them as incapable of holding their own in the debate. When Yochanan ben Zakkai asks why Shavuot must always fall on a Sunday, none of them is able to answer. Finally, one old man "babbles" (the Talmud's word!) a reason: Knowing that Shavuot lasts only one day, and loving Israel so much, Moses instituted it for the day after Shabbat, so that Israel may enjoy two consecutive days of celebration. Yochanan ridicules this notion, pointing out (rather sensibly) that if Moses was such a lover of Israel, he should not have led the people out of Egypt by a circuitous route that resulted in a forty-year journey. When the elder takes offense at this belittling response, Yochanan adds insult to injury by adding that "our perfect Torah" should not be like "your idle chatter"—meaning that he, Yochanan, can prove his position, whereas the elder has just a speculative (and specious) explanation.

Yochanan's proof is that the Torah says both "you should count fifty days" (Lev. 23:16) and that there should be seven complete weeks (Lev. 23:15), which is forty-nine days. This can be reconciled only if you count from a movable starting point (Passover). When Passover falls on Shabbat, the counting begins on Sunday and goes for seven complete weeks. When Passover falls during the week, the counting starts the day after and must not *exceed* fifty days. According to the Boethusian position, should Passover fall on a Monday, we cannot begin counting the Omer until the following Sunday, meaning that we would count fifty-six days until Shavuot—a violation of the fifty-day limit from Leviticus 23:16.

168

[2] *"Count"* The Talmud (Men. 65b) wonders why the command to count the Omer is phrased in the plural *(us'fartem lakhem)*, rather than in the singular *(us'farta l'kha)*. This question gains added force from the fact that elsewhere (Deut. 16:9) the Torah does indeed use the singular for "You shall count" *(tispar lakh)*. The answer is related to the previous discussion (see "The day after the holiday [*shabbat*]" above,) on the day that counting should begin. The singular of Deuteronomy 16:9 is taken to refer to the *bet din*, or rabbinic court, which, by dint of the fact that it sanctifies the months based on witness testimony, is ultimately responsible for determining when the counting of the Omer will begin. The plural formulation of Leviticus 23:15 is interpreted as placing the obligation of counting the Omer on the shoulders of all individual Jews.

[4] *"Today we are one day"* R. Barukh Halevi Epstein (1860–1941, Russia) asks why the first day of counting the Omer is given as *yom echad* ("one day") rather than as *yom rishon* ("first day"). One reason is that this phrase echoes Genesis 1:5—"There was evening and morning, one day" *(vay'hi erev vay'hi voker yom echad)*. The second reason he gives is that the Boethusians (whom he referred to as Sadducees) held that the counting of the Omer should always begin on a Sunday *(yom rishon* in Hebrew). To call the first day of counting *yom rishon* might inadvertently strengthen the force of the Boethusian (Sadducean) view.

◆

KUSHNER & POLEN (CHASIDISM)

s'firot here might best be understood not so much as the infrastructure of creation, but as dimensions of the divine psyche and therefore of our own personalities. And each of the seven weeks, each with its seven days, is inter-inclusive, that is, each week corresponds to a specific *s'firah*, which, in turn, contains that *s'firah's* version of all the other six *s'firot*. For example, the first week, *Chesed*, contains a *Chesed* version of all seven, just as the third week, *Tiferet*, contains a *Tiferet* version of all seven, and so forth. We can therefore describe each *s'firah* with its corresponding dimension of personality—and therefore its successive development through the seven weeks of counting the Omer.

1. *Chesed*, "love," means unlimited expansion and inclusiveness.
2. *G'vurah*, "rigor," means the setting of boundaries.
3. *Tiferet*, "beauty," means balance or harmony.
4. *Netsach*, "victory," means commitment, eternity, and showing up.
5. *Hod*, "splendor," means the reverberation that comes from making definitions, as these definitions ripple outward throughout our perception of the world.
6. *Y'sod*, "foundation," means the joy of creation, the (almost) orgiastic pleasure that is the foundational moment in every project.
7. *Malkhut*, "kingdom," means receptivity to take in the blessing that is given.

And, in this way, during each successive week of the counting of the Omer, in an ever-ascending spiral, we too can comprehend and begin to heal our own souls.

◆

LANDES (HALAKHAH)

brought the *omer* offering that is waved—they are to be seven complete weeks—until the morrow of the seventh week you are to count to fifty days and then offer a new meal-offering to God." I shall employ this verse to explain the halakhic understanding of this *mitzvah*:

1. "You *all* are to count": The Hebrew is *us'fartem lakhem*, the plural, from which the Talmud points out that the *mitzvah* rests upon each individual—unlike the counting to the jubilee year, where we find the singular, *us'farta l'kha*, referring to the obligation of the court as a single body to count forty-nine years (Men. 65b and the Tosafot there).

2. "Count": This is an actual, out-loud counting, unlike other countings in the Torah—again, like the court counting the years to the jubilee. There, you need not actually orally count; it is sufficient just to compute the amount of time that has passed and know how much more time is left. The *s'firat ha'omer*, however, is a conscious, articulated, and oral counting (*Arukh Hashulchan* 489:1).

3. "Count": Once you have counted you have fulfilled the *mitzvah*. Thus, even if someone asks you what number you are counting and you answer, you have fulfilled the *mitzvah*. The practical consequence is that you can no longer make a blessing over the counting in case you want to do it again in its full ritual form, for that would be a *b'rachah l'vatalah*, "a blessing made in vain" (*Bet Yosef* 489:2). Thus the custom is to answer, "Yesterday we counted …" and to supply the number of that day. According to the *TaZ* (*Torah Zahav*, commentary to the *Shulchan Arukh* composed by Rabbi David Halevi, 1586–1667, Poland), to fulfill the *mitzvah* one needs to say *Hayom* ("Today is…."). Saying just the number would not prevent one from saying the blessing and counting properly afterward.

4. "From the morrow … complete weeks": There is a disagreement regarding when the counting may start. (1) The *Tur*, based upon the *Rosh* (Rabbenu Asher, 1250–1327, Germany, Toledo), and the *S'MaG* (*Sefer Mitzvot G'dolot* by Moses of Coucy, thirteenth century, France, "Positive Commandments," 200) understand that one can count "at the beginning of the night, even as early as *safek chasheikhah*" ("doubtful darkness"). (2) *RaN* (Nissim ben Reuven, d. 1380, Spain, commentary on Alfasi) and *Rashba* (Solomon ibn Adret, 1235–1310, Spain, commentary on the Talmud) say that those who are careful will count only after *tseit hakochavim* ("when the stars emerge"). The *Bayit Chadash* (*BaCH*,

Joel Sirkes, Poland, sixteenth century, O. Ch. 489:1) concurs, but concludes that, nonetheless, the general custom is to count even in doubtful darkness. He draws the line there, disallowing a third view (3), *Sefer Hamanhig* (halakhic compendium by Abraham ben Nathan Hayarchi, Lunel, Toledo, 1155–1215) that one can count even earlier. The different *shitot* (opinions) can be explained in the following way: Opinion 2, the *Ran* and *Rashba* (it can be done only after the stars emerge), is obviously because they want to make certain that the day they are counting has actually commenced. Opinion 1, the *Tur* (one can count early), is that if one wishes the counting to be a "complete" day, it needs to be at the very beginning. Opinion 3, *Sefer Hamanhig* (it can be even earlier) is because if *Ma'ariv* is connected to an earlier *Minchah*, it may be recited earlier, implying that in some formal sense, night has begun. Again, the practical halakhah allows counting only as early as doubtful darkness. We urge that in late spring, when Friday night services may finish before twilight, the congregation should be reminded to count the Omer at home during the meal (as well as to recite again the *Sh'ma*, which also properly needs to be said at dark).

5. "Days … weeks": The verse speaks about counting both days and weeks. Which takes precedence? Jacob ben Asher (the *Tur*) provides several possibilities. He quotes his father, the *Rosh*, who says that some opine that days are counted as, primary only until one reaches a full week. At that point we say, "Today is seven days, which are one week." But from that point on we no longer count the total number of days separately. Thus at eight days, we say, "Today is one week and one day," not "eight days," as we have already counted seven of those days the prior week. We continue that way until reaching fourteen days, when we state, "Today is fourteen days, which are two weeks." At fifteen days we state, "Today is two weeks and one day," And so it goes.

Another opinion is to emphasize the days over the weeks, mentioning the latter only at multiples of seven. Thus at seven days we state, "Today is seven days, which are one week." At eight days we say only, "Today is eight days." At fourteen days we state, "Today is fourteen days, which are two weeks."

The dominant position follows Maimonides' opinion, as explained by Rabbi Joseph B. Solveitchik (the *Rov*, Lithuania, Berlin, Boston, New York; preeminent talmudist and Orthodox theologian of the middle and late twentieth century): "Don't be mixed up by their [the Sages'] saying that it is a *mitzvah* to count days and it is a *mitzvah* to count weeks so that you think that they are two [separate] *mitzvot*, rather … they are two parts of one mitzvah" [*Book of Commandments*, "Positive Commandments," 161]. Thus his practice, which is ours, was to count both days and weeks equally, starting with "Today is one day"; then, eventually, "Today is seven days, which is one week"; then, "Today is eight days, which is one week and one day"; and so on.

There is a custom to add to the counting either *la'omer* ("to the [counting of the] Omer") or *ba'omer* ("in the [counting of the] Omer.") Either is correct.

6. "Complete": One must count each and every day. If you miss the counting at night, you count during the next day, but without a blessing. If you miss counting the next day as well, you can no longer count the following nights with a blessing, but you should continue counting anyway, without it.

7. "From the day you brought the *omer* offering that is waved … offer a new meal-offering": The absence nowadays of the *omer* and of sacrifices, generally, leads the majority of halakhic authorities to consider the practice of counting rabbinic (*d'rabbanan*), commemorating the Temple service. Others, chiefly Maimonides, believe the counting is its own independent *mitzvah* that retains its Torah status (*d'ora'ita*), even though we lack the offerings that are made on each end.

This, I believe, has a practical implication. The counting is preceded by an explicit statement, "I am fully prepared to perform the positive commandment of *s'firat ha'omer*, in accordance with what is written in the Torah: Count.... " For those who follow Maimonides' opinion, this is not a problem, for indeed it is a positive commandment from the Torah. But if one follows the majority view that counting is now merely rabbinic, it is not only wrong but (I believe) halakhically problematic to say that introduction, since stating that a rabbinic enactment is a Torah law is a violation of *bal tosif*, the prohibition not to add to the commandments of the Torah. One suggestion (offered in conversation by Rabbi Aharon Adler of Jerusalem, synagogue rabbi and Rosh Yeshivah) is to consider the introduction ("I am fully prepared") as a *sh'ifah*—an articulated yearning for the return of this *mitzvah* in its full status. An explanation to worshipers in this manner would solve the legal problem and add considerably to their spiritual intention. I would also note that if one follows Maimonides, one should take comfort and strength in an interpretation that considers the independent spiritual integrity of counting days and weeks, even though the sacrificial system is no longer with us.

———◆———

L. HOFFMAN (HISTORY)

(as preferred by *Mishnah B'rurah*), rather than after it (following the custom of the *Gra*, the Vilna Gaon). The former custom (reflected here) is rooted in the desire to do the counting as soon as possible after nightfall occurs. The latter custom treats the counting as an independent *mitzvah* that should not interrupt the altogether separate *mitzvah* of reciting the evening service; it must therefore be delayed until after that service's conclusion (i.e., after *Alenu* and the final *Kaddish*).

[1] *"Fully prepared"* The remnants of a kabbalistic *kavvanah*. Nowadays, we use the

word *kavvanah* to imply inward spiritual intensity in prayer—the opposite of rote recitation. But kabbalists applied the term as part of their mystical system whereby every individual act of prayer has its own unique potential for bringing about a *zivvug* (pronounced zee-VOOG), a "union" of male and female aspects of God (see Volume 3, *P'sukei D'zimrah* [*Morning Psalms*], L. Hoffman, "With this do I prepare," pp. 53, 66–67). In this technical sense, a *kavvanah* is an introductory meditation in the first-person singular that enables worshipers to concentrate on the hidden purpose behind the prayer. We have only the bare outline of the meditation here, not the esoteric detail that the original kabbalistic *kavvanah* would have provided.

[3] *"Blessed"* The blessing is probably medieval, but of uncertain origin. It is certainly geonic, taken for granted by Saadiah (c. 920) and Hai Gaon (d. 1038). Unaccountably, however, it is absent from authentic manuscripts of *Seder Rav Amram* (our first known prayer book, c. 860). In Spain, Isaac Ibn Ghayyat (1038–1089) cites plenty of geonic precedent for it, including *Halakhot G'dolot*, which is generally (though not universally) attributed to Yehudai Gaon (eighth century); and it is normative among later Europeans. Maimonides (1135–1204) mentions it, but may imply that some people are not careful in saying it, since he goes out of his way to rule that counting the Omer without saying the blessing fulfills the *mitzvah* ("Laws of the *Tamid* and *Musaf* Sacrifices" 7:25). By the sixteenth century, Joseph Caro glosses Maimonides by adding, "That is obvious, since failure to say blessings does not invalidate *mitzvot*." In Caro's day, everyone said the blessing, no doubt, moving Caro to wonder why Maimonides had felt the need to stipulate the obvious.

In geonic times, question arose as to whether the entire congregation should stand during the blessing, a practice that Hai Gaon calls unnecessary bother *(tirkha)*. Everywhere, he says, congregations sit while the prayer leader stands and recites the blessing; then the seated congregation, in unison, answers *"Amen."* But European practice (e.g., Isaac ibn Ghayyat and Aaron ben Jacob of Lunel [thirteenth to fourteenth century, *Orchot Chaim*]) often had everyone stand during it. Solomon ibn Adret (the *RaSHBA*, c. 1235–c. 1310, Spain) differentiated the blessing from the counting itself, ruling that although everyone has to count the Omer, people need only listen to the blessing, but not stand while doing so.

The nineteenth-century *Arukh Hashulchan* (O. Ch. 489:4) exempts women from the entire commandment (it is a positive time-bound *mitzvah*), but notes that women are accustomed to participating in it, just as they are the *mitzvot* of "*shofar, sukkah,* and *lulav*."

We might also expect the blessing we call *Shehecheyanu* (pronounced sheh-heh-kheh-YAH-noo, "who has given us life"; known also as *Birkat Z'man*, pronounced beer-KAHT z'-MAHN, "the blessing of time"). Other cyclical events (like blowing the shofar and marking the onset of holidays) call for this blessing to celebrate their annual return. But tradition forbids it here because the Omer period mourns the Temple's destruction, and *Shehecheyanu* is reserved for joyful occasions.

[4] *"One day"* We include here only the formula for counting the first day. But the formula becomes more complex by the end of a week, because rabbinic interpretation demands that both days and weeks be included in the count (see Landes, "Counting the Omer," p. 161). Our current formula is medieval. Nissim Gerondi (the *RaN* [acronym for Rabbenu Nissim], c. 1310–c. 1375, Gerona, Spain) says explicitly (commentary to Alfasi, end of Pesachim), "The *mitzvah* is to count weeks just at the end of each week, but in most places, it has become customary to act stringently by saying every day, 'Today is day such and such of the Omer, which is so and so many weeks and so many days.'"

Yemenite Jews recite the formula in Aramaic—treating it like other legal formulas that are recited in Aramaic, such as *Kol Nidre* and *Ha lachma anya* (an introductory prayer at the Passover Seder acknowledging legal ownership by all present of the matzah).

Psalm 67 Recited during the seven weeks of counting because (omitting the superscription, verse 6 here), the psalm has seven verses (one for each week) and forty-nine words (one for each day).

[14] *"By the might of your great right hand"* A fascinating mystical composition, comprising an acrostic of a forty-two-letter name of God. For commentary, see Volume 8, *Kabbalat Shabbat (Welcoming Shabbat in the Synagogue)*, pp. 111–114.

[22] *"To cleanse us of our evil"* A kabbalistic addition, stipulating the esoteric meaning of the counting. *K'lipot* (pronounced k'-lee-POHT) are part of the kabbalistic myth of creation, impurities said to have embedded themselves in the universe when the light emanating from God (on its way to becoming material reality) smashed the successive waves of *s'firot* ("vessels") in which it was stored, leaving *k'lipot*, "shards," from which all existence must be purified in order to return to its desired end of complete divine and cosmic unity.

J. HOFFMAN (TRANSLATION)

quotation from Leviticus indicates when to begin counting the Omer, so it is important to know whether it refers to the day after the holiday (as we have it translated here, and as has become rabbinic tradition) or to the day after the Shabbat of the holiday (as the language seems to indicate). We translate in accordance with rabbinic tradition, noting that, while the Hebrew does support our translation, "Shabbat" was probably the original intention.

[2] *"Wave the Omer offering"* Birnbaum, "bring the sheaf of the wave offering." But "sheaf" is *omer* in Hebrew, and we want to show the connection between "counting the Omer" and the "*omer* offering."

[2] *"Full weeks"* The word for "full" here *(tamim)* usually means "unblemished," referring to animals. And the word for "week" here is *shabbat*. If "seven unblemished Sabbaths" made any sense, we would use that as the translation. But the Septuagint gives us "complete" (not "unblemished") here. Furthermore, this quotation is from Leviticus, but in Deuteronomy we find a review of the material, and there we find "seven weeks," not "seven Sabbaths." The Septuagint repeats, in part, the language from Leviticus, but uses "seven full weeks" in Deuteronomy. We thus suspect that our version of the text from Leviticus may be the result of a transmission error or may reflect a dialect of Hebrew with which we are not entirely familiar.

[2] *"Week,"* Again, the Hebrew reads *shabbat*.

[4] *"One day"* The formulation stays the same for the first six days, but then, reflecting the theme of "weeks," changes with day seven, giving us the translation (from day 10, for example): "Today we are ten days, which make up one week and three days, into the counting of the Omer."

[6] *"Conductor"* Others: "choirmaster" or "leader." Curiously, both here and in the many other psalms in which it appears, the Septuagint consistently translates this (today poorly understood) Hebrew attribution as "for the end." The Hebrew word is *m'natse'ach*, which we assume to be "leader" (in this case, leader of the orchestra, hence "conductor"). It comes from the root *n.ts.ch*, which gives us various meanings, including "brilliant/shining," "conquer," "lead," and "eternity." The Greek translation seems to presume that the word incorporates the "eternity" meaning, while other Jewish translations tend toward "lead."

Psalm 67 has exactly forty-nine Hebrew words, one, therefore, for each day of the Omer. Unfortunately, our English translation required more.

[6] *"Of instrumental music"* Again, we do not know enough about ancient music and musical terminology to know exactly what is meant here. The word *bin'ginot* means "with/in the *n'ginah*s," but we don't know exactly what a *n'ginah* is, or how the phrase "with/in *n'ginah*s" relates to the introduction of the psalm. The prevailing theory of the Hebrew word is that it refers to some sort of instrumentation. Our translation suggests that there were two types of professional conductor, one "of instrumental music" and one "of vocal music." As in our language today, although they involved different skills, they did not have different names. Of course, if this theory is right, it's not clear how the text of the psalm (which was presumably sung) relates to this purported instrumental work. Nor is it clear why other psalms that seem to mention specific instruments (see Volume 8, *Kabbalat Shabbat*, pp. 91–92) are conducted by the vocal-music conductor. Almost certainly we and other translators have missed something fundamental here.

[7] *"Treat us graciously"* Or "be gracious to us." In this poetic context, however, "treat" seems more appropriate than the bland "be."

[7] *"Shining his face among us"* This idiom of "face shining" appears most prominently in the Priestly Blessing (See Volume 2, *The Amidah*, pp. 176–177), where we also suggest the poetic translation: "May you be emblazoned by Adonai's face and treated graciously.") There, too, we find God's grace and God's shining face combined into one image. These themes, along with "peace" (also present in the Priestly Blessing), seem to have been popular in antiquity. In addition to their appearances in various formulations in the Bible itself, they surface in the most ancient surviving Bible-like material: silver scrolls dating perhaps to the seventh century B.C.E.: "May Adonai bless you and keep you. May Adonai shine his face upon you and give you peace."

[7] *"Forever"* Hebrew, *selah*. Elsewhere (see Volume 2, *The Amidah*, p. 85), we note that the term was probably something like the modern musical fermata, meaning "forever" to the Rabbis, but not to the psalmist. The Greek translators of the Septuagint also didn't know what it meant, inventing a unique Greek word (*diapsalma*, roughly "through the psalm," often translated "pause") to translate *selah*. We might do just as well to leave the word untranslated here.

[8] *"So that we know"* Others, "to make known." But the Hebrew is clearly "to know." At issue is who the inferred subject of the Hebrew infinitive is, that is, whether "God" or "us" is doing the verb. In the English, "God shines his face among us to know …," "God" is the only possible subject of "to know," but in Hebrew "us [we]" can also be the subject. (The details of how infinitives get interpreted in such situations are complicated. For example, in the English "I promised Mom not to call after 11:00 P.M.," I am doing the calling, whereas in "I persuaded Mom not to call before 11:00 A.M.," she's doing the calling.)

[8] *"Peoples"* We would prefer "nations" here, but because the Hebrew was three words (with nearly identical meanings), here and immediately below, we opt for synonyms in English, as well.

[10] *"Nationality"* Alas, "nationality," is related to "nation" in a way that the two Hebrew words are not, but we have run out of options in English.

[10] *"Greatly rejoice"* Hebrew, something like "rejoice and be happy."

[10] *"Guide"* Following Birnbaum. We assume that the word here, more often translated along the lines of "show comfort to," is in parallel with "rule," above.

[10] *"Forever"* Again, *selah*.

[22] *"Cleanse us"* Or "cleanse ourselves." The Hebrew is ambiguous as to who is doing the cleansing. Also, we would prefer "purify" here, but then would we have "purify … impurities," creating a poetic affect in the English absent in the Hebrew.

[22] *"Evil"* "Evil" is certainly the wrong word in English, but we hardly have a better one. The Hebrew word means "outer shells" and is often translated "husks." It refers to

the shells of the vessels that, according to the kabbalists, contain God and God's holy light. The shells hide what is in the vessels and keep us from what is holy.

[25] *"Amen"* Literally, *Amen. Selah.* We omit *selah* here.

◆ ◆ ◆

[Continue with Alenu and Kaddish Yatom (Mourner's Kaddish). For text and commentary, see Volume 6, Tachanun and Concluding Prayers, pp. 133–157. From Rosh Chodesh Elul until Simchat Torah, continue here, followed by Kaddish Yatom (Mourner's Kaddish). If services are being held in a house of mourning, continue on p. 190.]

H. Closing Prayers

I. Psalm 27

¹For David. Adonai is my light and my salvation. Before whom shall I fear? Adonai is the strength of my life. Before whom shall I tremble? ²When those who would do evil approached me to devour my flesh, my enemies and my foes, it was they who failed and stumbled. ³Even should a battalion engage me in battle, my heart will not fear. Even should I be engaged in war, in this do I trust. ⁴One thing do I ask from Adonai: it is what I request: That I might sit in Adonai's house all the days of my life, to gaze upon Adonai's beauty, and to see his Temple. ⁵For He will hide me in his shelter on bad days, protect me with the protection of his tent. He will set me high upon a rock. ⁶Then my head will be held high above my enemies about me, and in his tent I will offer offerings of triumph. I will sing and chant to Adonai. ⁷Hear, O Adonai! My voice calls out. Be gracious to me and answer me. ⁸My heart says to you, "Seek my face." I have sought your face, Adonai. ⁹Do not hide your face from me. Do not turn away your servant in anger, for You have been my help. Do not forsake me and do not abandon me, God of my salvation. ¹⁰For my father and mother have abandoned me, but Adonai took me in. ¹¹Adonai, show me your way, and lead me on a just path for the sake of my enemies. ¹²Do not hand me over to my foes, for false witnesses and unjust accusers have risen up against me. ¹³Had I only not believed I would see Adonai's goodness in the land of the living! ¹⁴Wait for Adonai! Be strong and steel your heart. Wait for Adonai!

לְ֜דָוִד. יְיָ אוֹרִי וְיִשְׁעִי, מִמִּי אִירָא; ¹
יְיָ מָעוֹז חַיַּי, מִמִּי אֶפְחָד. ²בִּקְרֹב
עָלַי מְרֵעִים לֶאֱכֹל אֶת בְּשָׂרִי, צָרַי
וְאֹיְבַי לִי, הֵמָּה כָשְׁלוּ וְנָפָלוּ. ³אִם
תַּחֲנֶה עָלַי מַחֲנֶה, לֹא יִירָא לִבִּי; אִם
תָּקוּם עָלַי מִלְחָמָה, בְּזֹאת אֲנִי בוֹטֵחַ.
⁴אַחַת שָׁאַלְתִּי מֵאֵת יְיָ, אוֹתָהּ אֲבַקֵּשׁ:
שִׁבְתִּי בְּבֵית יְיָ כָּל יְמֵי חַיַּי, לַחֲזוֹת
בְּנֹעַם יְיָ, וּלְבַקֵּר בְּהֵיכָלוֹ. ⁵כִּי יִצְפְּנֵנִי
בְּסֻכֹּה בְּיוֹם רָעָה, יַסְתִּרֵנִי בְּסֵתֶר אָהֳלוֹ;
בְּצוּר יְרוֹמְמֵנִי. ⁶וְעַתָּה יָרוּם רֹאשִׁי עַל
אֹיְבַי סְבִיבוֹתַי, וְאֶזְבְּחָה בְאָהֳלוֹ זִבְחֵי
תְרוּעָה; אָשִׁירָה וַאֲזַמְּרָה לַייָ. ⁷שְׁמַע,
יְיָ, קוֹלִי אֶקְרָא, וְחָנֵּנִי וַעֲנֵנִי. ⁸לְךָ אָמַר
לִבִּי, בַּקְּשׁוּ פָנָי; אֶת פָּנֶיךָ, יְיָ, אֲבַקֵּשׁ.
⁹אַל תַּסְתֵּר פָּנֶיךָ מִמֶּנִּי, אַל תַּט בְּאַף
עַבְדֶּךָ, עֶזְרָתִי הָיִיתָ; אַל תִּטְּשֵׁנִי וְאַל
תַּעַזְבֵנִי, אֱלֹהֵי יִשְׁעִי. ¹⁰כִּי אָבִי וְאִמִּי
עֲזָבוּנִי, וַיְיָ יַאַסְפֵנִי. ¹¹הוֹרֵנִי יְיָ דַּרְכֶּךָ,
וּנְחֵנִי בְּאֹרַח מִישׁוֹר, לְמַעַן שֹׁרְרָי. ¹²אַל
תִּתְּנֵנִי בְּנֶפֶשׁ צָרָי, כִּי קָמוּ בִי עֵדֵי
שֶׁקֶר וִיפֵחַ חָמָס. ¹³לוּלֵא הֶאֱמַנְתִּי
לִרְאוֹת בְּטוּב יְיָ בְּאֶרֶץ חַיִּים. ¹⁴קַוֵּה אֶל
יְיָ, חֲזַק וְיַאֲמֵץ לִבֶּךָ, וְקַוֵּה אֶל יְיָ.

BRETTLER (BIBLE)

Psalm 27 An unusually difficult psalm. The first six verses have the form of a psalm of thanksgiving, after being saved from enemies, while verses 7–14 are technically a "lament" (a complaint), in which the psalmist is in dire need of divine intervention. Perhaps two separate psalms have been combined, possibly because they both describe benefiting from the divine presence at the Temple. Their order, however, remains problematic—logically, thanksgiving should follow lament, implying the situation of someone who has been saved from danger.

Another problem concerns verses 7–14, where the person praying seems to be suffering from (p. 183)

DORFF (THEOLOGY)

[1] *"Adonai is my light and my salvation …"* From the onset of Elul, the month of spiritual and moral preparation preceding Rosh Hashanah, until the end of the penitential season (through Yom Kippur or Hoshanah Rabbah—custom varies), we pray that God will (p. 184)

ELLENSON (MODERN LITURGIES)

Psalm 27 A number of Reform prayer books include this psalm, though the *Union Prayer Book* (American Reform, 1895) renders it only in the vernacular. Reform liturgy generally looked favorably on biblical material (see "Announcement of Sacred (p. 185)

FRANKEL (A WOMAN'S VOICE)

"From Rosh Chodesh Elul" In the early eighteenth century, a small Yiddish prayer book was published under the title *Tkhines vos men zol zogn fun Rosh Khoydesh Elul to Yom Kipor* ("*Tkhine*s to be recited in synagogue from the beginning of Elul until Yom Kippur"). The author, Beyle Hurvits, offered the following prayer to be recited before the *K'dushah*:

> Near You, God, there is no night,
> And candles are not needed beside You,
>
> (p. 185)

[For prayer instructions, see page 179.]

I. PSALM 27

[1] For David. Adonai is my light and my salvation. Before whom shall I fear? Adonai is the strength of my life. Before whom shall I tremble? [2] When those who would do evil approached me to devour my flesh, my enemies and my foes, it was they who failed and stumbled. [3] Even should a battalion engage me in battle, my heart will not fear. Even

GRAY (OUR TALMUDIC HERITAGE)

[1] *"Adonai is my light* [ori] *and my salvation* [v'yishi]*"* Midrash T'hillim 27:2 explains this phrase beautifully in connection with Psalm 119:105 ("Your words are a candle to my feet and a light for my path"). The wicked are like people who stumble about in the darkness, tripping over rocks and falling into pits. But the righteous are like people who walk holding a bright light (the Torah), which enables them to avoid the rocks and pits. What are these rocks and pits that the (p. 186)

KUSHNER & POLEN (CHASIDISM)

[4] *"One thing do I ask from Adonai"* Throughout the thirty days of the month of Elul and the ten days between Rosh Hashanah and Yom Kippur, at the conclusion of *Ma'ariv*, it is customary to recite Psalm 27. Chasidic tradition, citing Rabbi Levi Yitzhak of Berditchev, takes the redundancy of the biblical parallelism (i.e., one thing I ask / that do I seek) as a distillation of every spiritual endeavor: "The one thing I'm asking for is precisely that I should always be seeking the presence of God."

L. HOFFMAN (HISTORY)

PSALMS, THE PART OF THE BIBLE MOST FREQUENTLY CITED IN THE PRAYER BOOK, OFTEN BRING SERVICES TO A CLOSE. CHOICE OF PSALMS VARIES WIDELY, HOWEVER. WE INCLUDE HERE PSALM 27, BECAUSE IT IS SO WIDELY ASSOCIATED WITH THE HIGH HOLY DAY PERIOD, AND PSALM 49 (P. 190).

Psalm 27 In Sefardi tradition (including Spanish-Portuguese), the evening service ends in a particularly striking way. Just before *Alenu*, Sefardim say Psalm 23 and then repeat the *Bar'khu*, a surprise for Ashkenazi visitors who readily recognize it only as a call *to* prayer, not a *(p. 186)*

א לְדָוִד. יְיָ אוֹרִי וְיִשְׁעִי, מִמִּי אִירָא; יְיָ מָעוֹז חַיַּי, מִמִּי אֶפְחָד. ב בִּקְרֹב עָלַי מְרֵעִים לֶאֱכֹל אֶת בְּשָׂרִי, צָרַי וְאֹיְבַי לִי, הֵמָּה כָשְׁלוּ וְנָפָלוּ. ג אִם תַּחֲנֶה עָלַי מַחֲנֶה, לֹא יִירָא לִבִּי; אִם תָּקוּם עָלַי מִלְחָמָה, בְּזֹאת אֲנִי בוֹטֵחַ. ד אַחַת שָׁאַלְתִּי מֵאֵת יְיָ, אוֹתָהּ אֲבַקֵּשׁ: שִׁבְתִּי

J. HOFFMAN (TRANSLATION)

[1] *"For David"* Once again, we find an attribution introducing a psalm. In this case, it seems fairly straightforward. The Greek version, however, begins, "For David, before he was anointed," raising the intriguing possibility that David needed the light and salvation (see below, "Salvation") only before he was anointed.

[1] *"Salvation"* Hebrew, *yesha*. This is not the usual Hebrew word for "salvation," *y'shu'ah*, though both words appear to come from the same root, *y.sh.ayin*. Of the few other times we see this word, twice it is in connection with clothing, in the metaphor that wearing *yesha* is a good thing. This opening line may mean something like *(p. 187)*

should I be engaged in war, in this do I trust. ⁴One thing do I ask from Adonai: it is what I request: That I might sit in Adonai's house all the days of my life, to gaze upon Adonai's beauty, and to see his Temple. ⁵For He will hide me in his shelter on bad days, protect me with the protection of his tent. He will set me high upon a rock. ⁶Then my head will be held high above my enemies about me, and in his tent I will offer offerings of triumph. I will sing and chant to Adonai. ⁷Hear, O Adonai! My voice calls out. Be gracious to me and answer me. ⁸My heart says to you, "Seek my face." I have sought your face, Adonai. ⁹Do not hide your face from me. Do not turn away your servant in anger, for You have been my help. Do not forsake me and do not abandon me, God of my salvation. ¹⁰For my father and mother have abandoned me, but Adonai took me in. ¹¹Adonai, show me your way, and lead me on a just path for the sake of my enemies. ¹²Do not hand me over to my foes, for false witnesses and unjust accusers have risen up against me. ¹³Had I only not believed I would see Adonai's goodness in the land of the living! ¹⁴Wait for Adonai! Be strong and steel your heart. Wait for Adonai!

בְּבֵית יְיָ כָּל יְמֵי חַיַּי, לַחֲזוֹת בְּנֹעַם יְיָ, וּלְבַקֵּר בְּהֵיכָלוֹ. ⁵כִּי יִצְפְּנֵנִי בְּסֻכֹּה בְּיוֹם רָעָה, יַסְתִּרֵנִי בְּסֵתֶר אָהֳלוֹ; בְּצוּר יְרוֹמְמֵנִי. ⁶וְעַתָּה יָרוּם רֹאשִׁי עַל אֹיְבַי סְבִיבוֹתַי, וְאֶזְבְּחָה בְאָהֳלוֹ זִבְחֵי תְרוּעָה; אָשִׁירָה וַאֲזַמְּרָה לַיְיָ. ⁷שְׁמַע, יְיָ, קוֹלִי אֶקְרָא, וְחָנֵּנִי וַעֲנֵנִי. ⁸לְךָ אָמַר לִבִּי, בַּקְּשׁוּ פָנָי; אֶת פָּנֶיךָ, יְיָ, אֲבַקֵּשׁ. ⁹אַל תַּסְתֵּר פָּנֶיךָ מִמֶּנִּי, אַל תַּט בְּאַף עַבְדֶּךָ, עֶזְרָתִי הָיִיתָ; אַל תִּטְּשֵׁנִי וְאַל תַּעַזְבֵנִי, אֱלֹהֵי יִשְׁעִי. ¹⁰כִּי אָבִי וְאִמִּי עֲזָבוּנִי, וַיְיָ יַאַסְפֵנִי. ¹¹הוֹרֵנִי יְיָ דַּרְכֶּךָ, וּנְחֵנִי בְּאֹרַח מִישׁוֹר, לְמַעַן שׁוֹרְרָי. ¹²אַל תִּתְּנֵנִי בְּנֶפֶשׁ צָרָי, כִּי קָמוּ בִי עֵדֵי שֶׁקֶר וִיפֵחַ חָמָס. ¹³לוּלֵא הֶאֱמַנְתִּי לִרְאוֹת בְּטוּב יְיָ בְּאֶרֶץ חַיִּים. ¹⁴קַוֵּה אֶל יְיָ, חֲזַק וְיַאֲמֵץ לִבֶּךָ, וְקַוֵּה אֶל יְיָ.

more than one problem—is he bothered by (military) enemies or by false accusations (vv. 11–12)? As psalms were reused, they may have been enlarged as "multipurpose" vehicles of expression for different situations.

[1] *"My light … my salvation"* A typical biblical poetic verse, divisible into two largely equal parts that are syntactically and semantically similar. God is the psalmist's "light," an image found elsewhere too, as in Isaiah 60:19–20. But connected to "my salvation," the reference may be more specifically to God's shining countenance, which will assure deliverance (see Pss. 31:17, 44:4, 80:4; 80:8, 80:20).

[2] *"To devour my flesh"* Enemies are depicted either as carnivorous animals or, worse, actual cannibals!

[3] *"My heart will not fear"* A return to the initial verse, "Before whom shall I fear?"

[4] *"Sit in Adonai's house all the days of my life"* Similar to the conclusion of Psalm 23: "and I shall dwell in the house of Adonai for many long years." It is uncertain if this is meant hyperbolically or if laypeople could literally camp out in the Temple, enjoying the proximity of the divine presence.

[5] *"Shelter … tent … rock"* Used elsewhere of the Temple, reflecting the belief that it was preceded by such temporary dwellings as the tabernacle and the sanctuary at Shiloh, where Samuel served as priest, and where Hannah came for her famous prayer (1 Samuel 2). The Temple was a place of refuge; Adonijah, for example, grasps the horns of the Jerusalem altar to claim sanctuary from Solomon (1 Kings 1:50).

[6] *"Sing and chant"* A suggestion that singing could accompany sacrifices, though this is never confirmed elsewhere in the Bible. It may mean a song accompanied by a stringed instrument—more intense than *ashirah*, which implies "I will sing," without suggesting musical accompaniment. The idiom always occurs with the same verb order, building from the less intense to the greater.

[7] *"Hear … and answer me"* In both structure and vocabulary, this is the typical opening of a lament. Compare, for example, Psalm 4:2: "Answer me when I call, Adonai, my vindicator! You freed me from distress; have mercy on me and hear my prayer." "Answer me" may be a general request for help, but it may also reflect a ritual where a cultic prophet would provide the petitioner with a divine answer.

[8] *"Seek my face"* Temples in antiquity often housed images of the deity that the worshiper might seek to see by offering petitions while standing near the deity's image. If, as we assume, the Jerusalem Temple held no such imagery, the expression should be understood metaphorically.

[10] *"My father and mother have abandoned me"* The image of God as parent is surprisingly infrequent in the Bible, but it occurs here.

God is the ideal parent, who would never abandon a child, reflecting Isaiah 49:15, which asks, similarly, "Can a woman forget her baby, or disown the child of her womb? Though she might forget, I never could forget you."

[11] *"Show me"* The psalmist assumes he deserves persecution for some unrighteousness on his part, so he requests divine instruction that will help him merit being rewarded with triumph over his enemies.

[12] *"False witnesses"* Bearing false witness is mentioned in the Decalogue and is punished severely in a measure-for-measure fashion (Deut. 19:16–21). The damage such a witness can cause is described most poetically in Proverbs 25:18: "Like a club, a sword, a sharpened arrow, is a man who testifies falsely against his fellow."

[13] *"Had I only not believed"* Some scholars believe that this verse reflects the confidence that the worshiper feels after receiving an oracle of reassurance that he will continue in "the land of the living," rather than die and descend to Sheol, the netherworld, where the dead go never to be heard from again.

[14] *"Wait for Adonai"* As often happens in psalms, the petitioner is so happy at this impending deliverance that he concludes with words of encouragement to the broader community. Psalm 37:34 too advises, "Wait for Adonai," but explains further, "Keep to his way, and He will raise you high that you may inherit the land; when the wicked are cut off, you shall see it."

◆

DORFF (THEOLOGY)

act as our "light and salvation."

[2] *"Enemies"* We ask God to help us overcome spiritual, not just physical, enemies.

[4] *"That I might sit in Adonai's house"* We pray that we may dwell in the shelter of God's home, received by God in mercy rather than anger, "for my father and mother have abandoned me, but Adonai took me in" (v. 10)—an especially poignant line indicating our trust in God's company and protection.

[14] *"Wait for Adonai! Be strong and steel your heart. Wait for Adonai!"* An especially ringing statement of trust and hope in Adonai, reiterating the theme of Elul and the penitential season: that we summon up faith and courage sufficient to confront our moral and spiritual failings, which are often enemies more difficult to overcome than physical adversaries.

◆

ELLENSON (MODERN LITURGIES)

Time," p. 105), especially psalms, which consist overall of spiritual prayers to and about God.

———◆———

FRANKEL (A WOMAN'S VOICE)

For You light up the whole world with Your light.
And the morning speaks of Your mercy,
And the night speaks of Your truth,
And all creatures acknowledge Your wonder.
God, You help us every day.

Who can speak of the great wonder
That You might impart to the pious on their day,
In the place where all the people of creation will sit.
For Your one day is a thousand years
And Your day is longer than the whole of the world's existence.
And You are forever in eternity,
You outlive all Your creation,
And You remain eternal,
And as You live eternally,
So, too, do Your servants
Live in eternal life.

And how holy You are.
Everyone sanctifies You
In heaven three times a day
And on earth.
And not only do the angels say
"Holy, holy, holy"
But so do Your holy people, Israel,
Sanctify Your name by saying
"Holy, holy, holy."
You are sanctified, Lord,
Amen.

(From Kay, *Seyder Tkhines*, pp. 224–25)

———◆———

GRAY (OUR TALMUDIC HERITAGE)

righteous are able to avoid? According to the midrash, David said, "When I was about to violate Shabbat, the Torah enlightened me, as it says, 'Remember the Shabbat day' (Exod. 20:8). This is what is meant by 'a candle to my feet and a light for my path.'"

The midrash also links *ori* ("my light") to Rosh Hashanah, and *v'yishi* ("and my salvation") to Yom Kippur, the day on which God saves us by forgiving our sins (Mid. T'hillim 27:4). It is likely that this midrashic connection between Psalm 27 and the Days of Awe accounts for the *minhag* of reciting this psalm during the month of Elul and the High Holy Day period.

[2] *"When those who would do evil approached"* Continuing the midrashic link between this psalm and the Days of Awe, the Rabbis interpret "evildoers" as the heavenly beings who accuse Israel so as to ensure Israel's being found guilty during the Days of Awe.

[2] *"My enemies and my foes ... failed and stumbled"* The letters that constitute the Hebrew *hasatan*, denoting our accuser before the heavenly tribunal, are numerically equivalent to 364, one less than the number of days in the solar year (365). The midrash deduces that he may accuse Israel for 364 days of the year, but not on Yom Kippur. On Yom Kippur, God withdraws permission to accuse us, but invites him instead to see what we are doing. When Satan sees Israel fasting and praying, wearing white garments, and wrapped in *tallitot*, he and his minions turn away in shame (*hemah kashlu v'nafalu*), acknowledging that on Yom Kippur, Israel is indeed like the ministering angels. At that point, God promises that He will forgive us for our sins, whereupon the psalm continues confidently with verses 3 on.

L. HOFFMAN (HISTORY)

conclusion of it. *Bar'khu* concludes the morning service also.

The custom is reported in the Palestinian work *Massekhet Sofrim* (10:7), so it goes back to eighth-century Eretz Yisrael (if not before). It was intended for people who arrived too late to say the early blessings. Hearing *Bar'khu* and the accompanying *Kaddish* just before it was considered equivalent to fulfilling the obligation to say even the prayers that had been missed. Isaac ben Sheshet Perfet (RiBaSH) of Barcelona (fourteenth century) does not especially like the practice, but allows it, especially on Friday night, since prayers start especially early then (in order to get them all done in time to go home and eat). Spanish-Portuguese Jews retained the custom. In Eretz Yisrael, it spread to some Ashkenazi synagogues also, under the influence of Sefardi kabbalists, as it did among Chasidim in Europe as well.

For other psalms frequently found at the end of *Ma'ariv*, but not included here, see "Introduction to the Liturgy: The Shape of *Minchah* and *Ma'ariv*," p. 11.

J. HOFFMAN (TRANSLATION)

"Cloaked in light and God's saving power, whom shall I fear?"

[1] *"Before whom"* More accurately, just "whom," but we will use "tremble" next to translate another Hebrew word meaning "fear," thereby getting, "Before whom shall I tremble?"; and we want to maintain the parallel structure of the Hebrew.

[1] *"Strength of my life"* We translate more or less literally, on the assumption that this is poetic imagery.

[1] *"Tremble"* More accurately, "fear." But we just used "fear," and no good synonym for "fear" in English presents itself.

[2] *"Those who would do evil"* Or "evildoers."

[2] *"Stumbled"* More accurately, "fell." But "failed and fell" would introduce (nicely poetic) alliteration in English where there is none in Hebrew.

[3] *"Battalion engage me in battle"* The Hebrew is similarly poetic, using the root "camp" twice, once to mean "army" *(machaneh)*, and once to mean "prepare for/engage in battle" *(tachaneh)*. Neither of these meanings is extraordinary, but we find the two juxtaposed nowhere else.

[3] *"This"* It is entirely unclear from the Hebrew, both here and below, what "this" is. Context, of course, strongly suggests God, but the pronoun is feminine, and without a feminine antecedent, it seems out of place. (The feminine pronoun generally refers only to a grammatically feminine noun or to a general situation.)

[4] *"One thing"* Or perhaps, "once...." Again (as with "this," in the comment above), the word "one" is feminine, and seems to lack a clear referent. The Hebrew for "thing" is missing; we supply it in English to give "one" some meaning. Also, after specifically mentioning "one [thing]," the psalm goes on to list more than one.

[4] *"See"* The Hebrew word (*ul'vaker*, from the root *b.k.r*), seems to have a variety of meanings, ranging from "see" to "inspect" to "ask for." We deduce its meaning here from the seemingly parallel verb "gaze upon." But it might equally mean "to [enter his Temple in order to] inquire...."

[5] *"He will set me high upon a rock"* One wonders what the connection between this line and the hiding (previous line) might be. This seems to be a turning point in the imagery, but the word indicating the change in status ("then") doesn't appear until immediately after this line.

[6] *"Triumph"* Hebrew, *t'ruah*, probably reflecting some loud noise connected with triumph.

[7] *"O Adonai!"* We retain the archaic "O Adonai" only because we want to emphasize

that this line mirrors the beginning of the *Sh'ma* ("Hear O Israel"). See Volume 1, *The Sh'ma and Its Blessings*, pp. 87 and 91.

[8] *"My heart says to you, 'Seek my face.' I have sought your face, Adonai"* This line seems to make no sense, though the English translation masks some of the problems. The first verb "seek" is plural, that is, it addresses more than one person. There is no reason for the psalm to address God in the plural here, having used the singular everywhere else. The Greek translation in the Septuagint reads, "... sought my face. Your face I will seek," but the official English translation of that Greek translation seemingly arbitrarily changes "my" to "your": "I sought your face. Your face I will seek." *JPS's* translation matches. However, but for the vowels (added only about thousand years ago) and the last word of the line, we might have "my face sought your face, Adonai," which has the benefits of almost matching the Greek as well as being grammatical and making sense. We therefore suspect that the line that has made its way to us is not the original.

[9] *"Salvation"* This is the same rare word for salvation that began the psalm.

[11] *"Show me"* This is a brilliant play on words, which we cannot capture in English. The word used here for "show me" looks like the word for "parent." So while the literal meaning of the phrase is as we have it, the Hebrew also poetically suggests "be a parent to me," just after the psalmist laments his loss of mother and father.

[11] *"Just path"* Or, perhaps, as in *JPS*, "level path."

[11] *"Enemies"* Here, too, the logic seems unclear. Why would this be done for the sake of enemies? The Hebrew word here, while commonly interpreted to mean "enemy" (and so translated in the Septuagint), also means "singer." Why might the same root mean "enemy"? The names of two musical instruments seem also to have roots that connect them to evil: a *chalil* (flute of some sort) shares its root with *chalila* ("cursed"), and a *nevel* (probably a harp) shares its root with the root meaning "disgrace." One wonders if we have missed something about the ancient view of music here.

[12] *"Foes"* Literally, my foes' *nefesh*. On *nefesh*, see Volume 1, *The Sh'ma and Its Blessings*, p. 100.

[12] *"False witnesses and unjust accusers"* As in *JPS*.

[13] *"Had I only not believed"* As it stands, this seems to be a cry of defeat on the part of one person, only to be countered by a second person, next. Without the "not," however, the line would make more sense ("I believe I will see Adonai's goodness ...!") Vexingly, this is what the Septuagint gives us.

◆ ◆ ◆

[In a house of mourning throughout the period of shivah, *continue here, followed by* Kaddish Yatom *(Mourner's Kaddish). For text and commentary, see Volume 6, Tachanun and Concluding Prayers, pp. 149–157.]*

II. Psalm 49

For the conductor, a psalm for the children of Korah. [2] Hear this, all nations; listen, all inhabitants of the world, [3] mortal and human, rich and poor together. [4] My mouth will speak wisdom, my speech be full of insight. [5] I will turn my ear to a message, expound my riddle by harp.

[6] Why should I fear in times of trouble, when I am encompassed by the guilt of my attackers, [7] who rely on their riches, and revel in their great wealth? [8] A man will not redeem his brother, nor pay his ransom to God. [9] Redeeming their soul costs money, and it ceases forever. [10] If he were to live forever, he would never see his grave. [11] He will see the wise die; the fool and the simple will perish together, leaving their riches to others. [12] Their grave is their eternal home, their resting place from generation to generation, those who call upon their own names on earth. [13] Not through money will one sleep, to be considered like the beasts that perish.

[14] This is the way of those who are foolhardy. After them they will delight in their own words. [15] Like sheep to Sheol, they have set Death to shepherd them. The upright will rule over them at daybreak. Their rock will dominate them in Sheol. [16] But God will redeem my soul from the hand of Sheol, for He will take me.

[17] Do not fear when a man becomes rich, when the wealth of his house grows, [18] for he will not take everything with him, and his possessions will not follow him. [19] For he will

לַֽמְנַצֵּֽחַ, לִבְנֵי קֹֽרַח מִזְמוֹר. [2] שִׁמְעוּ זֹאת, כָּל הָעַמִּים; הַאֲזִֽינוּ, כָּל יֹשְׁבֵי חָֽלֶד. [3] גַּם בְּנֵי אָדָם, גַּם בְּנֵי אִישׁ, יַֽחַד עָשִׁיר וְאֶבְיוֹן. [4] פִּי יְדַבֵּר חָכְמוֹת, וְהָגוּת לִבִּי תְבוּנוֹת. [5] אַטֶּה לְמָשָׁל אָזְנִי, אֶפְתַּח בְּכִנּוֹר חִידָתִי.

[6] לָֽמָּה אִירָא בִּֽימֵי רָע, עֲוֹן עֲקֵבַי יְסוּבֵּֽנִי. [7] הַבֹּטְחִים עַל חֵילָם, וּבְרֹב עָשְׁרָם יִתְהַלָּֽלוּ. [8] אָח לֹא פָדֹה יִפְדֶּה אִישׁ, לֹא יִתֵּן לֵאלֹהִים כָּפְרוֹ. [9] וְיֵקַר פִּדְיוֹן נַפְשָׁם, וְחָדַל לְעוֹלָם. [10] וִֽיחִי עוֹד לָנֶֽצַח, לֹא יִרְאֶה הַשָּֽׁחַת. [11] כִּי יִרְאֶה חֲכָמִים יָמֽוּתוּ, יַֽחַד כְּסִיל וָבַֽעַר יֹאבֵֽדוּ, וְעָזְבוּ לַאֲחֵרִים חֵילָם. [12] קִרְבָּם בָּתֵּֽימוֹ לְעוֹלָם, מִשְׁכְּנֹתָם לְדֹר וָדֹר; קָרְאוּ בִשְׁמוֹתָם עֲלֵי אֲדָמוֹת. [13] וְאָדָם בִּיקָר בַּל יָלִין; נִמְשַׁל כַּבְּהֵמוֹת נִדְמוּ.

[14] זֶה דַרְכָּם כֵּֽסֶל לָֽמוֹ, וְאַחֲרֵיהֶם בְּפִיהֶם יִרְצוּ, סֶֽלָה. [15] כַּצֹּאן לִשְׁאוֹל שַׁתּוּ, מָֽוֶת יִרְעֵם; וַיִּרְדּוּ בָם יְשָׁרִים לַבֹּֽקֶר, וְצוּרָם לְבַלּוֹת שְׁאוֹל מִזְּבֻל לוֹ. [16] אַךְ אֱלֹהִים יִפְדֶּה נַפְשִׁי מִיַּד שְׁאוֹל, כִּי יִקָּחֵֽנִי סֶֽלָה.

[17] אַל תִּירָא כִּי יַעֲשִׁר אִישׁ, כִּי יִרְבֶּה כְּבוֹד בֵּיתוֹ. [18] כִּי לֹא בְמוֹתוֹ יִקַּח הַכֹּל, לֹא יֵרֵד אַחֲרָיו כְּבוֹדוֹ. [19] כִּי נַפְשׁוֹ בְּחַיָּיו

bless his soul during life, and they will acknowledge you when it is good to you. [20] The soul will come to the generation of his ancestors. They will never see light.

[21] Not through money will one understand, to be considered like the beasts that perish.

יְבָרֵךְ; וְיוֹדֻךָ כִּי תֵיטִיב לָךְ. [20] תָּבֹא עַד דּוֹר אֲבוֹתָיו, עַד נֵצַח לֹא יִרְאוּ אוֹר.

[21] אָדָם בִּיקָר וְלֹא יָבִין, נִמְשַׁל כַּבְּהֵמוֹת נִדְמוּ.

BRETTLER (BIBLE)

Psalm 49 This extremely difficult psalm is usually characterized as a didactic or wisdom psalm; it shares vocabulary and ideas with the wisdom Books of Proverbs, Job, and Ecclesiastes. As a psalm, it is atypical in that it neither petitions nor thanks God, and it is difficult to establish whether, like other psalms, it was used in the cult.

[1] *"The children of Korah"* A branch of the Levites, mentioned in the superscriptions of two collections of psalms called "Korahite Psalms": 42–49 (except for 43), and 84–88 (except for 86).

[2] *"Listen …"* Invoking the entire world to *(p. 195)*

DORFF (THEOLOGY)

[7, 11] *"Who rely on their riches, and revel in their great wealth … the fool and the simple will perish together, leaving their riches to others"* Wealth has no enduring worth, for, as the saying goes, "You cannot take it with you when you die." The biblical Book of Ecclesiastes *(p. 197)*

ELLENSON (MODERN LITURGIES)

Psalm 49 The point made about Psalm 27 (see p. 180) is true here as well. Though other psalms or readings (e.g., Ecclesiastes in the *Union Prayer Book*) are offered as well, in a house of mourning, this traditional favorite is not deliberately excluded.

[For prayer instructions, see page 190.]

II. PSALM 49

[1] For the conductor, a psalm for the children of Korah. [2] Hear this, all nations; listen, all inhabitants of the world, [3] mortal and human, rich and poor together. [4] My mouth will speak wisdom, my speech be full of insight. [5] I will turn my ear to a message, expound my riddle by harp.

Psalms, the part of the Bible most frequently cited in the prayer book, often bring services to a close. We include here two of the most common: Psalm 27 (p. 179) and Psalm 49, the latter assigned for services in a house of mourning (a shivah minyan, *pronounced shee-VAH min-YAHN, but, commonly, SHIH-vah MIHN-y'n).*

◆

¹לַמְנַצֵּחַ, לִבְנֵי קֹרַח מִזְמוֹר. ²שִׁמְעוּ זֹאת, כָּל הָעַמִּים; הַאֲזִינוּ, כָּל יֹשְׁבֵי חָלֶד. ³גַּם בְּנֵי אָדָם, גַּם בְּנֵי אִישׁ, יַחַד עָשִׁיר וְאֶבְיוֹן. ⁴פִּי יְדַבֵּר חָכְמוֹת, וְהָגוּת לִבִּי תְבוּנוֹת. ⁵אַטֶּה לְמָשָׁל אָזְנִי, אֶפְתַּח בְּכִנּוֹר חִידָתִי.

J. Hoffman (Translation)

Psalm 49 Psalm 49 is at once enigmatic and uniquely intriguing.

The Hebrew is difficult, as indicated in the translation notes. *JPS*, too, laments more than once that the meaning of the Hebrew is "uncertain." Similarly, the superb *Jewish Study Bible* (Oxford University Press, 2003) notes that "this is an unusual and difficult psalm…. [It is] very difficult textually."

The Septuagint's version of this psalm varies considerably from our Hebrew version, suggesting that the authors of the Septuagint also didn't fully understand it. For example, the Septuagint offers "brother" in the Greek instead of "ah!" in Hebrew, "heel [of a foot]" instead of "attackers," and other surprising differences. (p. 197)

6 Why should I fear in times of trouble, when I am encompassed by the guilt of my attackers, 7 who rely on their riches, and revel in their great wealth? 8 A man will not redeem his brother, nor pay his ransom to God. 9 Redeeming their soul costs money, and it ceases forever. 10 If he were to live forever, he would never see his grave. 11 He will see the wise die; the fool and the simple will perish together, leaving their riches to others. 12 Their grave is their eternal home, their resting place from generation to generation, those who call upon their own names on earth. 13 Not through money will one sleep, to be considered like the beasts that perish.

14 This is the way of those who are foolhardy. After them they will delight in their own words. 15 Like sheep to Sheol, they have set Death to shepherd them. The upright will rule over them at daybreak. Their rock will dominate them in Sheol. 16 But God will redeem my soul from the hand of Sheol, for He will take me.

17 Do not fear when a man becomes rich, when the wealth of his house grows, 18 for he will not take everything with him, and his possessions will not follow him. 19 For he will bless his soul during life, and they will acknowledge you when it is good to you. 20 The soul will come to

⁶לָמָּה אִירָא בִּימֵי רָע, עֲוֹן עֲקֵבַי יְסוּבֵּנִי. ⁷הַבֹּטְחִים עַל חֵילָם, וּבְרֹב עָשְׁרָם יִתְהַלָּלוּ. ⁸אָח לֹא פָדֹה יִפְדֶּה אִישׁ, לֹא יִתֵּן לֵאלֹהִים כָּפְרוֹ. ⁹וְיֵקַר פִּדְיוֹן נַפְשָׁם, וְחָדַל לְעוֹלָם. ¹⁰וִיחִי עוֹד לָנֶצַח, לֹא יִרְאֶה הַשָּׁחַת. ¹¹כִּי יִרְאֶה חֲכָמִים יָמוּתוּ, יַחַד כְּסִיל וָבַעַר יֹאבֵדוּ, וְעָזְבוּ לַאֲחֵרִים חֵילָם. ¹²קִרְבָּם בָּתֵּימוֹ לְעוֹלָם, מִשְׁכְּנֹתָם לְדֹר וָדֹר; קָרְאוּ בִשְׁמוֹתָם עֲלֵי אֲדָמוֹת. ¹³וְאָדָם בִּיקָר בַּל יָלִין; נִמְשַׁל כַּבְּהֵמוֹת נִדְמוּ.

¹⁴זֶה דַרְכָּם כֵּסֶל לָמוֹ, וְאַחֲרֵיהֶם בְּפִיהֶם יִרְצוּ, סֶלָה. ¹⁵כַּצֹּאן לִשְׁאוֹל שַׁתּוּ, מָוֶת יִרְעֵם; וַיִּרְדּוּ בָם יְשָׁרִים לַבֹּקֶר, וְצוּרָם לְבַלּוֹת שְׁאוֹל מִזְּבֻל לוֹ. ¹⁶אַךְ אֱלֹהִים יִפְדֶּה נַפְשִׁי מִיַּד שְׁאוֹל, כִּי יִקָּחֵנִי סֶלָה.

¹⁷אַל תִּירָא כִּי יַעֲשִׁר אִישׁ, כִּי יִרְבֶּה כְּבוֹד בֵּיתוֹ. ¹⁸כִּי לֹא בְמוֹתוֹ יִקַּח הַכֹּל, לֹא יֵרֵד אַחֲרָיו כְּבוֹדוֹ. ¹⁹כִּי נַפְשׁוֹ בְּחַיָּיו יְבָרֵךְ; וְיוֹדֻךָ כִּי תֵיטִיב לָךְ. ²⁰תָּבֹא עַד דּוֹר אֲבוֹתָיו, עַד נֵצַח לֹא יִרְאוּ אוֹר.

²¹אָדָם בִּיקָר וְלֹא יָבִין, נִמְשַׁל כַּבְּהֵמוֹת נִדְמוּ.

the generation of his ancestors. They will never see light.

²¹Not through money will one understand, to be considered like the beasts that perish.

---

listen, an idea found elsewhere in the Psalter (e.g., 96:1, 98:4), but having an exaggerative character to it.

³*"Mortal and human, rich and poor together"* Biblical poetry typically uses parallelism, where one line follows another in order to elaborate upon it, but sometimes the second part seems to be a filler, as if the author could think of nothing better to add, but was stuck with the technical need to follow the usual poetic device. This is likely the case here, where *gam b'nei ish*, "human," is not discernibly different from the previous phrase, *gam b'nei adam*, "mortal." It may seem at first that the next part of the verse, *yachad ashir v'evyon*, "rich and poor together," just emphasizes the all-inclusiveness of the prior terms, but it quickly becomes obvious that it is meant to introduce one of the psalm's major themes: the relative status of poor and rich.

⁴*"Wisdom ... insight* [chochmot ... t'vunot]*"* A common word pair, especially favored in wisdom books. Of the twenty occurrences (always in this order), eleven are in Proverbs or Job. It is uncertain whether the two represent different types of knowledge or whether *t'vunot*, "insight," is just a fancier, less frequent word.

⁵*"Message ... riddle"* Occurs also in Proverbs 1:6: "For understanding message and epigram, the words of the wise and their riddles."

⁶*"Why should I fear in times of trouble"* Compare Psalm 23:4: "Though I walk through a valley of deepest darkness, I fear no harm, for You are with me."

⁷*"Who rely on their riches"* The theme of illegitimate trust in strength is especially common in the late biblical Book of Chronicles, which emphasizes that when Israel is righteous, they can defeat much larger and stronger armies. It is also found in wisdom literature, for example, Proverbs 21:31: "The horse is readied for the day of battle, but victory comes from Adonai."

⁷*"In their great wealth"* The privileges and problems of wealth are a major preoccupation of both Proverbs and Ecclesiastes. Attitudes vary, but the sentiment

expressed here is echoed in Proverbs 11:28: "He who trusts in his wealth shall fall, but the righteous shall flourish like foliage."

8–10 *"A man will not redeem his brother …"* The Hebrew of these verses is unusually difficult; it likely suggests that wealth cannot save its owner from the universal human fate of death and Sheol (the netherworld).

11 *"Wise … fool"* Contrasting the fates of the wise and (their opposite) of fools typifies wisdom literature. Both, however, must leave riches behind when they die. As Ecclesiastes puts it (6:1–2), "God sometimes grants a man riches, property, and wealth … but God does not permit him to enjoy it; instead, a stranger will enjoy it."

12–13 *"Their grave is their eternal home … like the beasts that perish"* These verses too have parallels in Ecclesiastes. For verse 12, see the story of the sage who saved a city, but was ultimately forgotten (Eccles. 9:13–16). For verse 13, compare Ecclesiastes 3:19, "For in respect of the fate of man and the fate of beast, they have one and the same fate: as the one dies so dies the other, and both have the same lifebreath; man has no superiority over beast, since both amount to nothing." How different this is from the attitude of Genesis 2:7, which highlights human uniqueness precisely because God provides human beings with lifebreath.

14 *"This is the way"* A verse so obscure that it is unclear even if it belongs with what precedes or follows.

15 *"Like sheep to Sheol"* A probable reference to the fate of the wealthy, who will find themselves without wealth in Sheol, like everyone else.

16 *"God will redeem … from … Sheol"* Given the biblical picture of Sheol as a netherworld where all people—rich or poor, righteous or wicked—go at death, it is likely that this verse refers to a *temporary* reprieve from death during life, perhaps being cured from severe illness. "Giving life to the dead" had that connotation biblically (see "Reviving the dead," p. 138).

20 *"The soul will come to the generation of his ancestors"* Whence we get the idiom, "to be gathered unto your fathers."

20 *"Never see light"* The netherworld, by definition, is dark, since the earth hides it from the sun. (Job 17:13 calls Sheol "the dark place.")

21 *"Not through money"* A refrain of verse 13, to close the psalm.

◆

DORFF (THEOLOGY)

(Kohelet) 2:4–12, 18–26 makes the same point, adding also that you cannot prevent your inheritors from squandering what you leave them.

12–13 *"Their grave is their eternal home … those who call upon their own names … like the beasts that perish"* Fame, like fortune, will be lost at death. Verses 17–21 repeat the theme. The psalmist believes that the rich and famous will be totally lost because, unlike the later Pharisees (the people later called "the Rabbis," who shaped the tradition that we know as Judaism), the psalmist does not believe in a life after death where one might enjoy one's fame or fortune. For the psalmist, as for all of the Bible except the Book of Daniel, people's "grave is their eternal home," and so fame and fortune cannot have ultimate worth.

15–16 *"Like sheep to Sheol* [the grave]*, they have set Death to shepherd them"* This psalm is used at a house of mourning to reinforce the lessons that fame and fortune are not of ultimate value; only faith in God is. On festive days, when *Tachanun* is not recited, Psalm 16 is substituted for this psalm in a house of mourning, for it speaks not of the negative lessons articulated in Psalm 49 but only of the positive message—namely, that "You will not abandon me to Sheol, or let your faithful one see the Pit. You will teach me the path of life. In your presence is perfect joy; delights are ever in your right hand" (Ps. 16:10–11).

———◆———

J. HOFFMAN (TRANSLATION)

Equally, the most likely interpretation of the Hebrew that we do understand seems nonsensical at times, again as indicated below in the translation notes. To consider but one example, *JPS's* translation of verses 9–10 contains the contradictory notions that "[9]… one ceases to be, forever. [10] He shall live eternally." (They solve this problem by making verse 10 into a question, though there is nothing in the Hebrew to suggest a question here.)

But perhaps the most intriguing part of the psalm is verse 5, which tells us that this psalm is a "riddle." When we find such seemingly odd Hebrew after the admonition that a riddle follows, we naturally suspect that the Hebrew is hard precisely because it is a riddle, one that we have not solved.

In addition to the possibility that the whole psalm is an allegory (as discussed immediately below), more than a few puns seem to grace this psalm. Two intertwined examples demonstrate.

In verse 13, we find the word *bikar* ("through money") next to "beasts," and one synonym for "beast" is *bakar;* continuing the word play, two verses later we find the word *boker* ("daybreak"). So we have *bikar/bakar/boker*. And verse 12 refers to "their *kereb*" ("inner" something, perhaps thoughts), though most translations assume that the word is supposed to be *keber* ("grave"). So in addition to *bikar/bakar/boker*, we have two anagrams of those words: *keber/kereb*. But if we are to allow anagrams (as in the widely accepted *keber* for *kereb*), we might reread the end of verse 15 as "they will go straight down to the grave [*keber*] with them," instead of the seemingly bizarre "they will rule over them at daybreak [*boker*]."

Secondly, the last verse of the psalm is a repetition of verse 13, but in place of *yalin* ("will sleep") we find *yavin* ("will understand"). While these similarities might be mere coincidence, after an introduction that promises a riddle, one wonders.

In terms of the content of the psalm, we seem to have more people involved than are mentioned by name. For example, in verse 12 we read about "their grave" (or "their inner thoughts") without any clear antecedent for "their." Who are "they"? Similarly, verse 15 seems to require two groups of people.

One possibility is that the psalm refers obliquely to Moses and Aaron, and to the Korah who was involved in the uprising against them (see Numbers 16). In Deuteronomy (31:29), we read that Moses is concerned that after his death, the people will act corruptly. This psalm could be about corruption, mentioning as it does "rich and poor," and using a word from the same root for "corruption" that we see in Deuteronomy (*sh.ch.t* both times). Perhaps Korah, instigator of the uprising, represents the corruption that Moses was worried about, and this psalm is a veiled warning to return to Moses's ways? In further support of this hypothesis, I note the following four points:

1. In Deuteronomy 32, immediately after expressing his concern about future corruption, Moses uses a now-famous poem to warn the people of Israel. That poem is called *Ha'azinu*, after its first word; Psalm 49, too, uses *ha'azinu*, and no other psalm uses this word.
2. The psalm seems to worry about "guilt by association" (v. 6), which is more in keeping with the Korah uprising than the usual theology of psalms.
3. The word translated by *JPS* as "ah!" might equally be read "brother" (as it is in the Septuagint), in which case we would find a reference to a brother, perhaps Moses's brother, Aaron.
4. The *Targum*, probably an eighth-century Aramaic translation of the Hebrew psalm, similarly introduces Moses, although he is not explicitly mentioned in the Hebrew.

If my guess is right, the first part of the psalm could be paraphrased as follows: "Here's a psalm for the corrupt children of Korah. Listen up, everyone, rich and poor together! I will speak in riddles: Why should I fear in times of trouble, though I am encompassed by the sin of those around me, who trust in their riches and glory, in their great wealth? A man cannot be redeemed by his brother, nor have his ransom to God paid by him. Money is their ransom. Moses is gone forever. Had Moses lived on, we would never see corruption…."

While the beginning of the psalm would then make sense, against this hypothesis we have to consider both the tenuous connection to Moses and the fact that it helps less toward the end of the psalm.

So we are left with a conundrum. Therefore, we translate the psalm as directly as we can, hopefully making it possible for a reader to unravel the riddle. Good luck.

[3] *"Rich and poor"* Coming after "mortal and human," we expect two synonyms, not opposites. One possibility is that we have misunderstood "mortal" and "human." Another is that already we see an oblique reference to the equality of rich and poor.

[4] *"Speech be full of insight"* More or less as in *JPS*. The Hebrew involves *lev* ("heart"), but as we have seen elsewhere (e.g., Volume 1, *The Shema and Its Blessings*, p. 100), the word "heart" is often best not translated literally.

[5] *"To a message"* Or, perhaps, "to an allegorical interpretation," a possibility made more likely by the parallel "riddle," next.

[5] *"Harp"* Others: "lyre." This may have been an instrument associated with psalms ("psalter"). It's not clear how the exposition of the riddle and the harp are connected.

[6] *"Fear in times of trouble"* Our English doesn't capture the particularly poetic Hebrew, which forms trochaic tetrometer with an internal near-rhyme.

[6] *"Attackers"* This is one possible interpretation of the Hebrew. Another, reflected in the Septuagint, is "my heel." Of course, "the guilt of my heel" makes little sense, but perhaps this is the riddle? If not, we are left wondering why being surrounded by the guilt of others should be a problem for the author, because in general, the theology of psalms does not worry about guilt by association. [See above, "Psalm 49," for more.] A final possibility is that the word refers to footprints and thus metaphorically to "what I have already done."

[8] *"His brother"* Following the Septuagint. The Hebrew means either "brother" or "ah," as in *JPS*: "Ah, it cannot redeem a man." But if so, what is "it" that cannot redeem a man?

[9] *"Redeeming their soul costs money, and it ceases forever"* Of course, this makes no sense. What ceases? Various attempts have been made to impose sense upon the Hebrew, including *JPS*'s "the price of life is too high, and so one ceases to be, forever," and *NRSV*'s "for the ransom of life is costly, and can never suffice." Again, see above, "Psalm 49."

[10] *"If he were to live forever"* Perhaps the "he" is Moses, as noted above, under "Psalm 49."

[10] *"Never see his grave [shachat]"* The Hebrew word *shachat* frequently means "grave"

in psalms, but may also refer to "corruption," as noted above, under "Psalm 49."

[12] *"Their grave is their eternal home"* The word for "grave" here is not the one we saw above ("never see his grave"), but rather an anagram of a more common word for grave. See above, "Psalm 49," for more information.

[13] *"Will one sleep"* This line will be repeated to end the psalm, with "understand" substituted for "sleep." Some people think our version has an error in this line, and that it, too, should be "understand."

[13] *"To be considered like the beasts that perish"* "To be considered" might mean "to be allegorically understood." It comes from the same root as the word we translated above as "message," in parallel with "riddle."

[14] *"After them they will delight in their own words"* Literally, "delight in their mouths." Either way, it doesn't make much sense. Perhaps this is the riddle?

[15] *"The upright will rule over them at daybreak"* Following *JPS*. But the word for "rule over" could also mean "descend," and "upright" could also mean "directly." The word for "at daybreak" is an anagram for "to the grave." If we substitute the anagram (see above, "Psalm 49," for why we might do this), we get something like the much more sensible "they will go directly to the grave."

[15] *"Their rock … Sheol"* One possibility for enigmatic Hebrew. *JPS* (after warning that the meaning of the Hebrew is uncertain) offers, "and their form shall waste away in Sheol till its nobility be gone."

[19] *"When it is good to you"* That is, when the soul is good to you. *JPS* offers, "They must admit that you did well by yourself," understanding the subject of the verb as "you," not "it." That is, they have "you will be good to you[rself]" instead of "it will be good to you." The Hebrew is ambiguous.

[20] *"The soul will come"* Literally, "it will come," which may also (as above) mean "you will come."

◆ ◆ ◆

2 | Minchah

Additions for Shabbat

A. The *Amidah*

I. The *K'dushat Hayom*, ("Sanctification of the Day") for Shabbat *Minchah*

[1] You are One and your name is One, and who is like your People Israel, one nation on earth! [2] You gave your people a diadem of greatness, a crown of distinction, a day of rest and holiness. [3] Abraham rejoices, Isaac celebrates, and Jacob and his children rest on it. [4] It is a rest of love and gifts, a rest of trust and trustworthiness, a rest of peace and repose and quiet and security, a complete rest that You love. [5] May all your children know for sure that their rest comes from You, and for their rest let them sanctify your name. [6] Our God and our ancestors' God, accept our rest, [7] sanctify us through your commandments, and grant us a share in your Torah. [8] Satisfy us with your goodness, and gladden us with your salvation. And purify our heart to serve You in truth. And, Adonai our God, lovingly and adoringly grant us as our inheritance your holy Shabbat, that all of Israel might rest on it and sanctify your name. [9] Blessed are You, Adonai, who sanctifies Shabbat.

אַ[1] תָּה אֶחָד וְשִׁמְךָ אֶחָד, וּמִי כְּעַמְּךָ יִשְׂרָאֵל גּוֹי אֶחָד בָּאָרֶץ. [2]תִּפְאֶרֶת גְּדֻלָּה, וַעֲטֶרֶת יְשׁוּעָה, יוֹם מְנוּחָה וּקְדֻשָּׁה לְעַמְּךָ נָתָתָּ. [3]אַבְרָהָם יָגֵל, יִצְחָק יְרַנֵּן, יַעֲקֹב וּבָנָיו יָנוּחוּ בוֹ. [4]מְנוּחַת אַהֲבָה וּנְדָבָה, מְנוּחַת אֱמֶת וֶאֱמוּנָה, מְנוּחַת שָׁלוֹם וְשַׁלְוָה וְהַשְׁקֵט וָבֶטַח, מְנוּחָה שְׁלֵמָה שָׁאַתָּה רוֹצֶה בָּהּ; [5]יַכִּירוּ בָנֶיךָ וְיֵדְעוּ, כִּי מֵאִתְּךָ הִיא מְנוּחָתָם, וְעַל מְנוּחָתָם יַקְדִּישׁוּ אֶת שְׁמֶךָ. [6]אֱלֹהֵינוּ וֵאלֹהֵי אֲבוֹתֵינוּ, רְצֵה בִמְנוּחָתֵנוּ. [7]קַדְּשֵׁנוּ בְּמִצְוֹתֶיךָ, וְתֵן חֶלְקֵנוּ בְּתוֹרָתֶךָ; [8]שַׂבְּעֵנוּ מִטּוּבֶךָ, וְשַׂמְּחֵנוּ בִּישׁוּעָתֶךָ; וְטַהֵר לִבֵּנוּ לְעָבְדְּךָ בֶּאֱמֶת; וְהַנְחִילֵנוּ, יְיָ אֱלֹהֵינוּ, בְּאַהֲבָה וּבְרָצוֹן שַׁבַּת קָדְשֶׁךָ, וְיָנוּחוּ בָה יִשְׂרָאֵל מְקַדְּשֵׁי שְׁמֶךָ. [9]בָּרוּךְ אַתָּה, יְיָ, מְקַדֵּשׁ הַשַּׁבָּת.

BRETTLER (BIBLE)

Minchah is the Hebrew word for "gift," more specifically, a gift to God, a sacrifice. In the context of the Temple cult, where *korban* is the general word for sacrifice, *minchah* refers to a grain offering. Typically wheat, though sometimes barley, it might be offered alone or alongside animal sacrifices, depending on context. Several texts (2 Kings 16:15; Ps. 141:2; Dan. 9:21; Ezra 9:4–5) mention a *minchah* offered before evening, but not by priests; *minchah* as "afternoon prayer," or even as the post-biblical word for "afternoon" alone, is probably derived from this offering.

[1] *"You are One ..."* This line incorporates *(p. 204)*

DORFF (THEOLOGY)

"Minchah" The Temple sacrifice that the *Minchah* service replaces occurred close to dusk *(tamid shel bein ha'arba'im).* For that historical reason, and also because it is hard to get a prayer quorum *(minyan)* for *Minchah* earlier in the afternoon and then again after sunset *(p. 205)*

ELLENSON (MODERN LITURGIES)

[3] *"Abraham rejoices"* While, as a whole, this prayer appears in neither the *Hamburg Temple Prayer Books* (1819, 1841) nor the *Olath Tamid* of David Einhorn (1858), more traditionally oriented Reform liturgists such as Abraham Geiger and Isaac *(p. 205)*

GRAY (OUR TALMUDIC HERITAGE)

[1] *"You are One and your name is One"* Abudarham gives two explanations of the oneness of God and his name. A Maimonidean interpretation is that God's oneness is unique, wholly unlike the oneness of created beings. Created beings are a self-contained unity composed of many parts, but God is one with absolutely no internal divisions whatsoever. God's name (the ineffable name "Y-H-W-H") is one because it belongs to God alone. The second explanation of God's *(p. 206)*

I. THE *K'DUSHAT HAYOM* ("SANCTIFICATION OF THE DAY") FOR SHABBAT *MINCHAH*

[1] You are One and your name is One, and who is like your People Israel, one nation on earth! [2] You gave your people a diadem of greatness, a crown of distinction, a day of rest and holiness. [3] Abraham rejoices, Isaac celebrates, and Jacob and his children rest on it. [4] It is a rest of love and gifts, a rest of trust and trustworthiness, a rest of peace and

KUSHNER & POLEN (CHASIDISM)

[1] *"You are One and your name is One"* Rabbi Yehuda Aryeh Lieb of Ger in his *S'fas Emes* (s.v. *T'rumah* 5660, 1900) cites *Tanchuma (T'rumah)*, which in turn reports the following metaphor, from Midrash Lekach Tov: It is like two merchants, one with a shipment of pepper and the other with a shipment of cumin. If they were to exchange their merchandise with one another, nothing except the owners of the respective spices will have changed. But, with two students of Torah, one of *(p. 207)*

L. HOFFMAN (HISTORY)

MINCHAH *(THE AFTERNOON SERVICE) FOR WEEKDAYS AND SHABBAT IS MOSTLY A REPETITION OF* SHACHARIT *(THE MORNING SERVICE), THE CONSTITUENT PARTS OF WHICH HAVE BEEN COVERED IN PREVIOUS VOLUMES. (FOR THE STRUCTURE OF* MINCHAH *PRAYERS, AND WHERE TO FIND DISCUSSION ON THEM, SEE PP. 22–23.) SHABBAT* MINCHAH, *HOWEVER, PRESENTS ALTERATIONS THAT HAVE NOT BEEN DISCUSSED PREVIOUSLY, SO ARE INCLUDED HERE.*

THE MOST SIGNIFICANT CHANGES ARE (1) THE INCLUSION OF A TORAH READING, BUT WITHOUT THE USUAL ACCOMPANYING LITURGY FROM THE (p. 208)

¹אַתָּה אֶחָד וְשִׁמְךָ אֶחָד, וּמִי כְּעַמְּךָ יִשְׂרָאֵל גּוֹי אֶחָד בָּאָרֶץ. ²תִּפְאֶרֶת גְּדֻלָּה, וַעֲטֶרֶת יְשׁוּעָה, יוֹם מְנוּחָה וּקְדֻשָּׁה לְעַמְּךָ נָתָתָּ. ³אַבְרָהָם יָגֵל, יִצְחָק יְרַנֵּן, יַעֲקֹב וּבָנָיו יָנוּחוּ בוֹ. ⁴מְנוּחַת אַהֲבָה וּנְדָבָה, מְנוּחַת אֱמֶת וֶאֱמוּנָה, מְנוּחַת שָׁלוֹם וְשַׁלְוָה וְהַשְׁקֵט וָבֶטַח, מְנוּחָה שְׁלֵמָה שָׁאַתָּה רוֹצֶה בָּהּ; ⁵יַכִּירוּ בָנֶיךָ וְיֵדְעוּ, כִּי מֵאִתְּךָ

LANDES (HALAKHAH)

[1] *"You are one"* An amazing choice for the *K'dushat Hayom* (the middle blessing of the *Amidah*), which is supposed to refer directly to Shabbat. Unlike the *Ma'ariv* and *Shacharit* parallels, this version of the middle blessing does not primarily do so. The School of Rashi (*Tosafot* to Hag. 3b, s.v. *Umi*; *Machzor Vitry*, p. 13) explains that it is chosen to demonstrate that God, Israel, and Shabbat testify regarding each other: God and Israel testify that Shabbat is *yom* *(p. 207)*

J. HOFFMAN (TRANSLATION)

[1] *"And"* Though it's stylistically odd to conjoin a statement ("You ... name is One") and a (rhetorical) question (who is ...?), that's what the Hebrew does, and we match it in English.

[2] *"Diadem"* Literally, "glory," but clearly in parallel with "crown."

[2] *"Distinction"* As in Birnbaum.

[4] *"Gifts"* The Hebrew, *n'davah*, connotes gifts or donations, but it is also a technical term for the "freewill" offering at the Temple.

[4] *"Trust and trustworthiness"* Recalling the language of *Emet Ve'emunah* (p. 69).

◆ ◆ ◆

repose and quiet and security, a complete rest that You love. [5] May all your children know for sure that their rest comes from You, and for their rest let them sanctify your name. [6] Our God and our ancestors' God, accept our rest, [7] sanctify us through your commandments, and grant us a share in your Torah. [8] Satisfy us with your goodness, and gladden us with your salvation. And purify our heart to serve You in truth. And, Adonai our God, lovingly and adoringly grant us as our inheritance your holy Shabbat, that all of Israel might rest on it and sanctify your name. [9] Blessed are You, Adonai, who sanctifies Shabbat.

הִיא מְנוּחָתָם, וְעַל מְנוּחָתָם יַקְדִּישׁוּ אֶת שְׁמֶךָ. [6] אֱלֹהֵינוּ וֵאלֹהֵי אֲבוֹתֵינוּ, רְצֵה בִמְנוּחָתֵנוּ. [7] קַדְּשֵׁנוּ בְּמִצְוֹתֶיךָ, וְתֵן חֶלְקֵנוּ בְּתוֹרָתֶךָ; [8] שַׂבְּעֵנוּ מִטּוּבֶךָ, וְשַׂמְּחֵנוּ בִּישׁוּעָתֶךָ; וְטַהֵר לִבֵּנוּ לְעָבְדְּךָ בֶּאֱמֶת; וְהַנְחִילֵנוּ, יְיָ אֱלֹהֵינוּ, בְּאַהֲבָה וּבְרָצוֹן שַׁבַּת קָדְשֶׁךָ, וְיָנוּחוּ בָהּ יִשְׂרָאֵל מְקַדְּשֵׁי שְׁמֶךָ. [9] בָּרוּךְ אַתָּה, יְיָ, מְקַדֵּשׁ הַשַּׁבָּת.

BRETTLER (BIBLE)

various biblical ideas and phrases, along the theological lines of Deuteronomy 12, where *one* God should be worshiped in *one* manner in the *one* place He will choose. "You are One" itself refers to the *Sh'ma* (Deut. 6:4), which became very important in the post-biblical period; it continues by quoting 2 Samuel 7:23.

[2] *"Gave … diadem … crown"* Neither "diadem" nor "crown" is used of Shabbat in the Bible, though the verb "to give" *(natan)* is found regarding Shabbat (Exod. 16:29; Ezek. 20:12).

[3] *"Rejoices … celebrates"* Two core biblical ideas about Shabbat are applied to the patriarchs. Neither usage occurs biblically, nor does the Bible allude to a heavenly Shabbat, as implied by this verse.

[4] *"Rest"* The liturgy emphasizes the positive aspects of Shabbat, not the biblical idea of capital punishment for those who violate it. This sentence exemplifies the law of increasing members, a device by which longer words and phrases follow shorter ones. Thus, two sets of two-word modifiers—"love and gifts" and "trust and trustworthiness"—are followed by longer phrases in the verse's second half.

[5] *"Know for sure"* Since Shabbat commemorates creation, observing Shabbat acknowledges God as creator and evokes our thanksgiving.

[5] *"Sanctify your name"* See "Who sanctify your name," p. 125.

[8] *"On it* [v'ah]*"* In some versions of the Siddur, we find "on them" *(vam)*, not "the Sabbath" (that is), but "the Jews." See L. Hoffman on same verse.

— ◆ —

DORFF (THEOLOGY)

for *Ma'ariv*, synagogues commonly schedule *Minchah* and *Ma'ariv* together, just before and after sunset. In some settings, though, *Minchah* is scheduled for the middle of the afternoon, with the pleasant consequence that it interrupts the day, reminding us in the midst of daily pressures and tasks that Jewish beliefs and values should affect even the most mundane things we do. Judaism is not restricted to the synagogue or special occasions; it is meant to influence every moment of life, including (perhaps especially) the times that one pays least attention to it.

[1] *"You are One and your name is One"* See "Blessed is Adonai forever …," p. 96, and "Creation of heaven and earth," p. 122.

— ◆ —

ELLENSON (MODERN LITURGIES)

Mayer Wise retained it in their Siddurim. However, for reasons that are unclear to us, Wise, and even the proto-Conservative prayerbook authors Jastrow and Szold (see "True and trustworthy," p. 68), omitted verse 3.

In the twentieth century, the 1948 *Union Prayer Book* (American Reform), the 1995 Reconstructionist *Kol Haneshamah*, the 1994 "gender-sensitive" *Gates of Prayer*, and the 1995 British Liberal *Lev Chadash* (1995) all follow the pattern established by Wise. They preserve the prayer in their entirety, without verse 3.

In contrast, the American Reform *Gates of Prayer* (1975), the Israeli *Ha'avodah Shebalev* (1982), the British Reform *Forms of Prayer* (1977), and the French *Siddour Taher Libeinu* (1997) all print the prayer in its entirety with no changes. (The Conservative *Sim Shalom* [1985], of course, retains the original, but Conservative liturgy almost always does so.)

As a result of "gender sensitivity," however, the most recent Conservative Siddur, *Va'ani Tefillati* (Israel, 1998), adds "with Sarah" (in brackets) after "Abraham," "with Rebecca" after "Isaac," and "with his wives" after "Jacob." In the proposed American Reform *Mishkan T'filah*, Sarah, Rebecca, Rachel, and Leah are inserted permanently without brackets, and "his children," in relationship to Jacob, are turned into "their children," thus indicating that these offspring are the children of the matriarchs as well as the patriarchs.

⁶*"Our God and our ancestors' God"* In the draft of the forthcoming *Mishkan T'filah* (American Reform), the word "our generations" is inserted in Hebrew. While neither *Lev Chadash* (British Liberal, 1995) nor *Kol Haneshamah* (Reconstructionist, 1995) alters the Hebrew here, the former translates *avotenu* as "our ancestors," while the latter states, "our ancients' God."

GRAY (OUR TALMUDIC HERITAGE)

oneness is that unlike created beings, who develop in stages throughout their lifetimes from child, to youth, and then eventually to old age, God is always one in the sense of remaining always unchanged. Relatedly, although human beings are viewed and addressed differently by the various people in their lives (parents call them one thing, peers another, and they refer to themselves in possibly yet another way), God's name is always the same, never changing.

¹*"And who is like your people ... "* The Talmud (Ber. 6a; Hag. 3a–b) transmits a tradition that God, like Israel, puts on *t'fillin*. They are said to contain 1 Chronicles 17:21 (= 2 Sam. 7:23): "Who is like your People Israel, one nation in all the earth?" The anonymous, editorial voice of the Talmud observes that Deuteronomy 26:17–18 ("You [Israel] have declared Adonai is your God. ... And Adonai has declared this day that you are ... His ... people") is fulfilled in God's and Israel's mutual daily declarations of each other's oneness: Israel recites the *Sh'ma* twice daily, and God declares, "Who is like your People Israel, one nation in all the earth?"

³*"Abraham rejoices ... "* Abudarham explains why the prayer attributes rejoicing to Abraham and Isaac, but resting to Jacob and his sons. Abraham and Isaac rejoice when Jacob and his sons (the Jewish people) observe Shabbat rest. Further, Abraham's joy is described with the verbal form of the Hebrew *gilah*, while Isaac's is indicated by *rinah*, which is indicative of greater joy (a lesson drawn from Isai. 35:2). Isaac's joy exceeded Abraham's because he lived closer in time than Abraham to the giving of the Torah and Israel's official acceptance of Shabbat. But Jacob and his sons, who were even closer in time than Isaac to the giving of the Torah, possessed more of the essential spirit of the day, and so are described in the prayer in terms of "rest."

⁵*"Know for sure"* What exactly is it that Israel is supposed to recognize (*yakiru*) or "know for sure"? According to Abudarham, it is that Shabbat is unlike other *mitzvot*, in that even God observes it; God's rest is our rest, as it says in *V'shamru*: "and on the seventh day He rested" (Exod. 31:17).

Tsidkat'kha Tsedek The recitation of these verses on Shabbat afternoon is not mentioned in the Talmud. The earliest discussion Abudarham can find is by Sar Shalom Gaon (ninth century, Babylonia), who notes its several references to *ts.d.k*, "justice," and describes it as a *tsiduk hadin*, a "justification," or acceptance, of God's decision to bring about the death of Moses, which, according to midrashic legend, occurred on a Shabbat afternoon. Rabbi Barukh Halevi Epstein refers to this legend in his explanation of why people are accustomed not to greet each other with *"Shabbat shalom"* after Shabbat *Minchah*, the way they do after Friday night *Ma'ariv* and *Shacharit* on Saturday morning. Refraining from this greeting is a tacit way to acknowledge the passing of Moses that occurred during that time of day.

◆

KUSHNER & POLEN (CHASIDISM)

whom has learned one topic and the other a different one, then when they exchange their "wares," the transfer is extraordinary. Now, each student has literally doubled the quantity of his or her knowledge.

In the same way, we understand that each and every Jew has a unique and indispensable portion in Torah. We each have a unique way of reading and understanding it. And when we take the trouble to share our own interpretations with one another, we all not only keep what we started with, but also receive the interpretations of everyone else. In this way we, collectively, become as one. Sharing unites us.

We share our uniqueness, not only with one another, but also, as it were, with God. As we read in the Talmud (Ber. 6a), God too wears *t'fillin*. This, of course, only raises the obvious (and mischievous) question of what is written on the parchments in God's *t'fillin*? Since it would make no sense for God to wear phylacteries proclaiming God's own unity, the solution is drawn from 1 Chronicles 17:21, "And who is like your People Israel, one nation in the world?" And it is this passage that has been woven into the *Amidah* for Shabbat afternoon.

◆

LANDES (HALAKHAH)

m'nuchah ("a day of rest"); Israel and Shabbat testify that *atah echad* ("You, God, are One"); God and Shabbat testify that Israel is *goy echad ba'arets* ("one nation on earth").

◆

L. HOFFMAN (HISTORY)

MORNING (SEE VOLUME 4, SEDER K'RIAT HATORAH (THE TORAH SERVICE) AND (2) THE INCLUSION OF K'DUSHAH D'SIDRA (SEE VOLUME 6, TACHANUN AND CONCLUDING PRAYERS, PP. 110–127), POSTPONED ON SHABBAT FROM THE MORNING SERVICE TO THE AFTERNOON. FOR DISCUSSION OF THESE CHANGES, SEE ABOVE, PP. 22–23. FOLLOWING THE TORAH READING, WE MOVE DIRECTLY TO THE AMIDAH. AS WITH EVERY AMIDAH FOR SHABBAT, THE MIDDLE THIRTEEN BLESSINGS (BLESSINGS 4–16), WHICH ARE CONSIDERED PETITIONARY, AND THEREFORE UNFITTING FOR SO SACRED A DAY, ARE REPLACED BY A SINGLE PRAYER CALLED K'DUSHAT HAYOM ("SANCTIFICATION OF THE DAY").

[1] *"You are One"* The *K'dushat Hayom* ("Sanctification of the Day") for *Minchah*. See "You sanctified [*atah kidashta*] the seventh day," p. 123.

[8] *"On it* [vah] *"* Literally, "on it." Some Siddur texts read "in them" *(vam)* not "in [on] it" *(vah)*. "On it" is clearly correct. It appears that way in every other *Amidah* for Shabbat, with the meaning, "Israel will rest on it [on Shabbat]." Indeed, most prayer books have amended the mistake by now. But for centuries, some Jews retained the error and then had to develop some rationale of what "in them" could mean. In so doing, they devised a midrashic understanding of Shabbat. "In them" implies "in Israel," with the potential meaning, "Shabbat will rest within the Jews who keep it."

◆

II. *Tsidkat'kha Tsedek* ("Your Righteousness Is Right") for Shabbat *Minchah*

[1] Your righteousness is forever right and your Torah true.

[2] Your righteousness, God, reaches the heavens; You have done wonders: who is like You?

[3] Your righteousness is like the mountains of God, your justice like a great depth. Save man and beast, Adonai.

צִדְקָתְךָ צֶדֶק לְעוֹלָם, וְתוֹרָתְךָ אֱמֶת. [1]

וְצִדְקָתְךָ אֱלֹהִים עַד מָרוֹם, אֲשֶׁר עָשִׂיתָ גְדֹלוֹת; אֱלֹהִים, מִי כָמְוֹךָ. [2]

צִדְקָתְךָ כְּהַרְרֵי אֵל, מִשְׁפָּטֶיךָ תְּהוֹם רַבָּה; אָדָם וּבְהֵמָה תוֹשִׁיעַ, יְיָ. [3]

BRETTLER (BIBLE)

[1-3] *"Your righteousness"* Three verses (Pss. 119:142, 71:19, 36:7) all beginning the same; only one other biblical verse (Ps. 40:11) begins with this word, and it is not contextually suitable here.

[3] *"God"* It is uncertain if *el* should be translated as "God." It may just be a superlative ("great," describing "great mountains"). It may also hark back to ancient Canaanite mythology, and refer to the divinity Il. *"A great depth"* goes back to the Ugaritic and biblical myth of the rebellion of the Sea after creation:

> It was you [the arm of God] that hacked Rahab into pieces,
>
> *(p. 212)*

DORFF (THEOLOGY)

[1] *"Your righteousness is forever right ..."* A set of biblical passages about justice, omitted if Shabbat or Sunday is one when *Tachanun* is not said (e.g., the New Moon, Passover, Chanukah), for then we think of the special theme of that occasion rather than focus on *(p. 212)*

ELLENSON (MODERN LITURGIES)

[1] *"Your righteousness"* This passage is omitted from most Reform prayer books. However, *Gates of Prayer* (American Reform, 1975) includes at least the first line in one of its evening services, and *Ha'avodah Shebalev* (Israeli Reform, 1982) contains all *(p. 212)*

GRAY (OUR TALMUDIC HERITAGE)

[1] *"Your righteousness ... right"* The Talmud (Shab. 118a) holds that whoever keeps the three meals of Shabbat will be saved from three afflictions: (1) the trials that will presage the coming of the messiah, (2) the apocalyptic war at the end of days between Gog and Magog, and (3) going to *Gehinnom* ("hell") after death. Our three verses, each about *tsedek* ("justice"), refer to the three acts of justice by which God will shelter us from these terrors. *(p. 213)*

II. TSIDKAT'KHA TSEDEK ("YOUR RIGHTEOUSNESS IS RIGHT") FOR SHABBAT MINCHAH

[1] Your righteousness is forever right and your Torah true.

[2] Your righteousness, God, reaches the heavens; You have done wonders: who is like You?

[3] Your righteousness is like the mountains of God, your justice like a great depth. Save man and beast, Adonai.

LANDES (HALAKHAH)

[1] *"Your righteousness ... right"* This passage fulfills the function of *tsiduk hadin*–"justifying the judgment," that is, accepting God's correct (if often incomprehensible) decision to bring death to individuals whom we love or admire in the world. The specific reference here is the deaths of Joseph, Moses, and David, who, traditionally, are thought of as dying on Shabbat. The *Bayit Chadash* (*BaCH*, Joel Sirkes, 1561–1640, Poland), however, maintains that Moses died on *(p. 213)*

THIS VERY SHORT PRAYER (COMPOSED OF THREE BIBLICAL CITATIONS) AFFIRMS GOD'S RIGHTEOUSNESS IN JUDGMENT AND FOLLOWS THE AMIDAH. *THEREAFTER, WE MOVE TO THE NORMAL CONCLUDING PRAYERS OF EVERY SERVICE, PRINCIPALLY* ALENU *AND* KADDISH.

[1] *"Your righteousness* [tsidkat'kha tsedek]*"* *Seder Rav Amram* (our first prayer book, c. 860 C.E.) has these lines, and they probably go back even farther, since Amram's gaonate spanned the years from 858 to 871, and the tradition of saying *Tsidkat'kha Tsedek* is cited in the name of one of his predecessors, Sar   *(p. 213)*

¹צִדְקָתְךָ צֶדֶק לְעוֹלָם, וְתוֹרָתְךָ אֱמֶת.

²וְצִדְקָתְךָ אֱלֹהִים עַד מָרוֹם, אֲשֶׁר עָשִׂיתָ גְדֹלוֹת; אֱלֹהִים, מִי כָמוֹךָ.

³צִדְקָתְךָ כְּהַרְרֵי אֵל, מִשְׁפָּטֶיךָ תְּהוֹם רַבָּה; אָדָם וּבְהֵמָה תוֹשִׁיעַ, יְיָ.

J. HOFFMAN (TRANSLATION)

[1] *"Your righteousness is forever right"* Commonly, "your righteousness is an everlasting righteousness," but the Hebrew actually has two related but not identical words here, so we opt for "righteousness" and "right."

◆ ◆ ◆

MINCHAH (ADDITIONS FOR SHABBAT)

BRETTLER (BIBLE)

that pierced the dragon.
It was You that dried up the Sea.

Isaiah 51:9–10

For other references to the myth, see Volume 8, *Kabbalat Shabbat (Welcoming Shabbat in the Synagogue)*, pp. 24 and 90.

——◆——

DORFF (THEOLOGY)

the ongoing need for justice in the world. *Tachanun* is omitted on Shabbat too, but as a non-holiday Shabbat draws to a close, we recite these lines anyway to reassert the need for justice in the weekday world that we are about to enter.

[1] *"Your Torah true"* This first verse links justice to Torah, since we have just read Torah as part of Shabbat *Minchah* (see diagram, p. 22).

[2] *"Your righteousness, God ..."* We link morality to one, powerful God, the theme of the middle section of the *Amidah* for *Minchah* on Shabbat. One just God establishes this single moral criterion for all humanity; human beings are to act morally because it is the right thing to do, not just to appease a God of power. (See "Blessed is Adonai forever," p. 96.)

[3] *"Man and beast"* Righteousness is necessary for saving the entire world, including even the animals. By inserting these lines here, the Rabbis remind us again of the need for morality in the weekday world that we will be reentering soon.

——◆——

ELLENSON (MODERN LITURGIES)

three verses. Conservative liturgies *Sim Shalom* (1985, 1998) and *Va'ani Tefillati* (1998) also include these passages in their entirety, as does the Reconstructionist *Kol Haneshamah* (1995). British Reform *Forms of Prayer* (1977) sides with the more liberal American Reform and Reconstructionist liturgies here.

——◆——

GRAY (OUR TALMUDIC HERITAGE)

R. Hamnuna taught (Sanh. 7a) that the first question a person will be asked after death relates to how much Torah the person studied in life. Verse 1 ("Your Torah [is] true") must, therefore, refer to being saved from *Gehinnom* (3).

Verse 2, "You have done wonders" *(g'dolot)* corresponds to the apocalyptic war of Gog and Magog (2), where God will indeed do "great things" *(g'dolot)*, for Ezekiel 38:23 describes God as being "magnified" *(hitgadilti*, from the same root as *g'dolot)* in connection with that war.

Verse 3, "Your justice like a great depth" *(mishpatekha t'hom rabbah)* denotes the afflictions of the messiah (1), whose coming will uproot evil, which is described in the Midrash as being "very deep."

◆

LANDES (HALAKHAH)

Erev Shabbat (Friday), so this prayer commemorates his actual burial, his being "put away" *(nignaz)*, on Shabbat afternoon.

Alternatively, *tsiduk hadin* refers to the tradition that those who are punished in *Gehinnom* are set free on Shabbat day. The end of *Minchah* heralds the soon-to-end Shabbat, when these souls return to their harsh punishment. We, who observe this harshness, respond by "justifying the judgment."

Certain days, like Rosh Chodesh or even *Erev Rosh Chodesh*, are considered to contain an "extra degree" of happiness, so that if they fall on a weekday, the normal weekday supplications we call *Tachanun* are not recited (*Shulchan Arukh*, O. Ch., 292:2 and *Mishnah B'rurah* 6 and 7 by Rabbi Israel Meir HaCohen Kagan [*Chofetz Chayim*], 1839–1933, Radin, Poland). We do not say *Tsidkat'kha tsedek* then either.

◆

L. HOFFMAN (HISTORY)

Shalom (848–853). Amram, however, has the sentences in reverse order. Fourteenth-century savant David Abudarham cites our order here as common throughout Spain, but he has heard that Provençal synagogues reverse them to match the order in which they appear in the Bible (Pss. 36:7, 71:19, 119:142). He knows also that his geonic predecessors (not just Amram, but Saadiah also) had it that way. But both orders were retained here and there, apparently, and by the thirteenth century, perhaps under Abudarham's influence, Sefarad (Spain) reverted to the original order as in Amram, while Ashkenaz (Northern Europe) did not.

All agreed, however, that the prayer (in whatever order) was like a *tsiduk hadin* (pronounced tsee-DOOK hah-DEEN, meaning "righteousness of [God's] judgment"),

213

the prayer for funerals that acknowledges death as just. Sar Shalom had connected the prayer with the death of Moses, who was held to have died on Shabbat at *Minchah*. Other traditions, however, think Moses died just before Shabbat began or just after it ended, so an alternative explanation is that souls being punished in the afterlife get a respite on Shabbat. By *Minchah*, they must think about returning, as if they are going to be reburied. So we say the equivalent of a funeral liturgy for them.

There is yet a third explanation known to Abudarham. Shabbat featured an extra third meal (*s'udah sh'lishit*, pronounced s'-oo-DAH shlee-SHEET—see Volume 7, "*Shabbat at Home, S'udah Sh'lishit*: A Rite of Modest Majesty," pp. 30–36). The Talmud (Shab. 119b) promises that those who keep these three Shabbat meals will be saved from three moments of suffering: the travail that precedes the coming of the messiah; the apocalyptic war of Gog and Magog, and personal suffering in *Gehinnom* (the Jewish equivalent of hell) after we die. Shabbat *Minchah* precedes the *s'udah sh'lishit*, a time when this threefold promise comes naturally comes to mind. So it includes three verses to denote the three moments of deliverance that we will enjoy because we keep a *s'udah sh'lishit*.

By the Middle Ages, other explanations had become normative. The *Zohar*, for example, added Joseph and David to the list of those who died on Shabbat—saying that is why we say three verses, not just one. Answering the suspicion that Moses died on Friday, not Saturday, the *Zohar* suggests that God cradled Moses under the wings of the *Shekhinah* until Saturday arrived; only then was he buried—in the peace of Shabbat *Minchah*.

———◆———

About the Contributors

MARC BRETTLER

Marc Brettler, Ph.D., is Dora Goldberg Professor of Biblical Studies and chair of the Department of Near Eastern and Judaic Studies at Brandeis University. His major areas of research are biblical historical texts, religious metaphors, and gender issues in the Bible. Brettler is author of *God Is King: Understanding an Israelite Metaphor* (Sheffield Academic Press), *The Creation of History in Ancient Israel* (Routledge), *The Book of Judges* (Routledge), and *How to Read the Bible* (Jewish Publication Society), as well as a variety of articles on the Bible. He is also associate editor of the new edition of the *Oxford Annotated Bible* and coeditor of the *Jewish Study Bible* (Oxford University Press).

ELLIOT N. DORFF

Elliot N. Dorff, Ph.D., is rector and Sol and Anne Dorff Distinguished Professor of Philosophy at the University of Judaism in Los Angeles. His book *Knowing God: Jewish Journeys to the Unknowable* (Rowman and Littlefield) includes an extensive analysis of the nature of prayer. Ordained a rabbi at the Jewish Theological Seminary of America, Dorff is vice-chair of the Conservative Movement's Committee on Jewish Law and Standards, and he contributed to the Conservative Movement's new Torah commentary, *Etz Hayim*. He has chaired the Jewish Law Association and the Academy of Jewish Philosophy, and he is now president of Jewish Family Service of Los Angeles. He has served on several federal government commissions on issues in bioethics. Winner of the National Jewish Book Award for *To Do the Right and the Good: A Jewish Approach to Modern Social Ethics*, he has written twelve books and more than 150 articles on Jewish thought and ethics. His latest books are *The Way Into Tikkun Olam (Repairing the World)* (Jewish Lights) and *The Unfolding Tradition: Jewish Law After Sinai* (Aviv Press of the Rabbinical Assembly).

DAVID ELLENSON

David Ellenson, Ph.D., is president of Hebrew Union College–Jewish Institute of Religion. He holds the Gus Waterman Herrman Presidential Chair and is the I. H. and Anna Grancell Professor of Jewish Religious Thought. Ordained a rabbi by Hebrew

Union College–Jewish Institute of Religion, he has served as a visiting professor at Hebrew University in Jerusalem, at the Jewish Theological Seminary in New York, and at the University of California at Los Angeles. Ellenson has also taught at the Pardes Institute of Jewish Studies and at the Shalom Hartman Institute, both in Jerusalem. Ellenson has published and lectured extensively on diverse topics in modern Jewish thought, history, and ethics. His most recent book, *After Emancipation*, was published by HUC Press in 2004.

ELLEN FRANKEL

Dr. Ellen Frankel is currently the CEO and editor in chief of The Jewish Publication Society. A scholar of Jewish folklore, Frankel has published eight books, including *The Classic Tales; The Encyclopedia of Jewish Symbols,* co-authored with artist Betsy Teutsch; *The Five Books of Miriam: A Woman's Commentary on the Torah; The Jewish Spirit;* and *The Illustrated Hebrew Bible.* Frankel travels widely as a storyteller and lecturer, speaking at synagogues, summer study institutes, Hillels, Jewish women's groups, Jewish community centers, museums, schools, retirement communities, and nursing homes, and to radio audiences.

ALYSSA GRAY

Alyssa Gray, Ph.D., J.D., is assistant professor of codes and responsa literature at Hebrew Union College–Jewish Institute of Religion in New York. She has also taught at The Jewish Theological Seminary in New York. Her principal research interests are Babylonian and Palestinian Talmuds, Jewish law and legal theory, and the history of Jewish law, especially the topics of *tzedakah,* Jewish–non-Jewish interactions, and martyrdom. She has completed a book entitled *A Talmud in Exile,* which is forthcoming from Brown Judaic Studies. Her current research focuses on wealth and poverty in classical rabbinic literature.

JOEL M. HOFFMAN

Joel M. Hoffman, Ph.D., lectures across the globe on popular and scholarly topics spanning history, Hebrew, prayer, and Jewish continuity. He has served on the faculties of Brandeis University; the Academy for Jewish Religion; and, currently, Hebrew Union College–Jewish Institute of Religion in New York, where he teaches advanced classes on Hebrew and on translation. Hoffman's research in theoretical linguistics brings him to a new approach to ancient Hebrew, viewing it not merely as a dead language, but as a spoken language of antiquity. Hoffman is the author of *In the Beginning: A Short History of the Hebrew Language* (NYU Press). In addition to his graduate-level teaching, Hoffman serves as scholar-in-residence at Temple Shaaray Tefila in Bedford, New York, and finds time to teach youngsters a few afternoons a week.

LAWRENCE A. HOFFMAN

Lawrence A. Hoffman, Ph.D., has served for more than two decades as the Barbara and Stephen Friedman Professor of Liturgy Worship and Ritual at Hebrew Union College–Jewish Institute of Religion in New York, where he was ordained a rabbi. Widely recognized for his liturgical scholarship, Hoffman has combined research in Jewish ritual, worship, and spirituality with a passion for the spiritual renewal of contemporary Judaism. He has written and edited numerous books, including *The Art of Public Prayer, 2nd Edition: Not for Clergy Only* (SkyLight Paths)—now used nationally by Jews and Christians as a handbook for liturgical planners in church and synagogue, as well as a revision of *What Is a Jew?,* the best-selling classic that remains the most widely read introduction to Judaism ever written in any language. He is also the author of *Israel—A Spiritual Travel Guide: A Companion for the Modern Jewish Pilgrim* and *The Way Into Jewish Prayer* (both Jewish Lights Publishing). Hoffman is currently a developer of Synagogue 2000, a transdenominational project designed to envision and implement the ideal synagogue of the spirit for the twenty-first century.

LAWRENCE KUSHNER

Lawrence Kushner is the Emanu-El scholar at congregation Emanu-El in San Francisco, an adjunct faculty member at Hebrew Union College–Jewish Institute of Religion, and a visiting professor of Jewish spirituality at the Graduate Theological Union in Berkeley, California. He served as spiritual leader of Congregation Beth El in Sudbury, Massachusetts, for twenty-eight years and is widely regarded as one of the most creative religious writers in America. Ordained a rabbi by Hebrew Union College–Jewish Institute of Religion, Kushner led his congregants in publishing their own prayer book, *V'taher Libenu (Purify Our Hearts),* the first gender-neutral liturgy ever written. Through his lectures and many books, including *The Way Into Jewish Mystical Tradition; Invisible Lines of Connection: Sacred Stories of the Ordinary; The Book of Letters: A Mystical Hebrew Alphabet; Honey from the Rock: An Introduction to Jewish Mysticism; God Was in This Place and I, i Did Not Know: Finding Self, Spirituality, and Ultimate Meaning; Eyes Remade for Wonder: A Lawrence Kushner Reader,* and *Jewish Spirituality: A Brief Introduction for Christians,* all published by Jewish Lights, he has helped shape the Jewish community's present focus on personal and institutional spiritual renewal.

DANIEL LANDES

Daniel Landes is director and Rosh HaYeshivah of the Pardes Institute of Jewish Studies in Jerusalem and was an adjunct professor of Jewish law at Loyola University Law School in Los Angeles. Ordained a rabbi by Rabbi Isaac Elchanan Theological Seminary, Landes was a founding faculty member of the Simon Wiesenthal Center and the Yeshiva of Los Angeles. He has lectured and written various popular and scholarly articles on the subjects of Jewish thought, social ethics, and spirituality.

NEHEMIA POLEN

Nehemia Polen is professor of Jewish thought and director of the Hasidic Text Institute at Boston's Hebrew College. He is the author of *The Holy Fire: The Teachings of Rabbi Kalonymus Shapira, the Rebbe of the Warsaw Ghetto* (Jason Aronson), as well as many academic and popular articles on Chasidism and Jewish spirituality and coauthor of *Filling Words with Light: Hasidic and Mystical Reflections on Jewish Prayer* (Jewish Lights). He received his Ph.D. from Boston University, where he studied with and served as teaching fellow for Nobel laureate Elie Wiesel. In 1994 he was Daniel Jeremy Silver Fellow at Harvard University, and he has also been a Visiting Scholar at the Hebrew University in Jerusalem. He was ordained a rabbi at the Ner Israel Rabbinical College in Baltimore, Maryland, and served as a congregational rabbi for twenty-three years. In 1998–1999 he was a National Endowment for the Humanities Fellow, working on the writings of Malkah Shapiro (1894–1971), the daughter of a noted Chasidic master, whose Hebrew memoirs focus on the spiritual lives of women in the context of prewar Chasidism in Poland. This work is documented in his book *The Rebbe's Daughter* (Jewish Publication Society).

List of Abbreviations

Artscroll	*Siddur Kol Ya'akov,* 1984.
Birnbaum	*Daily Prayer Book: Hasiddur Hashalem,* 1949.
FOP	*Forms of Prayer,* 1997.
Fox	Everett Fox, *The Five Books of Moses* (New York: Schocken Books, 1995).
GOP	*Gates of Prayer,* 1975.
HS	*Ha'avodah Shebalev,* 1982.
KH	*Kol Haneshamah,* 1996.
King James	*King James Bible,* 1611/1769.
JPS	*Jewish Publication Society Bible* (Philadelphia: Jewish Publication Society, 1985).
NRSV	*New Revised Standard Bible,* 1989.
SLC	*Siddur Lev Chadash,* 1995.
SOH	*Service of the Heart,* 1967.
SSS	*Siddur Sim Shalom,* 1985; revised, 1998.
SVT	*Siddur Va'ani T'fillati,* 1998.
UPB	*Union Prayer Book,* 1894–1895.

Glossary

The following glossary defines Hebrew words used regularly throughout this volume and provides the way the words are pronounced. Sometimes two pronunciations are common, in which case the first is the way the word is sounded in proper Hebrew, and the second is the way it is sometimes heard in common speech, under the influence of Yiddish, the folk language of Jews in northern and eastern Europe (it is a combination, mostly, of Hebrew and German). Our goal is to provide the way that many Jews actually use these words, not just the technically correct version.

- The pronunciations are divided into syllables by dashes.

- The accented syllable is written in capital letters.

- "Kh" represents a guttural sound, similar to the German (as in "sprach").

- The most common vowel is "a" as in "father," which appears here as "ah."

- The short "e" (as in "get") is written as either "e" (when it is in the middle of a syllable) or "eh" (when it ends a syllable).

- Similarly, the short "i" (as in "tin") is written as either "i" (when it is in the middle of a syllable) or "ih" (when it ends a syllable).

- A long "o" (as in "Moses") is written as "oe" (as in the word "toe") or "oh" (as in the word "Oh!").

Abraham ben Nathan Hayarchi of Lunel: See ***Manhig.***

Abudarham: David ben Joseph Abudarham, fourteenth-century Spanish commentator on the liturgy. His *Sefer Abudarham* (completed in 1340) is our primary account of Spanish (Sefardi) practice of the time.

Acharonim (pronounced ah-khah-roe-NEEM or, commonly, akh-ROE-nim): The name given to Jewish legal authorities from roughly the sixteenth century on. The word means, literally, "later ones," as opposed to the "earlier ones," authorities prior to that time who are held in higher regard and are called *Rishonim* (pronounced ree-shoh-NEEM or, commonly, ree-SHOH-nim). Singular: *Acharon* (pronounced ah-khah-RONE) and *Rishon* (pronounced ree-SHONE).

Adam harishon (pronounced ah-DAHM hah-ree-SHOHN): "The first man," that is, the biblical Adam.

Adon Olam (pronounced ah-DOHN oh-LAHM): An early morning prayer of unknown authorship, but dating from medieval times, and possibly originally intended as a nighttime prayer, because it praises God for watching over our souls when we sleep. Nowadays, it is used also as a concluding song for which composers have provided a staggering variety of tunes.

Adonai elohei yisra'el (pronounced ah-doh-NAH'y eh-loh-HAY yis-rah-AYL): Literally, "Adonai God of Israel." A common appellation for God, used in this series to designate the opening words, and hence, the name of a prayer, that is added to *Tachanun* on Mondays and Thursdays.

Adret, Solomon ben Abraham: The RaSHBA, Spanish commentator and halakhist (1235–1310). See ***Rashba***.

Akedah (pronounced ah-kay-DAH): Literally, "binding"; the technical term for the Genesis 22 account of the binding of Isaac on the altar; read liturgically as part of the *Birkhot Hashachar*. By extension, a genre of poem, especially for the High Holy Days, pleading for forgiveness on account of the merit of Isaac's near self-sacrifice.

Al chet (pronounced ahl KHEHT): Literally, "For the sin…" See ***Vidui Rabbah***.

Alenu (pronounced ah-LAY-noo): The first word and, therefore, the title of a major prayer compiled in the second or third century as part of the New Year (Rosh Hashanah) service, but from about the fourteenth century on, used also as part of the concluding section of every daily service. *Alenu* means "it is incumbent upon us…" and introduces the prayer's theme: our duty to praise God.

Amah (pronounced ah-MAH): A rabbinic measure, amounting, roughly, to a forearm: the distance from the elbow to the tip of the little finger.

Amidah (pronounced either ah-mee-DAH or, commonly, ah-MEE-dah): One of three commonly used titles for the second of two central units in the worship service, the first being the *Sh'ma* and Its Blessings. It is composed of a series of blessings, many of which are petitionary, except on Sabbaths and holidays, when the petitions are removed out of deference to the holiness of the day. Also called ***T'fillah*** and ***Sh'moneh Esreh***. *Amidah* means "standing," and refers to the fact that the prayer is said standing up.

Amora (pronounced ah-MOE-rah): A title for talmudic authorities and, therefore, those living from roughly the third to the sixth centuries. Plural: *Amoraim* (pronounced ah-moe-rah-EEM or, commonly, ah-moe-RAH-yim). Often used in contrast to a *Tanna* (pronounced TAH-nah), the title of authorities in the time of the Mishnah, that is, prior to the third century. Plural: *Tannaim* (pronounced tah-nah-EEM or, commonly, tah-NAH-yim).

Anshei K'nesset Hagd'olah (pronounced ahn-shay KNEH-seht hah-g'-doh-LAH): "The men of the Great Assembly," a title used by rabbinic tradition to describe the generations of leaders from Ezra (fifth century B.C.E.) to the first Rabbis (second century B.C.E.).

Arukh Hashulchan (pronounced ah-RUKH hah-shool-kHAN): Nineteenth-century law code by Yechiel Michal Epstein, 1829–1888, Russia.

Arvit (pronounced ahr-VEET or, commonly, AHR-veet): From the Hebrew word *erev* (pronounced EH-rev) meaning "evening." One of two titles used for the evening worship service (also called *Ma'ariv*).

Ashamnu (pronounced ah-SHAHM-noo): Literally, "We have sinned." See *Vidui Zuta*.

Ashkavah (pronounced ahsh-kah-VAH or, commonly, ahsh-KAH-vah): Sometimes spelled *Hashkavah* (pronounced hahsh-kah-VAH or, commonly, hahsh-KAH-vah). A traditional Sefardi prayer for the dead, recited by mourners following the reading of Torah during the regular service. Said also at the graveside and during the evening service of Yom Kippur.

Ashkenazi (pronounced ahsh-k'-nah-ZEE or, commonly, ahsh-k'-NAH-zee): From the Hebrew word *Ashkenaz,* meaning the geographic area of northern and eastern Europe; Ashkenazi is the adjective, describing the liturgical rituals and customs practiced there, as opposed to Sefardi, meaning the liturgical rituals and customs that are derived from *Sefarad,* Spain (see *Sefardi*).

Ashre (pronounced ahsh-RAY or, commonly, AHSH-ray): The first word and, therefore, the title of a prayer said three times each day, composed primarily of Psalm 145. *Ashre* means "happy" and introduces the phrase "Happy are they who dwell in Your [God's] house."

Atah chonantanu (pronounced ah-TAH choh-nahn-TAH-noo): Literally, "You have favored us," the first words and, therefore, the title of the *Havdalah* insertion (declaring a separation between Shabbat and weekdays) for the fourth benediction of the Saturday night *Ma'ariv Amidah.*

Atarah (pronounced ah-tah-RAH): A stole worn by some Reform service leaders (in place of an actual *tallit* with *tsitsit*) prior to the liturgical renewal of the late twentieth century that featured a recovery of tradition and the reuse of the traditional *tallit*. (See *tallit*.)

Avel (pronounced ah-VAYL): Mourner.

Av harachamim (pronounced AHV hah-rah-khah-MEEM or, commonly, ahv hah-RAH-khah-meem): Literally, "Father of mercy," a prayer composed in the wake of the Crusades to commemorate the death of German Jewish martyrs; now part of the weekly Shabbat service (after reading Torah) and one of the main prayers comprising the Memorial Service *(Yizkor)*.

Avodah (pronounced ah-voe-DAH): Literally, "sacrificial service," a reference to the sacrificial cult practiced in the ancient Temple until its destruction by the Romans in the year 70 C.E.; also the title of the third to last blessing in the *Amidah,* a petition for the restoration of the Temple in messianic times. Many liberal liturgies either omit the blessing or reframe it as a petition for divine acceptance of worship in general.

Avot (pronounced ah-VOTE): Literally, "fathers" or "ancestors," and the title of the first blessing in the *Amidah*. The traditional wording of the blessing recollects the covenantal relationship between God and the patriarchs: Abraham, Isaac, and Jacob. Most liberal liturgies also include explicit reference to the matriarchs: Sarah, Rebekah, Rachel, and Leah.

[The] BaCH (pronounced BAHKH): An acronym for Rabbi Joel Sirkes (1561–1640, Poland), formed by juxtaposing the two Hebrew initials of his major legal work, *Bayit Chadash* (BaCH).

Badei Hashulchan (pronounced bah-DAY hah-shool-KHAN or, popularly, BAH-day hah-SHOOL-khan): Contemporary halakhic commentary to the *Shulchan Arukh*, by Rabbi Feivel Cohen, Brooklyn, New York.

Bakashot (pronounced bah-kah-SHOTE; singular, *bakashah*, pronounced bah-kah-SHAH): Petitions; technically, the middle thirteen blessings of the daily *Amidah*.

Baleh busteh (pronounced bah-l' BUS-tah [the U of "BUS" rhymes with the OU of "could"]): A virtually untranslatable Yiddish phrase meaning "good homemaker."

Bar'khu (pronounced bah-r'-KHOO or, commonly, BOH-r'khoo): The first word and, therefore, the title of the formal Call to Prayer with which the section called the *Sh'ma* and Its Blessings begins. *Bar'khu* means "praise," and it introduces the invitation to the assembled congregation to praise God.

Barukh Adonai l'olam (pronounced bah-RUKH ah-doh-NA'i l'-oh-LAHM): Literally, "Blessed is God forever," the first three Hebrew words and, hence, the title of the paragraph following the *Hashkivenu* in the *Ma'ariv* service, and sometimes labeled here, "The Extended *Hashkivenu*."

Barukh k'vod (pronounced bah-RUKH k'-VOD): The first two words of a response in the third blessing of the *Amidah* taken from Ezekiel 3:12, meaning "the glory of Adonai is blessed from His place."

Barukh she'amar (pronounced bah-RUKH sheh-ah-MAHR): Literally, "Blessed is the One by whose speech [the world came to be]," the first words and, therefore, the title of the blessing that opens the *P'sukei D'zimrah,* the "warm-up" section to the morning service composed mainly of biblical material (chiefly psalms) that were intended to be sung as praise of God.

Bayit Chadash (pronounced BAH-yiht chah-DAHSH): Commentary to *Tur* by Joel Sirkes (1561–1640, Poland); both author and commentary are known also by the acronym *BaCH*.

Benediction (also called a "blessing"): One of two terms used for the Rabbis' favorite prose formula for composing prayers. The worship service is composed of many different literary genres, but most of it is benedictions. Long benedictions end with a summary line that begins *Barukh atah Adonai*… "Blessed are You, Adonai…" Short blessings have the summary line alone.

Ben Sirah (pronounced behn SIH-rah): Author of a book of wisdom similar in style to Proverbs, probably dating to 180 or 200 B.C.E., and containing, among other things, a moving description of the High Priest in the Jerusalem Temple. Although not included in the Bible, it is known because it became part of Catholic Scripture. The book carries the author's name, but it is called, by Catholics, Ecclesiasticus. A recently discovered Hebrew edition of Ben Sirah contains a prayer that some identify (probably incorrectly) as an early version of the ***Amidah***.

Bet avel (pronounced bayt ah-VAYL): House of mourning.

Bet hamikdash (pronounced BAYT hah-mik-DASH): The ancient Temple, either the one built by Solomon (the First Temple) or the one constructed after the return from Babylonian exile (the Second Temple) and sacked by Rome in the war of 70.

Bet Yosef (pronounced BAYT yoh-SAYF): Literally, "House of Joseph," title for sixteenth-century commentary to the *Tur*, by Joseph Caro.

Beys hamikdesh (pronounced BAYS ha-MIK-d'sh): Yiddish for *bet hamikdash* ("Temple").

Binah (pronounced bee-NAH or, commonly, BEE-nah): Literally, "knowledge" or "understanding," and the title of the fourth blessing in the daily *Amidah*. It is a petition for human knowledge, particularly insight into the human condition, leading to repentance. In kabbalistic circles, it is one of the uppermost *s'firot*, representing a stage of divine thought prior to creation.

Birkat (pronounced beer-KAHT): Literally, "Blessing of..." The titles of many blessings are known as "Blessing of...," for example, "Blessing of Torah" and "Blessing of Jerusalem." Some titles are commonly shortened so that only the qualifying last words are used (such as "Jerusalem" instead of "Blessing of Jerusalem"), and they are listed in the glossary by the last words, e.g., *Y'rushalayim* instead of *Birkat Y'rushalayim* ("Jerusalem" instead of "Blessing of Jerusalem"). Those blessings that are more generally cited with the full title appear under *Birkat*.

Birkat Hashir (pronounced beer-KAHT hah-SHEER): Literally, "Blessing of song," and the title, therefore, of the final blessing to the *P'sukei D'zimrah,* the "warm-up" section to the morning service composed mainly of biblical material (chiefly psalms) that were intended to be sung as praise of God. Technically, a *Birkat Hashir* concludes any *Hallel* (see **Hallel**), in this case, the Daily *Hallel,* which is the central component of the *P'sukei D'zimrah.*

Birkat Hatorah (pronounced beer-KAHT hah-toe-RAH): Literally, "Blessing of Torah," the title for the second blessing in the liturgical section called the *Sh'ma* and Its Blessings; its theme is the revelation of the Torah to Israel on Mount Sinai.

Birkat Kohanim (pronounced beer-KAHT koe-hah-NEEM): Literally, "Blessing of the Priests," but usually referred to as "the priestly benediction," a reference to Numbers 6:24–26. Also the title of the final blessing of the *Amidah*. See also **Kohanim.**

Birkhot Hashachar (pronounced beer-KHOT hah-SHAH-khar): Literally, "Morning Blessings," the title of the first large section in the morning prayer regimen of Judaism; originally said privately upon arising in the morning, but now customarily recited immediately upon arriving at the synagogue. It is composed primarily of benedictions thanking God for the everyday gifts of health and wholeness, as well as study sections taken from the Bible and rabbinic literature.

Birkhot mitzvah (pronounced beer-KHOT meetz-VAH): Blessings said upon performing a commandment; normally of the form, "Blessed are You, Adonai our God, ruler of the universe, who sanctified us with commandments and commanded us to...."

Birkhot nehenin (pronounced beer-KHOT neh-heh-NEEN): Blessings said upon enjoyment of God's world (e.g., eating food, seeing rainbows, hearing a thunderstorm, seeing a flower); normally of the form, "Blessed are You, Adonai our God, ruler of the universe, who…."

B'rakhah (pronounced b'-rah-KHAH): The Hebrew word for "benediction" or "blessing." See **Benediction**. Plural ("benedictions") is *b'rakhot* (pronounced b'-rah-KHOTE).

B'rakhah achat mei'ein shalosh (pronounced b'-rah-KHAH ah-CHAT may-AYN shah-LOSH): Literally, "a single blessing in the form of three," referring to an ancient form of the *Birkat Hamazon* ("Grace after Meals"), in which a single blessing contains all three mandated themes of the first three blessings in the standard Grace. It is reserved for special halakhic purposes today, appearing, for instance, at the end of the Passover Seder.

B'rakhah achat mei'ein sheva (pronounced b'-rah-CHAH ah-CHAT may-AYN SHEH-vah): Literally, "one benediction in the form of seven," known also as *Magen Avot*. See **Magen Avot**.

B'rakhah achat mei'ein sh'moneh esrei (pronounced b-rah-KHAH ah-CHAT may-AYN sh'-moh-NEH ehs-RAY, or, popularly, b-rah-KHAH ah-KHAT may-AYN sh'-MOH-n' EHS-ray): Literally, "one blessing in the form of eighteen." See **Havineinu**.

B'rakhah l'vatalah (pronounced b'-rah-KHAH l'-vah-tah-LAH): Generally translated as "a blessing [recited] in vain," and implying blessings that are unconnected to the act or event for which they were mandated, or that are said redundantly.

Challah (pronounced khah-LAH, or, commonly, KHAH-lah): Originally (in Temple times), following Numbers 15:20, a portion of the about-to-be-baked dough given to the priest *(kohen)*. It is still removed today, but because we no longer provide gifts for priests, it is burned. Secondarily, nowadays, *challah* is the name given to the twisted egg bread used on Shabbat and holidays.

Chanukah (pronounced khah-noo-KAH, or commonly, KHAH-noo-kah): An eight-day festival beginning on the twenty-fifth day of the Hebrew month of Kislev, corresponding, usually, to some time in December. Chanukah celebrates the miraculous deliverance of the Jews as described in the books known as *Maccabees* (pronounced MA-kah-beez). Although not canonized in the Bible, Maccabees is carried in Catholic Scripture and describes the heroic acts of a priestly family, known also as the Hasmoneans (pronounced has-moe-NEE-'ns), in 167 B.C.E.

Chanuki'ah (pronounced khah-noo-kee-YAH or, commonly, khah-noo-KEE-yah): An eight-branch candelabra for Chanukah candles.

Chasidei Ashkenaz (pronounced khah-see-DAY Ahsh-k'-NAHZ or, commonly, khah-SEE-day AHSH-k'-nahz): Literally, "The pious of Germany," a loosely knit philosophical school of thought from twelfth- to thirteenth-century Germany, which pioneered a mystical understanding of the liturgy and emphasized an ascetic way of life and a negative view of humanity. See **Kavod**.

Chasidism (pronounced KHAH-sih-dizm): The doctrine generally traced to an eighteenth-century Polish Jewish mystic and spiritual leader known as the Ba'al Shem Tov (called also the BeSHT, an acronym composed of the initials of his name B, SH, and T). Followers are called *Chasidim* (pronounced khah-see-DEEM or khah-SIH-dim; singular, *Chasid,* pronounced khah-SEED or, commonly, KHA-sid) from the Hebrew word *chesed* (pronounced KHEH-sed), meaning "loving-kindness" or "piety."

Chatimah (pronounced khah-tee-MAH): The final summary line of a benediction (see **Benediction**).

Chatzi Kaddish (pronounced khah-TSEE kah-DEESH or, commonly, KHAH-tsee KAH-d'sh): Literally, "Half *Kaddish,*" a short version of the *Kaddish,* a sort of "oral punctuation," in this case, an "oral semicolon," used to indicate a separation between one major rubric of the service and another.

Chazarat hashatz (pronounced khah-zah-RAHT hah-SHAHTS): Repetition of the *Amidah* by the prayer leader.

Chazzan (pronounced khah-ZAHN, or, popularly, KHAH-z'n): In antiquity, a synagogue official with many duties; now, a cantor.

Chazzanut (pronounced khah-zah-NOOT): The traditional art of the cantor (or *chazzan*).

Cheshvan (pronounced KHESH-vahn): A Hebrew month corresponding to late October or November.

Chiasm (pronounced KYE-asm): Also, *chiasmus.* A term for a poetic device widely used in psalms, from the Latinized version of the Greek *chiasma,* "crossing," as in the Greek letter *chi,* X. *Chiasm* is an inverted relationship between syntactic elements of parallel phrases.

Chiyuv (pronounced khee-YOOV): Halakhically, a *mitzvah* that is absolutely obligatory (as opposed to a *mitzvah* that is not a *chiyuv,* in which case some individual discretion exists as to whether to perform it or not). It is obligatory (a *chiyuv*) to eat matzah on the first day of Passover, for instance; but although it is a *mitzvah,* it is not a *chiyuv* to eat it every other day of Passover, and one may choose to do so or not.

228

Chokhmah (pronounced khokh-MAH or, commonly, KHOKH-mah): Literally, "wisdom," but in kabbalistic circles, one of the uppermost *s'firot*, representing a stage of divine thought prior to creation.

Chol Hamo'ed (pronounced khohl hah-moh-AYD): Literally, "the ordinary [part] of the festival," that is, the intermediary days of Passover and Sukkot, which contain fully holy days on each end, but intermediary days between them. Halakhically, these are considered partly sacred, but not altogether so.

Chovah (pronounced khoh-VAH); An "obligation" (synonym, *chiyuv* [pronounced khee-YOOV]); as opposed to *r'shut* (pronounced: r'-SHOOT), an "option," liturgically.

Confession: See ***Vidui Rabbah, Vidui Zuta.***

Daily Hallel (pronounced hah-LAYL or, commonly, HAH-layl): English for *Hallel Sheb'khol Yom.* See ***Hallel.***

David (pronounced dah-VEED): Literally, "David," a reference to the biblical King David, and the title of the fifteenth blessing of the daily *Amidah,* a petition for the appearance of the messianic ruler said by tradition to be a descendant of King David. Some liberal liturgies omit the blessing or reframe it to refer to a messianic age of perfection, but without the arrival of a human messianic ruler.

D'ora'ita (pronounced d'-oh-RYE-tah): Aramaic for "from the Torah," a category of *mitzah* said to spring directly from the Torah, rather than by rabbinic fiat (see its opposite, ***d'rabbanan***).

Doxology: Technical term for a congregational response to an invitation to praise God; generally a single line of prayer affirming praise of God forever and ever. Examples in the *Sh'ma* and Its Blessings are the responses to the Call to Prayer and to the *Sh'ma* itself. From the Greek word *doxa,* meaning "glory."

D'rabbanan (pronounced d'-rah-bah-NAHN): Aramaic for "from our Rabbis," a category of *mitzah* said to spring from rabbinic fiat, rather than directly from the Torah (see its opposite, ***d'ora'ita***).

Ein Keloheinu (pronounced ayn kay-loh-HAY-noo): Literally, "There is none like our God," a concluding prayer of the *Musaf* service.

Ein sof (pronounced ayn SOHF): Literally, "without end," a kabbalistic term for the absolutely unknowable transcendent God, as opposed to the knowable aspects of God, which appear through emanations called *s'firot* (see ***S'firah***).

El Adon (pronounced ayl ah-DOHN): An early medieval (or, perhaps, ancient) poem celebrating God as a king enthroned on high; it is arranged as an acrostic, that is, each line begins with a different letter of the alphabet. Nowadays, *El Adon* is a popular Sabbath morning hymn.

Elohai n'tsor (pronounced eh-loh-HA'y n'-TSOR): Literally, "My God, keep [my tongue from evil]"; the first words and, therefore, the title of a silent prayer following every *Amidah*, attributed by the Talmud (Ber. 17a) to a fourth-century Babylonian sage known for his piety.

Eretz Yisrael (pronounced EH-retz yis-rah-AYL): Hebrew for "the Land of Israel."

Gaon (pronounced gah-OHN; plural: *Geonim,* pronounced g'-oh-NEEM): Title for the leading Rabbis in Babylon (present-day Iraq) from about 750 to 1038. From a biblical word meaning "glory," which is equivalent in the title to saying "Your Excellence."

Gematria (pronounced g-MAHT-ree-yah): The system of assigning a numerical value to each Hebrew letter, then matching the total value of a word or phrase to another word or phrase of the same value, thereby applying the meaning implicit in one word or phrase to the other. *Alef,* the first letter, is 1, *bet,* the second letter is 2, *gimel,* the third letter, 3, and so forth until we get to *yod,* which is 10. From then on, letters increase by tens until we reach *kuf,* which is 100. The increments now progress by hundreds until we reach the last letter, *tav,* which is 400.

Genizah (pronounced g'-NEE-zah): A cache of documents, in particular the one discovered at the turn of the twentieth century in an old synagogue in Cairo; the source of our knowledge about how Jews prayed in the Land of Israel and vicinity prior to the twelfth century. From a word meaning "to store or hide away," "to archive."

Gra (pronounced GRAH): Acronym for the *Gaon Rabbi Eliyah* (Eliyahu begins with an *alef,* hence the final "a" in the acronym), the Vilna Gaon, Elijah of Vilna, 1730–1797.

Graveside Kaddish: See **Kaddish L'it'chad'ta.**

G'ullah (pronounced g'-oo-LAH): Literally, "redemption" or "deliverance," and the title of the seventh blessing of the daily *Amidah,* as well as the third blessing in the *Sh'ma* and Its Blessings; its theme affirms God's redemptive act of delivering the Israelites from Egypt and promises ultimate deliverance from suffering and want at the end of time.

G'ullah arichta (pronounced g'-oo-LAH ah-RIKH-tah): Literally, "great, large, or long *G'ullah,*" hence, the name bestowed by a halakhic legal fiction on all three blessings following the nighttime *Sh'ma*: the *G'ullah* ("blessing of redemption"), the *Hashkivenu* (blessings requesting a safe night's sleep), and *Barukh Adonai l'olam* ("Blessed is Adonai forever"). By linking these three blessings together as if they were one long single blessing for redemption, we are able to say that the *G'ullah* (the blessing immediately after the *Sh'ma*) flows uninterruptedly into the *Amidah*. See **Lismokh g'ullah lit'fillah.**

G'vurot (pronounced g'voo-ROTE): Literally, "strength" or "power," and the title of the second blessing in the *Amidah*. It affirms the power of God to bring annual rain and new growth in nature and, by extension, to resurrect the dead. Some liberal liturgies omit the belief in resurrection or replace it with wording that suggests other concepts of eternal life.

Haftarah (pronounced hahf-tah-RAH or, commonly, hahf-TOE-rah): The section of Scripture taken from the prophets and read publicly as part of Shabbat and holiday worship services. From a word meaning "to conclude," because it is the "concluding reading," that is, it follows a reading from the Torah (the Five Books of Moses).

Haggadah (pronounced hah-gah-DAH or, commonly, hah-GAH-dah): The liturgical service for the Passover eve Seder meal. From a Hebrew word meaning "to tell," because the Haggadah is a telling of the Passover narrative.

Hakafah (pronounced hah-kah-FAH): Literally, "going around [the room]," a procession in which the Torah is taken from the ark and carried to the *bimah* during the introductory prayers. As the procession winds its way to the *bimah,* people approach the Torah, even kiss it.

Halakhah (pronounced hah-lah-KHAH or, commonly, hah-LAH-khah): The Hebrew word for "Jewish law." Also used as an anglicized adjective, halakhic (pronounced hah-LAH-khic), meaning "legal." From the Hebrew word meaning "to walk" or "to go," denoting the way in which a person should walk through life.

Hallel (pronounced hah-LAYL or, commonly, HAH-layl): A Hebrew word meaning "praise" and, by extension, the name given to sets of psalms that are recited liturgically in praise of God: Psalms 145–150, the Daily *Hallel,* are recited each morning; Psalm 136, the Great *Hallel,* is recited on Shabbat and holidays and is part of the Passover Seder. Psalms 113–118, the best-known *Hallel,* known more fully as the Egyptian *Hallel,* are recited on holidays and get their name from Psalm 114:1, which celebrates the moment "when Israel left Egypt."

Hallel Sheb'khol Yom (pronounced hah-LAYL [or, commonly, HAH-layl] sheh-b'-khol YOHM): The Hebrew term for the Daily *Hallel*. See **Hallel**.

Halleluyah (pronounced hah-l'-loo-YAH, but sometimes anglicized as hah-l'-LOO-yah): A common word in Psalms, meaning "praise God," and the final word of a congregational response within the third blessing of the *Amidah* (from Ps. 146:10).

Hashkivenu (pronounced hahsh-kee-VAY-noo): Literally, "Lie us down [to peace]," the first few words and, therefore, the title of the fourth blessing in the nighttime *Sh'ma* and Its Blessings.

Hat'fillah (pronounced hah-t'-fee-LAH): Literally, "the *T'fillah*," another name for the *Amidah*. See ***T'fillah***.

Havdalah (pronounced hahv-dah-LAH or, commonly, hahv-DAH-lah): Literally "separation," hence, the name of the prayer that separates Shabbat from the following week, said as an insertion into the Saturday evening *Amidah* and at home later in the evening. The latter instance, which is accompanied by wine, is called *Havdalah al Hakos* (pronounced hahv-dah-LAH ahl hah-KOHS), "*Havdalah* over a cup [of wine]."

Havdalah al Hakos: See ***Havdalah***.

Havineinu (pronounced hah-vee-NAY-noo): Literally, "Grant us wisdom," the opening words and, hence, the title of an old version of the *Amidah*, now used for emergency situations when there is not enough time to say the prescribed one. Known also as *B'rakhah achat mei'ein sh'moneh esrei* (pronounced b-rah-KHAH ah-CHAT may-AYN sh'-moh-NEH ehs-RAY or, popularly, b-rah-KHAH ah-CHAT may-AYN sh'-MOH-n' EHS-ray), meaning "One blessing in the form of eighteen," referring to the fact that this single blessing contains references to all mandated themes of the middle blessings in the daily *Amidah*. These thirteen themes, along with those of the first three and last three blessings of the *Amidah*, actually total nineteen, but two of the themes were originally grouped together—hence "eighteen.").

Hefsek (pronounced hehf-SAYK, but popularly, HEF-sayk): Literally, "an interruption," so used halakhically to denote an interruption in consciousness. Some prayers, or parts of prayers, must be said immediately after one another; also, blessings must be said in immediate juxtaposition with the action or experience for which they are intended. In such cases, a *hefsek* constitutes an improper interruption that may nullify the virtue of the prayer or blessing in question.

Hoda'ah (pronounced hoe-dah-AH): Literally, a combination of the Hebrew words for "gratitude" and "acknowledgment," so translated here as "grateful acknowledgment." The title of the second to last blessing in the *Amidah,* an expression of our grateful acknowledgment to God for the daily wonders that constitute human existence.

Hoeche K'dushah (pronounced HAY-kh' k'DOO-shah): A Yiddish term combining German and Hebrew and meaning, literally, "the High *K'dushah*." Refers to a way to shorten the time it takes to say the *Amidah* by avoiding the necessity of having the prayer leader repeat it all after it is said silently by the congregation.

Inclusio (pronounced in-CLOO-zee-oh): A rhetorical style common to biblical prayer, whereby the end of a composition reiterates the theme or words with which the composition began.

Isserles, Moses: See *R'ma*.

Kabbalah (pronounced kah-bah-LAH or, commonly, kah-BAH-lah): A general term for Jewish mysticism, but used properly for a specific mystical doctrine that began in western Europe in the eleventh or twelfth centuries; recorded in the *Zohar* (see *Zohar*) in the thirteenth century, and then further elaborated, especially in the Land of Israel (in Safed), in the sixteenth century. From a Hebrew word meaning "to receive" or "to welcome," and secondarily, "tradition," implying the receiving of tradition from one's past.

Kabbalat Shabbat (pronounced kah-bah-LAHT shah-BAHT): Literally, "Welcoming Shabbat." The preamble to the evening synagogue service *(Ma'ariv)* for Friday night, climaxing in the well-known mystical prayer *L'khah Dodi* (see *L'khah Dodi*).

Kaddish (pronounced kah-DEESH or, more commonly, KAH-d'sh): One of several prayers from a Hebrew word meaning "holy," and therefore the name given to a prayer affirming God's holiness. This prayer was composed in the first century but later found its way into the service in several forms, including one known as the Mourner's *Kaddish* and used as a mourning prayer.

Kaddish D'rabbanan (pronounced d'-rah-bah-NAHN): A form of the *Kaddish* (see *Kaddish*) containing a unique paragraph requesting well-being for all who study Torah. It appears liturgically as a conclusion to study passages.

Kaddish L'it'chad'ta (pronounced l'-it-KHAH-d'-tah): Also called *Kaddish L'chad'ta* (pronounced l'-KHAH-d'-tah). Literally, *Kaddish* "of renewal," the only form of *Kaddish* that includes a reference to the resurrection of the dead and the rebuilding of Jerusalem at the end of days. Recited after concluding a tractate of the Talmud or after a funeral (nowadays, some Jews substitute the Mourner's *Kaddish* for it; see **Kaddish Yatom**).

Kaddish Shalem (pronounced shah-LAYM): Literally, "The Complete *Kaddish*," the same words as **Kaddish Yatom** (the Mourner's *Kaddish*), but with an added line asking that our prayers be accepted on high. A sort of "oral punctuation," in this case, an "oral period," marking the completion of the *Amidah*, which (other than the reading of Torah, on specific days only) is the final major rubric in the service. Known also as *Kaddish Titkabal*, from the first word of the added line *Titkabal* [*tsalot-hon*], pronounced tit-kah-BAHL [tsa-lot-HOHN], meaning, "[May our prayer] be accepted."

Kaddish Titkabal (pronounced kah-DEESH teet-kah-BAHL): The Full, or Reader's, *Kaddish*. Called *Kaddish Titkabal* after the first word of the line characteristic of this *Kaddish*, *titkabal*, "May [our prayer] be accepted…"

Kaddish Yatom (pronounced yah-TOHM): That version of the *Kaddish* that is said by mourners specifically to memorialize the deceased.

Kavod (pronounced kah-VOHD): Literally, "glory," but used philosophically and liturgically by the German pietists (see ***Chasidei Ashkenaz***) to refer to the manifest aspect of God, as opposed to the unknown and unknowable divine essence.

Kavod Shabbat (pronounced kah-VOHD shah-BAHT): Literally, "honor [due to] Shabbat."

Kavvanah (pronounced kah-vah-NAH): From a word meaning "to direct," and therefore used technically to denote the state of directing one's words and thoughts sincerely to God, as opposed to the rote recitation of prayer.

K'dushah (pronounced k'-doo-SHAH or, commonly, k'-DOO-shah): From the Hebrew word meaning "holy," and therefore one of several prayers from the first or second century occurring in several places and versions, all of which have in common the citing of Isaiah 6:3: *Kadosh, kadosh, kadosh…*, "Holy, holy, holy is the Lord of hosts. The whole earth is full of his glory."

K'dushat Hashem (pronounced k'-doo-SHAHT hah-SHEM): Literally, "sanctification of the name [of God]," and the full name for the prayer that is generally called *K'dushah* (see ***K'dushah***). Best known as the third blessing in the *Amidah,* but found also prior to the morning *Sh'ma*. Used also in variant form *kiddush hashem* (pronounced kee-DOOSH hah-SHEM) as a term to describe dying for the sanctification of God's name, that is, martyrdom.

K'dushat hayom (pronounced k'-doo'-SHAHT ha-YOHM): Literally, "the holiness of the day," hence, the technical name of prayers that express the presence of a sacred day (Shabbat or holidays). There are three instances: the *Kiddush* that inaugurates the day either at the dinner table or at the opening evening *(Ma'ariv)* service; the fourth benediction of the Shabbat or holiday *Amidah;* and the final benediction after the *Haftarah* is recited.

Keva (pronounced KEH-vah): A Hebrew word meaning "fixity, stability," and, therefore, the aspect of a service that is fixed and immutable: the words on the page, perhaps, or the time at which the prayer must be said. In the early years, when prayers were delivered orally and improvised on the spot, *keva* meant the fixed order in which the liturgical themes had to be expressed.

Kibbuts G'luyot (pronounced kee-BOOTS g'-loo-YOTE): Literally, "gathering the exiles," and the title of the tenth blessing of the daily *Amidah*, a petition for Jews outside the Land of Israel to return home to their land as a sign that messianic times are imminent. Some liberal liturgies omit the blessing or interpret it more broadly to imply universal messianic liberation, but without the literal belief that Jews outside the Land of Israel are in "exile," or that they need to or want to "return home."

Kiddush (pronounced kee-DOOSH, but commonly, KIH-d'sh): Literally, "sanctification," hence, a form of *k'dushat hayom* (see **k'dushat hayom**); in this case, the mealtime prayer for the eve of Shabbat and holidays, intended to announce the arrival of sacred time, and accompanied by *birkat yayin*, the blessing over wine. A second version occurs in the Friday evening *(Ma'ariv)* service.

Kiddusha Rabbah (generally pronounced kih-DOO-shah RAH-bah): Literally, "the Great *Kiddush*." The name for the *Kiddush* (see **Kiddush**) recited at noon on Saturdays and holidays and, ironically, consisting essentially of only the blessing over wine.

Kohanim (pronounced koe-hah-NEEM): Literally, "priests," plural of *kohen* (pronounced koe-HAYN), a reference to the priests who offered sacrifices in the ancient Temple until its destruction by Rome in the year 70 C.E. Also the name of modern-day Jews who claim priestly descent and who are customarily given symbolic recognition in various ritual ways—as, for instance, being called first to stand beside the Torah reader and to recite a blessing over the reading. It is also the title of the last blessing in the *Amidah*, which contains the priestly benediction from Numbers 6:24–26. Another more popular name for that blessing is *Shalom* (pronounced shah-LOHM), "peace," because the priestly benediction requests peace. See also **Birkat Kohanim**.

Kohen gadol (pronounced koh-HAYN gah-DOHL): Literally, "high priest"; first, in the Bible, and thereafter in rabbinic times until the destruction of the Second Temple (70 C.E.).

Korbanot (pronounced kohr-bah-NOHT; singular: *korban*, pronounced kohr-BAHN): Literally, "sacrifices," but used liturgically to denote passages from Torah and rabbinic literature that explain how sacrifices are to be offered. These are inserted especially in the *Birkhot Hashachar* and the *Musaf* service.

Koyen godl (pronounced KOY-n GU-d'l): Yiddish for the Hebrew *kohen gadol*, "high priest."

K'riat Hatorah (pronounced k'ree-AHT hah-toe-RAH): The public reading of the Torah.

K'riat Sh'ma (pronounced k'-ree-YAHT sh'-MAH): Literally, "reciting the *Sh'ma*," and therefore a technical term for the liturgical act of reading the prayer known as the *Sh'ma* (see ***Sh'ma***).

K'vod Shabbat (pronounced k'-VOHD shah-BAHT): Literally, "honor [due to] Shabbat."

Lismokh g'ullah lit'fillah (pronounced lis-MOKH g'-oo-LAH li-t'-fee-LAH): Literally, "to connect the *G'ullah* to the *T'fillah*," instructions demanding that the blessing on redemption that follows the *Sh'ma* be linked immediately to the following *Amidah* (i.e., the *T'fillah*, the Rabbis' preferred term for the *Amidah*).

Liturgy: Public worship, from the Greek word *leitourgia,* meaning "public works." Liturgy in ancient Greece was considered a public work, the act of sacrificing or praising the gods, from which benefits would flow to the body politic.

L'khah Dodi (pronounced l'-KHAH doh-DEE): Literally, "Come, friend." A mystic sixteenth-century prayer that climaxes the Friday night service of ***Kabbalat Shabbat*** (welcoming Shabbat).

L'khu n'ran'nah (pronounced l'-KHOO n'-rah-n'-NAH, but, commonly, l'-KHOO n'-RAH-n'-nah): Literally, "Let us sing to Adonai," the opening words of Psalm 95, and the common title by which the psalm is known liturgically.

Long Confession (in Hebrew, *Vidui Rabbah,* pronounced vee-DOO'y rah-BAH or, commonly, VEE-doo-y RAH-bah): A lengthy litany arranged alphabetically and recited on Yom Kippur. The acrostic is formed by the initial letter of the first word after the opening phrase for each line, *Al chet shechatanu* (pronounced ahl KHEHT she-chah-TAH-noo), meaning "For the sin that we have committed." Referred to also as *Al chet.*

Ma'ariv (pronounced mah-ah-REEV or, commonly, MAH-ah-reev): From the Hebrew word *erev* (pronounced EH-rev), meaning "evening": one of two titles used for the evening worship service (also called ***Arvit***).

Machzor Vitry (pronounced mahkh-ZOHR veet-REE or, popularly, MAHKH-zohr VEET-ree): Literally, the *machzor* (prayer book containing the annual cycle of liturgy) from Vitry (in France). The most significant early French commentary to the liturgy, composed in the tenth and/or eleventh century, primarily by Simchah of Vitry, a student of Rashi.

Magen Avot (pronounced mah-GAYN ah-VOHT): Literally, "Ancestors' Shield," a reference to God's being a shield to Abraham, a theme of the introductory blessing of the standard *Amidah.* By extension, the name of a version of the *Amidah* said communally at *Ma'ariv* of Shabbat eve, and known also as *B'rakhah achat mei'ein sheva* (pronounced b'-rah-KHAH ah-KHAT may-AYN SHEH-vah, "One blessing in the form of seven"), an allusion to the fact that this single benediction refers explicitly to all seven of the themes required for the Shabbat *Amidah*.

Mah Tovu (pronounced mah TOH-voo): Technically, the prayer to be said upon approaching or entering a synagogue; in practice, the first prayer of *Birkhot Hashachar*.

Maimonides, Moses (known also as Rambam, pronounced RAHM-bahm): Most important Jewish philosopher of all time; also a physician and very significant legal authority. Born in Spain, he moved to Egypt, where he lived most of his life (1135–1204).

Malkhut (pronounced mahl-KHOOT): Literally, "kingdom," but used technically in Kabbalah as the name of the tenth *s'firah*, representative of the feminine principle.

Malkhuyot (pronounced mahl-khu-YOHT): Literally, "kingships." The primary blowing of the shofar on Rosh Hashanah is divided into three parts, each of which features the recitation of biblical verses and surrounding prayers on a different theme. *Malkhuyot* refers to the verses on the theme of God's sovereignty, and, by extension, to the first third of the "shofar service" where the verses are found. The other themes are *zikhronot* ("God's remembrance of us") and *shofarot* (the role of the shofar in the Bible). The three units are commonly referred to by an acronym of their first initials: MaZaSH.

Manhig (pronounced mahn-HEEG, or, popularly MAHN-heeg): Short for *Sefer Hamanhig* (pronounced SAY-fehr hah-mahn-HEEG), called also *Manhig Olam* (pronounced mahn-HEEG oh-LAHM), liturgical compendium by Abraham ben Nathan Hayarchi of Lunel (Provence, c. 1155–1215).

Massekhet Sofrim (pronounced mah-SEH-khet sohf-REEM): an eighth-century work largely from Eretz Yisrael, meaning "Tractate on Scribes." But it also discusses liturgical custom from the Land of Israel, so is a primary source for early medieval practice there.

Menorah (pronounced m'-noh-RAH, or commonly, m'-NOH-rah): A candelabra, originally the one in the desert Tabernacle of Exodus, with seven branches. The term was once commonly used also for the eight-branch candelabra for Chanukah, but now the term ***chanuki'ah*** is preferred for that one.

Mid'ora'ita (pronounced mee-d'-oh-RYE-tah): Strictly speaking, commandments derived directly from Torah, which are of a higher order than those rooted only in rabbinic ordinance (called ***Mid'rabbanan***), but all are binding.

Mid'rabbanan (pronounced mee-d'-rah-bah-NAHN): Commandments rooted only in rabbinic ordinance. See ***Mid'ora'ita***.

Midrash (pronounced meed-RAHSH or, commonly, MID-rahsh): From a Hebrew word meaning "to ferret out the meaning of a text," and therefore a rabbinic interpretation of a biblical word or verse. By extension, a body of rabbinic literature that offers classical interpretations of the Bible.

Midrash Rabbah (pronounced meed-RAHSH rah-BAH, but commonly, MID-rahsh RAH-bah): Literally, "Great [or Large] Midrash," the name of a set of midrashic works covering the Five Books of Moses (the Torah) and the Five Scrolls (Esther, Ruth, Lamentations, Ecclesiastes, and Song of Songs), compiled in Eretz Yisrael between the fifth and thirteenth centuries.

Midrash T'hillim (pronounced meed-RAHSH t'-hee-LEEM, but commonly, mid-rahsh TILL-im): Literally, "Midrash to Psalms," a collection of midrashim variously dated, with material as early as the third century, but reaching final redaction only centuries later. Some scholars believe the psalms were read liturgically week after week (like Torah and the *Haftarah*), in which case this would be a collection of interpretive material once used to elucidate those readings. Also called *Midrash Shocher Tov* (pronounced meed-RAHSH sho-KHAYR TOHV or, commonly, mid-rahsh SHO-kheir TOHV), from the opening words of Proverbs 11:27, the first verse it quotes, "Whoever earnestly seeks what is right [*shocher tov*] pursues what is pleasing."

Mikvah (pronounced mik-VEH, but, popularly, MIK-v'h: A "ritual bath" used (1) in a variety of cases (a menstruant, for example) as a transformational agent from the state of *t'umah* to *tohorah* ("ritual impurity" to "ritual purity"); (2) for purposes of conversion; (3) generalized, through time, for other ends, such as preparing for Shabbat.

Minchah (pronounced meen-KHAH or, more commonly, MIN-khah): Originally the name of a type of sacrifice, then the word for a sacrifice offered during the afternoon, and now the name for the afternoon synagogue service usually scheduled just before nightfall. *Minchah* means "afternoon."

Minchah g'dolah (pronounced min-KHAH g'doh-LAH or, popularly, MIN-khah g'-DOH-lah: Literally, "the great *minchah*," in contrast to *minchah k'tanah*, the "small *minchah*," alternative ways of scheduling the afternoon *Amidah*, which corresponded to the time of the sacrifice it replaced (the *minchah tamid*). The *tamid* was normally offered from *minchah k'tanah*, 9½ halakhic hours (see **Sha'ot z'maniyot**) into the day, until the day's end. On the day before Passover, however, slaughtering the *tamid* began three hours early so as to leave time for the necessary Passover offerings for the Seder that night. Hence, *minchah g'dolah*, 6½ halakhic hours into the day, and an alternative way to fix the beginning time at which the *Minchah Amidah* might commence.

Minchah k'tanah (pronounced min-KHAH k'-tah-NAH or, popularly, MIN-khah k'-TAH-nah): Literally, "the small *minchah*," denoting the earliest time in the afternoon *(minchah)* when the afternoon *tamid* sacrifice and, hence, the afternoon *Amidah* that took its place could be offered—that is, from 9½ *sha'ot z'maniyot* until the day's end (see **Sha'ot z'maniyot**).

Minchat Chinukh (pronounced min-KHAT chee-NOOKH): An analytic commentary on the 613 commandments, by Yosef Babad, 1801–1874, Tarnapol, Safed.

Minhag (pronounced meen-HAHG or, commonly, MIN-hahg): The Hebrew word for custom and, therefore, used liturgically to describe the customary way that different groups of Jews pray. By extension, *minhag* means a "rite," as in *Minhag Ashkenaz,* meaning "the rite of prayer, or the customary way of prayer for Jews in *Ashkenaz*"— that is, northern and eastern Europe.

Minhag hamakom (pronounced min-HAHG hah-mah-KOHM or, commonly, MIN-hahg hah-mah-KOHM): "The usual custom of the community." In cases where liturgical or ritual practice varies, but where the alternative practices are equally permitted, the rule is to follow *minhag hamakom.*

Minim (pronounced mee-NEEM): Literally, "heretics" or "sectarians," and the title of the twelfth blessing of the daily *Amidah,* a petition that heresy be eradicated and heretics punished. Liberal liturgies frequently omit the blessing, considering it an inappropriate malediction, not a benediction at all, or reframe it as a petition against evil in general.

Minyan (pronounced meen-YAHN, but, popularly, MIHN-y'n): The recitation of prayers considered especially sacred require a *minyan,* a quorum of ten. A *minyan* is, therefore, the minimum number of worshipers required to recite an entire service. By extension, it refers to the gathering for services itself—one attends to "make up a *minyan.*"

Mi sheberakh (pronounced, commonly, MEE sheh-BAY-rakh): A standard blessing beginning, "May the One who blessed [our ancestors]…," which could be adapted for any number of instances. This set of prayers requesting God's blessing on those who receive an *aliyah* or on their family members is perhaps the best-known addition to the service.

Mishnah (pronounced mish-NAH, but, commonly, MISH-nah): The name of the definitive six-volume statement of Jewish law from the Land of Israel, ca. 200 C.E., that culminates the era called tannaitic (after the title we give the Rabbis to that point; see **Tanna, Tanna'im**). But equally, the name applied to any particular teaching in that statement, for which the plural, *mishnayot* (pronounced mish-nah-YOHT), exists also (more than one such teaching).

Mishnah B'rurah (pronounced meesh-NAH b'-roo-RAH or, popularly, MISH-nah B'ROO-rah): Halakhic commentary and compendium on laws in that portion of the *Shulchan Arukh* called *Orach Chayim* ("The Way of Life"), containing most of the laws on liturgy; by Rabbi Israel Meir Hakohen Kagan *(Chafetz Chayim)*, Radin, Poland, 1838–1933.

Mishneh Torah (pronounced MISH-n' TOH-rah): Code of Jewish law by Moses Maimonides (composed in 1180), called also the *Yad* (pronounced YAHD), a Hebrew word made of the letters that, together, stand for the number fourteen—a reference to the fact that the Code is divided into fourteen books. Unlike other Codes, the *Mishneh Torah* sums up every aspect of Jewish law, even hypothetical precepts relevant only in messianic times, as well as philosophical introductions on the nature of God and prayer.

Mishpat (pronounced meesh-PAHT): Literally, "justice," and the title of the eleventh blessing of the daily *Amidah;* a petition for just rulership, a condition associated with the messianic age.

Mitzvah (pronounced meetz-VAH or, commonly, MITZ-vah; plural: *mitzvot,* pronounced meetz-VOTE): A Hebrew word used commonly to mean "good deed," but in the more technical sense, denoting any commandment from God and, therefore, by extension, what God wants us to do. Reciting the *Sh'ma* morning and evening, for instance, is a *mitzvah.*

Mitzvah l'ma'alah min haz'man (pronounced meets-VAH l'-mah-ah-LAH meen hahz-MAHN): Literally, "a commandment that transcends time," a theological correction to *mitzvot* (commandments) that seem otherwise to be "commandments dependent on time" (see ***Mitzvat aseh shehaz'man g'ramah***), and which would then exempt women from required observance.

Mitzvah overet (pronounced meets-VAH oh-VEH-reht): Literally, a "passing *mitzvah,*" a *mitzvah* whose proper time of performance will pass if not done immediately.

Mitzvat aseh shehaz'man g'ramah (pronounced meets-VAHT ah-SAY sheh-hah-z'-MAHN g'rah-MAH): Literally, a "positive commandment dependent on time," a category of commandments from which women are normally exempt.

Modeh/ah ani (pronounced moh-DEH ah-NEE [for women, moh-DAH ah-NEE]): Literally, "I gratefully acknowledge [...that You have returned my soul to me]"— therefore, the standard prayer to be said upon awakening.

Modim D'rabbanan (pronounced moe-DEEM d'-rah-bah-NAHN, or commonly, MOE-dim d'-rah-bah-nahn): *Modim* is the first word of the second to last blessing of the *Amidah* and, therefore, a shorthand way of referring to that prayer. *Modim D'rabbanan* is the name given to the form of the prayer that is reserved for congregational recitation during the repetition of the *Amidah* by the prayer leader. Literally, it means "the *Modim* of our Rabbis," and refers to the fact that the prayer is composed of what were once several alternative responses, each of which was the custom of one of the Rabbis of the Talmud.

Mordecai [bar Hillel]: Thirteenth-century talmudic commentator, Germany.

Muktzeh (pronounced mook-TZEH, but, popularly, MOOK-tzeh): Literally, "on the sidelines." A legal term for items that cannot be moved on Shabbat because they are "alienated" from any positive use. This includes (a) items whose use would violate the Sabbath, like a cigarette lighter; (b) items which are repulsive, like garbage; (c) items that have no Shabbat use at all, like stones and dirt.

Musaf (pronounced moo-SAHF or, commonly, MOO-sahf): The Hebrew word meaning "extra" or "added," and, therefore, the title of the additional sacrifice that was offered in the Temple on Shabbat and holy days. It is now the name given to an added service of worship appended to the morning service on those days.

Musar (pronounced moo-SAHR, but, popularly, MOO-sahr): Literally, "ethics," but used specifically for a nineteenth- to twentieth-century movement that emerged in Lithuanian *yeshivot* stressing personal ethics, rooted in Halakhah.

M'zuzah (pronounced m'-zoo-ZAH or, commonly, m'-ZOO-zah): The Hebrew word in the Bible meaning "doorpost" and, by extension, the term now used for a small casement that contains the first two sections of the *Sh'ma* (Deut. 6:4–9; 11:13–21) and is affixed to the doorposts of Jewish homes.

N'filat apayim (pronounced n'-fee-LAHT ah-PAH-yim): Literally, "falling on one's face," and, therefore, a technical term for the *Tachanun*, the section of the daily service that features supplications and is said with head resting on forearm, as if "prostrate" before God.

Nidah (pronounced nee-DAH, or, commonly, NEE-dah): Menstruant.

N'illah (pronounced n'-ee-LAH or, commonly, n'-EE-lah): The concluding service for Yom Kippur.

Nishmat kol cha'i (pronounced neesh-MAHT kohl KHA'i): A blessing mentioned in the Talmud as one of two benedictions in use as the *Birkat Hashir* (pronounced beer-KAHT hah-SHEER), the blessing that ends a psalm collection known as *Hallel*. (See *Hallel*.) Nowadays, we use it (1) as part of a longer **Birkat Hashir**, after the Daily *Hallel,* that constitutes the central section of the ***P'sukei D'zimrah*** for Sabbaths and festivals; and (2) to conclude a similar *Hallel* in the Passover Haggadah.

N'kadesh (pronounced n'kah-DAYSH): The *Amidah* is first recited silently by each worshiper and then repeated aloud by the prayer leader, at which time its third blessing appears in extended form. *N'kadesh* (literally, "Let us sanctify...") is the first Hebrew word of that extended blessing and is thus, by extension, a common way of referring to it.

Notarikon (pronounced noh-TAH-ri-kohn): A system of acrostics, by which each letter of a single word is treated as the initial letter of another word, until a secret meaning is revealed by the set of new words.

Odem horishn (pronounced UH-d'm hah-RIH-sh'n): Yiddish for *adam harishon*, "the first man," that is, Adam.

Omer: See *S'firat ha'omer*.

Orach Chayim (pronounced OH-rakh KHA-yim): Abbreviated as O. Ch. Literally, "The Way of Life," one of four sections in the *Tur* and the *Shulchan Arukh*, two of Judaism's major law codes; the section containing the rules of prayer.

Payy'tan (pronounced pah-y'-TAHN; plural: *payy'tanim*, pronounced pah-y'-tah-NEEM): A poet; the name given particularly to classical and medieval poets whose work is inserted into the standard prayers for special occasions.

Perek (pronounced PEH-rek; plural: *p'rakim*, pronounced p'-rah-KEEM): Literally, a "section" or "chapter" of a written work; used liturgically to mean the sections of the *Sh'ma*. Each of its three biblical sections is a different *perek*.

Piyyut (pronounced pee-YOOT; plural: *piyyutim*, pronounced pee-yoo-TEEM): Literally, "a poem," but used technically to mean liturgical poems composed in classical and medieval times and inserted into the standard prayers on special occasions.

P'rishah (pronounced p'ree-SHAH, but, commonly P'REE-shah): Commentary on the *Tur*, by Rabbi Joshua Hakohen Falk, 1555–1614, Poland.

P'sukei D'zimrah (pronounced p'-soo-KAY d'-zeem-RAH or, commonly, p'-SOO-kay d'-ZIM-rah): Literally, "verses of song," and therefore the title of a lengthy set of opening morning prayers that contain psalms and songs and serve as spiritual preparation prior to the official Call to Prayer.

Purim (pronounced poo-REEM or, commonly, PU-rim): A festival falling on the fourteenth day of the Hebrew month of Adar, generally corresponding to late February or early March. It celebrates the miraculous deliverance referred to in the biblical Book of Esther. Literally, *purim* means "lots," as in the phrase "drawing of lots," because the date on which the Jews were to have been killed was chosen by lot.

RaN (pronounced RAHN): Acronym for *R*abbi *N*issim [ben Reuven], Spain, d. 1380, and his commentary on Isaac Alfasi (the *RiF*).

RaSHBA (pronounced rahsh-BAH or, popularly, RAHSH-bah): Acronym for *R*abbi *SH*lomo [Solomon] *B*en *A*vraham [Abraham Adret], Spanish halakhist and commentator on the Talmud, 1235–1310.

Rashi (pronounced RAH-shee): Acronym for *R*abbi *Sh*lomo [Solomon] ben *I*saac, French commentator on Bible and Talmud, 1040–1105; founder of school of Jewish thought and custom, whence various liturgical works came into being, among them *Machzor Vitry* and *Siddur Rashi.*

R'fuah (pronounced r'-foo-AH or, commonly, r'-FOO-ah): Literally, "healing," and the title of the eighth blessing of the daily *Amidah,* a petition for healing.

Riboyne shel oylem (pronounced ree-BOY-n' shel OY-l'm): A Yiddish version of a common appellation for God, *Ribono shel olam* (pronounced ree-boh-NOH shel oh-LAHM), meaning, "master of the universe."

RiF (pronounced RIHF): Acronym for *R*abbi *I*saac Alfasi (North Africa, 1013–1103) and his code of Jewish law by the same name.

R'ma (pronounced r'-MAH): An acronym for Rabbi Moses Isserles, sixteenth-century Poland, chief Ashkenazi commentator on the *Shulchan Arukh,* the sixteenth-century Sefardi code by Joseph Caro.

Rosh (pronounced ROHSH): The Rosh (1250–1328), otherwise known as Rabbeinu Asher, or Asher ben Yechiel, was a significant halakhic authority, first in Germany and later in Spain. His son, Jacob ben Asher, codified many of his father's views alongside his own in his influential law code, the *Tur.*

Rosh Chodesh (pronounced rohsh KHOH-desh): Literally, "the head of the month," and, therefore, the Hebrew name for the one- or two-day new moon period with which lunar months begin. It is marked as a holiday in Jewish tradition, a period of new beginnings.

[The] Rov (pronounced ROHV): Joseph B. Solveitchik, Lithuania, Berlin, Boston, New York. Preeminent talmudist and Orthodox theologian of middle and late twentieth century).

R'shut (pronounced: r'-SHOOT): An "option" liturgically, as opposed to a *chovah* (pronounced khoh-VAH) or *chiyuv* (pronounced khee-YOOV), meaning "obligation."

243

Rubric (pronounced ROO-brick): A technical term for any discrete section of liturgy, whether a prayer or a set of prayers. The *Sh'ma* and Its Blessings is one of several large rubrics in the service; within that large rubric, the *Sh'ma* or any one of its accompanying blessings may be called a rubric as well.

Seder (pronounced SEH-der or, commonly, SAY-der): The Hebrew word meaning "order" and, therefore, (1) the name given to the ritualized meal eaten on Passover eve, and (2) an early alternative term for the order of prayers in a prayer book. The word Siddur (see **Siddur**) is now preferred for the latter.

Seder Rav Amram (pronounced SAY-dehr rahv AHM-rahm): First known comprehensive Jewish prayer book, emanating from Rav Amram Gaon (c. 860 C.E.), a leading Jewish scholar and head of Sura, a famed academy in Babylonia (modern-day Iraq).

Sefardi (pronounced s'-fahr-DEE or, commonly, s'-FAHR-dee): From the Hebrew word *Sefarad* (pronounced s'-fah-RAHD), meaning the geographic area of modern-day Spain and Portugal. Sefardi is the adjective, describing the liturgical rituals and customs that are derived from *Sefarad* prior to the expulsion of Jews from there at the end of the fifteenth century, as opposed to Ashkenazi (see **Ashkenazi**), meaning the liturgical rituals and customs common to northern and eastern Europe. Nowadays, Sefardi refers also to the customs of Jews from North Africa and Arab lands, whose ancestors came from Spain.

Sefer Hachinukh (pronounced SAY-fehr hah-khee-NOOKH): Literally, "The Book of Instruction," a commentary on the Torah that arranges the discussion of the commandments in the order in which they appear in Torah, according to the weekly Torah portion; by Pinchas Halevi of Barcelona, Venice, 1523.

Sefer Mitzvot Gadol (pronounced SAY-fehr meets-VOHT gah-DOHL): Literally, "The Great Book of Commandments," the title of a halakhic compendium by Moses of Coucy, thirteenth century, Spain, Also called by its acronym *SMaG*.

Septuagint (pronounced sehp-TOO-a-jint): Latin for "seventy," reflecting the myth that King Ptolemy of Egypt asked seventy-two Jews to translate the Torah into Greek; refers, therefore, to the first Greek translation of the Bible, begun (probably) in the third century B.C.E. The original Septuagint included only the Torah, but now we use the term to include also translations of other biblical books that were added to it.

S'firah (pronounced s'-fee-RAH or, popularly, s'-FEE-rah): Literally, "counting," so shorthand for *s'firat ha'omer*, "counting the Omer." See **S'firat ha'omer.**

S'firat ha'omer (pronounced s'-fee-RAHT hah-OH-mehr): Literally, "counting the Omer." *Omer* (literally, "sheaf") refers to the sheaves of barley, the harvest of which coincides roughly with Passover. The Omer period extends from the eve of the second day of Passover to the night before Shavuot. Each day is counted liturgically as part of the evening *(Ma'ariv)* service.

S'firot (pronounced s'-fee-ROHT; singular: *s'firah,* pronounced s'-fee-RAH): According to the Kabbalah (Jewish mysticism, see ***Kabbalah***), the universe came into being by a process of divine emanation, whereby the divine light, as it were, expanded into empty space, eventually becoming physical matter. At various intervals, this light was frozen in time, as if captured by containers, each of which is called a *s'firah.* Literally, *s'firah* means "number," because early theory conceptualized the stages of creation as primordial numbers.

S'firotic (pronounced s'fee-RAH-tik): Relating to one or more *s'firot* or to the system of *s'firot.*

Shabbat (pronounced shah-BAHT): The Hebrew word for "Sabbath," from a word meaning "to rest."

Shabbat shalom (pronounced shah-BAHT shah-LOHM): Literally, "peaceful Shabbat," hence the greeting for Shabbat, "[May you have a] peaceful Shabbat." See also ***Shabb's.***

Shabb's (pronounced SHAH-b's): Yiddish for Shabbat, "Sabbath." *Guht* [or *Git*] *Shabb's* (pronounced guht ["uh" rhymes with "ou" in "could"] or git SHAH-b's) means "Have a good Shabbat," the Yiddish parallel to *Shabbat shalom.*

Shacharit (pronounced shah-khah-REET or, commonly, SHAH-khah-reet): The name given to the morning worship service; from the Hebrew word *shachar* (SHAH-khar), meaning "morning."

Shalom (pronounced shah-LOHM): Literally, "peace," and a popular title for the final benediction of the *Amidah,* more properly entitled *Kohanim* (pronounced koe-hah-NEEM), "priests," or, more fully, *Birkat Kohanim* (pronounced beer-KAHT koe-hah-NEEM), "blessing of the priests," "priestly benediction." See also ***Birkat Kohanim, Kohanim.***

Shalom Rav (pronounced shah-LOHM RAHV): Literally, "Great Peace," the first words and, therefore, the title of *Birkat Shalom* (technically, *Birkat Kohanim*), the final blessing in the *Amidah,* for *Ma'ariv* and, except on fast days for *Minchah,* too.

Shanim (pronounced shah-NEEM): Literally, "years," and the title of the ninth blessing of the daily *Amidah;* a petition for a year of agricultural abundance, such as that associated with messianic days.

Sha'ot z'maniyot (pronounced shah-OHT z'-mah-mee-YOHT): Halakhic hours. The rabbinic day was divided into twelve "hours," which varied in duration, since they were a mathematical result of dividing daylight by twelve. These were not solar hours then, but "halakhic hours," according to which sacrifices and prayer times were fixed.

Shatz (pronounced SHAHTS): Acronym for *sh'liach tsibbur* (pronounced sh'-LEE-akh tsee-BOOR), "agent of the congregation," that is, the prayer leader (frequently a trained cantor) charged with carrying the community's prayers to God.

Shefa (pronounced SHEH-fah): In kabbalistic worship, the plenitude of blessing that flows vertically through the *s'firot* to the world we inhabit.

Shekhinah (pronounced sh'-khee-NAH or, popularly, sh-KHEE-nah): From the Hebrew root *sh.kh.n*, meaning "to dwell," and, therefore, in talmudic literature, the "indwelling" aspect of God most immediately empathetic to human experience. As the feminine aspect of God, it appears in Kabbalah as the tenth and final *sefirah*, or emanation.

Shiltei Gibborim (pronounced sheel-TAY gee-boh-REEM, or, popularly, SHEEL-tay gee-BOH-reem): Commentary on Alfasi's code, by Joshua Boaz ben Simon, d. 1492.

Shirat Hayam (pronounced shee-RAHT hah-YAHM): Literally, "Song of the Sea," the song of praise and gratitude sung by Israel after the splitting of the Red Sea and, since the Middle Ages, a prominent constituent of the *P'sukei D'zimrah,* the "warm-up" section to the morning service composed mainly of biblical material (chiefly psalms) that were intended to be sung as praise of God.

Shivah (pronounced shee-VAH, but, commonly, SHIH-vah): Literally "seven," so used to designate the seven-day period of mourning, in which mourners remain at home to be visited by others. In such cases a *shivah minyan* (pronounced shee-VAH meen-YAHN or, commonly, a SHIH-vah mihn-y'n)—a worship service (normally held at synagogue)—occurs in the mourner's home. See *Minyan.*

Shivah d'n'chemta (pronounced shih-VAH d'-n'-KHEM-tah): "Literally, the seven weeks of comfort." The seven Sabbaths following Tisha B'av, which take us all the way to Rosh Hashanah, call for *Haftarot* that guarantee hope.

Sh'liach tsibbur (pronounced sh'-LEE-ahkh tsee-BOOR): Literally, the "agent of the congregation," and, therefore, the name given to the person who leads the prayer service.

Sh'lom bayit (pronounced shah-LOHM BAH-yit): Literally, "peace of the home."

Sh'ma (pronounced sh'-MAH): The central prayer in the first of the two main units in the worship service, the second being the *Amidah* (see **Amidah**). The *Sh'ma* comprises three citations from the Bible, and the larger unit in which it is embedded (called the *Sh'ma* and Its Blessings) is composed of a formal Call to Prayer (see **Bar'khu**) and a series of blessings on the theological themes that, together with the *Sh'ma*, constitute a liturgical creed of faith. *Sh'ma*, meaning "hear," is the first word of the first line of the first biblical citation, "Hear O Israel: Adonai is our God; Adonai is One," which is the paradigmatic statement of Jewish faith, the Jews' absolute commitment to the presence of a single and unique God in time and space.

Sh'mini Atseret (pronounced sh'-MEE-nee ah-TSEH-ret): Literally, "the eighth day of solemn assembly," and the name given to the eighth and final day of the autumn festival of Sukkot.

Sh'moneh Esreh (pronounced sh'-MOE-neh ES-ray): A Hebrew word meaning "eighteen" and, therefore, a name given to the second of the two main units in the worship service that once had eighteen benedictions in it (it now has nineteen), known also as the *Amidah* (see **Amidah**).

Shofarot (pronounced shoh-fah-ROHT): Shofar verses (see **Malkhuyot**).

Shomer Yisra'el (pronounced shoh-MAYR yis-rah-AYL or, commonly, SHOH-mayr yis-rah-AYL): Literally, "keeper of Israel," a designation of God and the opening words—hence, the title—of a medieval poem that is found in *Tachanun*.

Short Confession (in Hebrew, *Vidui Zuta*, pronounced vee-DOO'y ZOO-tah or, commonly, VEE-doo-y ZOO-tah): A short confession of sin, arranged alphabetically, so that each sin that is listed begins with a different letter of the Hebrew alphabet. Also referred to by the opening word, *Ashamnu* (pronounced ah-SHAHM-noo), meaning "We have sinned."

Shul (pronounced SHOOL): Yiddish for synagogue.

Shulchan Arukh (pronounced shool-KHAN ah-ROOKH or, commonly, SHOOL-khan AH-rookh): The name given to the best-known code of Jewish law, compiled by Joseph Caro in the Land of Israel and published in 1565. *Shulchan Arukh* means "The Set Table" and refers to the ease with which the various laws are set forth—like a table prepared with food ready for consumption.

Shulchan Arukh D'rav (pronounced shool-KHAHN ah-ROOKH d'-RAHV or, popularly, SHOOL-khan AH-rukh d'-RAHV): Halakhic compendium by Rabbi Shneur Zalman of Liady, eighteenth-century founder of Chabad Chasidism.

Siddur (pronounced see-DOOR or, commonly, SIH-d'r): From the Hebrew word *seder* (see **Seder**), meaning "order," and therefore, by extension, the name given to the "order of prayers," or prayer book.

Sim Shalom (pronounced SEEM shah-LOHM): Literally, "Grant Peace," the first words and, therefore, the title of *Birkat Shalom* (technically, *Birkat Kohanim*), the final blessing in the *Amidah*, for *Shacharit*, and for *Minchah* that falls on a fast day.

Sirkes, Joel. Polish halakhist and commentator (1561–1640). See **Bayit Chadash**.

S'lichot (pronounced s'-lee-KHOHT): From the root *s.l.ch*, "to forgive"; hence, liturgical poetry requesting divine forgiveness (sing., *s'lichah*, pronounced s'-lee-KHAH, the name given also to a blessing in the daily *Amidah* requesting forgiveness). Hence also, the title of penitential services held on Saturday night prior to Rosh Hashanah (or, if Rosh Hashanah falls in the first half of the week following, the Saturday before that).

SMaG (pronounced s'MAHG): An acronym for *Sefer Mitzvot Gadol*. See **Sefer Mitzvot Gadol**.

Synonymous parallelism: A biblical poetic device whereby the second part of a line *paraphrases* or "seconds" the first. See also **Synthetic parallelism**.

Synthetic parallelism: A biblical poetic device whereby the second part of a line *completes* the idea of the first half. See also **Synonymous parallelism**.

Tachanun (pronounced TAH-khah-noon): A Hebrew word meaning "supplications" and, by extension, the title of the large unit of prayer that follows the *Amidah*, which is largely supplicatory in character.

Tallit (pronounced tah-LEET; plural: *tallitot*, pronounced tah-lee-TOHT): The prayer shawl equipped with tassels (see **Tsitsit**) on each corner and generally worn during the morning *(Shacharit)* and additional *(Musaf)* synagogue services.

Tallit katan (pronounced tah-LEET kah-TAHN): Literally, "a little *tallit*," used originally as an undergarment to allow the wearing of *tsitsit* privately, all day long, in cultures where Jews wanted to look the same as everyone else.

Talmud (pronounced tahl-MOOD or, more commonly, TAHL-m'd): The name given to each of two great compendia of Jewish law and lore compiled over several centuries and ever since, the literary core of the rabbinic heritage. The Talmud Yerushalmi (pronounced y'-roo-SHAHL-mee), the "Jerusalem Talmud," is earlier, a product of the Land of Israel generally dated about 400 C.E. The better-known Talmud Bavli (pronounced BAHV-lee), or "Babylonian Talmud," took shape in Babylonia (present-day Iraq) and is traditionally dated about 550 C.E. When people say "the" Talmud without specifying which one they mean, they are referring to the Babylonian version. Talmud means "teaching."

Tanchuma (pronounced tahn-KHOO-mah): A midrashic collection of literary sermons covering the weekly Torah readings; probably compiled in Eretz Yisrael in the eighth to ninth century, but attributed to R. Tanchuma bar Abba, an earlier rabbinic figure.

Tanna (pronounced TAH-nah, plural: **Tanna'im**, pronounced tah-nah-EEM, but commonly, tah-NAH-yim): Aramaic for "teacher," referring to rabbinic authorities in the time of the Mishnah, that is, prior to the third century. Often used in contrast to *Amora* (see **Amora**).

TaZ (pronounced TAHZ): Acronym for *Torah Zahav*, commentary to the *Shulchan Arukh* composed by Rabbi David Halevi, 1586–1667, Poland.

Tetragrammaton: The technical term for the four-letter name of God that appears in the Bible. Treating it as sacred, Jews stopped pronouncing it centuries ago, so that the actual pronunciation has been lost; instead of reading it according to its letters, it is replaced in speech by the alternative name of God, Adonai.

T'fillah (pronounced t'-fee-LAH or, commonly, t'-FEE-lah): A Hebrew word meaning "prayer" but used technically to mean a specific prayer, namely, the second of the two main units in the worship service. It is known also as the *Amidah* or the *Sh'moneh Esreh* (see **Amidah**). Also the title of the sixteenth blessing of the *Amidah*, a petition for God to accept our prayer.

T'fillin (pronounced t'-FIH-lin or, sometimes, t'-fee-LEEN): Two cube-shaped black boxes containing biblical quotations (Exod. 13:1–10; 13:11–16; Deut. 6:4–9; 11:13–21) and affixed by means of attached leather straps to the forehead and left arm (right arm for left-handed people) during morning prayer.

T'hillah l'David (pronounced t'-hee-LAH l'-dah-VEED): Literally, "a psalm of David," and the first two words of Psalm 145; hence, the rabbinic name for Psalm 145, which eventually became known, more popularly, as *Ashre* (pronounced ahsh-RAY or, commonly, AHSH-ray). See **Ashre**.

Tiferet (pronounced tee-FEH-reht): Literally "glory," but used technically in Kabbalah as the name of the sixth *s'firah*, and representing the masculine principle.

Tikkun (pronounced tee-KOON): From the Hebrew root *t.k.n*, meaning "to repair," and used idiomatically by the second or third century to mean "repairing the [evils of] the world" (see **Tikkun olam**). Medieval kabbalists made it central to their doctrine of unifying the male and female aspects of God and, thereby, all the *s'firot* into which God and the universe-in-formation had been fragmented during creation. Hence, *Tikkun* became a specialized kabbalistic prayer service, held at midnight, and designed to bring about divine (and thereby universal) unification.

Tikkun chatsot (pronounced tee-KOON khah-TSOHT): Literally, a *tikkun* (kabbalistically devised service to correct the universe—see ***Tikkun***) held at *chatsot* (midnight).

Tikkun leil shavuot (pronounced tee-KOON layl shah-voo-OHT): A liturgy composed mostly of study passages, designed to be read throughout the night of Shavuot.

Tikkun olam (pronounced tee-KOON oh-LAHM): Literally, "repairing the universe." A phrase found in the second- or third-century prayer called the *Alenu*, in the sense of God's "repairing [the evils of] the universe [by bringing the kingdom of God]" *(l'taken olam b'malkhut shaddai)*—see Volume 6, *Tachanun and Concluding Prayers*, "Perfect the world," p. 137. Kabbalistically, it came to mean the mystical act of repairing the fragmented *s'firot*, which would unify the shattered Godhead and the universe simultaneously. Today, it is widely used generally to denote social action that corrects the evils of the world.

Tirkha (pronounced teer-KHAH but, commonly, TEER-khah): Literally, "burden"—making it so burdensome for worshipers to pray that they stop coming.

Tkhines (pronounced t'-KHI-n's): Literally, Yiddish for "supplications," but used technically to denote liturgies for women, common mostly in eastern Europe from the seventeenth to the nineteenth century. Sing., *tkhine* (pronounced T'KHI-n').

T'lata d'puranuta (pronounced t'-LAH-tah d'-poo-rah-NOO-tah): "The three readings of retribution." As the Rabbis saw it, God must have allowed, and perhaps even caused, the Temple to fall as punishment for Israel's sins. The three weeks prior to Tisha B'av, therefore, anticipate the fall, culminating in Shabbat *Chazon* (pronounced khah-ZOHN), "The Sabbath of 'the Vision,'" which features Isaiah's premonitory vision of Jerusalem's fall and the expectation of ultimate recovery (Isa. 1:1–27).

T'murah (pronounced t'-moo-RAH): A substitution code by which one letter takes the place of another, revealing new meanings.

Tosafot (pronounced toh-sah-FOHT or, popularly, TOH-sah-foht): Literally, "additional," referring to "additional" twelfth- to fourteenth-century Franco-German halakhists and commentators, the spiritual (and, to some extent, even familial) descendants of the French commentator Rashi (1040–1105).

Tosafot Yom Tov (pronounced toh-sah-FOHT yohm TOHV or, popularly, TOH-sah-foht YOHM tohv): Literally, "The Additions by Yom Tov," a fourteenth-century commentary on the Mishnah by Rabbi Yom Tov Lipman Heller.

Tsadikim (pronounced tsah-dee-KEEM): Literally, "the righteous," and the title of the thirteenth blessing of the daily *Amidah,* a petition that the righteous be rewarded.

T'shuvah (pronounced t'shoo-VAH or, commonly, t'SHOO-vah): Literally, "repentance," and the title of the fifth blessing in the daily *Amidah,* a petition by worshipers that they successfully turn to God in heartfelt repentance.

Tsidkat'kha Tsedek (pronounced tzeed-koht-KHAH TZEH-dehk or, commonly, tzeed-KOHT-khah TZEH-dehk): Literally, "Your righteousness is right," from Psalm 119:142. Liturgically, the first of three biblical verses recited after the Shabbat *Minchah Amidah* and taken to memorialize the death of Moses that is said to have occurred at that time.

Tsiduk Hadin (pronounced tzee-DOOK hah-DEEN): Literally, "justification of the judgment," hence, the technical term for the funeral service or, more specifically, the prayer that initiates it, beginning *hatsur tamim po'alo* … ("The rock [God], whose deeds are perfect …" [Deut. 32:4]). By extension, the term is applied to *Tsidkat'kha Tsedek* (see **Tsidkat'kha Tsedek**).

Tsitsit (pronounced tsee-TSEET): A Hebrew word meaning "tassels" or "fringes" and used to refer to the tassels affixed to the four corners of the *tallit* (the prayer shawl, see **Tallit**) as Numbers 15:38 instructs.

Tur (pronounced TOOR): The shorthand title applied to a fourteenth-century code of Jewish law, compiled by Jacob ben Asher in Spain, and the source for much of our knowledge about medieval liturgical practice. *Tur* means "row" or "column." The full name of the code is *Arba'ah Turim* (pronounced ahr-bah-AH too-REEM), "The Four Rows," with each row (or *Tur*) being a separate section of law on a given broad topic.

Tzitz Eliezer (pronounced TSEETS eh-lee-YEH z'r): Halakhic compendium by Eliezer Waldenberg, major Israeli responder and Head Judge of Rabbinical Courts.

Un'taneh Tokef (pronounced oo-n'-TAH-neh TOH-kehf): A *piyyut* (liturgical poem) for the High Holy Days emphasizing the awesome nature of these days when we stand before God for judgment. Widely, but incorrectly, connected with a legend of Jewish martyrdom in Germany, the poem more likely derives from a Byzantine poet, circa sixth century. It is known for its conclusion: "Penitence, prayer, and charity avert a bad decree."

Vay'khulu (pronounced vah-y'-KHOO-loo): Literally, "they were finished," the beginning of Genesis 2:1–2, announcing the end of creation; hence, the introductory paragraph of the Friday evening *Kiddush*, and part of the Friday *Ma'ariv K'dushat Hayom* ("Sanctification of the Day," the all-important middle benediction in the Shabbat *Amidah*). See *K'dushat Hayom*.

V'hu rachum (pronounced v'HOO rah-KHOOM): Literally, "He [God] is merciful," and, because of its sentiment, a common introductory line to prayers lauding God's gracious beneficence. The best example is a seven-paragraph penitential prayer that makes up the bulk of the version of *Tachanun* (pronounced TAH-khah-noon) that is said Mondays and Thursdays.

Vidui Rabbah (pronounced vee-DOO'y RAH-bah or, commonly, VEE-doo-y RAH-bah): Literally, "long confession." See *Long Confession*.

Vidui Zuta (pronounced vee-DOO-y ZOO-tah or, commonly, VEE-doo-y ZOO-tah): Literally, "short confession." See *Short Confession*.

V'shamru (pronounced v'-shahm-ROO, but popularly, v'-SHAHM-roo): Literally, "They shall keep," the beginning of Exodus 31:16–17, the commandment for Israel to keep Shabbat; hence, part of the *Shacharit K'dushat Hayom* ("Sanctification of the Day," the all-important middle benediction in the Shabbat *Amidah*). See *K'dushat Hayom*. Also the popular beginning form of *Kiddusha Rabbah* (Saturday noon *Kiddush*).

Yahrzeit (pronounced YOHR-tseit): A Yiddish word meaning the practice of marking the anniversary of a loved one's death by saying *Kaddish*. People speak of "having *yahrzeit*" on a given day, at which time the name of the person being memorialized may be mentioned aloud at services prior to the Mourner's *Kaddish* (see *Kaddish*).

Yichud (pronounced yee-KHOOD): Literally, "unification"; in kabbalistic worship, prayers have esoteric significance, generally the unification of the letters that make up God's name, but standing also for the conjoining of God's masculine and feminine aspects and, deeper still, the coming together of the shattered universe in which we live.

Yigdal (pronounced yig-DAHL): A popular morning hymn that encapsulates the thirteen principles of faith composed by prominent medieval philosopher Moses Maimonides (1135–1204). These thirteen principles were arranged poetically as *Yigdal* in the fourteenth century by Daniel ben Judah Dayan (pronounced dah-YAHN) of Rome.

Yishtabach (pronounced yish-tah-BAKH): The first word and, therefore, the title of the blessing used as the *Birkat Hashir* for weekdays (see *Birkat Hashir*). On Sabbaths and festivals, it is expanded by the addition of *Nishmat kol cha'i* (pronounced neesh-MAHT kohl KHA'i), a blessing mentioned in the Talmud (see *Nishmat kol cha'i*).

Yizkor (pronounced yeez-KOHR or, commonly, YIZ-k'r): The Memorial Service, said on Yom Kippur and the three Festivals (Passover, Shavuot, and Sh'mini Atseret).

Yom tov (pronounced yohm-TOHV): Literally, "good day," hence "festival, holiday."

Yotser (pronounced yoh-TSAYR or, commonly, YOH-tsayr): The Hebrew word meaning "creator" and, by extension, the title of the first blessing in the *Sh'ma* and Its Blessings, which is on the theme of God's creation of the universe.

Y'rushalayim (pronounced y'roo-shah-LAH-yeem): Literally, "Jerusalem," and the title of the fourteenth blessing of the daily *Amidah;* a petition for the divine building-up of Jerusalem, a condition associated with the imminence of the messianic age. Some liberal liturgies interpret it more broadly to include the restoration of modern-day Jerusalem, currently under way.

Y'sodai Y'shurun (pronounced y'soh-DAY y-shoo-ROON): Halakhic compendium by Gedaliah Felder, Toronto, mid- to late twentieth century.

Zikhronot (pronounced zikh-roh-NOHT): "Remembrance(s)" (see *Malkhuyot*).

Zivvug (pronounced zee-VOOG): Literally, a "union," implying a sexual union of male and female, and used by kabbalists to denote the esoteric impact of *mitzvot*, first and foremost prayer: the unification of male and female sides of God, symbolic of the larger unification of all that is—God and the universe—that had been fractured at the time of creation. See also *Tikkun*.

Zohar (pronounced ZOH-hahr): A shorthand title for *Sefer Hazohar* (pronounced SAY-fer hah-ZOH-hahr), literally, "The Book of Splendor," which is the primary compendium of mystical thought in Judaism; written mostly by Moses de Leon in Spain near the end of the thirteenth century and, ever since, the chief source for the study of Kabbalah (see *Kabbalah*).

AVAILABLE FROM BETTER BOOKSTORES.
TRY YOUR BOOKSTORE FIRST.

Bar/Bat Mitzvah

The JGirl's Guide: The Young Jewish Woman's Handbook for Coming of Age
By Penina Adelman, Ali Feldman, and Shulamit Reinharz
An inspirational, interactive guidebook designed to help pre-teen Jewish girls address the spiritual, educational, and psychological issues surrounding coming of age in today's society. 6 x 9, 240 pp, Quality PB, ISBN 1-58023-215-9 **$14.99**
Also Available: **The JGirl's Teacher's and Parent's Guide**
8½ x 11, 56 pp, PB, ISBN 1-58023-225-6 **$8.99**

Bar/Bat Mitzvah Basics: A Practical Family Guide to Coming of Age Together
By Helen Leneman 6 x 9, 240 pp, Quality PB, ISBN 1-58023-151-9 **$18.95**

The Bar/Bat Mitzvah Memory Book: An Album for Treasuring the Spiritual Celebration
By Rabbi Jeffrey K. Salkin and Nina Salkin
8 x 10, 48 pp, Deluxe Hardcover, 2-color text, ribbon marker, ISBN 1-58023-111-X **$19.95**

For Kids—Putting God on Your Guest List: How to Claim the Spiritual Meaning of Your Bar or Bat Mitzvah *By Rabbi Jeffrey K. Salkin*
6 x 9, 144 pp, Quality PB, ISBN 1-58023-015-6 **$14.99** *For ages 11–12*

Putting God on the Guest List, 3rd Edition: How to Reclaim the Spiritual Meaning of Your Child's Bar or Bat Mitzvah *By Rabbi Jeffrey K. Salkin*
6 x 9, 224 pp, Quality PB, ISBN 1-58023-222-1 **$16.99**; Hardcover, ISBN 1-58023-260-4 **$24.99**
Also Available: **Putting God on the Guest List Teacher's Guide**
8½ x 11, 48 pp, PB, ISBN 1-58023-226-4 **$8.99**

Tough Questions Jews Ask: A Young Adult's Guide to Building a Jewish Life
By Rabbi Edward Feinstein 6 x 9, 160 pp, Quality PB, ISBN 1-58023-139-X **$14.99** *For ages 13 & up*
Also Available: **Tough Questions Jews Ask Teacher's Guide**
8½ x 11, 72 pp, PB, ISBN 1-58023-187-X **$8.95**

Bible Study/Midrash

Hineini in Our Lives: Learning How to Respond to Others through 14 Biblical Texts, and Personal Stories *By Norman J. Cohen* 6 x 9, 240 pp, Hardcover, ISBN 1-58023-131-4 **$23.95**

Ancient Secrets: Using the Stories of the Bible to Improve Our Everyday Lives
By Rabbi Levi Meier, Ph.D. 5½ x 8½, 288 pp, Quality PB, ISBN 1-58023-064-4 **$16.95**

Moses—The Prince, the Prophet: His Life, Legend & Message for Our Lives
By Rabbi Levi Meier, Ph.D. 6 x 9, 224 pp, Quality PB, ISBN 1-58023-069-5 **$16.95**

Self, Struggle & Change: Family Conflict Stories in Genesis and Their Healing Insights for Our Lives *By Norman J. Cohen* 6 x 9, 224 pp, Quality PB, ISBN 1-879045-66-4 **$18.99**

Voices from Genesis: Guiding Us through the Stages of Life *By Norman J. Cohen*
6 x 9, 192 pp, Quality PB, ISBN 1-58023-118-7 **$16.95**

Congregation Resources

Becoming a Congregation of Learners: Learning as a Key to Revitalizing Congregational Life *By Isa Aron, Ph.D. Foreword by Rabbi Lawrence A. Hoffman.*
6 x 9, 304 pp, Quality PB, ISBN 1-58023-089-X **$19.95**

Finding a Spiritual Home: How a New Generation of Jews Can Transform the American Synagogue *By Rabbi Sidney Schwarz*
6 x 9, 352 pp, Quality PB, ISBN 1-58023-185-3 **$19.95**

Jewish Pastoral Care, 2nd Edition: A Practical Handbook from Traditional & Contemporary Sources *Edited by Rabbi Dayle A. Friedman*
6 x 9, 464 pp, Hardcover, ISBN 1-58023-221-3 **$40.00**

The Self-Renewing Congregation: Organizational Strategies for Revitalizing Congregational Life *By Isa Aron, Ph.D. Foreword by Dr. Ron Wolfson.*
6 x 9, 304 pp, Quality PB, ISBN 1-58023-166-7 **$19.95**

Or phone, fax, mail or e-mail to: **JEWISH LIGHTS Publishing**
Sunset Farm Offices, Route 4 • P.O. Box 237 • Woodstock, Vermont 05091
Tel: (802) 457-4000 • Fax: (802) 457-4004 • www.jewishlights.com
Credit card orders: (800) **962-4544** (8:30AM–5:30PM ET Monday–Friday)
Generous discounts on quantity orders. SATISFACTION GUARANTEED. Prices subject to change.

Holidays/Holy Days

Yom Kippur Readings: Inspiration, Information and Contemplation
Edited by Rabbi Dov Peretz Elkins with section introductions from Arthur Green's These Are the Words
An extraordinary collection of readings, prayers and insights that enable the modern worshiper to enter into the spirit of the Day of Atonement in a personal and powerful way, permitting the meaning of Yom Kippur to enter the heart.
6 x 9, 348 pp, Hardcover, ISBN 1-58023-271-X **$24.99**

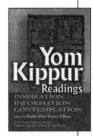

Leading the Passover Journey
The Seder's Meaning Revealed, the Haggadah's Story Retold
By Rabbi Nathan Laufer
Uncovers the hidden meaning of the Seder's rituals and customs
6 x 9, 208 pp, Hardcover, ISBN 1-58023-211-6 **$24.99**

Reclaiming Judaism as a Spiritual Practice: Holy Days and Shabbat
By Rabbi Goldie Milgram
Provides a framework for understanding the powerful and often unexplained intellectual, emotional, and spiritual tools that are essential for a lively, relevant, and fulfilling Jewish spiritual practice. 7 x 9, 272 pp, Quality PB, ISBN 1-58023-205-1 **$19.99**

7th Heaven: Celebrating Shabbat with Rebbe Nachman of Breslov
By Moshe Mykoff with the Breslov Research Institute
Explores the art of consciously observing Shabbat and understanding in-depth many of the day's spiritual practices. 5⅛ x 8¼, 224 pp, Deluxe PB w/flaps, ISBN 1-58023-175-6 **$18.95**

The Women's Passover Companion
Women's Reflections on the Festival of Freedom
Edited by Rabbi Sharon Cohen Anisfeld, Tara Mohr, and Catherine Spector
Groundbreaking. A provocative conversation about women's relationships to Passover as well as the roots and meanings of women's seders.
6 x 9, 352 pp, Hardcover, ISBN 1-58023-128-4 **$24.95**

The Women's Seder Sourcebook
Rituals & Readings for Use at the Passover Seder
Edited by Rabbi Sharon Cohen Anisfeld, Tara Mohr, and Catherine Spector
Gathers the voices of more than one hundred women in readings, personal and creative reflections, commentaries, blessings, and ritual suggestions that can be incorporated into your Passover celebration.
6 x 9, 384 pp, Hardcover, ISBN 1-58023-136-5 **$24.95**

Creating Lively Passover Seders: A Sourcebook of Engaging Tales, Texts & Activities
By David Arnow, Ph.D. 7 x 9, 416 pp, Quality PB, ISBN 1-58023-184-5 **$24.99**

Hanukkah, 2nd Edition: The Family Guide to Spiritual Celebration
By Dr. Ron Wolfson. Edited by Joel Lurie Grishaver.
7 x 9, 240 pp, illus., Quality PB, ISBN 1-58023-122-5 **$18.95**

The Jewish Family Fun Book: Holiday Projects, Everyday Activities, and Travel Ideas with Jewish Themes *By Danielle Dardashti and Roni Sarig. Illus. by Avi Katz.*
6 x 9, 288 pp, 70+ b/w illus. & diagrams, Quality PB, ISBN 1-58023-171-3 **$18.95**

The Jewish Gardening Cookbook: Growing Plants & Cooking for
Holidays & Festivals *By Michael Brown* 6 x 9, 224 pp, 30+ illus., Quality PB, ISBN 1-58023-116-0 **$16.95**

The Jewish Lights Book of Fun Classroom Activities: Simple and Seasonal
Projects for Teachers and Students *By Danielle Dardashti and Roni Sarig*
6 x 9, 240 pp, Quality PB, ISBN 1–58023–206–X **$19.99**

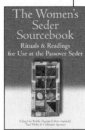

Passover, 2nd Edition: The Family Guide to Spiritual Celebration
By Dr. Ron Wolfson with Joel Lurie Grishaver 7 x 9, 352 pp, Quality PB, ISBN 1-58023-174-8 **$19.95**

Shabbat, 2nd Edition: The Family Guide to Preparing for and Celebrating the Sabbath
By Dr. Ron Wolfson 7 x 9, 320 pp, illus., Quality PB, ISBN 1-58023-164-0 **$19.95**

Sharing Blessings: Children's Stories for Exploring the Spirit of the Jewish Holidays
By Rahel Musleah and Michael Klayman
8½ x 11, 64 pp, Full-color illus., Hardcover, ISBN 1-879045-71-0 **$18.95** *For ages 6 & up*

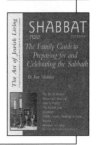

Inspiration

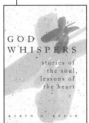

God in All Moments
Mystical & Practical Spiritual Wisdom from Hasidic Masters
Edited and translated by Or N. Rose with Ebn D. Leader
Hasidic teachings on how to be mindful in religious practice and cultivating everyday ethical behavior—*hanhagot*. 5½ x 8½, 192 pp, Quality PB, ISBN 1-58023-186-1 **$16.95**

Our Dance with God: Finding Prayer, Perspective and Meaning in the Stories of Our Lives *By Karyn D. Kedar*
Inspiring spiritual insight to guide you on your life journeys and teach you to live and thrive in two conflicting worlds: the rational/material and the spiritual.
6 x 9, 176 pp, Quality PB, ISBN 1-58023-202-7 **$16.99**

Also Available: **The Dance of the Dolphin** (Hardcover edition of *Our Dance with God*)
6 x 9, 176 pp, Hardcover, ISBN 1-58023-154-3 **$19.95**

The Empty Chair: Finding Hope and Joy—Timeless Wisdom from a Hasidic Master, Rebbe Nachman of Breslov *Adapted by Moshe Mykoff and the Breslov Research Institute*
4 x 6, 128 pp, 2-color text, Deluxe PB w/flaps, ISBN 1-879045-67-2 **$9.95**

The Gentle Weapon: Prayers for Everyday and Not-So-Everyday Moments—Timeless Wisdom from the Teachings of the Hasidic Master, Rebbe Nachman of Breslov
Adapted by Moshe Mykoff and S. C. Mizrahi, together with the Breslov Research Institute
4 x 6, 144 pp, 2-color text, Deluxe PB w/flaps, ISBN 1-58023-022-9 **$9.95**

God Whispers: Stories of the Soul, Lessons of the Heart *By Karyn D. Kedar*
6 x 9, 176 pp, Quality PB, ISBN 1-58023-088-1 **$15.95**

An Orphan in History: One Man's Triumphant Search for His Jewish Roots
By Paul Cowan. Afterword by Rachel Cowan. 6 x 9, 288 pp, Quality PB, ISBN 1-58023-135-7 **$16.95**

Restful Reflections: Nighttime Inspiration to Calm the Soul, Based on Jewish Wisdom
By Rabbi Kerry M. Olitzky & Rabbi Lori Forman 4½ x 6½, 448 pp, Quality PB, ISBN 1-58023-091-1 **$15.95**

Sacred Intentions: Daily Inspiration to Strengthen the Spirit, Based on Jewish Wisdom
By Rabbi Kerry M. Olitzky and Rabbi Lori Forman 4½ x 6½, 448 pp, Quality PB, ISBN 1-58023-061-X **$15.95**

Kabbalah/Mysticism/Enneagram

Seek My Face: A Jewish Mystical Theology
By Dr. Arthur Green
This classic work of contemporary Jewish theology, revised and updated, is a profound, deeply personal statement of the lasting truths of Jewish mysticism and the basic faith claims of Judaism. A tool for anyone seeking the elusive presence of God in the world. 6 x 9, 304 pp, Quality PB, ISBN 1-58023-130-6 **$19.95**

Zohar: Annotated & Explained
Translation and annotation by Dr. Daniel C. Matt. Foreword by Andrew Harvey
Offers insightful yet unobtrusive commentary to the masterpiece of Jewish mysticism. Explains references and mystical symbols, shares wisdom of spiritual masters, and clarifies the *Zohar*'s bold claim: We have always been taught that we need God, but in order to manifest in the world, God needs us.
5½ x 8½, 160 pp, Quality PB, ISBN 1-893361-51-9 **$15.99** *(A SkyLight Paths book)*

Cast in God's Image: Discover Your Personality Type Using the Enneagram and Kabbalah
By Rabbi Howard A. Addison
7 x 9, 176 pp, Quality PB, Layflat binding, 20+ journaling exercises, ISBN 1-58023-124-1 **$16.95**

Ehyeh: A Kabbalah for Tomorrow *By Dr. Arthur Green*
6 x 9, 224 pp, Quality PB, ISBN 1-58023-213-2 **$16.99**; Hardcover, ISBN 1-58023-125-X **$21.95**

The Enneagram and Kabbalah: Reading Your Soul *By Rabbi Howard A. Addison*
6 x 9, 176 pp, Quality PB, ISBN 1-58023-001-6 **$15.95**

Finding Joy: A Practical Spiritual Guide to Happiness *By Dannel I. Schwartz with Mark Hass*
6 x 9, 192 pp, Quality PB, ISBN 1-58023-009-1 **$14.95**

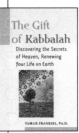

The Gift of Kabbalah: Discovering the Secrets of Heaven, Renewing Your Life on Earth
By Tamar Frankiel, Ph.D.
6 x 9, 256 pp, Quality PB, ISBN 1-58023-141-1 **$16.95**; Hardcover, ISBN 1-58023-108-X **$21.95**

The Way Into Jewish Mystical Tradition *By Lawrence Kushner*
6 x 9, 224 pp, Quality PB, ISBN 1-58023-200-0 **$18.99**; Hardcover, ISBN 1-58023-029-6 **$21.95**

Life Cycle
Marriage / Parenting / Family / Aging

Jewish Fathers: A Legacy of Love
Photographs by Lloyd Wolf. Essays by Paula Wolfson. Foreword by Harold S. Kushner.
Honors the role of contemporary Jewish fathers in America. Each father tells in his own words what it means to be a parent and Jewish, and what he learned from his own father. Insightful photos. 9½ x 9⅞, 144 pp with 100+ duotone photos, Hardcover, ISBN 1-58023-204-3 **$30.00**

The New Jewish Baby Album: Creating and Celebrating the Beginning of a Spiritual Life—A Jewish Lights Companion
By the Editors at Jewish Lights. Foreword by Anita Diamant. Preface by Sandy Eisenberg Sasso.
A spiritual keepsake that will be treasured for generations. More than just a memory book, *shows you how—and why it's important*—to create a Jewish home and a Jewish life. 8 x 10, 64 pp, Deluxe Padded Hardcover, Full-color illus., ISBN 1-58023-138-1 **$19.95**

The Jewish Pregnancy Book: A Resource for the Soul, Body & Mind during Pregnancy, Birth & the First Three Months
By Sandy Falk, M.D., and Rabbi Daniel Judson, with Steven A. Rapp
Includes medical information, prayers and rituals for each stage of pregnancy, from a liberal Jewish perspective. 7 x 10, 208 pp, Quality PB, b/w illus., ISBN 1-58023-178-0 **$16.95**

Celebrating Your New Jewish Daughter: Creating Jewish Ways to Welcome Baby Girls into the Covenant—New and Traditional Ceremonies
By Debra Nussbaum Cohen 6 x 9, 272 pp, Quality PB, ISBN 1-58023-090-3 **$18.95**

The New Jewish Baby Book, 2nd Edition: Names, Ceremonies & Customs—A Guide for Today's Families *By Anita Diamant* 6 x 9, 336 pp, Quality PB, ISBN 1-58023-251-5 **$19.99**

Parenting As a Spiritual Journey: Deepening Ordinary and Extraordinary Events into Sacred Occasions *By Rabbi Nancy Fuchs-Kreimer* 6 x 9, 224 pp, Quality PB, ISBN 1-58023-016-4 **$16.95**

Judaism for Two: A Spiritual Guide for Strengthening and Celebrating Your Loving Relationship *By Rabbi Nancy Fuchs-Kreimer and Rabbi Nancy H. Wiener*
Addresses the ways Jewish teachings can enhance and strengthen committed relationships. 6 x 9, 208 pp, Quality PB, ISBN 1-58023-254-X **$16.99**

Embracing the Covenant: Converts to Judaism Talk About Why & How
By Rabbi Allan Berkowitz and Patti Moskovitz 6 x 9, 192 pp, Quality PB, ISBN 1-879045-50-8 **$16.95**

The Guide to Jewish Interfaith Family Life: An InterfaithFamily.com Handbook
Edited by Ronnie Friedland and Edmund Case 6 x 9, 384 pp, Quality PB, ISBN 1-58023-153-5 **$18.95**

Introducing My Faith and My Community
The Jewish Outreach Institute Guide for the Christian in a Jewish Interfaith Relationship
By Rabbi Kerry M. Olitzky 6 x 9, 176 pp, Quality PB, ISBN 1-58023-192-6 **$16.99**

Making a Successful Jewish Interfaith Marriage: The Jewish Outreach Institute Guide to Opportunities, Challenges and Resources
By Rabbi Kerry M. Olitzky with Joan Peterson Littman 6 x 9, 176 pp, Quality PB, ISBN 1-58023-170-5 **$16.95**

The Creative Jewish Wedding Book: A Hands-On Guide to New & Old Traditions, Ceremonies & Celebrations *By Gabrielle Kaplan-Mayer*
Provides the tools to create the most meaningful Jewish traditional or alternative wedding by using ritual elements to express your unique style and spirituality. 9 x 9, 288 pp, b/w photos, Quality PB, ISBN 1-58023-194-2 **$19.99**

Divorce Is a Mitzvah: A Practical Guide to Finding Wholeness and Holiness When Your Marriage Dies *By Rabbi Perry Netter. Afterword by Rabbi Laura Geller.*
6 x 9, 224 pp, Quality PB, ISBN 1-58023-172-1 **$16.95**

A Heart of Wisdom: Making the Jewish Journey from Midlife through the Elder Years
Edited by Susan Berrin. Foreword by Harold Kushner. 6 x 9, 384 pp, Quality PB, ISBN 1-58023-051-2 **$18.95**

So That Your Values Live On: Ethical Wills and How to Prepare Them
Edited by Jack Riemer and Nathaniel Stampfer 6 x 9, 272 pp, Quality PB, ISBN 1-879045-34-6 **$18.95**

Meditation

The Handbook of Jewish Meditation Practices
A Guide for Enriching the Sabbath and Other Days of Your Life
By Rabbi David A. Cooper
Easy-to-learn meditation techniques. 6 x 9, 208 pp, Quality PB, ISBN 1-58023-102-0 **$16.95**

Discovering Jewish Meditation: Instruction & Guidance for Learning an Ancient
Spiritual Practice *By Nan Fink Gefen, Ph.D.* 6 x 9, 208 pp, Quality PB, ISBN 1-58023-067-9 **$16.95**

A Heart of Stillness: A Complete Guide to Learning the Art of Meditation
By Rabbi David A. Cooper 5½ x 8½, 272 pp, Quality PB, ISBN 1-893361-03-9 **$16.95**
(A SkyLight Paths book)

Meditation from the Heart of Judaism: Today's Teachers Share Their
Practices, Techniques, and Faith *Edited by Avram Davis*
6 x 9, 256 pp, Quality PB, ISBN 1-58023-049-0 **$16.95**

Silence, Simplicity & Solitude: A Complete Guide to Spiritual Retreat at Home
By Rabbi David A. Cooper 5½ x 8½, 336 pp, Quality PB, ISBN 1-893361-04-7 **$16.95**
(A SkyLight Paths book)

The Way of Flame: A Guide to the Forgotten Mystical Tradition of Jewish
Meditation *By Avram Davis* 4½ x 8, 176 pp, Quality PB, ISBN 1-58023-060-1 **$15.95**

Ritual/Sacred Practice/Journaling

The Jewish Dream Book: The Key to Opening the Inner Meaning of
Your Dreams *By Vanessa L. Ochs with Elizabeth Ochs; Full-color illus. by Kristina Swarner*
Instructions for how modern people can perform ancient Jewish dream practices
and dream interpretations drawn from the Jewish wisdom tradition. For anyone
who wants to understand their dreams—and themselves.
8 x 8, 120 pp, Full-color illus., Deluxe PB w/flaps, ISBN 1-58023-132-2 **$16.95**

The Jewish Journaling Book: How to Use Jewish Tradition to Write
Your Life & Explore Your Soul *By Janet Ruth Falon*
Details the history of Jewish journaling throughout biblical and modern times,
and teaches specific journaling techniques to help you create and maintain a vital
journal, from a Jewish perspective. 8 x 8, 304 pp, Deluxe PB w/flaps, ISBN 1-58023-203-5 **$18.99**

The Book of Jewish Sacred Practices: CLAL's Guide to Everyday & Holiday
Rituals & Blessings *Edited by Rabbi Irwin Kula and Vanessa L. Ochs, Ph.D.*
6 x 9, 368 pp, Quality PB, ISBN 1-58023-152-7 **$18.95**

Jewish Ritual: A Brief Introduction for Christians
By Rabbi Kerry M. Olitzky and Rabbi Daniel Judson
5½ x 8½, 144 pp, Quality PB, ISBN 1-58023-210-8 **$14.99**

The Rituals & Practices of a Jewish Life: A Handbook for Personal Spiritual
Renewal *Edited by Rabbi Kerry M. Olitzky and Rabbi Daniel Judson*
6 x 9, 272 pp, illus., Quality PB, ISBN 1-58023-169-1 **$18.95**

Science Fiction/
Mystery & Detective Fiction

Mystery Midrash: An Anthology of Jewish Mystery & Detective Fiction
Edited by Lawrence W. Raphael. Preface by Joel Siegel.
6 x 9, 304 pp, Quality PB, ISBN 1-58023-055-5 **$16.95**

Criminal Kabbalah: An Intriguing Anthology of Jewish Mystery & Detective Fiction
Edited by Lawrence W. Raphael. Foreword by Laurie R. King.
6 x 9, 256 pp, Quality PB, ISBN 1-58023-109-8 **$16.95**

Wandering Stars: An Anthology of Jewish Fantasy & Science Fiction
Edited by Jack Dann. Introduction by Isaac Asimov.
6 x 9, 272 pp, Quality PB, ISBN 1-58023-005-9 **$16.95**

More Wandering Stars: An Anthology of Outstanding Stories of Jewish Fantasy and
Science Fiction *Edited by Jack Dann. Introduction by Isaac Asimov.*
6 x 9, 192 pp, Quality PB, ISBN 1-58023-063-6 **$16.95**

Spirituality

Does the Soul Survive?: A Jewish Journey to Belief in Afterlife, Past Lives & Living with Purpose   *By Rabbi Elie Kaplan Spitz. Foreword by Brian L. Weiss, M.D.*
Spitz relates his own experiences and those shared with him by people he has worked with as a rabbi, and shows us that belief in afterlife and past lives, so often approached with reluctance, is in fact true to Jewish tradition.
6 x 9, 288 pp, Quality PB, ISBN 1-58023-165-9 **$16.95**; Hardcover, ISBN 1-58023-094-6 **$21.95**

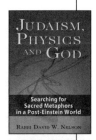

First Steps to a New Jewish Spirit: Reb Zalman's Guide to Recapturing the Intimacy & Ecstasy in Your Relationship with God
By Rabbi Zalman M. Schachter-Shalomi with Donald Gropman
An extraordinary spiritual handbook that restores psychic and physical vigor by introducing us to new models and alternative ways of practicing Judaism. Offers meditation and contemplation exercises for enriching the most important aspects of everyday life.   6 x 9, 144 pp, Quality PB, ISBN 1-58023-182-9 **$16.95**

God in Our Relationships: Spirituality between People from the Teachings of Martin Buber   *By Rabbi Dennis S. Ross*
On the eightieth anniversary of Buber's classic work, we can discover new answers to critical issues in our lives. Inspiring examples from Ross's own life—as congregational rabbi, father, hospital chaplain, social worker, and husband—illustrate Buber's difficult-to-understand ideas about how we encounter God and each other. 5½ x 8½, 160 pp, Quality PB, ISBN 1-58023-147-0 **$16.95**

Judaism, Physics and God: Searching for Sacred Metaphors in a Post-Einstein World   *By Rabbi David W. Nelson*
In clear, non-technical terms, this provocative fusion of religion and science examines the great theories of modern physics to find new ways for contemporary people to express their spiritual beliefs and thoughts.
6 x 9, 352 pp, Hardcover, ISBN 1-58023-252-3 **$24.99**

The Jewish Lights Spirituality Handbook: A Guide to Understanding, Exploring & Living a Spiritual Life   *Edited by Stuart M. Matlins*
What exactly is "Jewish" about spirituality? How do I make it a part of my life? Fifty of today's foremost spiritual leaders share their ideas and experience with us.
6 x 9, 456 pp, Quality PB, ISBN 1-58023-093-8 **$19.95**; Hardcover, ISBN 1-58023-100-4 **$24.95**

Bringing the Psalms to Life: How to Understand and Use the Book of Psalms
By Dr. Daniel F. Polish
6 x 9, 208 pp, Quality PB, ISBN 1-58023-157-8 **$16.95**; Hardcover, ISBN 1-58023-077-6 **$21.95**

God & the Big Bang: Discovering Harmony between Science & Spirituality
By Dr. Daniel C. Matt 6 x 9, 216 pp, Quality PB, ISBN 1-879045-89-3 **$16.95**

Godwrestling—Round 2: Ancient Wisdom, Future Paths
By Rabbi Arthur Waskow 6 x 9, 352 pp, Quality PB, ISBN 1-879045-72-9 **$18.95**

One God Clapping: The Spiritual Path of a Zen Rabbi   *By Rabbi Alan Lew with Sherril Jaffe*
5½ x 8½, 336 pp, Quality PB, ISBN 1-58023-115-2 **$16.95**

The Path of Blessing: Experiencing the Energy and Abundance of the Divine
By Rabbi Marcia Prager 5½ x 8½, 240 pp., Quality PB, ISBN 1-58023-148-9 **$16.95**

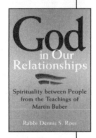

Six Jewish Spiritual Paths: A Rationalist Looks at Spirituality   *By Rabbi Rifat Sonsino*
6 x 9, 208 pp, Quality PB, ISBN 1-58023-167-5 **$16.95**; Hardcover, ISBN 1-58023-095-4 **$21.95**

Soul Judaism: Dancing with God into a New Era
By Rabbi Wayne Dosick 5½ x 8½, 304 pp, Quality PB, ISBN 1-58023-053-9 **$16.95**

Stepping Stones to Jewish Spiritual Living: Walking the Path Morning, Noon, and Night   *By Rabbi James L. Mirel and Karen Bonnell Werth*
6 x 9, 240 pp, Quality PB, ISBN 1-58023-074-1 **$16.95**; Hardcover, ISBN 1-58023-003-2 **$21.95**

There Is No Messiah ... and You're It: The Stunning Transformation of Judaism's Most Provocative Idea   *By Rabbi Robert N. Levine, D.D.*
6 x 9, 192 pp, Quality PB, ISBN 1-58023-255-8 **$16.99**; Hardcover, ISBN 1-58023-173-X **$21.95**

These Are the Words: A Vocabulary of Jewish Spiritual Life   *By Dr. Arthur Green*
6 x 9, 304 pp, Quality PB, ISBN 1-58023-107-1 **$18.95**

Spirituality/Lawrence Kushner

Filling Words with Light: Hasidic and Mystical Reflections on Jewish Prayer
By Lawrence Kushner and Nehemia Polen
Reflects on the joy, gratitude, mystery and awe embedded in traditional prayers and blessings, and shows how you can imbue these familiar sacred words with your own sense of holiness. 5½ x 8½, 176 pp, Hardcover, ISBN 1-58023-216-7 **$21.99**

The Book of Letters: A Mystical Hebrew Alphabet
Popular Hardcover Edition, 6 x 9, 80 pp, 2-color text, ISBN 1-879045-00-1 **$24.95**
Collector's Limited Edition, 9 x 12, 80 pp, gold foil embossed pages, w/limited edition silkscreened print, ISBN 1-879045-04-4 **$349.00**

The Book of Miracles: A Young Person's Guide to Jewish Spiritual Awareness
6 x 9, 96 pp, 2-color illus., Hardcover, ISBN 1-879045-78-8 **$16.95** *For ages 9–13*

The Book of Words: Talking Spiritual Life, Living Spiritual Talk
6 x 9, 160 pp, Quality PB, ISBN 1-58023-020-2 **$16.95**

Eyes Remade for Wonder: A Lawrence Kushner Reader *Introduction by Thomas Moore*
6 x 9, 240 pp, Quality PB, ISBN 1-58023-042-3 **$18.95;** Hardcover, ISBN 1-58023-014-8 **$23.95**

God Was in This Place & I, i Did Not Know
Finding Self, Spirituality and Ultimate Meaning 6 x 9, 192 pp, Quality PB, ISBN 1-879045-33-8 **$16.95**

Honey from the Rock: An Introduction to Jewish Mysticism
6 x 9, 176 pp, Quality PB, ISBN 1-58023-073-3 **$16.95**

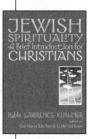

Invisible Lines of Connection: Sacred Stories of the Ordinary
5½ x 8½, 160 pp, Quality PB, ISBN 1-879045-98-2 **$15.95**

Jewish Spirituality—A Brief Introduction for Christians
5½ x 8½, 112 pp, Quality PB Original, ISBN 1-58023-150-0 **$12.95**

The River of Light: Jewish Mystical Awareness 6 x 9, 192 pp, Quality PB, ISBN 1-58023-096-2 **$16.95**

The Way Into Jewish Mystical Tradition
6 x 9, 224 pp, Quality PB, ISBN 1-58023-200-0 **$18.99;** Hardcover, ISBN 1-58023-029-6 **$21.95**

Spirituality/Prayer

Pray Tell: A Hadassah Guide to Jewish Prayer
By Rabbi Jules Harlow, with contributions from Tamara Cohen, Rochelle Furstenberg, Rabbi Daniel Gordis, Leora Tanenbaum, and many others
A guide to traditional Jewish prayer enriched with insight and wisdom from a broad variety of viewpoints—from Orthodox, Conservative, Reform, and Reconstructionist Judaism to New Age and feminist.
8½ x 11, 400 pp, Quality PB, ISBN 1-58023-163-2 **$29.95**

My People's Prayer Book Series Traditional Prayers, Modern Commentaries
Edited by Rabbi Lawrence A. Hoffman Provides diverse and exciting commentary to the traditional liturgy, helping modern men and women find new wisdom in Jewish prayer, and bring liturgy into their lives. Each book includes Hebrew text, modern translation, and commentaries from all perspectives of the Jewish world.

Vol. 1—The *Sh'ma* and Its Blessings
7 x 10, 168 pp, Hardcover, ISBN 1-879045-79-6 **$24.99**
Vol. 2—The *Amidah*
7 x 10, 240 pp, Hardcover, ISBN 1-879045-80-X **$24.95**
Vol. 3—*P'sukei D'zimrah* (Morning Psalms)
7 x 10, 240 pp, Hardcover, ISBN 1-879045-81-8 **$24.95**
Vol. 4—*Seder K'riat Hatorah* (The Torah Service)
7 x 10, 264 pp, Hardcover, ISBN 1-879045-82-6 **$23.95**
Vol. 5—*Birkhot Hashachar* (Morning Blessings)
7 x 10, 240 pp, Hardcover, ISBN 1-879045-83-4 **$24.95**
Vol. 6—*Tachanun* and Concluding Prayers
7 x 10, 240 pp, Hardcover, ISBN 1-879045-84-2 **$24.95**
Vol. 7—Shabbat at Home
7 x 10, 240 pp, Hardcover, ISBN 1-879045-85-0 **$24.95**
Vol. 8—*Kabbalat Shabbat* (Welcoming Shabbat in the Synagogue)
7 x 10, 240 pp, Hardcover, ISBN 1-58023-121-7 **$24.99**
Vol. 9—Welcoming the Night: *Minchah* and *Ma'ariv* (Afternoon and Evening Prayer) 7 x 10, 272 pp, Hardcover, ISBN 1-58023-262-0 **$24.99**

Spirituality/The Way Into... Series

The Way Into... Series offers an accessible and highly usable "guided tour" of the Jewish faith, people, history and beliefs—in total, an introduction to Judaism that will enable you to understand and interact with the sacred texts of the Jewish tradition. Each volume is written by a leading contemporary scholar and teacher, and explores one key aspect of Judaism. *The Way Into...* enables all readers to achieve a real sense of Jewish cultural literacy through guided study.

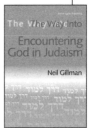

The Way Into Encountering God in Judaism   *By Neil Gillman*
6 x 9, 240 pp, Quality PB, ISBN 1-58023-199-3 **$18.99**; Hardcover, ISBN 1-58023-025-3 **$21.95**

Also Available: **The Jewish Approach to God: A Brief Introduction for Christians**
By Neil Gillman 5½ x 8½, 192 pp, Quality PB, ISBN 1-58023-190-X **$16.95**

The Way Into Jewish Mystical Tradition   *By Lawrence Kushner*
6 x 9, 224 pp, Quality PB, ISBN 1-58023-200-0 **$18.99**; Hardcover, ISBN 1-58023-029-6 **$21.95**

The Way Into Jewish Prayer   *By Lawrence A. Hoffman*
6 x 9, 224 pp, Quality PB, ISBN 1-58023-201-9 **$18.99**; Hardcover, ISBN 1-58023-027-X **$21.95**

The Way Into Torah   *By Norman J. Cohen*
6 x 9, 176 pp, Quality PB, ISBN 1-58023-198-5 **$16.99**; Hardcover, ISBN 1-58023-028-8 **$21.95**

Spirituality in the Workplace

Being God's Partner
How to Find the Hidden Link Between Spirituality and Your Work
By Rabbi Jeffrey K. Salkin. Introduction by Norman Lear.
6 x 9, 192 pp, Quality PB, ISBN 1-879045-65-6 **$17.95**

The Business Bible: 10 New Commandments for Bringing Spirituality & Ethical Values into the Workplace   *By Rabbi Wayne Dosick*
5½ x 8½, 208 pp, Quality PB, ISBN 1-58023-101-2 **$14.95**

Spirituality and Wellness

Aleph-Bet Yoga
Embodying the Hebrew Letters for Physical and Spiritual Well-Being
By Steven A. Rapp. Foreword by Tamar Frankiel, Ph.D., and Judy Greenfeld. Preface by Hart Lazer
7 x 10, 128 pp, b/w photos, Quality PB, Layflat binding, ISBN 1-58023-162-4 **$16.95**

Entering the Temple of Dreams
Jewish Prayers, Movements, and Meditations for the End of the Day
By Tamar Frankiel, Ph.D., and Judy Greenfeld
7 x 10, 192 pp, illus., Quality PB, ISBN 1-58023-079-2 **$16.95**

Jewish Paths toward Healing and Wholeness: A Personal Guide to Dealing with Suffering   *By Rabbi Kerry M. Olitzky. Foreword by Debbie Friedman.*
6 x 9, 192 pp, Quality PB, ISBN 1-58023-068-7 **$15.95**

Minding the Temple of the Soul
Balancing Body, Mind, and Spirit through Traditional Jewish Prayer, Movement, and Meditation   *By Tamar Frankiel, Ph.D., and Judy Greenfeld*
7 x 10, 184 pp, illus., Quality PB, ISBN 1-879045-64-8 **$16.95**
Audiotape of the Blessings and Meditations: 60 min. **$9.95**
Videotape of the Movements and Meditations: 46 min. **$20.00**

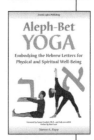

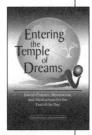

Spirituality/Women's Interest

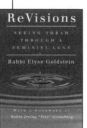

The Quotable Jewish Woman: Wisdom, Inspiration & Humor from the Mind & Heart *Edited and compiled by Elaine Bernstein Partnow*
The definitive collection of ideas, reflections, humor, and wit of over 300 Jewish women.
6 x 9, 496 pp, Hardcover, ISBN 1-58023-193-4 **$29.99**

Lifecycles, Vol. 1: Jewish Women on Life Passages & Personal Milestones
Edited and with introductions by Rabbi Debra Orenstein 6 x 9, 480 pp, Quality PB, ISBN 1-58023-018-0 **$19.95**

Lifecycles, Vol. 2: Jewish Women on Biblical Themes in Contemporary Life
Edited and with introductions by Rabbi Debra Orenstein and Rabbi Jane Rachel Litman
6 x 9, 464 pp, Quality PB, ISBN 1-58023-019-9 **$19.95**

Moonbeams: A Hadassah Rosh Hodesh Guide *Edited by Carol Diament, Ph.D.*
8½ x 11, 240 pp, Quality PB, ISBN 1-58023-099-7 **$20.00**

ReVisions: Seeing Torah through a Feminist Lens *By Rabbi Elyse Goldstein*
5½ x 8½, 224 pp, Quality PB, ISBN 1-58023-117-9 **$16.95**

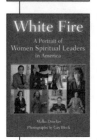

White Fire: A Portrait of Women Spiritual Leaders in America
By Rabbi Malka Drucker. Photographs by Gay Block.
7 x 10, 320 pp, 30+ b/w photos, Hardcover, ISBN 1-893361-64-0 **$24.95** *(A SkyLight Paths book)*

Women of the Wall: Claiming Sacred Ground at Judaism's Holy Site
Edited by Phyllis Chesler and Rivka Haut 6 x 9, 496 pp, b/w photos, Hardcover, ISBN 1-58023-161-6 **$34.95**

The Women's Haftarah Commentary: New Insights from Women Rabbis on the 54 Weekly Haftarah Portions, the 5 Megillot & Special Shabbatot
Edited by Rabbi Elyse Goldstein 6 x 9, 560 pp, Hardcover, ISBN 1-58023-133-0 **$39.99**

The Women's Torah Commentary: New Insights from Women Rabbis on the 54 Weekly Torah Portions *Edited by Rabbi Elyse Goldstein*
6 x 9, 496 pp, Hardcover, ISBN 1-58023-076-8 **$34.95**

The Year Mom Got Religion: One Woman's Midlife Journey into Judaism
By Lee Meyerhoff Hendler 6 x 9, 208 pp, Quality PB, ISBN 1-58023-070-9 **$15.95**

See Holidays for *The Women's Passover Companion: Women's Reflections on the Festival of Freedom* and *The Women's Seder Sourcebook: Rituals & Readings for Use at the Passover Seder.* Also see Bar/Bat Mitzvah for *The JGirl's Guide: The Young Jewish Woman's Handbook for Coming of Age.*

Travel

Israel—A Spiritual Travel Guide, 2nd Edition
A Companion for the Modern Jewish Pilgrim
By Rabbi Lawrence A. Hoffman 4¾ x 10, 256 pp, Quality PB, illus., ISBN 1-58023-261-2 **$18.99**
Also Available: **The Israel Mission Leader's Guide** ISBN 1-58023-085-7 **$4.95**

12 Steps

100 Blessings Every Day Daily Twelve Step Recovery Affirmations, Exercises for Personal Growth & Renewal Reflecting Seasons of the Jewish Year
By Rabbi Kerry M. Olitzky. Foreword by Rabbi Neil Gillman.
One-day-at-a-time monthly format. Reflects on the rhythm of the Jewish calendar to bring insight to recovery from addictions.
4½ x 6½, 432 pp, Quality PB, ISBN 1-879045-30-3 **$15.99**

Recovery from Codependence: A Jewish Twelve Steps Guide to Healing Your Soul
By Rabbi Kerry M. Olitzky 6 x 9, 160 pp, Quality PB, ISBN 1-879045-32-X **$13.95**

Renewed Each Day: Daily Twelve Step Recovery Meditations Based on the Bible
By Rabbi Kerry M. Olitzky and Aaron Z.
Vol. 1—Genesis & Exodus: 6 x 9, 224 pp, Quality PB, ISBN 1-879045-12-5 **$14.95**
Vol. 2—Leviticus, Numbers & Deuteronomy: 6 x 9, 280 pp, Quality PB, ISBN 1-879045-13-3 **$18.99**

Twelve Jewish Steps to Recovery: A Personal Guide to Turning from Alcoholism & Other Addictions—Drugs, Food, Gambling, Sex...
By Rabbi Kerry M. Olitzky and Stuart A. Copans, M.D. Preface by Abraham J. Twerski, M.D.
6 x 9, 144 pp, Quality PB, ISBN 1-879045-09-5 **$14.95**

Theology/Philosophy

Aspects of Rabbinic Theology
By Solomon Schechter. New Introduction by Dr. Neil Gillman.
6 x 9, 448 pp, Quality PB, ISBN 1-879045-24-9 **$19.95**

Broken Tablets: Restoring the Ten Commandments and Ourselves
Edited by Rachel S. Mikva. Introduction by Lawrence Kushner. Afterword by Arnold Jacob Wolf.
6 x 9, 192 pp, Quality PB, ISBN 1-58023-158-6 **$16.95**; Hardcover, ISBN 1-58023-066-0 **$21.95**

Creating an Ethical Jewish Life
A Practical Introduction to Classic Teachings on How to Be a Jew
By Dr. Byron L. Sherwin and Seymour J. Cohen
6 x 9, 336 pp, Quality PB, ISBN 1-58023-114-4 **$19.95**

The Death of Death: Resurrection and Immortality in Jewish Thought
By Dr. Neil Gillman 6 x 9, 336 pp, Quality PB, ISBN 1-58023-081-4 **$18.95**

Evolving Halakhah: A Progressive Approach to Traditional Jewish Law
By Rabbi Dr. Moshe Zemer
6 x 9, 480 pp, Quality PB, ISBN 1-58023-127-6 **$29.95**; Hardcover, ISBN 1-58023-002-4 **$40.00**

Hasidic Tales: Annotated & Explained
By Rabbi Rami Shapiro. Foreword by Andrew Harvey, SkyLight Illuminations series editor.
5½ x 8½, 240 pp, Quality PB, ISBN 1-893361-86-1 **$16.95** *(A SkyLight Paths Book)*

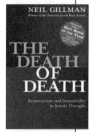

A Heart of Many Rooms: Celebrating the Many Voices within Judaism
By Dr. David Hartman 6 x 9, 352 pp, Quality PB, ISBN 1-58023-156-X **$19.95**

The Hebrew Prophets: Selections Annotated & Explained
Translation & Annotation by Rabbi Rami Shapiro. Foreword by Zalman M. Schachter-Shalomi
5½ x 8½, 224 pp, Quality PB, ISBN 1-59473-037-7 **$16.99** *(A SkyLight Paths book)*

Keeping Faith with the Psalms: Deepen Your Relationship with God Using the
Book of Psalms *By Daniel F. Polish* 6 x 9, 272 pp, Hardcover, ISBN 1-58023-179-9 **$24.95**

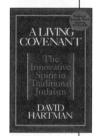

The Last Trial
On the Legends and Lore of the Command to Abraham to Offer Isaac as a Sacrifice
By Shalom Spiegel. New Introduction by Judah Goldin.
6 x 9, 208 pp, Quality PB, ISBN 1-879045-29-X **$18.95**

A Living Covenant: The Innovative Spirit in Traditional Judaism
By Dr. David Hartman 6 x 9, 368 pp, Quality PB, ISBN 1-58023-011-3 **$18.95**

Love and Terror in the God Encounter
The Theological Legacy of Rabbi Joseph B. Soloveitchik
By Dr. David Hartman
6 x 9, 240 pp, Quality PB, ISBN 1-58023-176-4 **$19.95**; Hardcover, ISBN 1-58023-112-8 **$25.00**

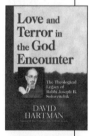

Seeking the Path to Life
Theological Meditations on God and the Nature of People, Love, Life and Death
By Rabbi Ira F. Stone 6 x 9, 160 pp, Quality PB, ISBN 1-879045-47-8 **$14.95**

The Spirit of Renewal: Finding Faith after the Holocaust
By Rabbi Edward Feld 6 x 9, 224 pp, Quality PB, ISBN 1-879045-40-0 **$16.95**

Tormented Master: *The Life and Spiritual Quest of Rabbi Nahman of Bratslav*
By Dr. Arthur Green 6 x 9, 416 pp, Quality PB, ISBN 1-879045-11-7 **$19.99**

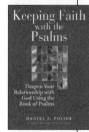

Your Word Is Fire: The Hasidic Masters on Contemplative Prayer
Edited and translated by Dr. Arthur Green and Barry W. Holtz
6 x 9, 160 pp, Quality PB, ISBN 1-879045-25-7 **$15.95**

I Am Jewish
Personal Reflections Inspired by the Last Words of Daniel Pearl

Almost 150 Jews—both famous and not—from all walks of life, from all around
the world, write about Identity, Heritage, Covenant / Chosenness and Faith,
Humanity and Ethnicity, and *Tikkun Olam* and Justice.
Edited by Judea and Ruth Pearl
6 x 9, 304 pp, Deluxe PB w/flaps, ISBN 1-58023-259-0 **$18.99**; Hardcover, ISBN 1-58023-183-7 **$24.99**
Download a free copy of the *I Am Jewish* Teacher's Guide at our website:
www.jewishlights.com

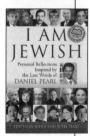

JEWISH LIGHTS BOOKS ARE AVAILABLE FROM BETTER BOOKSTORES. TRY YOUR BOOKSTORE FIRST.

About Jewish Lights

People of all faiths and backgrounds yearn for books that attract, engage, educate, and spiritually inspire.

Our principal goal is to stimulate thought and help all people learn about who the Jewish People are, where they come from, and what the future can be made to hold. While people of our diverse Jewish heritage are the primary audience, our books speak to people in the Christian world as well and will broaden their understanding of Judaism and the roots of their own faith.

We bring to you authors who are at the forefront of spiritual thought and experience. While each has something different to say, they all say it in a voice that you can hear.

Our books are designed to welcome you and then to engage, stimulate, and inspire. We judge our success not only by whether or not our books are beautiful and commercially successful, but by whether or not they make a difference in your life.

For your information and convenience, at the back of this book we have provided a list of other Jewish Lights books you might find interesting and useful. They cover all the categories of your life:

Bar/Bat Mitzvah	Life Cycle
Bible Study / Midrash	Meditation
Children's Books	Parenting
Congregation Resources	Prayer
Current Events / History	Ritual / Sacred Practice
Ecology	Spirituality
Fiction: Mystery, Science Fiction	Theology / Philosophy
Grief / Healing	Travel
Holidays / Holy Days	Twelve Steps
Inspiration	Women's Interest
Kabbalah / Mysticism / Enneagram	

Stuart M. Matlins, Publisher

Or phone, fax, mail or e-mail to: **JEWISH LIGHTS Publishing**
Sunset Farm Offices, Route 4 • P.O. Box 237 • Woodstock, Vermont 05091
Tel: (802) 457-4000 • Fax: (802) 457-4004 • www.jewishlights.com
Credit card orders: (800) 962-4544 (8:30AM–5:30PM ET Monday–Friday)
Generous discounts on quantity orders. SATISFACTION GUARANTEED. Prices subject to change.

For more information about each book, visit our website at www.jewishlights.com